BREATHING
MINDFULNESS

BOOKS BY SARAH SHAW

The Art of Listening: A Guide to the Early Teachings of Buddhism

Buddhist Meditation: An Anthology of Texts

Illuminating the Life of the Buddha: An Eighteenth-Century Siamese Chanting Manual, with Dr. Naomi Appleton and Toshiya Unebe

An Introduction to Buddhist Meditation

The Jātakas: Birth Stories of the Bodhisatta

Mindfulness: Where It Comes From and What It Means

The Spirit of Buddhist Meditation

The Ten Great Birth Stories of the Buddha: The Mahānipāta of the Jātakatthavaṇṇanā, with Dr. Naomi Appleton

BREATHING MINDFULNESS

Discovering the Riches at the Heart of the Buddhist Path

Sarah Shaw

SHAMBHALA

Shambhala Publications, Inc.
2129 13th Street
Boulder, Colorado 80302
www.shambhala.com

Cover Art: Wan/Adobe Stock
Cover Design: Daniel Urban-Brown
Interior design: Kate Huber-Parker

9 8 7 6 5 4 3 2 1

First Edition
Printed in the United States of America

Shambhala Publications makes every effort
to print on acid-free, recycled paper.
Shambhala Publications is distributed worldwide by
Penguin Random House, Inc., and its subsidiaries.

Library of Congress Cataloging-in-Publication Data
Names: Shaw, Sarah, 1955– author.
Title: Breathing mindfulness: discovering the riches at the heart of the
Buddhist path/Sarah Shaw.
Description: First edition. | Boulder, Colorado: Shambhala, [2025] |
Includes bibliographical references and index.
Identifiers: LCCN 2024027991 | ISBN 9781611807189 (trade paperback)
Subjects: LCSH: Buddhism—Study and teaching. | Mindfulness (Psychology)
Classification: LCC BQ156 .S36 2025 | DDC 294.3071—dc23/eng/20241107
LC record available at https://lccn.loc.gov/2024027991

The authorized representative in the EU for product safety and compliance is eucomply
OÜ, Pärnu mnt 139b-14, 11317 Tallinn, Estonia, hello@eucompliancepartner.com.

Contents

Acknowledgments

I feel indebted to many people for their help with this book. Some of them may not have realized they were helping me, but they were! It could have been through a remark, some information, a question, or simply through offering friendly encouragement. Here are some: Robert Adkins, Paul Baker, Bhikkhu Bodhi, Felipe Castro, Tian Chen, Dr. Potprecha Cholvijarn, Dr. Helen Close, Ilan and Avisag Cohn, Professor Kate Crosby, Andrew Dalkin, Ajahn Khammai Dhammasāmi (Oxford Sayadaw), Dr. Rajith Dissanayake, Graham and Helen Dixon, Donny Davino, Professor Jas Elsner, Che Garcia, Professor Rupert Gethin, Canon Dr. Robin Gibbons, Professor Georgios Halkias, Professor Charles Hallisey, Professor Peter Harvey, Professor Maria Heim, Dr. David Jolly, Dr. Jack Kornfield, Kyla Jane Krupke, Erin Lauer, Dr. Pyi Kyaw, Professor Thomas Lockhart, Sarah Mathieson, Keith Munnings, Anne Schilizzi, Ed Shea, Professor Eviatar Shulman, Professor Peter Skilling, Dr. Andrew Skilton, Professor Daniel Stuart, Dr. Nick Swann, Richard Teall, Venerable Nicholas Ṭhāṇissaro, Fiona Thomas, Venerable Tikkhañāṇa Thera, Briji Waterfield, Dr. Chris Westrup, and Sister Wanyu Zhang (Xian'gui Shi).

My thanks go to Leigh Brasington for so kindly agreeing to an online interview about his teaching methods and those of Ayya Khemā. Professor Halvor Eifring organized a conference in Norway in 2012 on meditation and its praxis that has continued to give me inspiration and cause for reflection. Over the last three years, participants in Professor Harold

Roth's Contemplative Studies group at Brown University have given constant feedback and comment, providing endless delight for their interest in breathing mindfulness. I would particularly like to thank Hal and his wife, Lis, for their friendship.

My mind went to trees after a wonderful, guided explanatory walk in the Loch Garten Nature Centre, Abernethy, in the Scottish Cairngorms. Since then, Claralynn Nunamaker, a licensed forester and Buddhist practitioner, has been generous in imparting her deep knowledge and her insights, which have informed my argument. I am grateful that she met me in the Highlands and explained some principles of forestry and sustainability. Other forestry tips have been provided by Dr. Francis Beresford and Chris Gilchrist, based on their experience at the Samatha Centre, Llangynllo, Wales.

As always, Nikko Odiseos, president of Shambhala, has offered support, friendship, and leads. Dr. Matt Zepelin has given wonderful editorial advice and comment. Thanks also to Dianna Able for her care in copyediting and to other editors involved in this script.

Special thanks are due to Boonman and Dang Poonyathiro for their quietly inspirational visits to the UK and to Dr. Paul Dennison for teachings and discussion. Friends in the Samatha Association, UK, and the Samatha Foundation, USA, whom I know in person or online, never cease to surprise me with their insights, background knowledge, and very varied expertise. All these people have shown me how friendship, practice together, and discussion makes things grow.

Lastly, I would like to thank my family and Charles, Jeremy, Roland, and Dechen for the happiness and company they bring.

Note on References

Some readers may be unfamiliar with Pāli referencing. To make things easier to look up, where a sutta or a story is numbered, the number is put in parentheses in the main text with an abbreviation. So, sutta 118 in the Majjhimanikāya is put as (M 118); sutta 2 in the Dīghanikāya is put as (D 2), and story 541 in the *Jātakas* is put as (J 541). Abbreviations for all other references to Pāli texts are given at the end of the book.

Prelude

The Forest

In order for us to breathe, we need the oxygen of woods. Along with our oceans, our woods are our planet's lungs, and we love to visit them. The Buddha and his followers liked to meditate there: it is said that all Buddhas find awakening under trees. In Scotland, there are vast swathes of land that were once ancient woodlands, ecological havens for numerous species of flora and fauna. If you visit one of the few left now, it feels magical, full of mysterious avenues and misty, gnarled groves, populated by multiple species of insects, butterflies, and birds. It is a great adventure to walk in such woods. If the weather is good, you can look around and find a shade-giving tree whose roots provide good openings for a sitter: rustles, movements of animals, dapplings of light, and the soft undercover make them a welcoming place to sit in meditation if you feel like it.

Woodlands like this used to be self-sufficient ecosystems. But throughout the nineteenth century they were eroded by the cultivation of a monoculture: pine and spruce for commercial production. Gradually, step by step, the old forests were almost entirely uprooted. Scotland's pines and spruces are beautiful. No one would begrudge them their space, as tall pines create such magnificent, peaked canopies of green, blue, gray, and olive throughout the mountains and glens. They are also good for the soil. But on their own they do not give the full diversity that is needed for all species to flourish and the soil to become "ancient," filled with different nutrients for all kinds of trees, plants, insects, birds, and animals. This variety makes forests that oxygenate us in mind, heart, and body.

As in so many places throughout the world, ancient forests, with their occasional rare species, and the little trees as well as the big ones, make the ecology of the whole area truly healthy. Forests breathe and need variety. Only when this starts to happen do rarer birds, like eagles and ospreys, find enough terrain to have hunting space and a chance for varied breeding with birds from other locations. In a joined-up area of forest all sorts of wildlife flourish. It takes time to cultivate such woodlands. It is not just as simple as planting a few of the right kinds of trees. Over a few decades, sufficient space needs to be filled at ground level with appropriate fruits, plants, and ground cover so that lichens, fungi, and insects can help to create anew the habitat of these woodlands. The soil needs to be steeped in this variety for a long time. In Scotland, as in other forests, it is a painstaking, careful process that will take decades. To cover the necessary space, blueberries, juniper, cowberries, and ling are needed to ensure a healthy, diverse growth. Fungi need to flourish to establish communications and ground soil; sensitive, flexible networks will then probe the ground, ensuring rootedness for trees. There is nothing wrong with any single tree. They are all good. We also might need new imported species, hybrids, or cross-fertilizations that will contribute and help. But for the countryside to breathe more freely, literally, we need plenty of species, and all the plant and animal life that flourishes alongside them.

The principles are exactly the same everywhere, from Scotland to California to Thailand. They apply to planting new forests and supporting old ones in any terrain. There is a need for ground cover, for richness, and for a soil that has seen generations of trees, all experimenting in their own way to find space, light, and nutrients. Different trees, even at different elevations, adjust to where they find themselves and adapt genetically, according to light, heat, soil, and nutrients. Their roots explore, adapt, and embed themselves to flourish. The species might be different in various places, but the needs are the same.[1]

This is a book about breathing mindfulness meditation and the many types of practice that have grown around it. I think we find the same principles there.

BREATHING MINDFULNESS

CHAPTER 1

Introduction

Some eighteenth-century Siamese texts open with an homage to "honorable breath," and the "holy practice" of mindfulness of breathing. It is a beautiful gesture of respect to a bodily function that keeps us going, all the time.

When I first started practicing breathing mindfulness, quite a few decades ago, my progress was unpromising. I did not feel my breath was at all holy. I wondered why I never seemed to be able to find it, let alone watch it. I went back to the class each week. I sensed some charged pool of stillness there. But I could not get the hang of this thing called "mindfulness," apart from knowing I probably needed more of it. I fidgeted and was convinced I could not be doing it right. Occasionally I did seem to find the breath and was able to watch it for a few moments. I just felt better. After only a week or so, I found if I noticed my breath during my day as well, things seemed more manageable. Then I managed to get regular practice in and found great benefits. I even found moments of composure and quiet at unexpected times.

One day when I was home visiting my parents, a completely new feeling came up. I actually *wanted* to do my meditation practice. This was quite unusual for me, so I went to meditate there and then. Everything came together. Within minutes I felt completely and utterly happy. My mind felt at home for the first time in my life. The breath, which had been with me all the time, was moving freely, so the body and mind felt at one. The experience was a recognition so complete it filled me with joy. How had this not been possible before? Now it is usual to say that such experiences arouse attachment. They certainly do! But there was also a new wisdom and knowledge of a path ahead: I knew what could happen and had found what I wanted to do. The experience was not in a great hurry to return to me, however. I went back to trying too hard, but I now knew what was possible.

My experience must have happened to countless people. Breathing mindfulness has become the most popular method of meditation internationally over the last hundred years. But it is hard to work out anything about its history, and it remains very difficult to find out more about the methods and styles of practice that have changed so many people's lives. Breathing mindfulness traditions, like so many others, are often unrecorded and private. Historically, people who practice what we now call "Southern Buddhism"—meaning, roughly, the Buddhisms of South and Southeast Asia—did not talk much about their practice. Some methods were not written down. For a number of reasons—which will be explored in this book—only now do we know more about the varieties of practice that used to flourish, some of which have come into the international sphere. But it is all still largely undocumented.

I have met many people in other traditions as well as mine who would like to know how their practice fits into a larger picture. Others, who do not meditate at all, just want to find out about the character and style of the Buddhisms of these regions without feeling that there is "only one" method. It was a puzzle to me that I had never found an account of the various different breathing practices nor a record of the one I practice. After quite a few years, I did find some. But many of them said I should definitely *not* be practicing some of the techniques, such as calm (*samatha*), that I found so necessary and helpful!

This book hopes to give a general historical survey of some varieties of breathing mindfulness and how they apparently developed. Breathing mindfulness is the most popular practice in Southern Buddhism. This is the meditation said by Pāli commentaries to have been undertaken by the Buddha on the night of his awakening.[1] According to the suttas, after following mortifications, he remembered spontaneously finding the first *jhāna* as a child, having been left under a rose-apple tree at the plowing festival. This is a meditation still practiced today. The Buddha said that remembering this had been the basis of his understanding of the middle way.

Breathing mindfulness brings about the balance of mindfulness and calm, so that various routes can then be undertaken.[2] As a way of obtaining calm (*samatha*), it operates through development of the *nimitta* (mental object) to take the mind to the meditation the Buddha found as a child and used as the basis for his awakening. It can then be used as the basis for formless meditation. Right *jhāna*, which can be a basis for that, is described as a lucid, alert, and deeply contented peace that envelops mind and body: a refreshing and restorative absorption inextricably linked to mindfulness and wisdom.[3] Some methods place considerable emphasis on this state. There are, however, insight methods as well. Because the breath is always moving—so it partakes of impermanence (*anicca*), has unsatisfactory elements (*dukkha*), and is not owned—it can also act as a constant reminder of nonself (*anattā*). So it allows meditation on the three signs that lead to insight as well as calm. Most meditations include some elements of both.

The breath is always there, somewhere, and we can always be aware of it in different ways. This book explores variations in the background and understanding of these practices, from method to method. Calm methods tend to work with feeling (*vedanā*), in finding the flow and softness of the breath. They often link breathing practices to careful differentiation of lengths of breath in a manner based on The Sutta on Breathing Mindfulness. Mantra, visualization, and chanting, as well as meditation on the four elements, support the breathing mindfulness practice in some methods, particularly those where there is a strong esoteric element. Insight methods might place more attention to noticing the breath as a means of changing how one perceives the world (*saññā*) as well as investigating the three signs and how the mind's constructings and labelings create the world for us in various ways. They all find their first principles in the sutta. Other theory systems, such as Abhidhamma, the canonical philosophical and psychological system, are also applied in all kinds of ways.

All these approaches based on the breath are felt to lead to awakening. The divine abidings of loving-kindness, compassion, sympathetic joy, and equanimity are found throughout and practiced before, after, or during the breath meditations. Underneath this is the breath. It can weave in all these approaches and, if handled with care, tends to cure problems and imbalances that might arise in any one person. The Buddha describes concentration based on this meditation as "peaceful and sublime, an ambrosial pleasant dwelling."[4] He compares such deep meditation to a welcome burst of a rain cloud after the dirt and heat of the hot season. A breathing practice can refresh by its inherent balance, whatever style you do.

Most practitioners enjoy the fact that there are other kinds of practice than their own. It still sometimes happens, however, that people are told by someone that they are doing the "wrong" method! This has been said to me, not just in some books, but in meditation centers I have visited, in Manchester, London, Bangkok, and Colombo. I thought this was just because I did a *samatha* practice. (As we shall see, these have been less esteemed by some.) Yet I am assured by various people who do various insight systems that they have had comparable experiences. So why this anxiety to lead people away from systems that are seen as less good and even less Buddhist? It was a puzzle for me for years. If someone is happy with their method, it is not a good idea to try and convert them to another. People new to the subject feel bemused by this lack of a broad perspective in what they read and hear. The Buddha was very careful in his instructions to his followers, asking them to give a suitable teaching only on request, at the right time, for the right person.[5] So why this insistence and standoffs between methods of practice?

The answer to the mystery seems to me to arise from a misapprehension of the early roots of Buddhism. The Buddha taught and needed to address many different kinds of people. In this book, I suggest that the very variety of methods, approaches, and theory systems associated with breathing mindfulness practice is a sign of its health. It was implicitly sanctioned by the Buddha himself. Again, the Buddha adapted his teachings according to the person and sanctioned many different practices as part of the Buddhist path.[6] He taught people according to their temperaments and adjusted his teachings to fit the person's needs; he accommodated variety constantly, clearly aware that different people needed different things.[7] Sometimes, it seems, he made up a meditation on the spot to suit a particular person.[8] Different traditions emerged almost immediately, a reflection of this potential for diverse seeding.

The breath itself is always new, replenishing, and endlessly restorative. It sorts out most problems on its own, with the right attitude of friendliness and respect. Different systems tend to evolve to ensure this happens for the people concerned. I feel the Buddha taught what was needed by particular people at a particular time. The various methods around now are simply a reflection of this sense of working with people's needs and characters.

It seems important to have an overview. How did different traditions, methods, and techniques emerge? How can we step back and look at them all? Many books on this subject, understandably, promote one method. This is good, but it is also good to appreciate and respect other styles as well. The forest helps us here: it offers a precise metaphor for the varied approaches to breathing mindfulness and the kind of people who do them. We need apt variety and can enjoy it. The Sutta on Breathing Mindfulness, which we will explore in this book and which is the canonical Buddhist text on breathing mindfulness, shows how this practice, and Buddhist principles, can take root in new places and be endlessly adaptable. Breathing mindfulness has been, and remains, the main form of practice in Southeast and South Asian Buddhism. There has been some deforestation, as we shall see, but the variety and potential of the breathing mindfulness traditions are still there to some degree.

The intention of this book is not to give an intensely academic analysis. Scholarly specialties are necessary for close scrutiny but can also be limiting: the high-resolution needs of the discipline involved can lose a rounded sense of the overall. I hope to give a feeling of what it is like just to walk through the forest, sensing the textures, feel, and atmosphere of the terrain.[9] It seems interesting just to encounter the traditions of practice, look at some of the figures from the past and present, and find out about some styles of practice that have shaped those that people do now. Throughout, I explore how and where various approaches evolved historically, and what we know about their ground cover and soil as well as their deep roots; all the methods here find some ancient validation but also have real freshness, and sometimes innovation, apt for our ever-changing, living breath. Information is sometimes scanty, but we can sense the fuller landscape. I hope the references help people who would like to find out more about any one system.

South and Southeast Asian Buddhisms are known now as Theravada. Buddhism has many creative tensions affecting approaches to practice. The ancient distinction between the Theriya tradition—which gave rise to what we call Theravada now—and the Mahayana tradition offers one major example. Perhaps in contrast to Buddhisms in other regions, what we now call Theravada schools regard breathing mindfulness as offering a complete path to awakening. Their methods provide the focus of this book. Most Buddhisms work with the breath, however, and understanding something of these varied emphases enriches our practice, whatever system we follow. The practice of breathing mindfulness is perhaps Buddhism's greatest gift to the world. It is fascinating to see its many varieties. I hope people who are practitioners feel that their method is fairly shown, and that people who know little about the subject find it is one they would like to investigate more.

CHAPTER 2

Vocabulary

A new practitioner in breathing mindfulness wrote me to say she felt she had "landed by small plane or helicopter into a vast landscape." She wanted to know more about how she could relate the Buddhist terms and vocabulary she was learning to her daily experience and meditation. It is strange to encounter words in Buddhism and not really see how they apply to one's own simple experience. If you go to a new terrain, you learn a new language—and the Buddha taught, not just meditation, but a new vocabulary to understand it.

As with any craft or skill, there are some terms that come up all the time that start to become reasonably familiar. Many are used for all stages of meditation practice and in keeping the breath in one's awareness during the day. One of the characteristics that the Buddha noted about breathing mindfulness is that it suppresses too much thinking.[1] In practice, that does not mean thoughts disappear but that labeling tends to stop when the breath becomes the sustained object of interest. The mind is placed in a new way, without so much fuss. Breathing mindfulness, even from the early stages, helps us to move away from the pull of buzzing thoughts, desires, and annoyances to be aware of the breath. The way it does this is helped through some of the terms that will be explained here. They are all simple states we experience in our daily lives, but they acquire new meaning and significance as the practice deepens.

In order to get a feeling for this process, we need to see the mind from a slightly different perspective. The ancients did not have the same view of breathing as we do. For them, breathing was our relationship and contact with one of the four great primaries: earth, water, fire, and air. Air is what allows us to breathe, and what keeps our body alive. It is everywhere in our body. In some ways it is like our physical experience of the breath. We can feel it coming in and going out throughout the body. Ajahn (Geoff) Ṭhānissaro says, discussing the teachings of Ajahn Lee Dhammadhāro, discussed in this book:

> For example, when he refers to the breath or breath sensations, he is speaking not only of the air going in and out of the lungs, but also of the way breathing feels, from the inside, throughout the entire body. Similarly, the "elements" (*dhātu*) of the body are not the chemical elements. Instead, they are elementary feelings—energy, warmth, liquidity, solidity, emptiness, and consciousness—the way the body presents itself directly to inner awareness. The only way to get past the strangeness of this sort of terminology is to start exploring your own body and mind from the inside and to gain a sense of which terms apply to which of your own personal experiences. Only then will these terms fulfill their intended purpose—as tools for refining your inner sensitivities—for the truth of meditation lies, not in understanding the words, but in mastering the skill that leads to a direct understanding of awareness itself.[2]

Finding our own vocabulary for events happening in meditation and in daily life and allowing ourselves to understand each of the key terms is a lifelong work. It means we can appreciate the texts we hear, read, or talk about with greater feeling and understanding; it also builds a language that is shared by other meditators in our own and in other traditions.

Ṭhānissaro compares Ajahn Lee's teachings to a recipe:

> If you simply read the recipe, you can't—even if you understand all the terms—get any flavor or nourishment from it. If you follow the first few steps and then give up when it starts getting difficult, you've wasted your time. But if you follow it all the way, you can then set it aside and simply enjoy the results of your own cooking.[3]

Many of the terms are features we know well from daily life but just have not isolated as qualities to cultivate—we have not learned to cook with them! If we can recognize them in daily life, and know them, they will help as we explore the unfamiliar territory of watching and learning from the breath. The meaning of these words deepens and changes as the practice of breathing mindfulness develops. The seven factors of awakening are primary in The Sutta on Breathing Mindfulness (M 118). Before we move to a close reading of that discourse in the next chapter, it is helpful to know what the seven factors are and how they can be seen in a breathing mindfulness practice. Here they are:

- Mindfulness

- Investigation

- Vigor

- Joy

- Tranquility

- Concentration

- Equanimity

Next I will give some interpretations. Meditators may explain each one slightly differently according to their own experience in meditation: again, terms acquire new dimensions as one's own practice develops. Different schools of breathing mindfulness might have a subtly different understanding too: if the practice is more inclined to an insight path, some terms relating to wisdom and discrimination may acquire particular weight. For those following a *samatha* path, it may be others.[4]

Understanding the Language of the Factors of Awakening

With a breathing practice, a great deal of one's alertness and sense of the body on the ground is simply to do with posture. It has an effect on the flow of breath, the state of mind, and the arousing of basic mindfulness:

where we are and how the body feels. Can I feel the ground? Ajahn Sucitto says: "The ideal . . . is one of having the backside firmly planted on the ground; then one can tune in to the sense of being supported."[5] One posture is the half-lotus. Westerners often have not grown up sitting on the floor or squatting so much, so variations on the half-lotus posture, with the right foot tucked into the left thigh, may be needed. Some people need a looser cross-legged posture or one with legs folded to one side. Many people find the legs get more used to this and gradually become more flexible. The half-lotus makes a steady, natural shelf, and is worth aiming for because it feels so stable. For any posture, you might need a cushion. A cushion under the right knee, with the foot under the thigh, can be helpful. At the outset of the meditation, just being aware of your contact with the ground makes you feel it is supporting you. It is always useful to be mindful of this contact during the meditation.

The back should be upright, neither hunched nor too rigid, which can strain the lower back. Mindfulness can be established a little before the meditation by slightly overstretching the shoulders back and overstretching forward. You can then imagine the sternum being pulled up a bit so that the chin stays up but not high. The vertebrae need to settle into one another, keeping verticality but also the right, easy balance so one does not lean forward.[6] Then the hands can rest comfortably. For this practice, this is usually with the right hand over left, with thumbs completely relaxed on the first finger of the right hand: the concentration posture. The hands feel like a boat, and the body feels steady. Ajahn Sucitto says:

> When you sustain this balanced and upright awareness, and centre your awareness of your body, there is a steady and spacious embodied sense that the breathing flows through. That current of breathing and the upright sense support each other. Then you are firmly established, like a wide-canopied tree rooted in the Earth. Well done! To have touched and stayed on your own ground is a huge step towards improving your clarity and calm.[7]

The main area of mindfulness is the breath itself. This can be tricky. Where is my breath? How do I find it? Most teachers suggest just waiting until you can feel it: "Let it arise rather than go hunting for it."[8] Some teachers suggest that welcoming the breath in and letting it go is like the relationship with a friend. It has always been there for us, and we can trust that and wait for it to become clear.[9] With a breathing practice, there are many techniques of investigation. But just finding how to keep the attention on the breath is usually the first kind of investigating we do, as the mind explores the breath. The five hindrances to calm meditation—of longing for the senses, ill will, sloth and torpor, restlessness and worry, and doubt—can come in at any time.[10] Some breathing mindfulness methods advise labeling them as a way of dealing with them and then moving back to the breath. Others do less labeling but are just aware of them as they come up. Ajahn Viradhammo gives encouraging advice as to how to keep this up, even when it seems to be going wrong:

> In this way, we learn to endure impatience, and that's transformative. We recognize the impatience, we watch it, and eventually it falls away. We do the same with restlessness and all of the other hindrances. We sense these things when they're coming up, but we're just with them, rather than willfully repressing them. We breathe with them and accept them. We accept them again and again.[11]

This is bringing into play a kind of investigation (*dhammavicaya*), the second factor of awakening. The mind can then start to investigate the breath, feeling, as Buddhadāsa says, the flavor of each breath as it comes in and out.[12] In Abhidhamma, this simple probing sense is equated to the investigation that is present when the mind attains enlightenment. It can be there at many levels as the mind explores the breath.

After a while, the third factor, vigor (*viriya*), can be naturally aroused by the breath. In sports we all know when vigor arises and we put effort in. It can be as much knowing how *not* to put in too much effort. In breathing mindfulness, that is the most common problem when people start. It is just like many sports. When you first start to play tennis, you wave your arms around too much and waste energy! But after a while, you learn just what effort is needed and where it comes from: the energy arises from different parts of the body, appropriate for what is needed.

In any sport or skill, one investigates, not in a cerebral way but with the body, finding the minimum effort for the most energy. The same applies to breathing mindfulness. The energy needed can sometimes be very gentle indeed. We do know how to breathe. We just have to listen to the movement of the breath, with a straight back, to find the kind of energy needed.

Then, interest and zest come in. This may take time, but the fourth factor, joy (*pīti*), when it is found with the breath, is the real game changer for the experience of breathing mindfulness. It starts to be pleasant sometimes. The joy, again, can be like the joy felt in a sport or something we just like doing, like painting or sculpting, where we find real delight. With patience, that joy can also come with the breath. In the teachings we are going to look at in this book, the amount of joy encouraged can vary greatly. Some do not pay that much attention to it all. Others take it as very important as a way of keeping the practice vivid and letting it change us. Either way, some joy is needed. If we substitute the word *love* for *joy*, as has been suggested, it is like doing something because you love doing it.[13] Everything changes. Ajahn Pasanno stresses "allowing" oneself to experience joy, as many people feel they should not be experiencing it.[14] It is part of the meditation. With some methods of breathing mindfulness, joy can be very intense and transformative: it purifies the whole mind and changes everything for people.

With awareness of the breath, often people who thought they could not experience joy feel that they can. The fifth factor, tranquility (*passaddhi*) then arises. It introduces an awake, engaged trust in the breath that softens the meditation: you are working with, not against, the breath. It is a bit like when doing a craft or a sport and everything is set in motion: the pot is going well when working on a potter's wheel, or you are enjoying doing a gardening job in a steady way, or you are even trusting the wave when surfing. Joy becomes tranquil, so the body relaxes, and the mind does too. Then the next stage, of concentration (*samādhi*), can come into play. Focus is needed and can be trained.

Concentration is often misunderstood as the kind of focus that is intent and sharp. In a breathing practice that is wrong concentration, without mindfulness and overall awareness. Ajahn Sucitto says, "Nor does 'concentration' (*samādhi*) mean holding attention onto a particular point—*samādhi* is a state that the mind enters into as it settles down and feels at ease."[15] In practice, many systems of breathing mindfulness do focus on one spot, throughout or for part of the meditation, as it is helpful to do so. In some systems, the tip of the nose or the abdomen is very important. But concentration itself means becoming even and unified: it is the state of the mind and body that is important, and whether it feels unified and settled. Venerable Bhikkhu Anālayo calls it a "natural converging, a coming together in an effortless unification of mind that rests within itself, composed and at ease."[16] It should not be rigid and can be felt as inner stillness: Ajahn Buddhadāsa describes it as known through three qualities: it is stable (*samāhito*), purified (*parisuddho*), and flexible (*kammaniyo*).[17] The mind is happily gathered.

Here, there are some points of difference between styles of practice. The breath, says Buddhaghosa, is the only meditation object pursued through touch: we feel the breath and know it through that.[18] Some of the traditions in this book pursue that contact in particular and use it as the basis for investigation, the second factor of awakening, which then becomes dominant. Contact with the breath is investigated for its impermanence, in its rise and fall and in the constant movement of phenomena in the body and mind. Or it might be pursued to be analyzed into different elements, scrutinized for their nature and the aspect of nonself: the four elements are not self. Such insight methods became very popular in the twentieth century.

Another, more traditional route is to develop the state known as *jhāna* on the basis of the breath. This is the meditation mentioned in the last chapter, which the Buddha experienced spontaneously as a child, and used as the basis of his awakening. The Buddha constantly teaches this meditation and practices it himself after he is enlightened. In the canon, right concentration is associated with the four *jhānas*.[19] The breath seems neutral in feeling at first, but in time, known with friendliness, it arouses joy, happiness, and tranquility. These feelings themselves can be explored with a different kind of investigation that allows them to develop and mature, so the whole mind and body experience happiness in the breath.

After a while, an image (*nimitta*) might develop in the mind as a sign of the mind becoming still. In *samatha* systems, this image is fostered and followed. The breath encourages the practitioner to develop five qualities as they explore its feeling and nature. These are placing or applying the mind (*vitakka*), exploring or examining (*vicāra*), joy (*pīti*), happiness (*sukha*) and one-pointedness or unification (*ekaggatā*).[20] These are all qualities that we can find and know in daily life in a milder form: that is, when we enjoy something and the usual "thinking" goes away. There is a joy, happiness, and singleness in what we are doing. When this arises in the meditation, with mindfulness, it is good.

In daily life this unified sense arises in things that we like, where we use a different kind of thinking. Some might find it while white-water rafting, when your body knows how to guide you and how to steer the waters. Sedentary activities can arouse it too. I find it in complicated Fair Isle knitting sometimes, when the usual thinking mind is suspended through an intuition of how to do the pattern: your body, not you, seems to know how to do it and the mind feels freed up from usual distractions. A university student of mine who is a champion rock climber said she could *only* do her extreme form of the sport if she let herself relax and allow the mind to go to a less cluttered state so that the body does the thinking. It is too dangerous otherwise! You need plenty of mindfulness inside and out, she said, all the time. Developing skills in the *nimitta*, and allowing body knowledge to arise, uses the same sort of intuitive capacity: it is not "thought" in our usual sense. This is the same for people who do not get an image, who find that the feeling of suffusion with the breath still develops such skills.

After a while, these five work with one another so that they feel inseparable and deepen beyond our usual experience. Together, they unify and purify the body and mind, creating the "limbs" to enter deep meditation, *jhāna*. As mindfulness and concentration on the breath deepen, hindrances dissolve, and the mind becomes completely unified in the breath. This is entry into the first *jhāna*. Then, the applying and exploring aspects of the mind are not needed as the mind moves to the second *jhāna*, which has joy, happiness, and unification as well as an internal silence. All discursive thought has dropped away. Joy, reaching its own fruition, is then dropped, and the practitioner attains the third *jhāna*, characterized by happiness and unification and a great increase in mindfulness and clarity. Finally, even happiness is no longer necessary, and the mind rests in a unification marked by great mindfulness and equanimity: the fourth *jhāna*. These states may take years to develop so that they can be entered and left at ease. They give fuel, confer steady strength, and ensure emotional stability. The practitioner can then move to practice formless meditation or to develop the higher knowledges (*abhiññā*) or insight and wisdom.

When anyone practices the divine abidings of loving-kindness, compassion, sympathetic joy, and equanimity, they are doing a calm (*samatha*) practice and developing concentration. To be aware of all beings, everywhere, wishing them well, is to open the mind infinitely and to stop scatteredness and distraction. Again, usual thinking about people and things drops away in the feeling of the meditation. These are not harsh but soft, suffusing practices that naturally work through intuition on the basis of feeling. They unify the mind, wherever it is felt, and wash away hindrances. They can be deepened to *jhāna* in meditation: they are also kinds of concentration. We know this stilling sometimes, in ourselves and others. In daily life the divine abidings are our signs of emotional maturity. We can recognize them in people with whom we feel at home: the capacity to empathize, to show compassion, to enjoy happiness in others, and sometimes to watch with feeling but without partiality. The last divine abiding, equanimity also acts as the seventh factor of awakening. It is not the rejection of feeling but a state whereby feeling is purified and simply becomes itself, fully mindful of what is going on, without partiality. This too is essential for enlightenment.

These are qualities we all might feel sometimes, perhaps momentarily. I think we would agree they are the things that give meaning and value in our lives. After a while, such terms acquire more significance. They are central to any breathing mindfulness practice. In Buddhist Abhidhamma, they denote what is there when the mind is healthy (*kusala*). They can arise in daily life when there is a skillful mind. They arise in deeper forms in meditation and, it is said, when the mind is approaching enlightenment. I feel they are best understood, on a mundane level, as qualities that are there when we feel happy and fulfilled, that we would wish for our friends and family in their daily lives. Sometimes they work as a process, with one leading naturally to the next. All seven factors are said to be needed to become enlightened. They are strengthened and purified until the mind is freed from the suffering of attachments and rejections, and investigation is transformed into deep wisdom. The Buddha, in the sutta we are about to discuss, clearly regarded them as key to breathing mindfulness, as qualities that can come into play at any stage, from beginning to end. In some Theravada meditations they are invoked and invited to arrive.[21]

All systems described in this book arouse mindfulness. Some emphasize joy, tranquility, and calm, while others stress investigation and vigor as they explore the breath. There is an ancient distinction between meditation approaches that tend to calm ("wet")—that develop *jhāna* and concentration—and those inclined to insight ("dry"), which sometimes do not. The breath tends to balance, in all methods. All are intended to arouse these seven factors, at some time, in mindfulness of the breath.

CHAPTER 3

The Sutta on Breathing Mindfulness

Ānāpānasati-sutta

One of the most economical and beautifully practicable pieces of crafts-manship in the Pāli canon is The Sutta on Breathing Mindfulness.[1] This text gives us the *locus classicus* for this practice, in all its stages—numbering sixteen. These stages, or pairs, have become the template, a series of basic markers, for most forms of breathing mindfulness found today.

The sixteen stages taught by the Buddha in this sutta offer a full path to awakening and show his attitude to teaching. As we see, it works on many levels. The Buddha does not spell everything out; however, he is precise. He does not give all the details as to how to undertake the prac-tice; he distills the essence of how to approach each breath and points out the happiness, peace, and insight this attention can bring. This text shows us how to be aware of the breath, explore it in manifold ways, and then see what happens to the mind and body as this exploration takes place.[2] The breath rises and falls, can be smooth but also happy, and can be lengthened or shortened. All the skills we need with the breath are in the sixteen stages.

Many interpretations and perspectives on these have been explored in teachings and commentaries inspired by this sutta, from the earliest times. Variation in understanding is authentic and ancient; there are very early debates and controversies on almost every word or phrase within the core stages described in this sutta.³ Our discussion here will not attempt to trace each commentary and varied reading of the phrases. Rather, we will look at the sutta and see if we can get a feeling for the different kinds of experiential contact the stages suggest. The question will not be primarily "what is the right way of interpreting this passage?" but more "how can the stages of breathing mindfulness act as a guide?" I hope this will show where so many modern schools of practice originate and explain how they have evolved the way they have.

At the outset of the sutta, an evocative image sets the tone, suggesting how breathing mindfulness and other meditations were taught to others. The discourse is given at Sāvatthi, at the grove belonging to Migara's mother, a notable lay disciple. It is the full moon of the Pavarana, toward the end of the Vassa, or the rainy season. This is the three-month period when monastics go into retreat, staying in one monastery rather than traveling and teaching. This full moon, before usual contact with the laity and outside world is renewed, is traditionally a time for confessing faults; the sangha needs to be whole and unified as it emerges from its seclusion. The monastics have all been practicing meditation together for a long time. Unusually, on this occasion we are told how many of the Buddha's chief disciples are present. It is a gathering of the core members of the sangha:

> At that time some elder monks were teaching and training. Some elder monks were teaching and training ten monks, some were teaching and training twenty monks, some were teaching and training thirty monks, some were teaching and training forty monks. The new monks, being taught and trained by the elder monks, became aware of the distinctive excellence of each stage in its sequence.⁴

The atmosphere is warm: the Buddha makes an unusual homage to his assembled community. He announces his great happiness at the meditation and teaching that has been going on during the rains and says that he will stay for the whole of this month to continue meditation and teaching with them.

The teaching of breathing mindfulness is given at the next full moon, the Komudī, the time when luxuriant white lotuses blossom everywhere. With the rains now ended, monks pour in from the surrounding countryside to hear the Buddha's teachings. The image of monks teaching younger ones, in different groups, is repeated. The Buddha starts his teaching by observing appreciatively that the assembly is the "heartwood" of the sangha. Recollecting the qualities of this great community with the traditional formulas of their homage and recollection, he reminds them of their purity of speech, action, and thought. He congratulates them, saying how rare it is to see such a community, anywhere. It contains those who are enlightened; those who will be never-returners and will be born in a refined heaven, called a Pure Abode, before attaining their goal, as they have rid themselves of five fetters; those who are once-returners and those who are stream-enterers, who will never be born in a lower realm again and who are heading for enlightenment.[5] They live dedicated to cultivating and developing the four foundations of mindfulness, the thirty-seven factors leading to awakening, and the divine abidings; they meditate on foulness and the perception of impermanence.

Amid these, the Buddha adds, there are those who are dedicated to mindfulness of breathing. This, he says, should be cultivated, made much of, and practiced frequently: it will fulfill all the foundations of mindfulness and hence all the seven factors of awakening.

The Buddha teaches to a highly select group. He starts off with a now famous instruction:

> Here, monks, a monk goes to a forest, or the roots of a tree, or an empty place, and sits, folding his legs in a cross-legged position, making his body straight, and sets up mindfulness in front of him.[6]

This instruction is given only for breathing mindfulness and is also found in The Sutta on the Fruits of Recluseship (*Sāmaññaphala-sutta*; D 2), the great sutta on the practice of concentration, its fruits, and its conclusion. There, it is given before the practitioner, having fulfilled ethical behavior (*sīla*), who sits and abandons the hindrances, attains the four *jhānas*, and develops the higher knowledges through to the final fruit of recluseship: enlightenment and arhatship.[7] The breath is not specified as the practice involved. As this formula is usually associated with breathing mindfulness, however, it was possibly intended here, suggesting that breathing mindfulness was the usual way to attain *jhāna*.[8] All Buddhas are said to teach this meditation, both as a concentration and as a mindfulness practice. The Buddha says that if anyone could speak of anything as "a noble abiding, a divine abiding, the Tathāgata's abiding," they could say it of breathing mindfulness as a concentration practice.[9]

Here, the practice of mindfulness of breathing does not have the word concentration (*samādhi*) attached, as it often does elsewhere. But as we will see, the instructions suggest the vocabulary of *jhāna* and make that association clear.[10] In some modern understandings of Buddhism, mindfulness and concentration are sometimes pitted against one another as if they are in some way opposed. They are not an "either/or." Right *jhāna*, in right concentration, is heavily dependent on mindfulness. Mindfulness is explicitly cited as the basis on which the *jhānas* are established in The Sutta on the Fruits of Recluseship. It is described as strong in the third *jhāna*, where the purification by happiness releases great alertness and clarity of mind. It is again cited for the fourth *jhāna*, where mindfulness is itself "purified by equanimity."[11] In the Abhidhamma, mindfulness is a determinant of the skillful *citta*: it is present in all occurrences of the mind that is free from defilements.[12] This consciousness also forms the basis of *jhāna*.[13] Mindfulness also needs and, in meditation, develops some calm and concentration.

Many people now speak of mindfulness as in some way opposed to the sense of flow. There is a convergence of all the energies of the mind and body when we are really enjoying something and, to use a modern expression, "in the zone." As I hope becomes clear, mindfulness and a sense of absorption can go together. In breathing mindfulness, when it is developed fully, they both need to be there and, with a little practice, can be, right from the first stages. If we come to know and like the breath, we can, sometimes, feel that we enjoy it. As so many teachers in this book suggest, that is the beginning of the full practice of breathing mindfulness.

Concentration is a factor in all consciousness, according to the Abhidhamma, but may be very weak.[14] Anyone who is practicing mindfulness exercises of the kind often given now will find some basic level of calm. A practice with the breath naturally arouses some calm, as one becomes more at ease with its rise and fall and finds just watching it lightly brings a sense of peace. This is concentration. So, a sense of that is usually present in the way the instructions are given—some calm and unification is needed for the mind to be settled and established in mindful alertness. Certainly, there is a difference between the alertness of mindfulness and the stillness and peace of concentration. But these two qualities blend together in right *jhāna* and need not be seen as opposed, a step that in itself suggests that a choice of meditation emphasis has to involve rejection. Most meditations include both elements to some degree. As Venerable Henepola Gunaratana says, ideally mindfulness and concentration work together as a team: "Mindfulness picks the objects of attention, and notices when the attention has gone astray. Concentration does the actual work of holding the attention steady on that chosen object."[15]

The Buddha moves on to the sixteen stages, or sixteen pairs—the classic formula. They are a kind of encoded guide for practicing breathing mindfulness through to its goal: awakening. In a moment we will look at the sixteen stages: they often occur in suttas on their own.[16] But it is worth remembering that in this sutta the Buddha does not end his discourse there; it is not just about the sixteen stages. He follows with an account of the seven factors of awakening (chapter 2): these arise on the basis of the four foundations of mindfulness found through the sixteen. Words connected with four factors occur in the sixteen: mindfulness, joy, tranquility, and concentration. Equanimity is suggested. These are key to our appreciation of the sixteen. All these factors can be aroused through the stages; the stages have an intimate link with them. Developed, he says, these simple qualities lead in the end to knowledge and liberation.

In early texts, breathing mindfulness is given as a practice for those who think a lot.[17] Too much discussion and commentary can be off-putting! So, before we look more at the four clusters of instructions involved in the sutta, I suggest that the sixteen are read, in order, as a light exercise. It need only take a few minutes. But just take a few moments to sit, cross-legged if that is comfortable. A straight back, as the text suggests, can help this, as it helps in experiencing the passage of the breath. When the body is settled, it is possible to be aware of the sounds, the touches on the skin, and the feeling of the ground or floor underneath. Just read through the list and try each stage for a few breaths, seeing how each one feels. It is helpful not to try and work it out intellectually or to feel concern about getting it wrong, but just to see whether each one is something that can be explored with the breath immediately, with a feeling of openness to what comes up. It may well be that one or other stage does not really resonate or feels odd: that is fine, and just worth noticing. If one stage does not feel approachable, simply move on to the next.

The text says the preliminary to the sixteen stages is to summon up mindfulness "in front" (*parimukha*). This has been the subject of great interpretative discussion.[18] In practice, it helps to be reasonably alert to where you are sitting—the contact with the ground and a sense of the area around. The practice is usually conducted with the eyes closed. It is possible to read the stage, then try it. But if you prefer just trying it with the eyes open here, that also works.

The First Tetrad: The Body

1. Mindful, he breathes in; mindful, he breathes out. Either, breathing in a long breath, he knows, "I am breathing in a long breath," or, breathing out a long breath, he knows, "I am breathing out a long breath."

2. Either, breathing in a short breath, he knows, "I am breathing in a short breath," or, breathing out a short breath, he knows, "I am breathing out a short breath."

3. He trains in this way: "Experiencing the whole body, I shall breathe in." He trains in this way: "Experiencing the whole body, I shall breathe out."

4. He trains in this way: "Making bodily activities tranquil, I shall breathe in." He trains in this way: "Making bodily activities tranquil, I shall breathe out."[19]

The first cluster relates to the body and how we experience it. For these four, it is helpful to try and be aware of where you are and how your posture feels and to get your bearings so you feel comfortable. At first, just try and bring a general awareness to your breath, whatever it is doing, as the opening of the first stage indicates: by following its passage in and out of the body. Then, when you have got a feel for how it is going today, allow the breath to deepen gradually and try doing a few longer, deep breaths at the longest length that is comfortable. See if you can enjoy it and sense the effect of a deep, long, and unstrained breath.

For the second stage, try doing a few short breaths, and see if you can still do that and relax—still keeping the back straight and the posture settled—with the short inbreath and short outbreath. It may feel slightly different and be associated in daily life with a tense, very active state of mind: if so, it is interesting to relax the shoulders and attention and see if one can feel calm too, just while doing this short breath. The breath might feel slightly lighter, and for some this stage is easier. It has a different tone. There is no need to judge! Some days a long breath feels more comfortable, some days a short.

Then go to the third stage and see if it is possible to be aware of the whole body while taking in the breath and breathing out, whatever length of breath that may arise. You might find that it is indeed possible if you imagine it is.

Then, last, see if it is possible to breathe in a sense of tranquility and breathe it out, calming the activities in the body. It is helpful not to think any of the stages through, but just try doing them and trusting that you can. If not, it is no problem—you can just see how you do with moving between the four and see if you can find something working. If not, just move on.

The Second Tetrad: The Feelings

5. He trains in this way: "Experiencing joy I breathe in." He trains in this way: "Experiencing joy I breathe out."

6. He trains in this way: "Experiencing happiness I breathe in."
   He trains in this way: "Experiencing happiness I breathe out."

7. He trains in this way: "Experiencing the activities in my mind
   I breathe in." He trains in this way: "Experiencing the activities
   in my mind I breathe out."

8. He trains in this way: "Making the activities in my heart and
   mind tranquil I breathe in." He trains in this way: "Making the
   activities in my heart and mind tranquil I breathe out."[20]

This cluster is associated with mindfulness of feeling. Is it possible to
breathe in joy and breathe out joy? It is an interesting and sometimes
surprising thing to try. Rather than assuming joy is not there, it is worth
assuming it is! And if not, you can make some space for it to arise if it
wishes to. At first this might not seem to work, but after a few breaths it
can seem possible.

After that, one tries the next pair: breathing in happiness and breathing it out again. Again, if one assumes it is there, one might just find it. If
not, it does not matter. It might make you smile.

From there, one can become aware of the activities that are going on
in the whole mind; the breath can be felt to envelop it all. *Citta* is usually translated as mind or consciousness but especially heart. It is worth
knowing that, for the ancients as for many peoples now, consciousness
was understood to reside in the heart base (*hadaya*).[21] The seat of "mind"
can start there and move outward. Just as the first tetrad suggests making
the bodily activities tranquil with the breath, this cluster allows attention to include a larger sense of heart and the whole mind, and if you get
the right feeling of playful experimentation, you may find that the breath
can feel happy too.

The Third Tetrad: Heart and Mind

9. He trains in this way: "Experiencing the mind I breathe in."
   He trains in this way: "Experiencing the mind I breathe out."

10. He trains in this way: "Gladdening the mind I breathe in." He
    trains in this way: "Gladdening the mind I breathe out."

11. He trains in this way: "Stilling the mind I breathe in." He trains in this way: "Stilling the mind I breathe out."

12. He trains in this way: "Freeing the mind I breathe in." He trains in this way: "Freeing the mind I breathe out."[22]

The third cluster concerns mindfulness of this mind. For many people, if the mind is understood as having its basis in the heart, it is just much easier to open the attention to the whole and see it as the heart—but, if you prefer, "mind" is also good. It is an immediate way of understanding the stages 7 and 8 as well as this tetrad. Others might feel the mind simply as a kind of spacious expansion out from the body. The movement to "the mind" rather than the "activities of the mind" can be felt as an opening out so awareness envelops the mind as a whole, including all the bits of trailing thoughts.

Just as with joy and happiness, it is possible to try and gladden the whole heart and mind, as if the breath is enveloping it and cheering it up. Then, one can have a sense that the breath is stilling the mind on the inbreath and the outbreath. The last stage can be freeing: it is interesting to see if one can feel that the breath is releasing this larger sense of mind, on the inbreath and the outbreath. Again, it is helpful not to think it through, but just to try and see if one can get an intimation of that simply by suggesting it to oneself.

The Fourth Tetrad: Dhammas, *"things as they are."*

13. He trains in this way: "Watching impermanence I breathe in." He trains in this way: "Watching impermanence I breathe out."

14. He trains in this way: "Watching the fading away of passion I breathe in." He trains in this way: "Watching the fading away of passion I breathe out."

15. He trains in this way: "Watching ceasing I breathe in." He trains in this way: "Watching ceasing I breathe out."

16. He trains in this way: "Watching letting go I breathe in." He trains in this way: "Watching letting go I breathe out."[23]

The fourth tetrad opens up a new field: everything, with nothing left out. A new verb brings us to the fourth foundation of mindfulness as each stage now involves watching: being aware of the continuous flow of *dhammas*, events or phenomena, in the body and mind and the world around, as they arise, come into being, and fall away. Rise and fall are activities that the breath does through instinct; indeed, it is this very manifestation of impermanence in the breath that keeps us alive. It is always rising, coming into being, and falling, and attention can gently move to this aspect of it, seeing how impermanence, in practice, can be one of the most reassuring aspects of our existence and experience. Our breath needs to change so that it can come in and go. It is, paradoxically, why we can feel so stable in our lives and the experience of the breath. This foundation of mindfulness is a way of seeing things as they are (*yathābhūtaṃ*) and responding to them. As a grouping, this tetrad may be more difficult to sense immediately. But with an open attitude, it can be done by feeling a sense of a larger letting go. One is still mindful of the body, which is "things as they are," just as the feelings and the state of the mind are. The new verb denotes a new attitude to the breath. The meditator is not doing anything other than actively "watching."

As this goes on, it is possible to be aware of the whole body as well, and the feelings, and the mind: events in each rise and fall while others come into being. One can then feel awareness of the constant, rippling waves of the impermanence of the breath and body, like waves coming into the shore and ebbing. In the Vinaya, the word *nicca* means regular. The first stage of this tetrad is watching things as *a-*, which means "not," and *nicca*: permanent, regular. So, this stage can be seen as observing that events in the body and mind are changing and not quite regular. There is always something changing. This perception itself changes the perspective completely: it helps one feel the falling away of passion, with the emergence of a peace in the ceasing of activities. Just being aware of the rise and fall, and enjoying and appreciating it, is enough, like enjoying watching waves crashing on the beach. Finally, it is possible to suggest to oneself, with the physical and emotional sense of the breath, the release and letting go that simple awareness and observation of these movements can bring.

The Sixteen Stages as Sequence

It is possible to find a feeling for many of these stages straightaway; some may not be obvious, but there are usually some that can be sensed. Do the sixteen make a sequential process? The clusters describe how the breath can be known through four areas of attention, each in four ways. Elements within each cluster seem to work together, so you can cycle them. For the first four, as I hope this exercise makes clear, just turning the attention to the bodily sensation of the breath—being aware of it—changes perspective, as does being aware of a very long inbreath and a long outbreath: it shifts our minds to the area of the breath and the whole body. Putting aside physiological notions of where the breath "should" be in the body, it is experientially possible to feel it pervade the whole body. One can then become familiar with the very different quality of the short breath and find that it can be peaceful too. "Making tranquil" activities in the body sounds odd, but in a few breaths it is possible to sense what it feels like to let the mind feel tranquil, through the act of observing the breath as it comes in and out of the body.

The first four stages, under the category of body mindfulness, establish a ground and set the tone of what follows. Each subsequent cluster also has its own character and changes the quality of the attention: one starts to be aware of feeling in the second four. It can be surprising to find that it is sometimes possible both to experience feelings differently and to let them transform, by breathing joy in and out and then happiness in and out. This opens up a possibility. One can become aware of the immense domain of the mind itself, in four ways: by experiencing the mind, gladdening it, stilling it, and freeing it. Trying each in turn, with the inbreath and the outbreath, sustains that possibility. The last four stages culminate in letting go. By watching, they take a different perspective altogether, like viewing all one's experience in a different way. It is possible to step back and see the whole, with events in body, feelings, and mind rising and falling, all the time.

Becoming aware of impermanence, the transcending of passion, then ceasing and finally letting go changes one's relationship to the breath and the body. There is a being that is practicing, with a body, feelings of all kinds, moods, and thoughts, who has a chance of finding freedom. This principle, a kind of evocation that allows one to be open to the possibility of experiencing joy and happiness before gently letting go of them, and then being open to impermanence and release before letting them go too, is found in many systems of breathing mindfulness. The key is in the way attention is applied, and in seeing if it can be soft, noninsistent, and appropriate to the breath at the time.

Every detail of the wording of these sixteen stages has been subjected to philological scrutiny, argued and debated among practitioners, commentators, and scholars in the now over two millennia that have passed since they were composed. This process seems to have started from the earliest days. These debates are important, and their perspectives enrich our understanding. Even so, there is some quality about all these stages that many people feel intuitively and immediately, if they are open to them. You are the taster of each breath you take; you can see how each one works for you, on that day, and how it feels. Each stage has its own feeling and flavor. I hope doing the exercise first shows how the sixteen have possibilities and meanings that can apply on multiple levels, from the first few tries at being aware of the breath until, I suspect, the final attainment of one's goal.

The stages are like openings, or windows, to further exploration. Chinese scholar Tse-fu Jeff Kuan suggests that in this sutta, the Buddha unified teachings on mindfulness and concentration and wisdom: the sixteen stages, he posits, are different ways, all skillful, of perceiving and understanding the breath.[24] They seem like beads you can feel on a string, which circles around. Each one has a different qualitative feel that you can encounter, again and again, from meditation to meditation. Each one helps us to experience the breath differently. People sometimes say the greatest poetry has precision but is susceptible to interpretation on many levels. This list of sixteen, although not poetry, also has that capacity. Together, it makes a series and offers a repertoire of sixteen very simple ways we can look at and experience the breath.

CHAPTER 4

How a Small Detail Reflects the Whole

Calm and Insight

The Buddha invites us to experience the breath, repeatedly, in different ways, and so to train our minds. From early on, the sequence of sixteen was applied in all sorts of ways to stages of the Buddhist path. Early commentaries understood them as a causal sequence, corresponding to stages of progress in the path. That is how they have often been taught: one naturally gives rise to the next. Within that, the way that different methods frame this flow and movement, as well as the character and nature of each stage, varies.

Many of these reflect an old tension: between breathing mindfulness primarily used for calm, and breathing mindfulness primarily used for insight. All systems encourage some calm, but some methods do not encourage the practice of those four deep states of calm known as *jhāna*. This is the meditation said to form right concentration: the cultivation of the states the Buddha experienced and practiced on the night of his awakening.[1] Systems that depend on these are discussed particularly in chapters 8 and 9. The usual path suggested in the canon involves a movement from ethics, to meditation and *jhāna*, and then to insight.[2] Not all Buddhist schools historically took that approach, however, and many popular methods found today likewise do not take that route. Rather, they develop attention to the breath primarily for insight. This means that the rise and fall of the breath, its impermanence, and its unsatisfactoriness are soon the main, foreground awareness. Calm may arise as a preliminary background to this, but the state of *jhāna* is not the intention or the objective at the outset and, for some methods, not considered so important.

Before we move on to some ways breathing mindfulness was understood in the early days, it will be helpful to consider a few small areas where wording can influence style and method. This will involve taking just two stages of the sixteen. Each stage has had comparably varied interpretations. But, as we shall see, simple adjustments in practice sometimes reflect profoundly different approaches to the Buddhist path. What follows in this chapter is an account of the general tenor and direction of some modern methods. Getting a sense of the different routes you can take with one practice is helpful in understanding not only our own practice, whatever it is, but importantly, those of other people too. There really are different species of breathing mindfulness practice, and some suit different people. I think that sense of possibility was there right at the beginning.

Long and Short Breaths

The sutta says:

1. Mindful, he breathes in; mindful, he breathes out. Either, breathing in a long breath, he knows, "I am breathing in a long breath," or, breathing out a long breath, he knows, "I am breathing out a long breath."

2. Either, breathing in a short breath, he knows, "I am breathing in a short breath," or, breathing out a short breath, he knows, "I am breathing out a short breath."

These short instructions introduce an interesting question: choice. Does the verb "he knows" (*pajānati*), whether there is a long or a short breath, involve some conscious decision to take a long or short breath? The breath is our most conspicuous bodily function and lies at the middle point between our conscious control and our unconscious instinct. We can just let it be as it is, or we can find a way of making it go long or short. Can or should a breathing mindfulness practice involve this choice at the outset? What are a long breath and a short breath? It is worth just looking at this one question here, as an example of how rich a few simple lines of instruction can prove to be. The commentators Buddhaghosa and Upatissa and an early commentary, "The Treatise on Breathing," do not have much to say on this; they differentiate between long and short breaths as separate stages but say little to distinguish them apart from the obvious: one is long, and one is short.[3] We will look at their observations later. Here, however, let us look at three recent teachers—Ajahn Buddhadāsa Bhikkhu (1906–1993), Ajahn Lee Dhammadhāro (1907–1961), and Venerable Nyanaponika Thera (1901–1994)—for their preliminary instructions.

Buddhadāsa, the highly influential twentieth-century teacher, suggests noticing very carefully the difference between a long and a short breath, as they feel so different. As a preliminary to meditation, he suggests just "following" it:[4]

> For example, we can feel the long and the short duration of the breath. Thus, we learn naturally about the long breath and the short breath. We can observe the coarse and fine nature of the breath. Further, we can observe its smoothness and bumpiness . . . we contemplate the different kinds of breath: long and short, coarse and fine, easy and uneasy. Begin to observe the various kinds by experiencing them with sati.
>
> We must learn to observe in greater detail, that is, to observe the reaction or influence of each on each different kind of breathing. What reaction do they cause? How do they influence our awareness? For example, when each breath is long, how does that affect our awareness? What reactions do short breaths cause? What are the influences of coarse and fine breathing, of comfortable and uncomfortable breathing? We should observe the different types of breath and their various influences until we can distinguish clearly

how the long and the short breaths, coarse and fine breaths, and comfortable and uncomfortable breaths differ. We must learn to know the reactions to these various properties of the breath. Likewise, we must learn to know when these qualities influence our awareness, our sensitivity, our mind. . . . It is also important for us to note the effect or flavor of each kind of breath.[5]

These instructions, given at the beginning of his work *Mindfulness with Breathing: A Manual for Serious Beginners*, are intended as an introduction to the practice of breathing mindfulness. His manual, a great classic of this meditation, is worth reading for anyone, whatever their chosen system. Taking each one of the sixteen stages in turn, he invites the meditator to explore them sequentially, yet also appreciate their individual taste. He notes differences between the long and the short breath, but the distinction is downplayed in service to his primary purpose: simply to get people to notice the breath with even and relaxed attention. He invites practitioners to notice how intimately the breath reflects one's mental state, and how, just by observation, the breaths start to change and become finer and quieter.

In contrast, the old meditations of Southeast Asia, which used to be normative there, do often make a choice. There is a deliberate distinction between the long and the short breath at the outset, in a way that is particularly significant for their methods. Some teachers, like Ajahn Lee Dhammadhāro, developed all kinds of exercises mixing long and short breaths, presumably developing and acting within older traditions. We will look at some of Ajahn Lee's teachings more in chapter 11. Here, however, is just one of his descriptions of a possible breathing practice:

There are seven basic steps:

1. Start out with three or seven long in-and-out breaths, thinking *bud* with the in-breath, and *dho* with the out. Keep the meditation syllable as long as the breath.

2. Be clearly aware of each in-and-out breath.

3. Observe the breath as it goes in and out, noticing whether it's comfortable or uncomfortable, broad or narrow, obstructed or free-flowing, fast or slow, short or long, warm or cool. If the breath doesn't feel comfortable, change it until it does. For instance, if breathing in long and out long is uncomfortable, try breathing in short and out short. As soon as you find that your breathing feels comfortable, let this comfortable breath sensation spread to the different parts of the body.

To begin with, inhale the breath sensation at the base of the skull and let it flow all the way down the spine. Then, if you are male, let it spread down your right leg to the sole of your foot, to the ends of your toes, and out into the air. Inhale the breath sensation at the base of the skull again and let it spread down your spine, down your left leg to the ends of your toes and out into the air. (If you are female, begin with the left side first, because the male and female nervous systems are different.) Then let the breath from the base of the skull spread down over both shoulders, past your elbows and wrists, to the tips of your fingers, and out into the air. Let the breath at the base of the throat spread down the central nerve at the front of the body, past the lungs and liver, all the way down to the bladder and colon. Inhale the breath right at the middle of the chest and let it go all the way down to your intestines. Let all these breath sensations spread so that they connect and flow together, and you'll feel a greatly improved sense of well-being.[6]

This shows a radically different approach: the long breath is the basis of the practice, but the short breath gives another basis at a different level. These breaths are consciously measured. Mindfulness is still aroused at each long and short breath, but in a different way from the one explained by Buddhadāsa. The syllables BU-DDHO feature as an anchor for the mind.[7] The sense of the breath is pervasive, including the whole body. Then, the next pair of the sixteen stages are involved: mindfulness of bodily activities comes through the movement of the attention through the body. The sensations are made tranquil through the instruction to "let all these breath sensations spread so that they connect and flow together, and you'll feel a greatly improved sense of well-being." In the list of sixteen, the next stage after this tetrad, the fifth pair, is arousing joy with the breath: we can see how the practice encourages this.

Ajahn Lee Dhammadhāro's teachings here, arising from the forest traditions of Thailand, show the stamp of old Cambodian and Siamese meditations (*borān kammaṭṭhāna* or *kammatthan boran*), where the healing power of the *nimitta* from breath meditation is allowed to suffuse the whole body (see chapter 9). This is calm, or *samādhi*, breathing mindfulness. The breath is taken as an object for the pursuit of concentration and *jhāna*, linked with insight. As we will see in chapter 12, Boonman Poonyathiro's method, from Thailand, is also largely based on old meditations. It too makes a careful distinction between the long and the short. The length of breath is key in allowing entrance in and out of *jhāna*; the long breath begins and ends the practice. This is the "longest breath one can comfortably take" and is not strained or forced. Part of the exercise is finding a long length that feels comfortable and natural. Pa Auk Sayadaw, who teaches *jhāna* in a systematic manner, also starts with the deliberately long breath described in the sutta and makes a clear differentiation between that and the short breath, which is his next stage.

Yet another approach is given by Venerable Nyanaponika Thera, an insight (vipassana) teacher. It derives from another classic exposition of Theravada meditation, *The Heart of Buddhist Meditation*:

> . . . for Mindfulness of Breathing, the Lotus Posture and fully crossed legs is preferable though it is not of absolute necessity. We have also given a warning not to interfere with the breath in any way: in Buddhist practice there should be no holding or stopping of the breath, no deliberate deepening nor attempts to force it into a definite time rhythm. The only task here is to follow the natural flow of the breath mindfully and continuously, without a break or without an unnoticed break. The point where one should fix one's attention is the nostrils against which the breathing air strikes, and one should not leave that point of observation because here one can easily check the entry and exit of the breath.[8]

Later in his book, he also explains a variation of what he calls the Burmese method—a product of the innovations in Burma in the nineteenth century—but says that, by its focus on the abdomen rather than the breath, it is not breathing mindfulness.[9] Nyanaponika is wary of any form of breath guidance or adjustment, describing it with vocabulary like "holding or stopping" and "force" that indicates his caution: the emphasis is on a simple and uninterrupted flow. What he terms a Buddhist approach does not include adjustment of the length or following the breath in the whole body.

Nyanaponika was a deeply experienced theoretician as well as a practitioner. Adopting language clearly derived from commentaries, he suggests looking at the beginning, middle, and the end of the breath with unwavering attentiveness and mindfulness of the various ways the breath can be distracted at each stage—a very ancient distinction (see chapter 6). This method, he said, leads to the culmination at the second pair of the first tetrad of The Sutta on Breathing Mindfulness: here, he explains, a *samatha* school moves to deepen *jhāna* on the breath; an insight school will move to insight. This interpretation of the sixteen stages of breathing mindfulness is found frequently in the twentieth and twenty-first centuries. This was in part influenced by Burmese teachers Ledi Sayadaw and Mahāsi Sayadaw, with whom he spent some time (chapters 13 and 14).

I have chosen the foregoing three teachers as representatives of quite different skills and approaches to the breath, reflected in their understanding of the path and the theory associated with it. Their teachings have all earned reverence throughout Southeast and South Asia and are taught internationally. They are all known for great meditative experience but in different practices. Nyanaponika, who suggests no adjustment to the length of the breath, teaches in the "dry" style, associated from ancient times with insight methods. There is not an emphasis on *jhāna*. The breath is interesting because it is changing and not self. Buddhadāsa suggests calm for exploratory purposes and encourages peace and joy. Ajahn Lee, here and elsewhere, uses deliberate mixes of long and short breaths as part of his repertoire of tools for entering and leaving meditation. One can sense the intuitive style of a *samatha* practice: the breath includes the whole body and has healing properties that can be circulated all around it, consciously. These styles have far more affinities than differences, as for each the breath gives a path to liberation. All trace their methods back to traditional Buddhist texts and commentaries and teach breathing mindfulness as a full path to enlightenment. Yet each gives slightly different advice: how one looks at the breath affects how one enters different meditations.

One can see how richly diverse and sophisticated the pool of South and Southeast Asian breathing techniques had become by the early to mid-twentieth century. We will not compare each stage for each method! But diversity of expression, understanding, and intent permeate their understandings of later stages. This is not a forest monoculture. Rather, it is a highly varied ancient woodland, where many species of indigenous trees, supported by the ground cover of *sīla* and the supportive customs associated with meditative practice in Asia, all flourish. Despite quite major differences of style, content, and delivery, all these approaches show the stamp of The Sutta on Breathing Mindfulness. The wording of that discourse validates them all.

The first two pairs, unlike subsequent stages, use the verb "he knows," or "he understands" rather than the "he trains"; they also use the present tense. L. S. Cousins suggests that that wording structure is quite usual.[10] But many would say the phrasing "he knows" or "he understands" suggests simple observation rather than the intention implied by the use of the words "he trains" and the future tense in subsequent stages: "I shall breathe in . . . I shall breathe out. . . ." In this way, Nyanaponika's method and those of the many popular insight schools find early vindication.[11]

Those who follow a practice that adjusts the breath do so, usually, for attaining calm. They encourage not strain but mindfulness and respect for the nature of the breath and its inclination. There is no forcing or straining. They will, correctly, point out that ancient commentaries make some distinctions between long and short breaths. Cousins notes that deliberate differentiation between lengths was current in ancient India: "But others say, 'Breathing long or short,' i.e., long is [breathing that is] deliberately made to exceed the normal, short is less than normal."

Clearly different applications of the instructions started early.[12] There is an old association of the long breath with joy, while the short breath is associated with happiness.[13] It is certainly striking that there is no mention of a normal, middle-length (*majjhima*) breath, the one we usually have in everyday life. Some sort of conscious breath adjustment is then suggested.[14]

For those who follow a practice that *does* make a distinction between the long and short breath, there is a very helpful image associated with this first tetrad: the woodturner. This is found in both versions of the suttas on the foundations of mindfulness (M 10; D 22), though not in the breathing mindfulness sutta. The attention of the meditator for the first pair of the sixteen is compared to a skilled woodturner who knows if he is turning a long turn or a short one.

Just as, bhikkhus, a skilled turner or turner's apprentice, while making a long turn, knows "I am making a long turn," or, while making a short turn, knows "I am making a short turn," just so, monks, a monk while breathing in long, knows "I am breathing in long," or, while breathing out long, he knows "I am breathing out long"; or, while breathing in short, he knows "I am breathing in short," or, while breathing out short, he knows "I am breathing out short."[15]

The lathe-worker or woodturner[16] uses a knife or a chisel to smooth, say, a table leg, a wooden joint for a house, or a bowl, presumably the main purpose of woodworking in ancient India when the sutta was composed. The woodturner is one who "works with revolving." If a woodturner is making something like a table leg on a lathe, they chisel in a long, sweeping line, shaving the whole way down the leg to get a smooth run. For joints, carved knobs, and bowls, they use a finer chisel to feel their way for the roundedness of the object or decoration, or to pare the ends of joints. They would certainly know that they are doing a long or a short turn. Would they make that choice beforehand? The image suggests they would. So, the practitioner who makes a distinction between the long and the short breath is doing so like the woodturner: choosing what is needed to deal with the breath at the time.

It is fun to find a traditional woodturner and watch them. You can see why breathing mindfulness is compared to woodworking. The woodturner feels their way along the wood as it turns, easing the chisel down to find a smooth finish. Such workers show great love and feeling for the wood itself, knowing not just whether to make a long or a short cut, but also how to adjust to a soft, malleable wood like pine or a hard one like cherry or oak. Each wood requires a different kind of attention: the soft surface of pine needs only a light touch, so the chisel skims the surface; cherry or oak require a more focused, deliberately renewed attention at each stage. A knobby kind of wood needs patient turning, again and again, for the knot to be dispersed. The woodworker's sense of appreciation for the wood, the job, and the product they are making on the lathe is palpable. They are aware of what they are doing and its context at each stage and work with mindfulness of their natural materials and tools. Complete bodily engagement shapes the outcome of the task. It is a delight to see such craftsmanship.

The breath, like different woods, offers materials that can be different on different days and different times. A soft, smooth breath on one day requires lightness of touch. A tough, knotty one at another time needs patient, long smoothing. As with woodturning, a long breath to the area below the navel can have a broad, satisfying feeling, while a short one might feel more finely tuned.

For some *samatha* breathing mindfulness methods that help us enter and exit *jhāna*, it is important to develop a baseline: a long or short breath, which becomes natural to begin and finish each practice.

This is rather like the neutral positions of some yoga and martial arts systems. If you are exerting great flexibility and stamina in the use of your body, you need to be able to return to a good stabilizer, perhaps a tabletop or mountain pose in yoga or the ready position in kung fu. These neutral positions—not our normal ones—are important to allow the practitioner to feel a point of balance and stability within the system they are using. The positions also act as a bridge that you can return to and use to make the mental and bodily adjustment back to your normal life. In physical movements they are essential: if any move feels wrong or strained, or just if you feel a need to stabilize and get back to normal, they are there to let things balance out. Such positions are a bit like a base camp on a mountain hike: somewhere to restore yourself, get ready for the climb, and then return at the end to take stock and rest before returning back to the world. All martial arts have such postures and need them.

For meditators entering *jhāna*, the ability to come back to the very long breath often serves as a reassurance and steadier. At the beginning of any meditation practice, you can feel the longest breath that feels comfortable within the body and use it tune in to the meditation practice. Then, at the end of the meditation, you know you can come back to the body using the same long breath and restore your sense of where you are. Like the neutral position in physical practices, the baseline breath acts as a bridge between the meditation and ordinary life; you can return to your normal breath and pick up your day as before. Ajahn Lee suggests this natural point of equipoise in his instructions. In his system, it can be a long breath or a short one. He also uses the BU-DDHO mantra with the breath as such a stabilizer for keeping mindful attention firm (see chapter 11).

Conscious adjustment of breath length is usually associated with calm methods, but it also occasionally serves a comparable function in vipassana systems.[17] In the Burmese Sunlun method, discussed in chapter 14, a short, rapid breath is set as the measure to which one can always return, at any stage of the practice, to ensure that the mindfulness and concentration are balanced for the next stage and before the return to your usual day.[18] It also, importantly, sustains mindfulness and prevents the mind from slipping into what is known as *bhavaṅga* in Abhidhamma. *Bhavaṅga* is the state that the mind is said to enter in deep sleep, which is not helpful. It is possible, in meditation systems that raise some energy, for the meditator to enter an unmindful *jhāna*, an absorption without mindfulness, for quite long periods. Maintaining awareness of the breath at a baseline length makes this highly unlikely.

All of this can sound like the place in *Gulliver's Travels* where there is heated debate over whether you should eat your boiled egg with the big side up or the little! But the discussions do have implications. In the system I practice, taught by Boonman Poonyathiro, we deliberately do both long and short breaths. Both can be peaceful; both can be even. If we translate that into our experience of the breath, we can see that instructions to adjust the length of breath make sense—for the method involved. If there is a differentiation between lengths of breath, and one can feel peaceful and relaxed at any stage of the breath, there is an important life skill.

We associate short breaths with being anxious or agitated. If you have just done a meditation practice that includes a deliberately shortened breath and you found peace there, then this will have an effect on daily life too: situations like running for the bus, being agitated before giving a presentation, or being anxious about meeting someone can all be experienced differently. Oddly enough, the short breath, when it arises spontaneously in our daily life, can bring peacefulness too, even if you are in a hurry. It just needs to be observed and allowed to do what it wants at such times.

Why should so much depend on something so simple? Throughout the twentieth century, most books on breathing mindfulness said the breath should never be guided or adjusted. They also often advised against *jhāna*. For some new insight systems, any kind of control over the length of breath was felt to be not only unnecessary but possibly unhelpful. This background helps explain why there remains today some wariness, and even hostility, toward many *samatha* practices, along with the use of any kind of breath control and certain somatic ways of experiencing the breath.[19]

The anti-control approach was probably correct for the aforementioned insight systems. But for other methods, breath adjustment offers an important aid. The practice is designed around the distinction between long and short. A stable base length gives a way of offering protection for the practitioner. It also means it is easy to move out of deep meditation, by going back to a normal breath.

Those who oppose guidance of breath in breathing mindfulness stress that the Buddha tried exercises relating to breath control before his awakening and did not find them conducive to awakening. In the *Mahāsaccaka-sutta* (M 36), in the midst of his self-torments, he certainly records some very bizarre breath control practices:

> Why don't I practice *jhāna* without any breath? So I cut off my breathing in and my breathing out through my mouth and nose. But then winds came out my ears making noise. It was like the snorting of a blacksmith's bellows! My energy was roused up and unflagging. My mindfulness was indeed established and not confused. But my body was disturbed, not tranquil, because I had pushed too hard with that painful effort.[20]

Further excesses are tried. Eventually the Buddha-to-be, Gotama, realizes this is just useless self-mortification. It is important that the Buddha describes such practices as a wrong form of *jhāna*. As he says, they do not lead to peace and liberation. His description also offers a good object lesson for anyone working on breathing mindfulness: it shows how not to do it!

This is a vivid example of how breathing mindfulness can be too forced, with no real attention paid to what the breath and the body need. I have heard it suggested that this passage constitutes a rejection of using breath length to enter breathing mindfulness *jhāna*. But here, absurdly, Gotama forces the breath to stop and hence follows a dead-end path. This is not like the steady, mindful craftsmanship of a woodturner. The commentaries say that his experience under the rose-apple tree, where the Buddha spontaneously finds *jhāna* as a child, was based on breathing mindfulness concentration: it led him to a quite different experience, the great joy and balance of right *jhāna*.[21] This is the meditation that he is said to have remembered on the night of awakening to send him on a path where there was no "fear of the happiness that is outside the senses." This, it seems, is what led him to awakening.

For practitioners in any method, it is helpful to know something about the wide variety of interpretations of and approaches to long and short breaths so that one can respect this diversity. All kinds of readings seem to be possible from the text. Whole, thriving systems, all true to the text, have arisen from such varied interpretations—different species of trees, to use the metaphor we have been using, flourishing alongside one another.

With something so powerful, instinctive, and innate as the breath, quite small changes of emphasis and attention can help to direct the natural forces of the mind in differently appropriate ways. The breath is one of few bodily functions that has the possibility of an attention that is both instinctive and consciously manageable. Finding the point at which the observer and meditator appreciates the breath changes the character and taste of the style of meditation you follow.

It is a bit like choosing a boat and learning to steer and guide it when you take it out. Systems of working with the breath have their own integrity and are like different kinds of boats for different kinds of water. Some require a lot of steering, like sailing boats; these may have controls that need monitoring. Others follow winds and currents and need less steerage. Sometimes, if the boat has sails, they have to be set to catch the wind the right way; the rudder needs to be working at the appropriate angle. Such boats, of course, are designed that way by those who want to use them differently.

It is the same for a whole, coherently complete system of breathing mindfulness: you just need to know the boat you are in and follow the system. For some extensive and systematic practices of *jhāna*, finely tuned controls are often important; the alterations of breath length are a way of helping: the practice becomes maneuverable, like a flexible boat that might need more steerage. An insight vehicle might need less. One needs to recognize that the method was designed that way, and if one changes the system they follow, one may need to unlearn some habits and develop new ones, just as if changing from a sailboat to a rowboat, or a kayak to a canoe.[22]

This discussion has been about one small detail: I hope it shows how significant and fruitful various readings can be.

CHAPTER 5

Sixteen Ways of Knowing the Breath

We can now look at the stages as a causal, linear process. They can feel like steps, where the momentum of finding one step gives the lift to the next. They do not always have to be taken as a sequence, however. Some systems place considerable emphasis on certain stages and perhaps come back to some of the early stages later; some traditions lightly go over some stages that others explore in depth. Other meditations are described in the canon in such a way. The divine abidings, for example, always appear as separately enumerated items in the same sequence but are not necessarily undertaken in that way.

The factors of awakening offer another helpful comparable. They also have the sense of a causal process: after mindfulness, each one is described as arising naturally on the basis of the fulfillment of the one before.[1] But the factors also have an existence that is independent of one another: one can, for instance, arouse vigor or tranquility as one wishes when meditation is well established. They "can be developed interactively" so that one acts on another.[2] One sutta describes them as like the different-colored clothes of a monarch, who can choose which colored garment to wear on a particular day: the monarch can "dwell" in one for a morning, and then another in the afternoon, and yet another in the evening.[3]

The First Tetrad

Practice traditions vary greatly in how they interpret even the first few lines of the sixteen stages. It is worth looking at some differing accounts, just for the first tetrad, to see how this works: at each stage, their attitude to techniques involving the breath is reflected in different emphases.[4]

Some discussion has occurred as to the role of the introductory words—"mindful he breathes in, or mindful he breathes out"—which are given before the instructions that start with the long breath. It is taken by some as itself a stage in the meditation; others see it simply as a mnemonic opener device that became incorporated as part of the text.[5] Whatever the reason, it works well in Pāli and even in English— perhaps it is the same in other languages. Giuliano Giustarini observes there is a meditative pace in the repeated ending *gato*, meaning the one who goes to a wilderness or a forest (*araññagato vā rukkhamūlagato vā suññāgāragato*). This alliteration and assonance of repeated sibilants in the Pāli leads to a breathlike rhythm in this first line, which you can feel even if you do not know Pāli: *so sato va assasati sato va passasati.*[6] This sort of wordplay to echo effect was popular in ancient India and permeates the suttas. If this line was added later and became part of the text, perhaps it was for good reason: it helps the reader, or listener then, to get ready. In practice, many people find that it takes a while before they feel comfortable following the breath and need to give it a few goes.[7]

Most practitioners like to get a feeling for the breath before they begin the meditation—just being aware of it, seeing how it goes that day, whether it feels bumpy, light, smooth or shallow. These factors change during the course of any hour or minute of any day. If you are listening to the sutta, the words "mindful, he breathes in, or mindful, he breathes out," is a good way of tuning in.

We examined the long and the short breath in the last chapter. We can now move on to another point of interesting debate, this time concerning the third pair that follows these first two stages: "He trains in this way: 'Experiencing the whole body, I shall breathe in.' He trains in this way: 'Experiencing the whole body, I shall breathe out.'" What body is meant? Does it mean the breath, or does it mean the whole physical body? There are a number of theories on this.

I feel it is simpler just to try and do it: to imagine or feel that the breath is indeed in the whole body and is permeating it completely. It is matter (*rūpa*), physically there; the consciousness that senses and moves with the breath is mind (*nāma*). As we will see later, the commentator Upatissa suggests a slightly different approach, but this works well at the start. There is an experiential sense that one can feel the breath suffusing the whole body.

At the time of the Buddha there was no scientific understanding of gas or oxygen. Rather, there were supposedly seven winds moving in different areas and directions in the body.[8] These constitute the element of air, one of the four elements—earth, water, fire, and air—that make our physical experience. These were believed to move about the body as a whole. There was no physiological sense of the whereabouts of oxygen in the lungs and a sense of where the breath goes from an anatomical point of view: the pervasion refers to a sense of the breath's effects in the whole body.

Experientially, the words suggest something simple in essence: that it is possible to feel the breath in the whole body, if one is open to the idea, and that this is what this stage means. This understanding applies on many levels of meditation: the "body" known by the breath can change as the practice develops and becomes more refined.

The fourth stage invites an openness just to try something out: is it possible to feel tranquility being breathed in on the inbreath and out on the outbreath? I think one just has to try it for oneself. Allowing a space for this to happen, even if one does not feel it immediately, seems to create the possibility that it can. It is a different understanding of the mind and what it can do: for when that happens, the body itself starts to feel calm.

The Second Tetrad

The first cluster is seen as completing the basic work of experiencing the breath in the body. The first tetrad is the basis for most breathing mindfulness systems; a groundedness within the body is then something that is always there and to which we can return. The next moves to the area of feeling: "experiencing" joy, happiness, and the activities of the mind and "making them tranquil."

Here, there is a clear allusion to the *jhānas*: joy is present in the first and second *jhāna*, according to the sutta system; happiness is a product of that, present in the first and second *jhāna* but becoming full and reaching its peak in the third. Joy in this tetrad appears to replace the measuring and groundedness of the first tetrad and forms the basis for these four stages. The body tetrad had a sense of an implicit *vitakka* and *vicāra*, the application of the mind, and its propensity to explore, to the lengths of breath and to direct attention to the body. An internal voice may still be murmuring in the background. This one now moves to the experience of joy as a way to understand and know the "body" that is being described. Joy allows one to become aware of feeling at a more subtle level, our guide to a *samatha* way of knowing of the breath.

As well as following an inherent sequence, the stages in this cluster can work together. Ajahn Sucitto says: "in practice the tetrads interplay, rather as a thumb would interact with the fingers of a hand."[9] The structure reflects the first tetrad: the first two set a basis in joy, then happiness, which allows awareness of all the activities that are going on in the mind and heart: these are then made tranquil.

The second tetrad relates to feelings and how we experience them: joy in the breath is the basis for this process to occur. It may seem strange to suggest that one can, for instance, breathe in joy and breathe it out, but it can be very surprising just to try it! Smiling relaxes the muscles on the face and can help. Throughout this and the following tetrads it is worth remembering that the breath can be experienced in the whole body, and is itself physical, experienced by touch. This helps one feel grounded: this experience may itself change as the practice develops. When joy arises as the basis of the second tetrad, it serves the same function with regard to the experience of feeling that the length of breath did for the body.

This can be experienced at any level of practice. If one is very unhappy indeed, even in grief, this very emotion can bring great softness in one's attention to the breath: that softness, in turn, can shift the tone to joy, even for a few moments. This stage gives an opening into the world of feeling, and allows sadness, grief, anger, or tension to be dissolved at that very basic level of how one experiences them. Joy is a factor of awakening and can arise with the breath: at such times unhappiness is transformed.

From there, happiness can arise, quietening the joy into simple contentment in the breath. Beginners in meditation feel this sometimes at times of great stress and unease, and often say how surprised they are. It can be experienced too at the level of deep meditation. It seems to me that the first tetrad of the sixteen is like the basic bodily appreciation that arises with the breath. It is like a violinist coming to know their instrument, making sure the notes are even and full and finding a bodily basis with their violin. The second tetrad shows the depth of feeling a violinist can bring to the touch of the bow: the mellow sound that is created transforms deep feeling into joy.

Then, when it comes to stages 7 and 8, there is a basis of calm. The "activities" of mind can be seen as anything that is going on in the feelings and now the mind itself—one's whole mood and sense of what is happening in the mind. This is so much easier if there has been even a moment of joy and then happiness, which is a more stable sense of contentment. Things may have been turbulent before, or blocked, or twisted into the mind and body with shoulder tension, apprehension in the stomach, or general unhappiness: any sense of enjoyment in the breath helps us to feel our way through that.

For the eighth stage, the breath can bring in a sense of tranquility and calm. You breathe that tranquility in, and then out on the outbreath. This is the fifth factor of awakening—a factor that, traditionally in the factors of awakening, does indeed arise after joy and its by-product, happiness. The tranquility here is different from that within the body but may include it: like some great music, the movements that arise show a great sense of activity, including often violent emotions, dramas, and turbulence. This tetrad transforms such emotions through joy, through happiness, and then through quiet. The word *jhāna* is not mentioned, but it does not have to be. This cluster is about feeling and emotion, and we may feel that in any breathing practice, whether as a beginner or an advanced practitioner.

The Third Tetrad

By now the meditator has settled into the world of body and feeling. From this area of support, the meditator can move to a large sense of the mind as a whole: it can be experienced, gladdened, stilled, and freed with the breath. The sense here is of great spaciousness. The heart and mind open out and are not confined, as a subtler contact with the breath opens up the experience of the body and heart and loses a sense of boundaries and limits. Buddhadāsa says: "By practicing this, we learn to know ourselves and the kind of thoughts that are typical for us. Then we understand ourselves well. What kind of *citta* is habitual in us?"[10] He suggests going back to the beginning and finding gladness there and using that to gladden the heart. When the *citta* "knows how to be happy," it works better and becomes settled and concentrated. Then you can liberate and free the mind from attachments with each in- and outbreath.

The Fourth Tetrad

This cluster takes a new perspective: the breath trains us to be a "watcher" (*ānupassī*) of impermanence, the fading away of passion, ceasing, and letting go in the breath. Sometimes perhaps, as with hearing great music or being moved to stillness watching a tragedy or great drama or just suddenly seeing an extraordinary view, one steps back and starts to experience the world from a vaster perspective.

The world of the breath is an ever-changing, irregular field of motion and movement, the means by which the body and mind are being sustained. The field of experience opens out. If other living beings come into awareness, their sorrows and joys are seen too with equanimity, as the breath is. Differentiations of "me" and "that" dissolve. In the peace this brings, the breath may subside so that it is almost imperceptible. The meditator is "witnessing," as Ajahn Sucitto translates this verb, movements inside, outside, and both inside and outside. Ajahn Pasanno emphasizes that this is engaged, not passive. This is not the observation that limits but which frees, like letting a kite or a bird go. The meditation is released from the weight of "I" to spoil it all. Venerable Anālayo gives the image of the condor, who flies through the air and who then merges, freed, into the landscape, as an emblem of the principles of breathing mindfulness.[11]

I have not assigned to any stage certain meditative attainments or stages of insight. This is not because those associations are absent, but because the wording, simply as it stands, is potent and does something extraordinary. It suggests how the breath can be a way of finding out how any event in the mind and body can be viewed and understood through itself, the breath. A new perspective is found on "things as they are." There are many resonances and internal echoes within the sixteen. There are four tetrads, which follow a pattern of establishing a new domain, examining it, and then finding resolution in the fourth element.[12] There are also eight pairs: the long and the short breath establish a polarity between two quite different activities. Such polarities can be seen throughout the subsequent seven pairs of the stages, as one stage balances the next. It is a bit like when walking one balances the body through the movements of the right and left leg. Being aware of a long breath, then a short, creates a momentum. This is followed by an awareness of bodily activities, which are then stilled. This is followed by the experience of joy in the breath, balanced by the quiet of happiness, and so on.

There are allusions to terms used to describe particular stages of meditative attainment elsewhere. But the Buddha makes no overt mention of any meditative state, or of the stages of arhatship and insight. The vocabulary and terms that suggest these attainments are crucial and, at some stage, involved. But the list of sixteen does not seem designed to be limited or pinned down. If the Buddha had wanted to make associations explicit and spell them out, he would have. I am grateful he did not.

The sixteen stages feel like an evocation of the path itself, at many levels, from the beginner finding a few moments' respite when they are feeling sad to the very advanced practitioner subtly fine-tuning their awareness with deeply established mindfulness and wisdom. The listener, in the Buddha's time, and now the reader can respond to the many echoes that those at the time would have heard and recognized—they would have sensed and known where words like joy and happiness usually occur; they would have known also where words like *anicca* and *virāga* usually appear. In a few minutes, they would feel, as we can, a sense that mindfulness of breath offers everything they need.

A Formula for Any Time and Place

This mnemonic formula offers a distillation of basic instructions, almost like a recipe, for breathing mindfulness: each stage has multiple levels of meaning. Seeing each stage working as a process, repeated in different ways, again and again, shows some essential feature of Buddhist practice. Our breath rises and falls all the time, always giving a new chance. For the mind to be healthy, there are certain features that need to be present in our meditation and certain things that need to be done somehow, in some way.

The factors of awakening can be introduced at any time, as the sutta suggests. Mindfulness and alertness are always needed. Investigation, of the quality and feeling of the breath, can always be there. One might take this investigation to insight through continued observation of the mark of impermanence, or one can investigate the softness of the breath, taking the meditation to the experience of greater calm. We also need to find the right effort and vigor for the time. Joy is clearly important: we cannot go far in anything without liking it! It is essential to allow us to continue but also to let the experience of the breath change us and to let go of pride or attachment. Tranquility eases and settles the joy as the mind finds stillness in concentration. At the end, a new perspective—seeing the mind and body with equanimity and "middleness" (*tatramajjhattatā*)—is made possible. Within these, there is room for creativity and exploring. This is a protective series, its verbs showing ways that the breath can be approached: as we practice breathing mindfulness we can train, experience, find joy, gladden, make tranquil, and watch. It feels like a balanced path.

It is worth hearing the sixteen stages chanted. They appear to be ancient, part of the oldest layer of Buddhist canonical literature and distinctively Buddhist.[13] From a compositional and literary point of view, they work, particularly but not only in Pāli, as a "heard" piece of meditational advice, as their form evokes as well as describes the basis of the practice. The breath goes round and round: the instructions feel like they do as well. In an analysis of the verbal patterns of the sixteen stages, Giustarini demonstrates how the rhythmic, mnemonic designs often found in the suttas characterize breathing mindfulness in particular, where what is described is itself so repetitive. The sibilants, onomatopoeia, and patterns of the words in Pāli all suggest that reciting this text was itself an aspect of a ritual designed to elicit the experience of the breathing mindfulness practice as one listened to it. One does not need to know Pāli to feel the effects of the first pair:

> *dīghaṃ vā assasanto dīghaṃ assasāmī ti pajānāti dīghaṃ vā*
> *   passasanto*
> *dīghaṃ passasāmī ti pajānāti rassaṃ vā assasanto rassaṃ*
> *   assasāmī ti*
> *pajānāti rassaṃ vā passasanto rassaṃ passasāmī ti pajānāti.*

Giustarini observes, "the present participle and the present indicative of the verb *assasati* [he breathes] dance together through the progression of the modalities of *ānāpānasati* at the beat of the occurrences of the verb *pajānāti* [he knows]."[14]

It is possible the sixteen are a later development of an earlier, shorter pair; if so, it seems likely that the development was made by the Buddha himself.[15] The text shows how, in practice, the four foundations of mindfulness work to offer a complete path to awakening. There are, in effect, thirty-two stages, as "The Treatise on Breathing" in *The Path of Discrimination*, discussed in the next chapter, notes. Thirty-two is a particularly significant number in Buddhism, suggesting an organism and wholeness within a complexity of parts. There are thirty-two marks of the Buddha, from his feet to the crown of his head. There are thirty-two parts of the human body. Buddhist cosmology has the thirty-one realms of existence, from the depths of the lowest hell up to the rarefied formless heavens; the thirty-second element is implied: the possibility of nirvana and no more rebirth.[16] Eviatar Shulman has suggested that the core of the Buddha's teachings lies in formulas, themselves devised as starting points for sutta development.[17] This principle appears to apply to how the practice traditions explored and developed the sixteen.

Historically, many of the schools described in this book define themselves within the terms of these sixteen recommendations, often interpreting their applicability to different kinds of practice and stages of the path by arranging their own method in accordance with the four tetrads of body, feeling, mind or heart, and *dhammas*, things as they are. Most styles described in the book are in some way dependent on them. Many modify or emphasize certain areas. The fact that this happens so much suggests that the sixteen could have been designed with that very purpose in mind: to be used as a template to ensure that breathing mindfulness can do certain, different things as you practice it. Hearing it reminds the chanter and listener of this.

How can we gain a sense of the sixteen as a world of possible approaches? A simple example helps me. With any musical instrument, like the guitar, violin, or clarinet, you need to get the body right. You need to adjust the posture, come to know the instrument, look after it so it is in tune or oiled, and feel its measure. Then, you train: you get a physical instinct as to how to make the body feel comfortable and erect, receptive to an instrument that feels attuned to temperature, posture, and your mood that day. Then you practice and practice and practice. It goes wrong. But tranquility of body comes when the balance is right. You start to explore feeling and find the instrument can arouse joy through the way it is played, and that, with appreciation, eases into happiness. As you play, you explore the "mind" of what is going on: the music's variations, movements in and out, depths, and range. You might feel your mind and the music are becoming one. If you are lucky, you feel linked inextricably to your musical piece and your instrument: differentiations between subject and object dissolve. Notes and chords arise and fall in a field of change, moving and alive. A sense of self drops away. Silence, or cessation, occurs sometimes in music, all the more powerful for what has gone on before. At the end, you relinquish, and the music comes to an end. The quiet that is left is quite different from the one before.

Breathing meditation is often mundane, a way of, in musical terms, going through your scales, feeling you might not be doing it right and hitting the wrong note. But sometimes you find that the music and you seem to work together. You let go: the practice feels like a complete work, and the music leaves you changed.

CHAPTER 6

The Treatise on Breathing

Some Old Debates

The Buddha thought highly of his followers. The image of them teaching others in The Sutta on Breathing Mindfulness demonstrates a vibrancy and willingness to communicate in the early community of the sangha. A creative and flexible teacher himself, the Buddha frequently praises others for their fresh use of simile and their methods of teaching; such homages are found throughout the early suttas.

Good craftspeople like to develop methods and techniques. Conversations and discussions on the craft of meditation, as well as meditative experiments themselves, must have started in the Buddha's own lifetime, for we see evidence of this diversity very early on. A number of works show the interpretations and explanations of early commentators and practitioners, who started composing commentaries soon after their teacher's death. Meditation teachers of the time had the job of teaching and transmitting what they had learned. Then, as now, they would have needed to be flexible. Some commentaries assigned particular attainments and stages of the path to different kinds and types of meditation practice. But some practitioners, I imagine, just tried it all out, looking for what worked for themselves and with their students.

It is inevitable—and healthy—that there were divergent evolutions in this process. The Buddha had very varied followers, a fact he noted. There is a sutta where he observes that those of comparable interests tend to like each other's company and walk together in groups: those with a taste for insight walk together; those with a taste for *samatha* walk together.[1] I imagine that also went on afterward. There were so many paths sanctioned by the Buddha; those who had followed one route would interpret the suttas and teachings accordingly. It is not surprising then that, as evidence shows, debates about various aspects of the *jhānas*, the progression to insight, and the fulfillment of insight began early, nor that they have come through to us as ongoing discussions.

One big question, then and now, is: how do the sixteen stages work with the broader stages of the path to awakening? The sutta's association with the four foundations of mindfulness seems to have been the primary means of understanding this relationship since ancient times, providing a template many liked: the path to the first *jhāna* in the first tetrad, of body; the path to the completion of the *jhānas* and formless spheres in the second tetrad, of feeling; the path to the development of insight in the third tetrad; and the path to stream-entry in the fourth.

This pattern is broadly followed in most old Theravada understandings. But there were several others. As one might expect of those who enjoy the Abhidhamma, the Abhidharmikas move rapidly to insight: they interpret the fulfillment of the first four stages as, not just a quietening of the breath, but the complete tranquility of the breath—the fourth *jhāna*, where breathing seems almost to have disappeared and may be imperceptible.[2] The second and third tetrads are then associated with developing insight, and the fourth tetrad with stream-entry or, in some interpretations, the four stages of path. Many interpret the completion of each tetrad as leading to the fulfillment of all the factors of awakening, and thus leading to enlightenment.[3] Others read the sequence very differently, seeing calm and insight combined throughout, with insight coming to fruition only at the end. It is likely that such divergences emerged as early as the latter years of the Buddha's teaching career.

From early times, exponents of breathing mindfulness came to different conclusions and ways of working. Some of these have taken fruit across the subsequent centuries, often in combination with local understandings of, for instance, the nature of wisdom or local symbologies and rituals. The overall result is that manifold ways of developing breathing mindfulness practice are in evidence both textually and in living practice. Commentaries give important clues and guidance as to how and why this variety developed. But throughout South and Southeast Asian Buddhism, one finds comparable, if somewhat divergent, traditions of interpretation and practice. Whole schools of practice have built their understandings around different interpretations, so that they acquire a life of their own. Knowing the original philology and likely reading is informative. But it is also worth just appreciating a sense of the characters involved, their histories, and their background to understand why and how they adapted what they learned: these impressions show a larger picture and help us to step back and see the whole.

In this and the next two chapters, we will look briefly at some early commentaries: they set a pattern for what is to come. I have chosen those that appear to have been most consulted in the Buddhist cultural regions of South and Southeast Asia. Again, the intention here is not to explain all the detail but rather to show how the practice traditions started to express their different methods and to interpret breathing mindfulness as a craft.

"The Treatise on Breathing" in *The Path of Discrimination* (*Paṭisambhidāmagga*)

With the deaths of great Buddhist figures in modern times, it can take years for full accounts of their teachings to filter through into manuals and systems and thus reach a wider audience. This seems to have been the case with the specifics from much earlier eras of Buddhism about how to conduct a meditation practice on the breath. One imagines that techniques and teachings on how to do practices passed from one teacher to the next quite naturally. Methods might have started to be recorded only when there were a number of possible approaches or at times when people felt other practitioners might not have easy access to teachings and would need to be steered in the right direction.

After the loss of the Buddha, the early sangha worked on assembling his teachings—the most important thing that needed doing. The first wave saw the composition of the Vinaya, the code of conduct for monks, and the suttas, the Buddha's discourses on particular occasions. But in the two or three centuries after that, other works emerged, like the Abhidhamma. Some elements in these works could well date from the time of the Buddha; some may be later commentary.

One or two of these works give evidence about early variations in practice. Such is the case with "The Treatise on Breathing," an early teaching on breathing mindfulness that is tucked into a larger work, *The Path of Discrimination* (*Paṭisambhidāmagga*).[4] This oral work, composed sometime between the third century B.C.E. and the first century B.C.E., is included in the Minor Texts (*Khuddanikāya*). It is ascribed by old Pāli traditions to the Buddha's chief disciple, Sāriputta, who was distinguished by his great insight and powerfully analytic mind. Whether or not it was composed by Sāriputta, either literally, or in spirit by one of his followers, *The Path of Discrimination* adopts the methods we recognize from this great disciple. Highly systematized, though structured in a more fluid, open-ended way than the Abhidhamma texts, it arranges factors in lists and asks questions as Abhidhamma texts do, but with its own style and character. Although complex and theoretical, it offers a few curious resting places that simply examine technique—the "how to" of various canonical practices. "The Treatise on Breathing" is one such place, but there is also, for instance, a treatise wherein many different ways of practicing loving-kindness are described, as well as their place in the teaching as a whole.

"The Treatise on Breathing," while composed in the style of the other treatises in *The Path of Discrimination*, feels like walking in on a long-standing discussion about how to help new meditators, how the breath can be perceived, problems likely to arise, and how experienced practitioners can come to understand the way of breathing mindfulness in full. It seems the treatise's author or authors wanted to record a complete repertoire of ways you can know and work with the breath. Clearly the practice was very popular. Here, the sixteen stages of breathing are examined in high resolution; each one is explained and scrutinized but also seen for its role in a larger path to awakening. There is a sense of sequence in the sixteen: one leads to another. But there is also a sense that each stage has value for its own sake. Each stage has an inbreath and an outbreath:

this can be known and appreciated. So, the sixteen is made, nicely, into a thirty-two. The stages are described as thirty-two "makers of mindfulness" or "workers in mindfulness."[5] This number, thirty-two, is usually associated in Buddhism with a body, a group, or a full organism. In any organism, each part is important and has its own role.

The treatise looks as if it is intended for very experienced meditators, but some of it is helpful for anyone at any stage. It is divided into four sections on breathing mindfulness. Section 1 describes features that can obstruct or aid concentration during this practice. Section 2 describes stages and potential problems that can arise while seeking calm, always coming back to one strategy: maintaining unwavering attention to the breath, in the present. Section 3 describes how to avoid these problems, finishing with a verse from the canon about the one who has reached arhatship based on breathing mindfulness. Section 4 takes the thirty-two stages one by one, considering the possibilities and potential of each and indicating, at the end, their opening out to a full path. Its style lets the variations of possible approaches fan out, apparently endlessly. No one stage is presented as more important than the others.

Here, I will just pick out some sections that seem useful in understanding how breathing mindfulness appeared to earlier meditators, which I simultaneously find to be very rich and useful information about how breathing mindfulness works.

Concentration meditation needs seclusion from the senses (*viveka*). The first section, taking breathing mindfulness as a calm (*samatha*) practice, starts by noting things that pose an "obstacle," or literally, a "place of ambush" (*paripantha*), to the mind's willing entry into seclusion. The word is associated with dangers on the road or a forest path, such as wild animals or robbers. As any meditator knows, as soon as attention goes inward, the "I" can perceive a real threat from leaving the usual sensory world. It starts to put up barriers.[6] These obstacles can feel just like ambushers lying in wait to prevent us from following the breath! Indeed, it is said we all have them lurking around, latently, until we reach the first stage of awakening, when the obstacles start to be eroded. The list gives some sense of how the breath can encounter these ambushers, but it also says how to overcome them. Each obstacle is placed alongside things that are an aid, or a "help" (*upakāra*)—their antidote.

- Longing for the senses is an obstacle to concentration; giving up (*nekkhamma*) is an aid to concentration.

- Hatred is an obstacle to concentration; the absence of hatred [in Abhidhamma, loving-kindness and the potential for loving-kindness] is an aid to concentration.

- Sloth and torpor are an obstacle to concentration; the perception of light is an aid to concentration.

- Restlessness (*uddhacca*) is an obstacle to concentration; balance (*avikheppa*) is an aid to concentration.

- Doubt (*vicikicchā*) is an obstacle to concentration; defining of events as they occur (*dhammavavatthāna*) is an aid to concentration.

- Ignorance (*avijjā*) is an obstacle to concentration; knowledge (*ñāṇa*) is an aid to concentration.

- Boredom (*arati*) is an obstacle to concentration; gladness (*pāmojja*) is an aid to concentration.

- All unskillful phenomena are an obstacle to concentration; all skillful phenomena are an aid to concentration.[7]

This short list, rather like that of the five hindrances to meditation, might be helpful to anyone at any level of experience,[8] but it feels, in particular, like a description of subtle barriers that can arise at the threshold of deep absorption: things that seem to try and stop us from leaving our usual world behind, and from trusting the new one, perhaps just before the first *jhāna*.

The first obstacle, longing for the senses, is fairly obvious to anyone who has tried watching the breath. Other attractive things can immediately crowd in the mind. "Giving up" can be a literal renunciation, as in taking up the monastic life.[9] But it also means, just for that moment, willingly relinquishing the tempting object, whatever it is at that time. Placing attention elsewhere, meaning being able to turn the mind to the breath and to let go of usual sensory distractions, is not always hard. If attention is placed on the breath and some pleasure is found there, it can capture the mind's interest so that a giving-up of the preoccupation really does take place. The breath just becomes more interesting than whatever was wanted before. When this happens, it is like closing the door when you are at a busy party: the hum of what was so exciting just before recedes into the distance.

Absence of hatred—the practice of loving-kindness—is the antidote to the next obstacle: ill will. Trying to love or accept a person, a difficulty, or a particular situation we do not like is a challenge we all recognize. It is possible to spend a whole meditation practice struggling with this obstacle in its various forms: being hungry, annoyed, bad-tempered, or in the midst of a conflict that just will not go away. With regard to the breath, an immediate strategy is to arouse a sense of loving-kindness, even to and with the breath itself. Hatred feels painful to the body; its mark is that it is just so unpleasant. It is possible sometimes to let a space arise where the breath can be breathed in in loving-kindness, then loving-kindness can be felt for the outbreath. It is like the woodturner discussed in chapter 4, who loves the material with which he works. If treated with love, the breath soon makes us aware of just how unpleasant ill will feels, in the tensing of the shoulders, the coldness of the mind, and the turbulence in the lower stomach. Hatred creates knots inside us and becomes a genuine obstacle to what we are doing. We do not have to focus on the tension—though some traditions work directly with that, actively probing painful sensation; the breath, if there is friendliness to it, can help this process as it washes through and transforms the tension. But it can also be helpful just to avert the attention from the object of our ill will and toward the easing of loving-kindness, letting the breath carry that loving-kindness to those knots in the whole body, again and again. It disperses the symptoms and gives something else for the mind to do; this also helps to prevent us from wanting to return to that hatred again.

The perception of light as an antidote to the hindrance of sloth and torpor is a canonical recommendation. The Buddha suggests it to the follower who became his second chief disciple, Mahāmoggallāna, who eventually became renowned for his great psychic powers and praised by the Buddha for his great mastery in this area.[10] Recurrent sleepiness was, however, a persistent problem for him at each prior stage of the path. His story acts as a reminder that practices with an emphasis on concentration can sometimes become sleepy if mindfulness is lost. The Buddha gave him, as he did others, this simple recommendation: be aware of light in the outside world.

In the United Kingdom, where our ever-changing shifts in weather remind us of the way ebbs and flows just come and go in the mind, a surprise burst of sunshine in the outside world lifts the spirits, even when the eyes are shut. It brings a vitality that can lift us out of sloth or torpor. Being aware of light around, as the Buddha encouraged Mahāmoggallāna to do, can help to lift this hindrance. If sunshine is there, you can sense how it filters through to the eyes under closed lids to brighten the mind, which can serve as an effective antidote to sluggishness, if it is only a little more mindfulness that is needed. But it is worth remembering that sometimes one is genuinely overtired, and it may be that sleep is what is really needed. Indeed, the Buddha suggested a nap to Mahāmoggallāna as a last port of call if nothing else worked. Many laypeople just push things too much in daily life and start pushing in their meditation, too, perhaps not realizing that some rest, at least as a precursor to meditation, would be more appropriate than exerting themselves in yet another domain of activity. Yet there is a circular aspect here too, as it often takes quietening the mind in meditation to let the consciousness of one's underlying energy emerge cleanly, in a straightforward way.

The usual canonical hindrance of restlessness and worry is here reduced to one obstacle: restlessness. The antidote is given as balance, or the absence of scatteredness (*avikkhepa*). If for any one moment the breath becomes interesting, this balance starts to arise naturally; if that is sustained, the scatteredness just falls away as the mind instinctively tires of all the impatient impulses to go to anything other than the experience of the breath itself.

Another obstacle, doubt, the last of the usual hindrances, has the characteristic of deliberately avoiding the object. If one doubts something—and the teacher, the teaching, and oneself are usually cited as the main things one is likely to doubt—the mind sheers away all the time. The antidote for this distracting inner commentator is investigation, in defining events as they occur (*dhammavavaṭṭhāna*). What is the breath doing, and how does it feel? Does it feel full of hiccups, jagged so it seems to catch at certain points? If so, is it possible just to accept that and to keep some flow? Can it feel smooth and move in a less constricted way? If the breath is investigated in this way, there is no room for doubt. Any problems we find with the breath we find in our daily lives: investigating something can work to get rid of doubt in many other spheres too.

After that, ignorance is listed as an obstacle. In meditation, it is difficult to see it working. We are ignorant of our ignorance! In practice, at a basic level, I feel it means the sense of turning away from what you are doing and not listening to any knowledge about yourself and your body that arises at the time. Ajahn Chah talks of the "earthworm" knowledge, or intuition, which has no pride but recognizes the situation as it is and acts accordingly. Knowledge can also arise as the knowledge of the rise and the fall of breath, the changes going on, and the understanding of how to work with what is there and accept it as it is, as the carpenter knows what is there when he is working with some wood. Trusting this deeper area of knowledge, accessible to us all sometimes, is a kind of honesty that is realistic about what is here this day, without being unkind to ourselves. We tend to think of factors on the Buddhist path, like the eradication of ignorance, as unreachable to beginners or the "ordinary" meditator. But even at early stages of meditation we often have seeds of wisdom in the things we know from our own experience in meditating, perhaps for a few months or years.

The last single obstacle is curious but easily relatable to our experience: boredom. It is a new addition to the canonical list. It has to be said that in meditation boredom can descend without notice, like a chance gloomy cloud, sometimes just when things are about to change. It just happens sometimes! So what does this mean in a practice? It may arise just when it is time to let go, and it arrives in this form to let you know that. Or it may be that too much strain has come into the whole meditation; the mind understandably switches off as it becomes too unpleasant.

The word used for boredom, *arati*, literally means an absence of delight. *Rati*, its opposite, is almost always associated with sexual or sensual pleasure. In this context, there is no delight in the breath: it is not enjoyed. This can be the symptom of a kind of unhappiness. But we do not get bored if we are interested. Gladness (*pāmojja*), the aid or antidote to boredom, is used in its verbal form, "to gladden," in the tenth pair in the sixteen stages discussed in the previous chapter. Gladdening the breath—or consciously cheering it up, as one might say—helps. In practice, I have found that if the breath becomes uninteresting it is usually because I am not looking at it with a friendly attitude and have been trying to impose something on it, not letting it breathe in its own way. A kind of boredom comes through overstraining, or bringing agendas to the meditation, or not liking what is found in the breath and pretending it is not there. Something that one is feeling sad about can hide behind boredom. The breath is usually happy to provide gladness or some restorative power if it is allowed to be itself, and the sadness can be revealed and eased.

This obstacle may also suggest that more gladness is needed in daily life, which could be brought to the meditation. For laypeople there are plenty of routes. Skillful consciousness (*kusala citta*) can arise in all sorts of situations: swimming, playing tennis, cooking, painting the walls, having a chat with a friend, or laughing with the family. If any of these bring gladness and freshness, those will come into the breathing practice too, and it will not become boring. It is interesting that this antidote is the last of the single ones. The breath can gladden and bring genuine cheerfulness and a wish to watch it more. For a concentration practice this phenomenon is not just an added extra but an important part of how meditation works: by willingness and an enjoyable wish to do more.

This leads naturally to the last in the whole list. "All unskillful *dhammas*" get in the way of meditation; "all skillful *dhammas*" are antidotes. The Abhidhamma style of opening out a list to all kinds of possibilities, "or anything else," is found throughout this text. So here, "all skillful phenomena" offer a natural concluding antidote and aid. Sometimes in meditation, it involves too much thought to identify a hindrance. This category is then very helpful: the obstacle can be recognized before you move on. It covers everything. And it also points to a helpful feature of the list: that *all* skillful *citta* can be an aid to meditation. This simple statement is worth unpacking.

What we do in daily life affects meditation. It should not be an endless labor, particularly for laypeople. If we do something we really enjoy and have fun with in daily life, that arouses skillful *citta*; it is overcoming hindrances. Going swimming with friends or walking the dog alone may be just the antidote that is needed for the breathing practice too. The word "obstacle" is an important one and used throughout the treatise for things that get in the way of the meditation. It does mean simply that: that there are obstacles that prevent us from turning to the breath, but there are aids and antidotes to that process too, which may be found and developed in daily life. It works the other way around as we also experience exactly the same obstacles in things we do in our active interactions. The breath helps us know and transform them. Whatever hindrances we encounter on the mat, we meet in life and feel in the sensation of the breath: background mindfulness of the breath in the day helps ease them.

Section 2 of "The Treatise on Breathing" details various imperfections that can arise in attentiveness to the breath. For instance, if there is too much longing for the inbreath, then that is a problem; too much longing for the outbreath is a problem also. At every point, from the beginning to the middle to the end, both the inbreath and the outbreath can feel pulled away or disjointed. The text says any hankering for the breath that has just gone is a hindrance, as is anticipating the next one.

Section 3 examines how the various obstacles and hindrances to this attention can be addressed through the breath, again with a fine scrutiny that deals with each obstacle and hindrance as it arises, from the beginning to the middle to the end of the breath. This is technical! In practice this can mean just feeling the whole breath and noticing a little if the mind does not like the inbreath or the outbreath or some part of either. Taking a few breaths easily can make that clearer, and the feeling can come in for the whole breath as a kind of enjoyment. In time, form and formless *jhānas* are described as the result.

The Role of *Nimitta* in "The Treatise on Breathing"

Characteristically for this treatise, amid its theoretical enumeration there is emphasis on its practice, including how to work with the *nimitta*, the sign or image of breathing mindfulness meditation as a *samatha* practice. The word *nimitta*, as we shall see, does not lend itself to being pinned down even in its original linguistic context—it seems to work better as a field of possibilities, having its own, finely tuned precision for each person. Throughout this discussion and the book, I will leave it untranslated.

The *nimitta* is the object that, if you are lucky, spontaneously arises in the mind of the practitioner when pursuing breathing mindfulness for calm. It is how we intuit our consciousness at the time. In most insight methods, if it arises it is usually either discarded or not developed fully. It is mentioned occasionally in the canon, though without much description: one sutta, for instance, says when it arrives this is an important time to consult a teacher.[11] To this day, *samatha* breathing mindfulness is recommended to be practiced with such personal guidance. The *nimitta* acts as a reflection of the mind's stillness and mindfulness. It is something to enjoy, without chasing after it—which we can easily and often do. It sometimes happens when there is less effort: it likes space and freedom. It mirrors the mind's balance and quiet so it can be known and understood. It needs gentle mindfulness of the breath at all times to be sustained in a balanced way. Then, because of its beauty and steadiness, it can act as a support and guide for the quietening of the mind. Boonman, my teacher, describes it as our "boat through the unconscious mind."

Ways of keeping a balanced attitude to the *nimitta* are discussed in detail in "The Treatise on Breathing." It offers ways of ensuring that mindfulness of the breath and a sense of equipoise are sustained when it arrives: for instance, the manifestations of strong joy are described, as well as how to deal with them. It is worth noting, however, that not everyone gets a *nimitta*, and their practice may be marked by other landmarks, such as calm and peace—a point Ajahn Thate, a forest teacher, stresses.[12]

In the treatise, work with the *nimitta* is described with a vivid image. I think it is the first time it occurs in Pāli literature:[13]

> Suppose there is a tree trunk placed on an even area of ground, and a man cuts it with a saw. The man's mindfulness is established by the saw's teeth where they touch the tree trunk, without his giving attention (*manasikaroti*) to the saw's teeth as they come and go. But they are not unknown (*na . . . aviditā*)[14] by him as he does so. And he shows effort, carries out his job and achieves a distinctive effect. As the tree trunk placed on an even area of ground, so is the *nimitta*, the sign, for the anchoring of mindfulness. As the saw's teeth, so the inbreaths and outbreaths. As the man's mindfulness, established by the saw's teeth where they touch the tree trunk, without his giving the attention to the saw's teeth as they come and go. And they are not unknown by him as he does so.[15]

For anyone who has tried sawing a tree trunk the analogy strikes immediate chords. It is possible, and necessary, to be engaged and aware of the whole body while doing something that requires intentness. When you cut the wood, you need to have a sense of both the edge and the larger movement of the saw and the body. Your foreground awareness is on the edge of the cut, but it is important that the rest "is not unknown." Otherwise, you will not saw well! The swing and the weight need to be stabilized as coming from the lower part of the body, not the arm and shoulders, for the saw to cut clean. The sense that a background, inclusive awareness, can be felt through the whole "body" of the breath while there is foreground attention on one place, the tip of the nose or the *nimitta* that arises in the mind, is central to *samatha* breathing mindfulness. If you are aware of the breath moving throughout the whole of the lower part of the body, sustaining a sense of contact with the cushion or ground, the attention will come from a grounded base. The arising of any image in the mind's age will be steadier and, gradually, through this overall awareness of the breath, become stable. The image of the saw shows how the meditator can be conscious of a number of things, within a large domain of mindfulness as a background awareness, while maintaining focus on one—a happy balance of mindfulness and concentration. Some modern insight teachings, such as the Goenka methods, also adopt something like this principle with an importantly different recommendation: to keep mindfulness during the day steady by being aware of the tip of the nose, in the *background*, while doing other things.

In section 4, the text explores each stage of breathing mindfulness in turn. This part is highly technical, with lists that open out into other lists, like fractals echoing the shape of other lists in the canon. But there are immediately recognizable elements that appear, based on close experiential observation. To give some flavor, here is a part of the fourth section of "The Treatise on Breathing," just one small part of the exegesis of just one stage, the first pair: breathing in a long breath and breathing out a long breath.

How is it that, in breathing in a long breath, they know "I breathe in a long breath"? and, breathing out a long breath, they know, "I breathe out a long breath"?

1. They breathe in a long breath, measured by its length (*addhānasaṅkhate*).

2. They breathe out a long breath, measured by its length.

3. As they breath in and out long inbreaths and long outbreaths measured by their lengths, desire (*chanda*) arises.

4. Through the power of desire, they breathe in a long breath, measured by length, that is finer than before.

5. Through the power of desire, they breathe out a long breath, measured by length, that is finer than before.

6. Through the power of desire, they breathe in and out long breaths, measured by length, that are finer than before. As, with desire, they breathe in and breathe out long inbreaths and long outbreaths, measured by length, finer than before, gladness (*pāmojja*) arises.

7. Through the power of gladness they breathe in a long breath, measured by length, finer than before.

8. Through the power of gladness they breath out a long outbreath, measured by length, finer than before.

9. Through the power of gladness they breathe in and breathe out long breaths, measured by length, finer than before. As, through gladness they breath in and breathe out long inbreaths and long outbreaths, measured by length, finer than before, the heart (*citta*) turns away from long inbreaths and outbreaths, and equanimity becomes settled.[16]

As the text continues:

Long inbreaths and outbreaths, in these nine aspects, are a body. The foundation is mindfulness. The contemplation is knowledge. The body is the foundation, but it is not the mindfulness. Mindfulness is both the foundation and the mindfulness. By means of that mindfulness and that knowledge he contemplates that body.[17]

Behind the circles of the reiterative style there are some crucial aspects of breathing mindfulness. First, that the breath is our "body" in a breathing practice: it can be felt everywhere; the experience of that body changes as the practice develops. But also, the passage points out, it is possible, and indeed preferable, to want to do and to like breathing mindfulness. This may seem odd to anyone who has tried and not enjoyed it. But after a while and with patience, it is sometimes possible to watch the breath with great attentiveness and interest, simply because the object is so engaging. An underlying assumption that desire is naturally aroused through the breath and is important to keep our attention sustained persists throughout the commentaries.

The commentary on this practice in the *Satipaṭṭhāna-sutta* also regards the first four stages described there primarily as a calm (*samatha*) practice and as a preliminary to insight.[18] As here, it says that during the first stage—practicing long breaths—observation of the breath becomes finer: repeatedly taking a long breath, desire or wish-to-do (*chanda*) also arises in the meditation.

Chanda means something like "wish," "desire," or "willingness," yet it is a word that is not really possible to translate. An important element in Buddhist meditation practice, *chanda* is very closely associated with many accounts of breathing mindfulness. According to Buddhist psychology, it can arise with unskillful thoughts—during meditation or in daily life when we crave something not needed, like a drink or too many chocolates, or want to do something illegal like speeding. Indeed, as such, when it appears as "longing" or "desire" for the sense pleasures, it is the first of the five hindrances and the obstacles to meditation. It is often thought of entirely in those terms by modern Buddhist practitioners. But this quality is also considered a positive aspect of the mind, and this is the sense for which we have no real English translation. It is the first of the four bases of spiritual success (*iddhipāda*) and considered essential to the path to awakening. The problem is that the English language conflates "wish" with a desire that we assume must be based on greed: we think *any* desire must be unskillful and arise from craving. We do not have a word to suggest a wish without that implication. It is not the same in Pāli. *Chanda* can be based on unskillful states—but does not have to be. In the Vinaya, the word is used to mean "consent," which provides a helpful dimension.[19] Nyanatusita translates it, with regard to the same passage translated here, as "motivation."[20]

Chanda is often a wish to pursue or undertake something from a skillful base, or simply because it is good. When we spontaneously want to help someone out or to continue doing something like a sport or hobby because it is so fulfilling and makes us happy, or when we wish to carry on a meditation, there may be this kind of desire. It may be very strong and arise as a deep and powerful wish. It does not need to be unskillful: people who become interested in Buddhist practice sometimes feel they should distrust such basic enjoyments and the sense of play their fun gives us. But in the case of these activities, it is probably not unskillful: certainly, some mild sense-desire might come in, but if the desire is based on mindfulness, it is usually skillful and healthy, one meaning of the word *kusala*. The enjoyment is part of this "wish-to-do."

It is what makes us continue with things simply because they are worth doing or we enjoy them, if they do not cause harm. As such it is a key factor in the thirty-seven factors contributing to awakening: it is that which makes us wish for skillful consciousness, peace, and the path. The extract we have just looked at takes us through this. It goes from such desire to gladness. This quality (*pāmojja*) appears later in the list of the sixteen, at the tenth stage, under mindfulness of mind. Here, it is included in the long breath too, where the mind is gladdened through the stages of the long breath. The qualities aroused by the long breath then move to equanimity, where the breaths subside. This suggests the fourth *jhāna*, where breathing becomes so serene it is apparently imperceptible, though it does not specify that.

Just this one stage has the seeds of all the others, it seems. The discussion of the long breath fills several pages of insights and attainments that can arise: it arouses all the foundations of mindfulness; it develops insight into dependent arising, the subsiding of discursive thought, the five faculties of meditation, the five powers, the factors of awakening, and the path; and it culminates in equanimity, as the mind brings to bear "upon the object, *nibbana*." The key word is *samodhāneti*, "brings together": the object is brought together with the breath, so it does not seem different. Enlightenment is not stated explicitly as a possibility. But it is not denied. The potential of this one stage, or pair of stages, flows through all the factors contributing to awakening and "combines" or "brings together" (*samodhāneti*) factors in that direction.[21] Just one pair from the sixteen stages is filled with endless possibilities. No level of the path appears to be excluded. The possibilities are all exactly the same for the short breath—the second pair, or stage, of the sixteen. All of this will be of great importance when we look at the Burmese insight movements: right from the outset of Buddhist practice, no one stage of breathing mindfulness seems limited.

There is also plenty of fresh observation about the breath in this section. Directionality in connection with the passage of the breath is introduced. The breath is described as going up and down in the body, from the tip of the nose downward; an end point of the inbreath is not explicitly located. Such detail is not found in *The Sutta on Breathing Mindfulness*.

It is sometimes suggested that the preliminary to the sixteen, where "mindfulness is aroused before him," indicates that the mouth or the tip of nose is involved, but no mention is made of the breath going "down" or "up." Here there is, and each stage of the breath is subjected to a fine exploration. Another section elaborates and describes how different qualities and stages of the path can support, be themselves strengthened, and flourish through the breath: the possibilities open for the breath are endless. This treatise holds a microscope up to the breath at each stage as its qualities are explored in real time, moving in and out of the body with a beginning, a middle, and an end.

One lovely image evokes very precisely the sense of constant refinement associated with this process. It is like the striking of the gong, the text says. This analogy occurs in the discussion of the long breath, to describe the kind of quietening effect of making the activities of the body tranquil. Such tranquility is included as a possibility in this very first stage, as the breath becomes finer and finer until it is almost imperceptible. Mindfulness and concentration are needed for ever-more sensitive appreciation of the movement of the breath. At first the gong's sounds are obvious and easy to pick up. But then they become more subtle as the sign of the obvious sounds ceases and a more subtle sound is heard, then that sound becomes even more subtle. Through unwavering attention to the inbreath and outbreath, "the wise enter into and emerge from that attainment."[22] Even the description of the simile is itself long and repetitive, like the long, rolling reverberation of the gong. This is still an oral literature, using repetition and rhythm as aids for its effects.

This passage says something that is important for anyone practicing *samatha* breathing mindfulness. As you watch the breath over a period, it becomes finer and softer all the time. It can seem that you have lost it, or you try to put the same effort in that was needed before. But, as with listening to the gong's sound, by keeping awareness sustained it is still possible to discern it and be aware of the whole body. It just requires a lighter and gentler quality of attention. The breath does not need the repeated application it needed at the beginning. Sensing its movement can feel like hearing.

The image adds another dimension. Hearing and listening are also important parts of *samatha* breathing mindfulness. As it proceeds, a sense of peaceful silence, like a *nimitta*, is the way many meditators sense mindfulness and concentration coming into balance. The breath may indeed become almost imperceptibly subtle, like a whisper, as the thoughts and distractions that are usually present subside too. Breathing mindfulness leading to concentration is usually described in terms of touch, of the sensation in the body, and of vision: the *nimitta* acts as a guide as the breath becomes increasingly subtle. For many, however, this subtlety is felt in the area of hearing, in what feels like the active presence of silence: the roar of an ocean far away, a reassuring quiet. For some meditators this can offer the best indication that the mind is becoming purified through the breath. It is worth noting that another crucial point is being made here too: the "wise" emerge cleanly from the meditation, just as they entered it.

The author or authors of *The Path of Discrimination* clearly felt breathing mindfulness to be of utmost importance; only the meditation on loving-kindness and the four foundations of mindfulness as a grouping receive such systematic attention in the text. The Abhidhamma and its related texts, with their stress on the factors present in any one moment of consciousness or matter, are sometimes said to subject the teaching to excessive codification. In practice, this treatise does just the opposite: it uses images with precision. It feels very systematic and immensely analytical, yet by showing how a breathing practice operates in real time, as it is experienced over several minutes or an hour—its descriptions feel like the similes of the suttas, such as the woodturner discussed in chapter 4. The treatise allows for many possibilities, which seem to stream outward, on the basis of each stage of breathing mindfulness in turn, as it occurs. Each of the sixteen stages is presented as a door to the possibilities of the whole path. Within "The Treatise on Breathing," none of the thirty-two "mindful craftsmen" or "mindful actions" seems limited in its potential.

Breathing mindfulness is pursued to the form *jhānas* and the four formless spheres. The eighteen insights are described as well as the four paths. The work lists twenty-four kinds of knowledge through concentration; seventy-two kinds of knowledge through insight are also described. The twenty-one pleasures of freedom (*vimutti*) start with stream-entry and end with arhatship. The treatise gives a curious mixture of categorization and discussion of technique. It can feel cerebral and is not an easy read. But it demonstrates that excellences and results are possible at any stage; each stage, it seems, can lead to awakening. The treatise says the one who works with the breath "combines *samatha* and insight through their meaning of a single taste."[23] Behind its technicalities, it appears to suggest: Why not explore one? It might show the way to others.

In section 3 of the treatise, there is a description derived from the canon, of the one who has attained awakening through breathing mindfulness:

> The one whose mindfulness of breathing, in and out, is perfect,
>   well developed, gradually brought to growth, according to the
>   Buddha's teachings:
> They illuminate the world
> like the full moon released from a cloud.[24]

CHAPTER 7

The Path to Freedom (*Vimuttimagga*) by the Arhat Upatissa

The next work we'll consider is by a mysterious author, Upatissa, said to have been enlightened. We know almost nothing about him, other than that he probably came from Sri Lanka or India, perhaps associated with the Abhayagirivihāra school. Buddhism went to Sri Lanka early, brought by the Indian King Aśoka's son, Mahinda. In the immediate centuries after the Buddha, various schools of understanding started to emerge, as they also did in the Indian mainland. The magnificent temples, stupas, and great monastery buildings of Anuradhapura are testament to this and to those who followed the teachings of "the elders." Abhayagirivihāra, "The Fearless Mountain Monastery," was possibly influenced by the teachings developing in India that eventually gave rise to the Mahayana. It represents, however, a line of understanding that accords with ways the Pāli canon describes meditation and breathing mindfulness.

The Path to Freedom is a meditation manual; it has recently been retranslated into English.[1] It must have been widely consulted, for in early days it spread as Buddhism did. While there are no versions left of Upatissa's original, presumably in Pāli, there is a sixth-century C.E. translation into Chinese. Some parts were translated into Tibetan. The practices he described were, presumably, undertaken in many forms of early Buddhism. It is a work intended to describe the whole way to en-lightenment and the freedom (*vimutti*) in the title and follows the tra-ditional pattern of starting with ethics and morality, moving through to concentration, and culminating in the steps to the attainment of the path.

Breathing mindfulness comes under the meditation section. It is one of Upatissa's thirty-eight objects of meditation, all based on canonical practices. It is fortunate we have it; the canon, while constantly advo-cating meditation, does not give much in the way of specific guidance. This was presumably on the assumption that guidance would be given by teachers or by fellow practitioners, mostly monastics. The writer—by this time writing was well established—was clearly very influenced by "The Treatise on Breathing" and frequently quotes and draws inspira-tion from it.

He opens by explaining mindfulness of breathing, and that its char-acteristic is to make manifest the *nimitta*. Attending to touch, the phys-ical contact of the breaths, he says, is the function of this practice. It has its footing in eliminating thinking (*vitakka*). He extols its benefits: the practitioner "accomplishes the peaceful, the excellent, the sublime, and the lovely, delightful pleasure." Bad or unhappy states of mind disappear. The body and mind do become tired, yet they do not waver or tremble. It also fulfills all foundations of mindfulness, seven factors of awakening, and finds freedom.

Going through each stage in turn, he recommends first arousing mindfulness at the tip of the nose or the upper lip, which is one inter-pretation of the expression that mindfulness "is established before him."[2] Following an instruction in "The Treatise on Breathing," he says the meditator then does not attend to the different phases of each breath—that is, the beginning, the middle, and the end.[3] Of the original passage Cousins suggests that this means not being distracted by any particular stage or focusing on any one too much, for unwavering attention to the whole breath is encouraged as well.[4] This instruction, which also appears in "The Treatise on Breathing," seems intended to ensure that the med-itator does not get *stuck* on some point, either in the inbreath or out-breath, so that it becomes more important than any of the others. The meditator is recommended not to attend to "different *nimittas*," perhaps the variety of images that might arise in the mind's eye that are not the *nimitta* of breathing mindfulness, because "manifold obstacles" can arise at that time and draw attention away. Attention to the breath *nimitta* is encouraged.

We now have, possibly for the first time in Pāli Buddhism, a description of the breath *nimitta*, the product of this practice. This is the object that arises in the mind when it is cleared of nine unspecified "afflictions."[5] When it does arise, he says, it is "like the pleasant touch of a tuft of silk or a tuft of cotton wool touching the body, or it is like the pleasant touch of a cool breeze touching the body." Upatissa then gives new and adventurous instructions. When this *nimitta* appears, it can be extended outward: at the tip of the nose, in the area between the eyebrows (*glabella*), up around the forehead, and many places until the entire head is pervaded with it. Then one can pervade the whole body with the joy and happiness it produces. This is called "success" (*samāpatti*). Such flexibility and mastery of skills with the breath *nimitta* is a common feature of some of the meditations discussed later in this book (chapters 9, 11, and 12).

At this stage other *nimittas* may arise, such as smoke, mist, dust, gold sand, or the sensation of needles pricking. If the meditator is not fully and clearly aware of these, there will be various perceptions and potential distortions of perception (*vipallāsa*; *vipariyāya*). By keeping mindful of the inbreath and the outbreath, these are not attended to. This means that a more subtle, purer breath *nimitta* can then arise.[6] Then, drawing on the list of nine ways of working with the breath discussed in the last chapter, stillness is obtained and, from there, all four *jhānas*.

This discussion has introduced us to the visual and sometimes tactile element that is so central to the practice of breathing meditation as a concentration (*samādhi*) practice. It stresses pleasantness of contact, like the touch of soft cotton or a breeze: this is, after all, an object known primarily by touch. This pleasantness is not just a happy by-product of watching the breath. Rather it is the means by which the mind becomes unified and allows the practitioner to enter *jhāna*. A subtle area of feeling is aroused, beyond our usual sensory enjoyments or displeasures, which acts as a guide through the unconscious mind as the meditation acquires depth, with an increase of both mindfulness and concentration. As this happens, the faculties of faith, vigor, mindfulness, concentration, and wisdom start to work together: the pleasant feeling is the means by which one's meditative skills can be used, with the breath, to bring the faculties into balance. Such a process is something that the practitioner feels they can control.

For the *nimitta* to arise for the meditator, obstacles and hindrances need to be overcome. Upatissa suggests that the *nimitta*, though it arises spontaneously from this process, can be subject to our wishes and feelings too, as we move it around and extend it. As one canonical text says of such skill: "a meditator can make the mind turn according to their wish and not according to the mind's wish."[7]

We are now introduced to a new element, a system of aids that, with variations, seems to have accompanied the practice of breathing mindfulness from early on. They are still practiced in some systems today. Upatissa gives them as (1) counting, (2) following, (3) settling, and (4) observing.[8] They can be seen as techniques and as ways of implementing the recommendations of The Sutta on Breathing Mindfulness into a daily practice. Upatissa does not say much about them, except that they are specific techniques to apply to observation of the breath. We will look at them within the terms of a fuller list that includes these four when considering Buddhaghosa in the next chapter.

Where he does conduct detailed exploration is in the practice of the sixteen stages, which he places as part of a systematic, graduated training. The sixteen "training grounds," as the text calls them, lead gradually to entry into the path. The first two, of the long and the short breath, he says, arouse non-delusion. This is because, as the practitioner becomes increasingly aware of ever-subtler manifestations of the breath, the *nimitta* arises. Non-delusion refers to this event, and to the necessary attending to its nature.[9] The meditator can then experience the body in the third stage through non-delusion and through the object. Non-delusion arises as the whole body is pervaded with joy and happiness. The hindrances are, it seems, washed away in the intensity of the experience. The whole body is experienced through the breaths as the matter-body (*rūpakāya*).

But the mind that is experienced is consciousness, the mind-body (*nā-makāya*). This interaction between what he calls "non-delusion" and the mind and body form the basis of his analysis.

This is one interpretation: I am sure there are others. But this interpretation, for me, opens up a fascinating and accessible field of experiential inquiry.

Mind and matter are different: in the breath we feel them meet. Being aware of both *rūpakāya* and *nāmakāya*, it is possible to become aware of the breath as a moving field of interaction, its impermanence and irregularity showing different terrain and different textures. From the outset in practicing breathing mindfulness, one notices how precisely one's mental state is reflected in the breath. Jagged movements and catches show very exactly where tensions are being felt in the body and mind; when they ease, the mind and body also do. The converse also applies: as one works with the breath, the mind's state is gradually changed and mental states transformed. The breath is the way of, through that very relationship, loosening the hold that unhelpful states in the mind exert. Irritation will have an exact location in the body and breath; joy changes the breath and the state of the mind. With mindfulness, little areas of tension are discerned in the breath, but these can be smoothed out, and the knots change into quite a different kind of experience. Happiness and contentment lie hidden in knots, unlocked when the mind quietens; intuition helps the exploration in and around the breath.

At the end of his commentary Upatissa compares mindfulness of breathing to walking alongside a river or the banks of a reservoir, "since the mind is focused, and mindfulness is settled on one object without moving." It seems like a long walk, with different kinds of treading involved: on mountains, screes, marshy riverbanks, and rocks. You need to remember where the riverbank is to find your way. The feet find out how to balance and feel the texture of the ground; the body learns how to find balance there at each stage. Following the breath, one also gets a feeling of the terrain that day. We are treading the area where the mind and the "matter" of the breath influence each other and work together.

We do not own our breath, but we can discern it. So, it is possible to see the breath as a means of loosening tensions at different points of the breath, just as you ease your way along a riverside path that is sometimes overgrown or blocked but sometimes pleasantly easy.

Upatissa recommends awareness of nonself at the third stage. The fourth stage takes the meditator, he says, to the first *jhāna*—and from there to all four *jhānas* as the bodily activities are stilled. Here, if there is a *nimitta* there, it has a crucial role to play. As he says, it is through the *nimitta* that this practice can still be continued. In practice, many people, as teachers throughout this book reassure, do not find a *nimitta*; they still find out how to progress through other "signs," like smoothness or quietness in the breath.[10] Eventually, the mind and breath seem to work in union. Still separate, it is then possible to discern in their relationship how, together, with the help of the *nimitta*, they can take one into deeper stages of calm and then insight.

Through the subsequent stages, as non-delusion grows, the relationship between the mind and matter, perceived through the breath, becomes more finely attuned. Upatissa sees the first twelve stages as working with calm and insight; the last four work with insight alone. The seven factors of awakening are described, seeing the development of the stages through to the attainment of the path. Impermanence as a condition is seen as a disadvantage during stage 13; on seeing this, equanimity emerges, and the meditator "is established in peace." Then, ceasing and relinquishment occur as the mind is "Inclining towards [abiding in] ease (*phāsu*) of mind." When the meditator reaches the sixteenth stage, nirvana is mentioned.

Upatissa also says that this practice allays discursive thought: "Thinking is like a divine musician who follows a sound when hearing it. Therefore, thinking is eliminated." Finally, he answers why the touch of the air element is so pleasant. "Because it pleases the mind."[11] This subtle pleasure, derived from the relationship between the breath experienced in the whole body and the mind, appears to be his guide through the sixteen stages.

CHAPTER 8

Buddhaghosa: *The Path of Purification (Visuddhimagga)*

At some time in the fifth century, a high-caste brahmin converted to Buddhism and became a monk. Bravely, he took the sea voyage from India to the island that is now Sri Lanka. It must have felt like a great adventure. Brahmins were not supposed to travel at all, and sea journeys were considered polluting to their high caste. From early times, however, merchants had been attracted to Buddhism. Buddhist traders embraced travel by land and sea, opening up the early maritime trade routes.[1] Arrival at his destination would have seemed to this traveler, Buddhaghosa, like making safe landing in a new home. Lanka had, by then, become the spiritual center for the Theriya practices and teachings, much later known as Theravada. Buddhaghosa was literate and learned, with a liking for writing things down: As he got off the boat, stories say, he observed an act of vandalism by one woman on another in the dockside area. His meticulous version of events purportedly became the first written legal evidence used on the island.[2]

Sri Lanka had already become a center for monastic and Buddhist life in the maritime regions of South and Southeast Asia. The Great Monastery (Mahāvihāra), where Buddhaghosa stayed, had become a hub for the Theriyas, the people who felt they were sustaining the oldest teachings. To this day, though many of the buildings are of later date, the temple complex retains its magnificence. Stone *kasiṇa* discs have been found in the archaeological sites there: it must have been a place of meditation, study, and discussion. But Anuradhapura, the major city located in the north central plain that was home to the Great Monastery, had a troubled history. The monks had to leave at one point and lost patronage. Buddhaghosa must have felt he was part of a great movement: writing down the commentaries for future generations so that teachings were not lost. Perhaps that impelled him to make his voyage. It was hoped that the great endeavor of creating written records would keep the Pāli tradition alive and flourishing and sustain this center as the protector of "old" Buddhism. The fact that his manual, and commentaries attributed to him, has stood the test of so many centuries is testament to the success of this venture.

When requested—for receiving an invitation was regarded as an important perquisite for such an endeavor—Buddhaghosa undertook a great task: asking around and collecting all the material available on the meditative life in order to commit it to writing. The setting was a scholar's, as well as a meditator's, dream. Beautifully appointed rooms had been arranged, while the monastery had a plentiful water supply and places of cool shade, including a Bodhi tree grown from a sapling from the one under which the Buddha had gained awakening. Writing the teachings would have been a physical and emotional practice (*bhāvanā*); it was considered to bring merit to all around. One can imagine him sitting comfortably alert as he carefully inscribed his words in curvy, often circle-based letters, always avoiding the straight line: constant mindfulness was needed, as the pen could catch in the grain of the palm leaves used at the time. The sounds of chants would have filled the monastery around him; their winding rhythms can be caught in his style.

Buddhaghosa was an assiduous and methodical chronicler, as his account on his arrival in Sri Lanka showed. *The Path of Purification* (*Visuddhimagga*), his magnificent guide to morality, concentration, and the attainment of the path, is characterized by extensive storytelling, simile, and references to the "ancients" as well as a discursive, even meandering, style. His descriptive method also avoids the straight line, placing us in a richly rounded world of incident and literary context.[3] The manual's varied guidance has been central to Buddhist meditative practice ever since. It is a compendium of all the accumulated advice, information, experience, and meditative procedures that had become accepted and were clearly current at the Great Monastery. Buddhaghosa does not much express his own teaching as authoritative: rather, to borrow an image deployed by Pāli scholar Maria Heim, he is communicating navigational advice for meditators from many experienced "sailors," knowledgeable in the weather conditions and tides of their native waters.[4] By the twelfth century teachings and practices emanating from this school had spread throughout the Buddhist regions of what are now Thailand, Myanmar (Burma), Cambodia, and Laos, as well as Sri Lanka. Where meditation was practiced, Buddhaghosa's instructions became a touchstone for understanding and putting into practice the meditation systems that had clearly become well established at this time, and which continue to be practiced now.

Legend says that Buddhaghosa had to write his manual three times. The first time he completed it, he read it out. The gods, in order to demonstrate his great mastery, stole his copy. He wrote it all out again. But the gods stole it once more. So, he wrote it out again. The gods brought back the other two copies; there was no difference between them. The story reveals how deeply his contemporaries regarded the teachings of the "men of old." Buddhaghosa had retained their teachings and could remember them all. According to one legend, Buddhaghosa then returned to India and went to Bodh Gaya to pay homage to the enlightenment tree, the original of the one where he had found shade in Anuradhapura.

The manual is compiled on the lines of Upatissa's, which seems to have been composed slightly earlier. Buddhaghosa never mentions it, perhaps feeling it was suspect, though he appears to draw heavily on its structure and content. He also extended the scope of Upatissa's work with more material, structuring his own manual around the seven stages of insight found in The Relay Chariots Sutta, the *Rathavinīta-sutta* (M 24). This text describes each stage of spiritual progress as like the stint in a relay of carriages, with one taking over from one before but each ceding to the next, until enlightenment.

The guidance on breathing mindfulness is found in the second section, after ethics and morality (*sīla*). It is concerned with developing *citta*, consciousness or the heart. In many ways, his elucidation of the sixteen stages echoes "The Treatise on Breathing" and *The Path to Freedom*. He quotes from the former frequently. It is when we come to the stages Upatissa had mentioned in part briefly—the different ways of approaching the breath—however, that the manual offers extensive and, for practitioners, most helpful advice. The purpose of this section seems to be to offer practical guidance, perhaps for teachers of meditation. It is not clear whether Buddhaghosa himself was a meditator—opinion tends toward that he was not, or at least not an expert one. Heim demonstrates, however, that he saw pursuing teachings *as* his practice. He lovingly records methods from now long-established exegetical and meditative traditions: for him, the vastness of methods of the teaching is like the ocean itself but, unlike that, measureless.[5]

It is a monastic manual, though the principles may have been taught to laypeople. Throughout we can see evidence of the author's literary and somewhat Sanskritic style, marked by leisured exploration of background stories, practical possibilities, and a discursive interest in richly varied interpretations. It is the work of someone who liked to listen, discuss, and by that time, read. This literary style still can be found in many Sri Lankan monks to this day. He says that someone who wants to attain a full path should first work on ethical behavior (*sīla*). Then they should approach a teacher—something that is stressed by both Buddhaghosa and Upatissa—and work on the breath. They should first pay devotions to the Triple Gem, and then approach the breath in four successive stages:

1. Counting

2. Following

3. Touching

4. Settling or fixing

These are followed by four further stages:

5. Observing-insight

6. Turning away—the path

7. Purification—the fruition of path

8. Looking back, or reviewing

The list gives complementary aids to help breathing mindfulness. It is not clear what relationship they have with the sixteen: they are usually associated with the first tetrad of the breathing mindfulness sutta. I suspect there have been all sorts of ways of adapting them.

The Counting

The counting (*gaṇanā*) stage, for Buddhaghosa, is necessary for beginners because it helps to keep the mind attached to the breath, all the time. Anyone who has tried watching the breath recognizes the problem: you want to do something else; the mind wanders; you lose the breath; you cannot remember what you are doing. All sorts of distractions, hindrances, obstacles, or whatever one wants to call them, keep on coming into the mind. Having something "to do" with the mind helps keep its attention on the breath. Buddhaghosa suggests more than the count of five and less than the count of ten. Too many numbers compressed together, he says, will not help the beginner. He uses the analogy of a herd of animals contained within too small a pen. Too many, and the mind becomes distracted by the numbers and forgets to be aware of its primary concern, the breath itself.[6]

Another agrarian image communicates a sense of relaxed attention to the numbers. He says that the skilled cowherd drops pebbles in his pocket to count the cows going into their pen early in the morning. It is a restfully rural image: the pebbles are presumably a good idea for the cowherd, so he can keep an eye on the cows rather than get too absorbed in the numbers themselves. As he implies, the numbers help to keep the mind on the breath but do not have to become a great area of interest themselves.

Many meditations adopt this basic method. Buddhaghosa loves simi-les, and he comes up with another one here: that the numbers taken in this way are like a rudder steering a boat; it keeps it on track. The meditation that I do, a Thai breathing mindfulness system, takes the longest breath one can comfortably manage—and it may take a couple of minutes to find this good, long breath that fills the whole body. Whereas Buddha-ghosa counts breaths, in this practice the meditator counts to nine on the inbreath itself and from nine back to one again on the outbreath. Again, the attention is very light. The breath can be forced if the numbers are too slow. The intention is just to keep the mind on the breath for that long breath, the first of the sixteen stages, and allow it to become even and relaxed as you do so. The long breath is the baseline of the method I know: a long breath is where you start any meditation practice, perhaps even just for a few breaths, and where you end any meditation practice too, so you can make sure the practice is completed and can let it go at the end. Then you return to the normal breath.

Buddhaghosa echoes the careful instructions of "The Treatise on Breathing" and *The Path to Freedom* to not get distracted—away from the outbreath or the inbreath or becoming engaged with objects outside on the outbreath. He understands this to mean that one should not fol-low the track of the breath but rather keep the counting at the tip of the nose, the point of entry of the breath.[7] This is an interesting interpreta-tion. "The Treatise on Breathing," as we have seen, certainly says that one should not get distracted by any particular phase of the inbreath or the outbreath. But while some modern meditators follow Buddhaghosa and suggest awareness should remain solely on the point of contact, others feel that the guidance suggests, not keeping one's attention *away* from the passage of the breath. Rather, it suggests being aware of obstacles that may arise as one *does* follow each stage of the breath: one should accord each stage the same careful and even attention one accords to the oth-ers. In many methods the breath is felt through the body. Some people "place" the numbers down the passage of the breath. Southeast Asian meditations, discussed in the next chapter, identify up to nine areas along this passage. But numbers do not have to be "located" anywhere at all. This shows how different interpretations can arise: one method may work very well for some and not for others. People in my tradition say that counting can be like feeling beads on a rosary or taking stepping stones over a river so you do not get sunk in the mud at a ford.

Buddhaghosa says one does not have to stay long in this phase. As he says, it is just a device to get the mind aware of the breath all the time. Nowadays, many practitioners find it serves as more than that. There is something very stabilizing and satisfying about this very first stage when it is done with the right kind of attention, neither too light nor too heavy. The breath and the mind can be felt to become unified in the body, and there can sometimes be deep joy. There is mindfulness of the whole body and a feeling of being tranquil in that. The important thing regarding any method, I would say, is not to be heavy-handed. Although counting breaths might seem odd and cumbersome at first, it is only a light attention that is needed to keep the mind on the object.

The Following

A new relationship with the breath is established in the next stage: the following (*anubandhanā*). Numbers are no longer necessary. If you are doing a very long breath and want to sustain that throughout the meditation, it becomes easier after a while to drop the numbers and simply follow the passage of the breath in and out of the body. We now have more specific bodily details suggested: the outbreath begins at the navel, the heart is at the middle, and the nose-tip is at the end, and vice versa for the inbreath. Buddhaghosa is uncomfortable with this instruction, however, and interprets the advice of "The Treatise," often understood as not to get *distracted* by any stage of the breath so that it arouses perturbation, as being that this stage itself is unsatisfactory and requires some of the next two.[8] Perhaps this is evidence that Buddhaghosa was an active meditative practitioner. The only thing I can say is that many methods actively encourage following the breath in and out of the body, from the outset.

As "The Treatise" suggests, the skill lies in not being distracted at any stage, but to keep the attention unwavering while gently keeping an all-around awareness of the body. An even attention to the breath is certainly possible, in my own and in others' experience, and it is very pleasant when it is found. There is no need to try other stages at this point: it is pleasing and stabilizing just as it is. Great mindfulness of feeling can be aroused at this stage. Indeed, when Buddhaghosa talks about the stages of the breath in the third stage of the sixteen—experiencing the bodily activities—he in effect describes the meditator addressing this problem. To some meditators, he says, the beginning of the breath's passage is plain, but not the end. To others the end is plain, but not the middle and the beginning, and so on. "I shall breathe in, experiencing the whole body, and I shall breathe out, experiencing the whole body" is the antidote that eventually addresses this lack of evenness.[9] When this happens in practice, the breath starts to feel very pleasant indeed.

The Touching

The touching (*phusanā*) phase involves keeping the attention on the tip of the nose while being "not unaware" of the breath moving in and out of the rest of the body. Buddhaghosa takes the saw image, discussed earlier in consideration of "The Treatise on Breathing," as an illustrative image for this and adds two others. The first is that of a man who cannot walk and who is rocking a seesaw for the amusement of some children. He stays firm in the middle—presumably why he is said to be unable to walk—and keeps the center of the seesaw stable and grounded with his foot.[10] He can still then keep an awareness of the motion of the whole seesaw; he keeps its weight balanced, seeing the swinging up and down is going well. The breath is like the movement of the seesaw; the foot holding it is keeping it steady. Buddhaghosa also offers the image of the gatekeeper of a town. The gatekeeper does not ask each person where they are from and where they are going, but rather keeps on eye on them as they arrive and leave. The gatekeeper to a town is an ancient simile for mindfulness, here applied more specifically to the movement of the breath in and out of the body.[11]

These three images all suggest focus, for the object is kept in foreground awareness, but all also require and involve a larger mindfulness, an awareness of the background of mind and body. In the system in which I practice, this stage involves keeping attention steady on the tip of the nose while still being aware of the full body as the breath enters and leaves it. This sense of the point of contact with the breath found through the tip of the nose forms the basis of many subsequent systems. Some in the Burmese insight methods take a variation on this as their primary practice.

The Settling or Fixing

Buddhaghosa notes that after the touching stage, the *nimitta* can appear. It is time to move the attention gently from the tip of the nose to the visual sphere. This is the stage of settling, or fixing, as it is more commonly translated. The word is *ṭhapanā*, from the word meaning "to establish, settle, or fix." With mindfulness and concentration developed, the more obvious problems that have been besetting the mind have been allayed. The body becomes lighter and more buoyant: "the physical body is as though it were ready to leap in the air." This is aided by the sense of an increased fineness in the breath. Citing the image of the gong (chapter 6), Buddhaghosa says it is like the increasingly subtle awareness needed to discern the breath that arises as breathing mindfulness develops. He suggests that, when the breath appears imperceptible, one just waits at the place normally touched by the breath for it to be sensed.[12]

Buddhaghosa points out that this practice is "not a trivial matter, nor can it be cultivated by trivial persons."[13] For a meditator who comes to this stage there is a feeling that trivia has gone from the mind or, if it has not, that one feels it will and needs to be. What is going on requires awareness and, in our modern terms, a very relaxed effort. This is like what a potter feels when the basic shape is there, and now it is a case of trusting the movement of the wheel as you coax the shape into the right form; fussing too much will not help this, as the pot takes its own time to find its shape. For a breathing mindfulness practitioner, at this point great patience and relaxation is required: as Buddhaghosa says, "strong mindfulness and understanding are needed now."[14]

With a series of beautiful images, he evokes both the sensation and the quality of the work that it is now possible to undertake with the breath from a such an easy basis, in an alert body and mind. The first is an evocatively tactile image of doing needlework with a very fine cloth and a fine needle. This meditation object, Buddhaghosa says, is like such a fine cloth. Mindfulness is like the needle that goes to the exact spot where the breath contacts the tip of the nose. The fine appreciation of the nature of the "cloth," the breath, is then possible. This rings true to me, as there is something so satisfying about working with fine cloth, if you enjoy it, and the needlework on it feels like a gentle movement that is subtle, yet very relaxing too. When there is awareness of the touch of the breath, with good background awareness, people often feel a kind of tingling and a pleasant, even icy, touch.

The second is again a bucolic image, apt for regions where farmwork must have been going on all around. A plowman sends his oxen to roam one morning to the forest. Rather than take too much trouble to track them down for work, he takes his rope and goad and just waits where they like to meet, by their drinking place. Eventually they will turn up, so he can let them come in their own time and drink as much as they want before attaching them to the yoke. The "rope" is mindfulness, and understanding is the "goad" that knows where they need to be led. The ease of this vigilant but unfussed approach, of waiting for things to emerge and settle down, then allows the *nimitta* to arise.

Buddhaghosa gives more descriptions of the *nimitta*. Upatissa had focused on its pleasantness and the physical sensations that may be felt in it: the touch of a breeze or the feeling of cloth. Buddhaghosa includes this element, with greater attention to the visual manifestations by which this touch may be known. It appears quite differently to different people, he says. For some it is visual, like a cluster of jewels or pearls. Yet to others it is like a braid, or garland of flowers, or a puff of smoke, or a cobweb, or a film of cloud, or a lotus, or a chariot wheel, or the disc of the sun or the moon. But for some it is tactile, like the touch of cotton or a breeze, or even, he says, like the feeling of rough silk-cotton seeds or a peg made of heartwood. The point, he argues, is that people experience it so variously. It is like people talking about the different effects they feel when they hear a sutta: they also differ, so to some it is like a torrent in a mountain, to others like enjoying the shade of a fruit tree. In practice, many meditators find the *nimitta* may not be visual: a sense of mild touch or a wave of peace or a gentle rushing sound may mark its appearance.

A great deal of concern has been expressed recently that Buddhaghosa apparently depicts the *nimitta*, and hence the entrance into *jhāna*, as exclusively visual, making it inaccessible for some who feel they do not "see" anything. Read carefully, however, it is clear that Buddhaghosa actively acknowledges the great diversity of ways people experience this stage; subsequent forest teachers support this wide approach.[15] This *nimitta* should be guarded as a woman carrying the embryo of a universal monarch guards her child. This, Buddhaghosa says, will let it grow, develop, and mature.[16] This mindfulness—a subtle sense of the feeling of something growing, that one looks after but with which one does not try to interfere too much and allows to gestate—lies at the heart of a *samatha* breathing mindfulness, however the *nimitta* manifests itself.

Buddhaghosa says the settling or fixing stage will then lead the meditator into all *jhānas*. For those who undertake breathing mindfulness as a *samatha* practice, these descriptions feel apt. Perhaps, as some have suggested, Buddhaghosa was not a *jhāna* practitioner. In any event, he was an exceptionally good listener. His accounts and similes, perhaps told to him by others, evoke the feeling of experiential contact with the breath as an object that arouses peacefulness and joy. Practitioners, or commentaries by practitioners, must have communicated that to him. Indeed, he seems to have been the recipient of all kinds of teachings from the various chanting lineages and the reciters (*bhaṇakas*), who are the custodians of particular collections of texts. This receptivity to variation applies to his discussion of a new stage: access, or neighborhood, concentration (*upacāra samādhi*). This is a level of *samatha* meditation when the hindrances are suppressed, while some joy, happiness, and one-pointedness are experienced. The counterpart sign (*patibhāganimitta*) arises, which has been described as the reflection of the mind's unification on the breath. But the meditator does not yet have the strength of the five faculties and powers to enter the *jhāna* itself. This stage comes to be considered by later insight traditions as a key landmark in the practice of breathing mindfulness (chapters 14 and 15). Its occurrence here is new, but even by this time, there had appeared some difference of interpretation, in ways suggesting longstanding controversies.[17]

Four Further Stages

After that, *The Path of Purification* examines four more stages. Observing and turning away involve mastering these states of deep meditation: being able to enter, stay in, leave meditation, and reviewing it afterward. There are risks the meditator becomes attached. These stages address that, and a purification takes place, so there is no hankering after them. The meditator then recollects them all, enters on the knowledge that arises as a result of that recollection, and finds the stages of path and arhatship. They are "ready to receive the highest gifts of the world with its gods."

This is just the first tetrad. Buddhaghosa goes through the others based on earlier commentarial observations. It is sufficient here to say that he concludes by saying that the first three tetrads show calm and insight combined; the last tetrad shows insight. This alignment is perhaps one to which most schools now adhere. What he seems to be doing, however, like commentators before, is placing no particular limits on the stage any one of the tetrads can attain. There is discussion of the fourth *jhāna*, for instance, and the subsiding of the breath so that it is imperceptible, at the third stage of the first tetrad. The subsiding of the breaths is compared to a man running or carrying a burden, strenuously exerting his breath, then finding relief in the shade, putting down all burdens. His breath now becomes so subtle that he has to wait to see if it occurs. Insight is also possible as the relative subtleties of form and formlessness are discerned.[18] Arhatship is discussed at the fourth stage of the sixteen.

Buddhaghosa's discursive, extended discussions on small matters of practice suggest that meditators and commentators liked to discuss, and often disagreed on, matters of technique, procedure, and levels of attainment. Certainly, there are commentarial positions that align each tetrad with one particular set of meditations and degrees of path. Clearly from early times, however, quite different understandings about these were being expressed. These manuals suggest that the situation was already fluid and subject to variation. This flexibility seems to apply particularly to the possibilities open to the meditator with the completion of the first tetrad. Each stage of breathing mindfulness has its own excellence; many are described with a notably undefined and unlimited potential.

In the last three chapters I have tried to explain some ways breathing mindfulness was understood and applied in the early centuries of Buddhism. The sixteen stages in the breathing mindfulness sutta were interpreted, reapplied, and helped by different methods, right from the time when the commentaries were first composed. If breathing mindfulness was practiced historically, as I assume it was, there must have been all sorts of variations in different places and at different times. Meditation on the breath is a craft. It seems understandable and apt that there are so many possibilities suggested by these commentaries, just as we find variations in textile working, pottery, house building, and weaving throughout these regions and the world. A new development does not mean a school deviated from the original: rather, it may have worked out a system of developing the necessary skills that is slightly different from those before.

At the beginning of this book, I compared the variety of breathing mindfulness traditions to the diversity of forests, with the supporting ground cover, bushes, and herbs of ancient woodland. Different kinds of trees and different individual trees need different sources of nourishment and encouragement. As I hope to make clear across the next chapters as we look at a few current systems of breath meditation, these commentaries established many paths of development. We now have a good foundation in the canon and commentaries to appreciate how this growth and evolution began.

CHAPTER 9

Thailand

The Old Meditations

We know little about the historical development of most meditations in South and Southeast Asian Buddhist regions, including breathing mindfulness, for hundreds of years after the compilation of the commentaries. However, we know that these areas were in contact with one another. In the early days of Buddhism, to get from India to other parts of South Asia—or further afield to Southeast Asia—you needed to go by boat: through the seas and bays that separated the serrated edges of Burma and Thailand from Sri Lanka, or along the rivers and streams that make a network of arterial connections amidst the forests, arid rocky terrains, and mountainous areas of what are now Cambodia and Laos. Trade, contacts, and teachings flourished throughout this riverine and maritime culture: from the early days of Buddhism, monastic and textual influences, sailors, traders, and government officials traveled in waves and crosscurrents across regions with networks of trade and diplomatic routes that were already sophisticated by the early centuries of the first millennium. There are plentiful Pāli inscriptions throughout Burma and Thailand from the fifth century onward, demonstrating that there were vibrantly active Buddhist communities. Various forms of Buddhism seem to have been practiced. By the twelfth century, however, ordination lines from Sri Lanka, where Buddhism arrived first, had spread throughout these areas, and the Theriya traditions, what we now call Theravada, started to be prevalent.[1] The teachings and commentaries associated with the Great Monastery were disseminated, though we do not know how nor in what capacity they were used.

Sri Lanka had great monasteries, but after the commentaries it is difficult to ascertain their practices. Southeast Asian Buddhisms have left little written record of meditation per se. By the second millennium, however, contacts between all these regions seem to have worked toward a loose Buddhist consensus. In practice it meant that the Pāli canon, post-canonical texts, commentaries, some models of art and temple construction, ordination procedures, and practices such as almsgiving became comparable everywhere. Buddhist hubs, linking coasts to hinterlands, and to forests and mountains, started to develop around particular monasteries and temples. Among these there were great regional variations in practice, chanting styles, narrative, vernacular Buddhist myths, legends, and accompanying customs. "Meditation" in the sense of a sitting practice is still not well documented, but it must have gone on sometimes.

The history of breathing mindfulness meditation practice can be divined only incidentally, as popular chants, inscriptions, and manuscripts say little about personal practice. The term *bhāvanā*, or practice, covers many activities that were seen as crucial to healthy development in meditation: chants, devotions, offerings, memorized *gāthas*, lists that were repeated again and again as an aid to practice. These have historically also been considered essential to support breathing mindfulness.[2] Of these, there is some record in Sri Lanka in particular. Personal practice, however, was probably largely transmitted through word of mouth.

Throughout, there seems to have been a sense of confidentiality, respect for privacy, and careful caution regarding claims of meditative attainment. In South and Southeast Asia, literacy was not widespread until the twentieth century; most women were nonliterate. The background to meditative culture, of *bhāvana* in a larger sense, which we can identify in the folding books (*samut khoi*), palm-leaf manuscripts, chant and ritual manuals, and the inscriptions that come from before two hundred years ago, is rich; until the eighteenth century, however, details of what we would call now meditative practice remained largely hidden.[3]

There are good reasons for this reticence and for why it started to change over the last two hundred years. In this and following chapters, we look at some of the meditation manuals, records, accounts, biographies, and great meditation teachers that emerged in Southern Buddhism since the eighteenth century. For the first time, we gain a varied picture of meditators, their preferences, and in some cases, their personal practices. Their testaments indicate how richly varied and diverse meditation had become. Ways various traditions interpreted the Pāli canon and commentaries were highly differentiated. Hybrids, adaptations, and fertile investigations produced all kinds of settings for breathing mindfulness, which by the nineteenth century was becoming one of the most popular practices for both monastics and laity.

The regions of Theravada are now defined by countries: Thailand, Myanmar (Burma), Cambodia, Laos, Sri Lanka. Most of these national identities were only formalized in the nineteenth century. So, it is worth bearing in mind that until the twentieth century many regions would have operated in ways that do not accord with modern boundaries. The borders of Laos, Cambodia, and Thailand cover areas where meditative practice has been strong. Much of what applies to one applies to the others, so far as we know. For the purposes of this discussion, I will use modern national boundaries, but there are many overlaps and cross-influences.

For what is now Thailand, we will look at two loosely defined meditative lines. Again, what is said here also applies to much of Laos and Cambodia, though histories there are less clear.[4] The first strand is what has been called *borān kammaṭṭhāna*, the "old meditation," which was predominant in most of Southeast Asia and possibly Sri Lanka.[5] There is no satisfactory term for these approaches and collections of practices but here it is called the Borān, or old, tradition.[6] The second is the forest movement, a monastic tradition that emerged in Thailand, Laos, and to a certain extent Cambodia in the late nineteenth century (chapters 10 and 11). This represented an attempt to go back to the early days of monastic wandering, asceticism, and meditation thought to have operated in the centuries after the Buddha's death. These two lines are considered distinct in their attitude to meditation and practice but, as we see, there are many overlaps.

These traditions, and many others less easily categorized, employ breathing mindfulness. The way they do so is different in style, but both take the breath meditation as a unifying element. The systems associated with these old meditations were taught as a full path to awakening, with calm and insight acting as means of changing the body and mind of the practitioner so it is ready. The breath, the passage of the breath within the body, and the use of the *nimitta* that arises on the breath, are central; the *nimitta* provides the stability to access ever deeper stages of meditation. This chapter looks at the feeling and style of these practices. They were—and still are, in the few places where they are practiced—complex, sophisticated and, broadly speaking, follow principles suggested and inspired by the earliest Buddhist texts. Those described here employ the breath as a primary element. The sixteen stages are nearly always in there somewhere; they are just not spelled out.

Borān: The Old Meditations
(*Borān Kammaṭṭhāna* or *kammatthan boran*)

The best way to see old Bangkok is still by boat. At the first stop, you walk through a covered market where a closely packed series of stalls display amulets, small figures, medallions, clay votive plaques, tablets, seals, and cloths for sale. The market is atmospherically placed against the lapping of the river and the quay where the boats stop. This sacred area is the heart of Thai Buddhist culture: the major temples and the palace complex are just a few minutes' walk away. You can browse the often-crowded market as you wait; the extraordinary array of objects and curiosities on display in the stalls always tempts buyers. The objects are covered with yantras, circling and looping designs of the human body, and depictions of Buddhas. These designs are known as Sak Yant, recognized by everyone as symbols bringing luck and good fortune. But the diagrams painted, carved, or imprinted on these artifacts give little indication of their origins: they are a physical expression of the old meditation systems of Southeast Asia—their methods, techniques, and diagrammatic explanations. As such, they are evidence of some of the most distinguished and widespread meditation teachings in South and Southeast Asia, once prevalent throughout these regions: we can call these systems, loosely, the Borān meditations.

As breathing mindfulness became the most popular meditation from the Southeast Asian Buddhist traditions spreading internationally, it was often taught simply, without stages or sequence, and with more emphasis on insight and simplicity. This was a deliberate strategy, as we shall see (see chapter 13). It also involved what some would say was a necessary adaptation to a more secular, now global society that felt it required greater emphasis on the direct and the immediately practicable.

The old meditations suggest a very different perspective, only now being pieced together. The history of breathing mindfulness, like other great meditative traditions, remains largely mysterious and undocumented. In the last fifty years, however, research and translation of meditation manuals, diagrammatic expositions, chanting books, and manuscripts of the old meditations are giving a much fuller picture of what happened on the ground with meditation in Thailand, Cambodia, and Laos before the late twentieth century. The Borān systems were the predominant meditative practice tradition throughout most of Southeast Asia before the nineteenth century and, in some cases, well into the twentieth century.[7] Their methods are imbued with mythology, symbolism, and a rich exploration of the full powers of the potential of breathing mindfulness. They investigate areas of meditation and emotional development in ways that feel quite different from most of the practices that went to the West.

The amulets and sheets of cloth in the market are evidence of this. Amulets are the distillation of the great auspiciousness of solitary and collective *bhāvanā*: the cultivation of many qualities that include sitting meditation and many aspects of devotion and daily practice.[8] They are talismans, good luck charms, and reminders of the qualities of the Buddha, the Dhamma, the Sangha, a favorite temple, a teacher, or a practice. Often used in conjunction with chanting, a popular Thai practice, they offer protection but also invite many other levels of engagement. They are often empowered by practitioners known or understood to be highly skilled in *jhāna* and, sometimes, the path.[9] They show encoded meditative instructions.[10]

Yantras and diagrams express the magical transformation of energies and the movement of the breath. Southeast Asian material, spiritual, and emotional culture draws on a pool of these for horoscopes, divination, good luck, blessings, and protection.[11] Some are not esoteric at all; some are—there are many layers of secrecy pertinent to different symbols, mantras, and practices.[12] Some mantras are known by only a few, who know the magical meanings and how to use them.[13] Buddhist scholar Justin McDaniel calls such features part of a "common logic that links the body of the Buddha and the body of the human being in a universal algebraic net."[14] Thai culture expresses itself through these flowing lines, adorned with the syllables, diagrams, and Khmer letters that plot out, carefully and precisely, unknown territory. They are a field of auspiciousness, recognized and enjoyed by everyone and once, if not much now, used to help meditation.

These graceful loops comprise some of the main texts of the old meditations. Yantras swoop down and coil around before soaring upward on the page of manuals, like the flight path of a descending and ascending bird—or indeed the circulation of the breath in meditation. They emanate from teachings that are often esoteric. Meditation, chanting, and other forms of *bhāvanā* are associated with initiation and a strong emphasis on the person-to-person imparting of a teaching, sometimes in a ceremonial context. Personal contact, at the right time and place, is crucial. The use of particular symbols is linked with areas of the body and mind to make a living map: a basis for visualization, enumeration, and cosmological evocation, linked through the manipulation of energies around the body. Ritual operates as a preliminary and as a protective mechanism to ensure the safety and well-being of the practitioner. The first steps in a particular meditation are taken in the presence of a teacher and others. They are also sequential: specified stages are given at appropriate times when the meditator is felt to be prepared. Paul Dennison notes, importantly, the constant use of invocation (*ārādhana*): a quality, a *nimitta*, or a meditation state is invited into the practitioner. Invocations dissolve usual linguistic and cognitive boundaries, and the state is allowed to arise.[15] Invocation is used at every level of practice, through to the formless spheres.[16]

Breath Meditation in Borān Lineages, Texts, and Symbols

The Borān meditation schools had, and some still have, distinct lineages closely associated with particular temples and teachers: some can trace documented ancestries back for centuries. All fall under the umbrella of "old" meditation, and thus share or draw from a common pool of symbologies, techniques, canonical practices, commentarial guidelines, and imagery, but each seems to have quite distinctive features that mark its particular style of teaching.[17]

Borān meditations are the oldest lineages in Southeast Asia. There are traditions recorded in Sri Lanka and some evidence of the practice in Mon regions of old Burma. Sometimes known as esoteric, Tantric, or pre-reform Theravada, they place the practices of calm and insight within a distinctive ritual and narrative framework, accompanied by a complex array of techniques, chants, body mapping, symbols, and the magical use of letters from the alphabet.[18] Throughout the history of Buddhism, practices have shifted and evolved, often in accordance with local customs and mythologies, which are themselves shaped by the texts, meditations, and theories that inspired them. These older traditions show how South and Southeast Asia received and worked with the Buddha's teachings on meditation, particularly those to do with breathing mindfulness. Yantras are just one part of a language of spiritual change found in old meditations, termed by Kate Crosby a system of "technology of transformation."[19] She outlines some of the principal features of these: the creation of the presence of the Buddha through ritual; the use of sacred language; correspondences between the macrocosm and microcosm; and the substitution of qualities to represent *dhammas*, initiations, and esoteric readings of traditional canonical terms.[20]

These systems were, however, largely unknown outside Southeast Asia until recently. French scholar François Bizot brought a corpus of texts from Cambodia, loosely known as the "Fig Tree" material, to international scholarly attention in the 1970s.[21] These practices were both monastic and lay and were living traditions before the troubles of war in the area. They combine ritual, narrative, mythology, canonical text, number systems—based on, for instance, the number of syllables in particular chants or the numbers of parts of the body—and meditations, all of which are intended to enable the transformation of the mind and body to work together.[22] These practices are used both for healing purposes and for calm (*samatha*) as well as insight (*vipassana*). Fig Tree texts are associated with emotionally compelling symbolic narratives whereby the "prince and princess of the heart" find their happiness and freedom through a search for the crystal spheres to be found on a magical fig tree: the human body. The tree is attacked all the time by terrible vultures, the six senses. In one text the prince is related to consciousness and the princess to mental states; these attributions vary.[23] The process of meditation is compared to nurturing an embryo, whose "limbs" are the five *jhāna* factors, grown and developed through practice.[24] The breath is often primary to old meditations:

> Behold! Here also, I practice worship in the form of meditation practice in accordance with the teaching of the holy omniscient Gotama in order that the acquired sign in the sphere of the holy mindfulness of breathing is born in me by virtue of the words that I pronounce: *araham sammāsambuddho bhagavā*! [three times]; *bud-dho*! [three times].[25]

Another, possibly associated, work was found by Anagārika Dhammapāla in Bambaragala Vihara, Teldeniya, Sri Lanka, in 1893 and translated by T. W. Rhys Davids as *The Yogāvacara's Manual of Indian Mysticism as Practised by Buddhists*.[26] It may date from sixteenth-century attempts by Siamese monastics to revive Buddhist traditions in the region, though the presence of other manuals of this kind means that we cannot rule out a Sri Lankan origin for such meditations.[27] It shows a meditation system practiced throughout Theravada regions, by monastics, the court, and rural laity, including women. The practices had already been marginalized and mostly lost when the manual was found. Whatever its origins, it contains elements also found in Borān meditations. Qualities are actively invoked and allowed to come into the body of the practitioner through meditative practice. As in so many of these meditations, breathing mindfulness is linked strongly to joy. The divine abidings of loving-kindness, compassion, sympathetic joy, and equanimity are also emphasized. Consequential factors of meditation, such as a lighter and more flexible feeling of the body and mind, follow. The whole sequence follows Borān patterns, and features such as the five joys and the six pairs, which we find in this chapter. The *nimitta* is drawn into the body, circulates, and is attached to areas like the heart and, in particular, the navel, from where it fans open into a mandala to explore and then attain stages of insight and path.[28]

The word "esoteric" is correctly applied to these systems of meditation, but the term applies in a remarkable way. Southeast Asian culture was soaked in the pool of the old meditations for so long that it remains, at certain levels, saturated by them. Their symbology is everywhere. Everyone is familiar with the aesthetics and style of tattoos, with their swirls of graceful designs known as *anuloms* and boxed diagrams filled with Khmer letters and signs.[29] These denote correspondences that relate directly and specifically to meditation practice, for those who know what they are.[30]

Mystery, potency, and auspiciousness are distilled in the differentiated yantras that make up the amulets, votive tablets, small clothes, and tiny bases for Buddha figures found in temples, hairdresser shops, and taxis. A seated meditative figure, circulating the qualities of the syllables NA MO BU DDHA YA around each loop, is an emblem of a healing magic that protects, blesses, and gives good luck, often in highly specific and particular ways. Many Thais have such amulets and charms, either to wear, have around their person, or keep in the house or car. Chant and song are filled with these traditions. As McDaniel has shown, the greatly popular *Jinapañjara* chant, dating from the nineteenth century, emerged from them.[31] The Peak of Tipitaka chant, sometimes taught at the main insight temple in Bangkok, Wat Mahathat, is also associated with Borān meditation. It offers an aural cornucopia of mantras, *gāthās*, evocations of auspiciousness, and enumerations of the books of the *dhamma*, all chanted in a free-form way. It is a joyful invocation of teachings whose syllables and arrangements are so potent, it is felt, they will pervade all channels and areas of the body and inform our relationships with others.[32] Cambodian songs celebrate such symbologies:

> With NA and MO I pay homage
> to the virtues of my parents.
> BU stands in for the pure Dharma
> DDHĀ the virtues of my dear kin.

And YA those of my wise teachers.
The All-knowing Buddha devised
these syllables for us to chant
as acts of worship, day by day.[33]

The discovery of rituals, manuals, and narratives relating to meditation has meant this evidence, seen by everyone, is being read in new ways.[34] Research is ongoing on the many complex Borān lineages and schools. In most, breathing mindfulness is a constant thread, often steering the meditator through other practices. The breath pervades the whole body and includes it, and it has increasing levels of refinement; by its very nature it is inclusive and provides a means of encircling, encompassing, and refining the energies associated with different areas of the body, heart, and mind of the practitioner. It unifies the mind as well as the body; it can be regulated if needed. Borān practices take the breath as a guide to explore earth, water, air, and fire and to investigate the body. The breath suffuses other meditations, which use it in various ways. The practices are certainly *samatha* based in their association with *jhāna* but also involve insight throughout. The breath sustains mindfulness, thus protecting and ensuring the balance and equipoise of the meditator as they enter states of calm and insight and then let go. The breath as healer is also emphasized, as areas of light (*nimittas*) can be circulated and allowed to penetrate the body.

Suk Kai Thuean's Manual as an Example of Borān Meditation

Thai as well as Western scholars have, thankfully, now conducted extensive research on these systems, some of which survive. Phibul Choompolpaisal has traced one still extant lineage back through the Ayutthaya period to sixteenth-century Thonburi.[35] This line is particularly associated with the Saṅgharāja Suk Kai Thuean (1733–1822). Its meditation is believed to have been predominant in the areas during the reigns of Rama I (1737–1809), Rama II (1767/8–1824), Rama III (1788–1851), and Rama IV (1804–1868).[36] The system continues to be practiced at Wat Ratchasittharam in Thonburi.[37]

In his doctoral dissertation on the SAMMĀ ARAHAṂ chant, another Thai scholar, Potprecha Cholvijarn, explains and translates several Siamese meditation manuals, including those pertaining to this lineage. These manuals date from the eighteenth century onward. They give us a glimpse into once widespread meditative practices undertaken by monastics and laity. Suk's manual, whose recommendations on the breath are discussed by Andrew Skilton and Phibul Choompolpaisal, offers a key example of this tradition and appears to have influenced several lineages.[38]

Suk Kai Thuean lived through great turmoil in Thai political and cultural life. He was born in the reign of King Boromakot of Ayutthaya (1733–1758) when the capital of the regions was Ayutthaya, before it was sacked by the Burmese. Suk taught meditation to the first king in the new dynasty after King Taksin was deposed. He died during the reign of King Rama II (1809–1824), when the court and capital were in Bangkok. He was abbot of Wat Thahoi, a forest tradition temple in Ayutthaya, and was invited by the new king to Bangkok as head of the sangha. As head of the sangha (sangharājā) Suk was in a position of considerable power. His meditation method was, for a time, greatly popular and enduring. He taught all four of these monarchs, two before they acceded to the throne. Rama IV, the last, known also as Mongkut, spent twenty-seven years as a mendicant monk before becoming king. Suk was famous also for empowering and creating amulets, skills traditionally associated with monastics.

The practices Suk taught were based in Borān traditions. Cholvijarn describes them as involving visualization and flexibility in moving nimittas, placing of them at centers in the body that follow the passage of the breath, and allowing the mind to settle at a particular physical base, usually the navel. From here, and by means of the nimitta, the meditator's mind becomes increasingly subtle yet ever expansive, exploring bodies within bodies as the spheres of the nimittas open up more layers of teaching through the center of the body. Increasingly refined manifestations of the Buddha's teachings, emerging from within, lead to awakening.[39]

These systems are distinctive, but it is important to stress they make no major departures either from the canon or the commentaries. They are, rather, inspired by them. Skill in mastering *nimittas* is suggested in the canon by the recommendations for practicing with meditation "devices" known as *kasiṇas*, which are used to focus the mind as objects of calm meditation.[40] There are eight skills in concentration, involving flexibility in moving, extending, and maneuvering the sign.[41] Skill in moving and extending the breath *nimitta* is encouraged from early times (see chapter 6). Borān meditation, extending many elements found or suggested in earlier commentaries, tends to "realize" them with physical and immediate detail. It brings canonical practices into a different light; for instance, Abhidhamma lists are used for visualization of the seven books and letters associated with each. Principles taught in earlier works, while framed differently, animate the guidance. In many particulars and in principle, Borān meditation is informed and shaped by the oldest teachings of the canon particularly, and the commentaries to some degree.

This applies also to the guidelines for breath work and breathing mindfulness. Borān traditions operate both as an explication and an enactment of the principles of The Sutta on Breathing Mindfulness. Its meditations show how the breathing mindfulness practice can infuse the cosmologies, understandings, medical systems, and bodily perceptions of the meditators. These systems are ordered, understood, and known in quite a different way as part of the path. The sixteen stages are not necessarily spelled out; their modes are, however, all used to conduct the breathing practice properly. The richness of these methods is testament to the very effectiveness of The Sutta on Breathing Mindfulness. Its principles were absorbed into a new culture, and in turn new styles emerged, shaped by them. The Sutta on Breathing Mindfulness is reembodied, with practices that accord to its principles and sixteen stages.

The Role of Nimitta in the Borān Meditation Tradition

The growing scholarly record of the Borān meditation tradition suggests that the *nimitta* features prominently, so before we look at the manual in more detail, we should look again at this word so central to the practice of breathing mindfulness as a calm meditation.[42] Mentioned occasionally in the Pāli canon, as we have seen, as the sign or mental image of calm meditation, it was described and explained in manuals.[43] In *The Path to*

Freedom, the purified *nimitta* is associated with "non-delusion," and its appearance offers the means by which the practitioner can steer their way through discerning the contact between the body of the breath (*rūpa*) and the mind (*nāma*) in the stages of breathing mindfulness. The *nimitta*, poised between them and created by both, is presented as a guide for the meditator, inviting them and leading them to the next stage, then it stabilizes the mind at a particular level.

Manuals throughout South and Southeast Asia detail colors, qualities, and particular attributes of different *nimittas* as various stages of practice. They are helpful diagnostic tools: the teacher can understand how the practice is going by hearing meditators describe their attributes. Such phenomena are like landmarks on the way: they allow the meditator to recollect, after a meditation, and so remember the route *nimittas* offer to deeper stages of calm.

The *kammaṭṭhāna* is the "place of work" or the theme of the meditation, such as the breath or the *kasiṇa* disc. The *nimitta* is the sign that arises on that theme. But *nimittas* are also considered *dhammas*, really existent entities. The breath *nimitta* described by Buddhaghosa denotes breathing mindfulness; it arises from that practice and is identified with it. Such a *nimitta* has a real existence as an event (*dhamma*). In Borān meditations, specific *nimittas* are used interchangeably with the meditation theme that produces them.[44] There is a process of substitution: the *nimitta* embodies the quality of the meditation concerned, which is then absorbed and understood by the practitioner before being allowed to dissolve.[45] The "places of work" (*kammatthānas*) are "experienced directly in the form of the *nimittas*." They are all "experienced by a successful practitioner as really existent 'presences' that appear to them and with which interaction is possible."[46] There are also *nimittas* for decay, old age, death, and corpses: all calm meditation objects can be understood with and through them. There is even a *nimitta* for the Buddha.

In *samatha* breathing mindfulness traditions the *nimitta* is a sign of progress, an indicator of the balance of mindfulness and concentration. In many Borān texts, refined *nimittas* are conceived of as honorable presences, to be named with honorifics such as Phra and Chao and deeply revered.[47] When one appears, it suggests appropriate effort: too much forcing and it disappears. As Buddhaghosa recommended, it should be guarded like the embryo of a universal monarch.[48] *Nimittas* offer ways of viewing consciousness. Boonman calls the *nimitta* a "friend" who sometimes turns up when least expected; as a sign of meditation, it has come to help. In these old practice traditions, a *nimitta* is often breathed in through the tip of the nose and drawn to the "womb" of the practitioner, bringing its qualities with it.[49]

Nimitta, *Joys, and Natural Elements in the Manual*

We can see how this works in Suk Kai Thuean's manual. The calm (*samatha*) stage of the practice has thirteen objects, taught in succession. All of these arise from the canon and commentaries in some form.

As in other manuals, first, there is the arousing of the five kinds of joy; each is perceived as a sphere of light. These five are an early list and are fully explained by Buddhaghosa in his manual, in connection with calm (*samatha*) meditation. They are minor joy (felt as prickling in the body), momentary joy, showering joy, uplifting joy, and pervading joy.[50] In this manual, each has a corresponding sphere; each of the five joys is also personified and given an honorific, such as Phra and Chao, used also for corresponding *nimittas*. These are titles accorded to venerable monastics and people of great stature. Each sphere is called a *dhamma* sphere (*duang tham*). Once manifest, such spheres can be moved around the body along the channel of the breath, from the nose-tip to the navel, in different sequences.

In many or most old meditation systems such bodily joy is felt to be the basis for the practice. In accordance with canonical and commentarial tradition, this joy, encapsulated in the *nimitta*, is said to purify the body, mind, and heart. Joy is the fourth and central factor of awakening. Once established, it acts as a platform for, and a means of accessing, the experience and appreciation of increasingly subtle visual and physical manifestations, or "bodies." This occurs when the *nimitta* has been transformed and stabilized in one physical location. In the Borān method, a system of correspondences gives added dimensions to these five joys. Each has one of the five Buddhas of this eon associated with it: the three who preceded Gotama—Kakusandha,

Koṇāgamana, Kassapa—then Gotama, our body, and then finally the Buddha-to-be, Metteyya, whose manifestation is associated with the completion of joy: full pervasion. Such joy is said by Buddhaghosa to allow the meditator to leap up and float in the air. He tells a story of a pregnant woman who stays at home instead of making a visit to the temple one full-moon night, but she is so enraptured to see the lamps glowing she floats through the air to join her family.[51]

There are multiple, interrelated folds of meaning. The five joys are also denoters of the five elements, shown so often in amulets, tattoos, and ceremonial drawings now. Yantras are usually drawn with the five syllables of NA (water), MO (earth), BU (air and the breath), DDHA (fire) and YA (space or consciousness) on one of the five limbs. YA sits above the head. According to the ancient Buddhist understanding, "hard" things like mountains, rocks, and tables have a predominance of the earth element. Watery phenomena like lakes, rivers, rain, streams, and ponds have a predominance of water. Fire is seen in its manifestations as flames and also as heat and light. Air is found everywhere, in the motion of leaves on trees, in ripples on water, and in the breath. So, the twenty-one parts of the body that are hard are linked to the first joy and the element of earth. The second is linked to the fire element with six attributes; the third to the element of water, the twelve moist aspects of the body; the fourth to the seven winds in the body; and the fifth to space, or consciousness. The many levels of association involved in these five elements show the layering of affinities that is characteristic of Borān meditation: the elements are found at an obvious physical level but have more rarefied manifestations, and perhaps different arrangements, at different levels of the meditative process.[52]

In Cambodian, Laotian, and Siamese meditation, the five elements are associated with the five-limbed *jhāna* factors: placing the mind (*vitakka*; MO) for earth, exploring (*vicāra*; NA) for water, joy for fire (DDHA), happiness for air and breath (BU), and one-pointedness or concentration for space, or sometimes consciousness (YA) unifying them all. The exploration of the five elements, and the association of the literal five elements—found, according to Buddhist understanding, in all matter—with states of mind and qualities that one cultivates for oneself in meditation, is canonical.

In The Sutta about Teaching Rāhula (*Rāhulovāda-sutta*; M 62), the Buddha teaches his son, Rāhula, to find each one of the elements in his body and in his mind. He tells him to be like the earth element, the element manifest in the hard parts of the body as bones and the skeleton. He should have that quality in himself and his mind. Water is the moist features of the body: blood, phlegm, saliva, pus, and so on. He should be like water. Fire is found in the heat aspects of the body. Air is found in the winds that circulate, including the breath. Space is found in the cavities in the body and around the whole. For each, Rāhula is told to find the quality in his mind too: the acceptance of earth, for instance, and the washing by water can be found in mental states as well. Later, he is taught breathing mindfulness.[53] At one temple, Wat Ratchasittharam, a relic of Rāhula is kept, as he is regarded as the first person to have received the Borān teachings taught at the temple.[54]

In Thai practice, the system is also used for healing, both in the sense of medicinal substances to address imbalance and in the therapeutic manipulation of *nimittas* within the body.[55] The breath, as air, is often employed to enable that process. Other fives are associated with NA MO BU DDHA YA: the five-limbs of a human and the five aggregates. The breath often acts as the mediator through the experience of these.

The five joys are followed by the six pairs (*yugala*). These are the twelve attributes of the skillful mind and body described in the Abhidhamma: tranquility of body and mind, lightness of body and mind, softness of body and mind, flexibility of body and mind, proficiency of body and mind, and uprightness of body and mind.[56] They are features that can arise when the mind is skillful. According to the Abhidhamma understanding, they are also said to be present in *jhāna* and at the moment of the four stages of the path. Abhidhamma was not attached to these systems as a kind of validation after the event. Rather, it offers an informing principle in their very formulation and the processes whereby they can be applied. In the Abhidhamma, skillful consciousness and unskillful consciousness have certain attributes particular to the level and quality of each. By a process of substitution, unskillfulness is replaced by skillfulness. Crosby demonstrates how this follows the principles of Sanskrit generative grammar: skillful consciousness, with wisdom, gradually supplants unskillful consciousness, until its momentum washes unskill-fulness away.[57]

The next stage is happiness in the body and happiness in the mind (*kāyasukha* and *cittasukha*). The fourth stage is breathing mindfulness.

Nimitta *and the Body*

For those interested in the practice of breathing mindfulness as a calm (*samatha*) as well as an insight meditation, the associations are clear: joy, readiness of the body and mind, and the experience of a somatic happi-ness, felt in the entire body, contribute to and are aided by a gentle train-ing in attentive appreciation of the fullness of the breath. This is not a sentimental avoidance of unpleasant feeling. Rather, the sense of easeful happiness (*sukha*), which has been described as a characteristic of the breathing meditation from early times, acts as a guide to the meditation and renders the body and the mind of the practitioner soft, pliable, and receptive. It also ensures that the mind is both upright and strong—the "six pairs" act as a group together: tranquility, lightness, softness, flex-ibility, proficiency, and uprightness, in the body and in the mind, bal-ance and modify each other.[58] They provide an essential support for the pursuit of *jhāna* and insight, ensuring the body and mind do not become rigid or unbalanced. It is worth noting the role of joy in this process. Together, joy and happiness that pervade the body and mind strengthen them for meditation, if the practice is correctly undertaken, with the back straight and the legs crossed. The body and mind work together and, through integrating joy and happiness, are made ready for the changes that arise from breathing mindfulness and for the steady ap-preciation of increasingly subtle manifestations both of the breath and the path.

This is evident in the great emphasis placed on the physical body as the basis for other "bodies" that emerge within it. In Suk's manual, the passage of the breath through the body is examined in detail.[59] It describes the appearance and visualization of the spheres of light—the *nimittas*—and the placing of them along nine bodily bases located on the passage of the breath, from the nose-tip through to the area around the navel. Each one is suitable for cultivating the breath *nimitta*.[60] The physical body provides the ground for working out the whole practice. Assigning the nose-tip as the beginning of the breath is commentarial, and if the *Ānāpānasati-sutta* instruction of arousing mindfulness "before one's face" is to be taken to mean, as some feel, the front of the nose or mouth, it was there from the beginning. But the physical location of the breath passage had not been greatly explored in the commentaries.

For mindfulness of breathing, the meditator rests the mind at the nine specific bodily bases along the breathing passage. Awareness of these points is aimed at "helping the practitioners mindfully to follow the breath as it moves in and out of the body while contacting these specific areas."[61] The nine, or sometimes seven, bodily bases of Borān meditations are a new development from canonical descriptions. They appear, in part, to be intended to ensure that the meditator does not fall into the trap of losing awareness of any part of the breath. Although the commentaries do not discuss bodily locations of the breath, it seems likely that "The Treatise on Breathing," which speaks in detail of the hindrances likely to follow one at the beginning, middle, and end of the breath, meant the passage of the breath through the body in some way: the manual speaks of problems in the apprehension of the breath along the route from "beginning" to "middle" to "end."[62]

In this manual, developments of the mind and consciousness have auspicious landmarks: the appearance of specific *nimittas* at each stage. *Dhamma* spheres appear at each stage of progress, from the first, joy; to the *nimitta* of the human body, when there is purity of body, speech, and mind; to the Brahma, or divine body, that appears at each one of the four *jhānas*. Within Buddhism, one can be born after death as a Brahma on the basis of *jhāna* meditation. Gods of this level are of such fine materiality that they often appear in suttas to humans, or sense-sphere gods, as sparkles of light or radiance.[63] The "spheres" discussed here are also too subtle to be apparent until one has attained the appropriate level of meditation, when the intimation of that sphere will appear through the *nimitta*. When one abandons false views of self, doubt, and attachment to precepts and vows at the level of stream entry, the sphere of stream entry, understood as *dhammakāya sotāpanna*, emerges.

The term *dhammakāya* has complex levels of meaning. It has been described as a "a truer mode of the Buddha's existence than any imper-manent, physical body of his that was seen and heard in the world."[64] It is, in effect, an enlightenment "body," still accessible and knowable in this world, and accessed, when the practitioner is ready, through an area around the navel. Nirvana is comparably realized, evoked by being de-scribed as "a place." Each level is associated with a new body based on a sphere: bodies within bodies are accessed by the mind that is stable and has rid itself of hindrances enough to find them, and they become man-ifest as the practice deepens and greater purification is achieved. Beings of this level and above, such as arhats and Buddhas, may appear in order to greet and welcome the practitioner, as we see in regard to Ajahn Mun Bhūridatta (see chapter 10). The principles of the sutta are observed; the formulation is creative and fresh.

In the modern teachings of the Wat Ratchasittharam temple, the stages described by Buddhaghosa are involved as a preliminary in breath-ing mindfulness. They are counting, following, touching, and settling, and they help to steer attention to the breath and sustain mindfulness awareness of the object.

Suk Kai Thuean's manual also included meditation on the loath-someness of the body, a practice common to Borān traditions, and perhaps a necessary counterweight to the sense of increasingly refined beauty and subtlety. It seems like the old monastic practice of drinking urine: a reminder of some basic facts about our human existence! The canonical *samatha* corpse practice arouses urgency (*saṃvega*) that is stilled to calm, to loosen craving for bodily pleasures.[65] After these *sa-matha* meditations, the practitioner moves to formless meditation and then insight, given with nine levels. The manual discloses no higher teachings of *samatha* and insight. To this day, they are still not openly revealed in this system, regarded as esoteric and advanced practices for advanced practitioners ready to move to them. This is a characteris-tic found in many breathing mindfulness schools, whether technically esoteric or not: appropriate protective and introductory measures are required formally or as an assumption; people are taught skills when they are ready. The understanding is that it is better that such advice is given at the right time.

In sum, this meditation path bases the teaching within the physical and experiential sense of one's own body. Happiness found in good feeling (*vedanā*) is its way of progress. Mindfulness of breathing acts as a support, steadier, and enabler. The perception of what the "body" involves is made increasingly subtle and becomes more finely tuned as the meditations develop. First, there is transformation and purification of the energies of the body and mind through joy. Then, the bodily base diagrams are employed at several levels of *samatha* practice. Once the meditation has become established, ever subtler "bodies" can be discerned within the meditator, each within the other, each more spacious, until the attainment of the stages of path.[66] The Buddha said, "In this fathom-long body is the arising of the world, the ceasing of the world."[67] This system takes this literally. Each stage is described within the physical experience of the body, even when that is being transcended. The *nimitta* allows the wisdom of each stage to develop and reveals deeper layers of meditation, and of mindfulness within the body.

The recital of the word BUDD-HO with the breath, to sustain mindfulness and attention, is found in many of these systems. The most common variation is BU on the inbreath and DDHA on the out. The Manomayiddhi system, popular today, uses breathing mindfulness with NA MA on the inbreath and BU DDHA on the outbreath as a means of keeping awareness of the body. The practices are said to develop knowledge (*vijjā*). Different realms of beings are visited, while mindfulness of the breath, with the mantra, ensures that an awareness of the physical body is sustained at all times. The meditator is always inducted carefully, guided by protective chants, and the breath acts as support throughout.[68]

Bases within the body where the breath goes each have their own meaning and function: in one Borān manual the nose-tip is the "origin of joy and delight" while the top of the head is the home of "graciousness and patience"; the base of the navel is the "appeasing of all suffering."[69] Sequence, meaning, and locations vary between systems. Some start with the navel and move up the body via the back to the top of the head, then to the back of the head, before moving down the body to just above the navel. Choompolpaisal explores comparable practices for another manual and temple. The basic technique consists of breathing mindfulness, with the visualization of a sphere *nimitta* at the end of the breath passage—around the stomach—until a vision of bright light (*ong bhāvanā*) appears. As the meditation develops, the light and its sphere are circulated backward and forward through the body and back again, so that they also go through nine bodily bases along the passage of the breath.[70]

Cholvijarn describes how Wat Rattchasitaram, the temple so heavily influenced by Suk, continues his practice in some form, fragile though the survival of such meditations now are. This lineage is known now as Kammatthan Majjima Baeb Lamdub, "Progressive (Mind)-Training in the Middle Way Employing Meditation Subjects."

The SAMMA ARAHAM Chant

The Sammā Araham meditation school is another example of a now popular practice closely related to the Borān tradition. The school was founded by a *samatha* teacher renowned for his psychic mastery, Luang Pho Sot (also known as Phra Mongkhon Thepmuni and Sot Candasaro; 1884–1959), a key figure in the transmission of Buddhism to the West. He interpreted the canonical instruction in The Sutta on the Foundations of Mindfulness to be aware of the "body in the body"—as working quite literally, so that Buddhahood and awakening are uncovered, like layers on an onion, from a base point around the navel.

One day as he sat in meditation "his mind [suddenly] became still and firmly established at the very centre of his body," and he experienced "a bright and shining sphere of Dhamma at the centre of his body, followed by new spheres, each brighter and clearer than the one before."[71] This experience of the *dhammakāya* prompted him to develop the new method. In 1916, he took on an old and half-abandoned temple, Wat Pak Nam, and remained there for forty-three years teaching SAMMĀ AR-AHAM recitation to numerous followers. Those spread it to a number of other centers, and it is still practiced widely today.

The mantra SAMMĀ ARAHAM is recited and linked, in many cases, to the passage of the breath. As with Suk's method, visions of bright spheres, or *nimittas*, are linked to various attainments; *nimittas* are visualized at the bodily bases of the breath. These lead to the attainment of spiritual bodies and the *dhammakāya*. Other old meditation methods are downplayed or not included. The sacred syllables, evoking levels of cosmology and linking microcosm to macrocosm, do not feature; presumably the SAMMĀ ARAHAM mantra is felt to be all that is needed. Substitution, whereby an element is taken as a substitute for something else, does not occur either. There is no Abhidhamma nor any of the initiation rituals that sometimes accompany old meditations. Yantras are not involved. While it shares much of the symbology and uses comparable techniques to Borān meditation, this is a quite distinct lineage of practice. But it too is closely linked to the breathing mindfulness practice and the stages as outlined in the *Ānāpānasati-sutta*.

The informing presence of the sutta can be seen. The allaying of the breath in that system is described as the calming of the bodily activities—the fourth of the sixteen breathing mindfulness stages, completing mindfulness of body. Mental activities (*cittasankhāra*) are also stilled. It is said, "The mind stops still at the centre of the dhamma sphere of the human body":

> The breath ceasing at the same place is called *ānāpāna*, which means the breath stopping still or having no breath. When the three activities [*sankhāra*] stop there, it is called *kāyānupassanā satipaṭṭhāna*. When the activities are calmed, there is the arising of joy. This is called *vedanāupassanā satipaṭṭhāna*. The mind thinking that it has joy is called *cittānupassanā satipaṭṭhāna*. When the three *satipaṭṭhānas* are together right there, a luminous sphere will appear, the size of an egg yolk, the moon or the sun, pure and clear like a mirror. This is called *dhammānupassanā satipaṭṭhāna*. Some call this sphere "Phra Dhamma the crystal sphere."[72]

Cholvijarn points out that the pattern follows that of The Sutta on Breathing Mindfulness, connecting the practice with the four foundations of mindfulness: body, feelings, mind or heart, and *dhammas*.

He suggests that the word "peace" (*santi*) refers to the *jhāna*, and the *ānāpāna* to the breath, ceasing at the fourth *jhāna*. Progress to enlightenment occurs at this place in the navel. He concludes:

> . . . if one strips Sammā Araham meditation of its *borān kammatthāna* aspects, what is left is essentially the practice of mindfulness of breathing, the recollection of the Buddha and the contemplation of one's body, feelings, mind and *dhamma*s, but extended to the inner bodies as well as the human body.[73]

The Past and Possible Futures of Thai Borān Lineages

There are many distinct Borān lineages of practice: they have roots and understandings derived from the old meditations, but each line of practice interprets them in distinctive ways. It seems to me that these methods constitute a way of approaching meditation rather than a single system; they draw on a pool of techniques, practices, and myths that encourages ever exploratory, creative investigation.[74] The ones described here take breathing mindfulness as a primary object and support in the meditations involved, but some do less. Some groups known abroad have less emphasis on the breath now but retain old features.

Wat Pak Nam, once understood as a center for these meditations, has many branches now, both within Thailand and at an international level. It has a justified reputation for encouraging lay practitioners, who are actively involved. There are many distinguished female practitioners. Mae Chee Puk, from this temple, founded the National Thai Nuns' Institute, which has numerous nuns attached.[75] Mae Chee Chandra Khon-nok-yoong (1909–2000), perhaps the most influential female teacher in twentieth-century Thailand, was a pupil of Luang Pho Sot Candasaro at Wat Pak Nam. She founded Wat Phra Dhammakāya, one of the largest temples in Thailand. Wat Dhammakāya meditation still bears the imprint of old meditations.[76] It has spread internationally and now has centers worldwide. In this system, seven bodily bases along the breath passage are often taken, but breath observation itself, oddly enough, is not so involved.[77] Perhaps less significant for a discussion of modern breathing mindfulness, the systems nevertheless demonstrate the continued heritage of old meditations.

Why are these methods less well known in the West in their old forms? Certainly they are esoteric, in the sense that the higher levels of practice are reserved for those who have had considerable experience and are ready for the next step. There are other, more troubling reasons, however: most of their marginalization has arisen, as it so often does, from politics. This started back in the early nineteenth century, when the prince who later became King Mongku attempted to reform the sangha. In 1833 he established the Thammayut, or Dhammayut, Nikāya of the monastic ordination, which, in time, started to control monastic power, education, and the teachings of meditative schools. Some parties within that movement, both royal and political, became opposed to traditional mythologies, storytelling, and systems of practice. Various attempts were made to discredit or marginalize them. No single cause appears to be paramount, but the effects have been widespread.[78] Many other influences also operated: a general movement toward scientism within Southeast Asia, a perceived need for a "rational" Buddhism, and a stress on the cognitive and apparently scientific, rather than the emotional or intuitive. A liking for more direct, even secular, practices less associated with ancient narrative, myth, and ritual was involved. Less emphasis on old magical understandings, with their ever-present backdrop of surrounding manifold realms, also perhaps helped turn the tide.

For whatever reason, modernity largely effaced these once allpervasive teachings. It seems possible that in time the tide will turn again. These old systems of meditation involve constant mindfulness of body, feeling (*vedanā*), and unwavering mindfulness in experiencing the mind and events that arise in it. Their appreciation of our human capacity for invocation is inspiring. By assuming one can find tranquility, joy, happiness, and letting go simply through one's apprehension of the breath, it becomes possible: the breath works on all foundations of mindfulness. The calm and the emotional steadiness produced by these and related systems, even in the midst of great uncertainty, grief, and loss, could look increasingly important in the twenty-first century.

Assuming these forms of practice survive and that Western interest in them continues to grow, it will be interesting to see how they are integrated into international meditative settings. At the moment they are fragile and local, strong enough to survive in part, but their centrality to Southeast Asian practice and meditation has been significantly eroded.

These are lineages to inspire awe, derived from centuries of practice and careful exploration. Honoring the breath to invite in and release restorative and healing qualities, pervading the body with the breath, and an intimate, ever-refined appreciation of the relationship between body and mind: what here is *not* suggested in The Sutta on Breathing Mindfulness?

> The person who venerates and practices this holy *Kammaṭṭhāna* considers his own body as a place of establishing (*ṭṭhāna*), for which he dare not have contempt. Such a one will attain the paths and fruits that will lead him to heavenly good and to the good of *nibbāna*.[79]

CHAPTER 10

Thailand Forest Traditions, Part One

Modern Emergence

In recent times, the forest meditator has become a symbol of meditative calm. In this and the following chapter, we move to discussion of the Thai forest traditions and their meditations and explorations around the breath. This chapter begins with an overview of the resonance of forest meditation in Thai and Southeast Asian Buddhism and culture, as well as how such traditions evolved in the modern era.

In the twentieth century the forest tradition burgeoned with positively arboreal growth in a now fertile soil: there are many great teachers and renowned figures, all with quite distinctive excellencies and teachings, who encourage and nurture new meditators in sometimes very different ways. These were often at the outset closely knitted into Borān methods, discussed in the last chapter. Before we consider this wide spectrum, this chapter takes a look at two figures, Ajahn Sao Kantasīlo and Ajahn Mun Bhūridatta, early pioneers in creating new perspectives on teaching meditation and, frequently, practice with the breath.

From early times, the forest has been a place for retreat, meditation, and monastic settlement. Forests and wildernesses were a natural home for the Buddha and his followers' meditations.[1] In suttas, gods from the heavens visit meditators in woodland groves.[2] For meditation, a mountain, a ravine, a mountain cave, a charnel ground, a jungle thicket, an open space, or a heap of straw is recommended.[3] The instructions for breathing mindfulness suggest a wilderness or, perhaps especially, "the roots of the tree." One commentary says the practitioner, by going to such places, is like a leopard, because "like the leopard he lives alone, in the forest, and accomplishes his aim, by overcoming those contrary to him, namely, the passions."[4]

Despite some deforestation, woodlands, jungles, and groves are still spread throughout Southeast Asia. The region's cultures are informed by a sense of the forest as the place of restoration, enchantment, and also livelihood. For Thais, the forest is certainly full of danger and wild animals. But in mural art found throughout all these regions, the forest also forms the dark, restful background for the imagination. Brilliantly colored animals, mythical creatures, gods, and humans enact the jatakas, tales of the bodhisatta's many past lives preparing for Buddhahood, set in a timeless "once upon a time," against the dark greens, blacks, and blues of an all-encompassing forest backdrop.

Historically, rivers were fished, wild fruits and vegetables were used for food, roots and herbs used for herbal remedies, and wood used for construction. Such settings were imbued with supposed supernatural properties as well as healing herbs and plants and sources of nourishment. Forests were not necessarily quiet or safe, however. Aside from the danger of large wild creatures, there were, as there still are today, loud noises from geckos and bullfrogs after rain, mosquitoes that bite, and poisonous snakes that can slither by at any time.[5]

Monasteries in forests offer seclusion, a natural setting very different from urban life. An ancient distinction between two kinds of monastic practice, that of town dwellers and of forest practitioners, persists to the present day, though many monastics now move between them.[6] Jungle regions would have felt more remote in the past than they do today, as transport links were solely riverine until the early twentieth century. Most jungle areas in Thailand, however, were never completely cut off from people and settlements.[7] Monastics were in friendly symbiotic relationships with the laity, benefiting from mutual support. Villagers were grateful for their teachings and protection, and the monks discussed in this chapter constantly expressed gratitude for the support they received from the laity.[8]

Modern Thai Forest Traditions and the Spirit of Reform

Such areas in Northeast Thailand and the Laotian borders have long been regarded as the "powerhouse" of monastic meditative practice. Breathing mindfulness has, in varying degrees, always played a central part. This tradition is old, but its recent popularity dates from the nineteenth century, in a group of monasteries scattered around Sisaket, Isaan, and Thonburi. Notable figures include Ajahn Sao, Ajahn Maha Boowa, Ajahn Lee, Ajahn Chah, and Ajahn Thate. The forest movement, as it is known, transformed monastic norms of the time by establishing in associated forest monasteries strict observance of the Vinaya, the monastic rules, with what was also, at that time, an unusually strong meditative element.

In the nineteenth century seismic changes were occurring in those regions. Deforestation had started, and roads were being built that connected the regions to the rest of Thailand. King Mongkut had been a monk himself for twenty-seven years and, unhappy with what he regarded as folk customs, superstitions, and a less rigorous attitude to the Vinaya, started the Dhammayut order of monks in 1833. This influential movement, which spread to Laos and Cambodia, promoted what was intended to be a reformed and streamlined Buddhism with a stricter adherence to monastic practice and a strong dependence on the Pāli canon, which King Mongkut felt had been neglected.[9] Thailand was never colonized, but the king wanted a modern approach to Buddhist understanding, which he felt could be achieved in part through a return to an earlier monastic ethos. He questioned the possibility of attaining nirvana or even *jhāna* in modern times.[10] In time, it started to be felt, wrongly, that traditional meditation systems, alongside those loosely called Borān, were not based on canonical principle.[11] The forest movement emerged amid this reformist mood. True to their pioneer spirit, however, those involved never felt their meditative possibilities were limited, whatever the monastic ordination line involved.

Because of the impact of Western cultures, there were attempts at the same time in outlying areas of Thailand to suppress local and much-loved cultures of ritual, jatakas, myths, and trust in supernormal powers derived from meditation. But in forest regions, so dependent on an intimate relationship with the wildlife, woods, and rivers where magic, spirits, and stories were seen as natural elements of the surrounding geography, they were not successful. Monastic emissaries from Bangkok, charged in 1898 with assessing the state of teachings in Northeast Thailand—then only accessible by river—noted with disfavor the strong emphasis on the ancient staples of village life: everywhere they found folk customs, jataka stories as models and disseminators of doctrine, and homages to beings living in trees, rivers, and mountains. In the rationalist mood, these posed an embarrassing reminder of "superstitions." Jatakas had always articulated a sense of the interdependency of the natural world and of all kinds of beings, such as gods, animals, humans, and the spirits of trees, rivers, caves, and mountains, all of whom chat to one another and interact. The new Dhammayutta Nikāya authorities felt the tales were unrepresentative of what was hoped to be a new, scientific Buddhism, able to withstand Western challenges.[12]

The reformist mood was constantly reinforced by missionary activity and a scientific worldview that was overthrowing traditional Thai systems of all kinds. Despite the cheerful imperviousness of many Thais to these influences, the mood affected attitudes to meditation, in particular *jhāna*. While not at first specifically aimed at meditative practice, the reforms started to be linked to a shift to vipassana and a growing sense that meditation should be "scientific."[13] Borān meditation, like so many other aspects of traditional Buddhism, was less emphasized. As Crosby shows, meditation had always been embedded in Thai, Cambodian, and Laotian medical science, but such associations were also now discredited.[14] The changes were bolstered by the influx of Burmese insight methods during the twentieth century, which became increasingly popular (see chapter 14 and 15). This proselytizing spirit led to the devaluation and, sadly, the active suppression of *samatha* practices.

At first, such influences were not strong. For forest meditators, a wish for an unencumbered lifestyle and Vinaya, along with ascetic practices sanctioned by the Buddha for some monastics who chose them, was at the fore.[15] They undertook periods of simple wandering or long extended walks, as would have been the case in ancient India.[16] In the long walks known as *dhutaṅga* practice for which this school is renowned, a monk simply takes his begging bowl and walks through regions that are genuinely more remote and rarely visited. This lifestyle was atmospherically defined by the fifth-century commentator Buddhaghosa as "always meeting the dawn in the forest."[17] For such walks, tents are made from robes and placed at the foot of the tree, a practice still popular in forest monastery retreats today.

The movement arose in this spirit of reform. While it is often seen as a separate lineage of meditation, it is defined more by its Vinaya code than any one practice. In the midst of such changes, breathing mindfulness was always at the core, but this seems to take more simplified forms during the twentieth century. An implicit assumption of the natural radiance of the mind also becomes more prevalent, though the goals of meditation exceed that.[18]

When considering the histories of meditations in these areas, we need to bear in mind how much had been unrecorded before. In the Thai context, information is scant about personal meditation practice before the nineteenth century. In Tibet and many parts of East Asia, knowing the life stories of great meditative figures is considered an essential accompaniment to sustaining a lineage holder's reputation, and knowing and reading their inspiring and encouraging biographies is itself a practice. But until the twentieth century, Southeast Asian monks and, even more so, nuns would not think it proper for their lives or practice histories to be recorded in biographies.[19] Those regarded as attaining arhatship were certainly the subject of myths, legends, and local admiration, but life stories and practice histories were rarely outlined in detail. A strong factor in this was South and Southeast Asian reverence for ensuring there was no breach in the most serious Vinaya rules. The fourth of four serious (*pārājika*) offenses that immediately exclude a monastic from their order is false claim to any meditative state.[20] In practice, this means that teachers, monastic and indeed lay, rarely discuss their meditative attainments in public. It is a graceful custom that still, for the most part, persists. People do not usually describe their own practice to others or reveal anything about their personal meditation to anyone except their preceptor or spiritual guides.

The situation is even more marked for female renunciates, traditionally more reticent in Thai culture. While many Thai nuns, or *mae chees*, of the twentieth century had shrines and stupas erected on their death—a great honor accorded to those felt to have the highest spiritual attainments—there is little record. Boys learned to read at local monasteries, but in most regions, female literacy was rare before the 1920s. Many of the great practitioner nuns born in the early part of the twentieth century did not learn to read until late in life, if at all.

Spiritual Biography as Teaching in Twentieth-Century Thai Buddhism

There are, however, plentiful records of the experiences of early twentieth-century forest monastics, for another trend accompanied the movement's success, and perhaps contributed to it. Prompted, perhaps, by a wish that went quite counter to the reforms, a stream of spiritual biographies and autobiographies emerged throughout the twentieth century to demonstrate that higher states were indeed possible and that the highest Buddhist goals could be achieved: others could try these spiritual paths. These accounts describe deep meditative states and, if only briefly, the methods that were taken to find them. They were often written by students and disciples of particular teachers, but also, in one or two famous cases, by the practitioner monastic themselves. Here life stories become interspersed with first-person accounts of meditation experiences, often through quotes of what the subject has said or, controversially, in claims by the authors themselves. Although often framed carefully, their discussion about the kinds of meditation they have been practicing and how it affects them often includes their description of what it is like to be liberated: the breath is often key to these.

Printing and distributing these records is seen as a compassionate gift and the greatest kind of generosity, for Asians the basis of all meditation.

Lay donors ensured that the dissemination of such biographies and teachings was wide. There is a custom throughout Southeast Asia for those with sufficient wealth to publish *dhamma* books and pamphlets for free distribution, and to dedicate the ensuing merit (*anumodana*) formally to relatives, parents, and teachers. Most of the figures discussed in this and the following chapter have biographies now freely accessible on the internet. As modernity made such an impact on the regions, with visitors to temples and monasteries coming from the international community and contact with the West becoming routine, Anglophone biographies also started to be composed, and those in Thai were translated. Such books have been distributed extensively to Buddhist centers around the world.[21]

The effects of these records have been far-reaching. Visitors from the West became monastics; many went on to be renowned teachers, starting monasteries and teaching centers outside Thailand. The reputation of the area as a center of meditative excellence has grown worldwide. Esoteric old meditations, conducted largely among non-Anglophone Thais, still remained little publicized or discussed internationally. The world at large, however, soon gained a vivid picture of the kinds of practices, struggles, and achievements that characterize the new forest monasticism of Northeast Thailand, Laos, and Cambodia. Jack Kornfield, who traveled in these regions in the 1970s, gives a now classic account of meetings with many of these practitioners, including their meditation techniques.[22] The immediacy of such accounts, along with other biographies and writings, helps to build up a picture of multigenerational practice, from multiple angles and perspectives. We find out about the teachers as living people, of quite different characters and styles. For the first time, perhaps in any Buddhist region, we can now trace the experiences of lines of teachers and practitioners and follow their interrelated paths, both in their regions and in time: meditation is being recorded in the first person, as lived experience. People's characters and likings for different meditations emerge; we feel their thoughts, struggles, and extraordinary achievements.

In these records, forest teachers are considered quite distinct from those following Borān methods. The meditation techniques of forest meditators, as described, appear less structured than those found in Borān meditative systems. This could, of course, simply be because they did not want to say too much about them. There is less of an obvious sense of sequential mapping or defined esoteric stages. The teaching method is direct and anecdotal, as life events are constantly used as teaching enactments of *dhamma*.

Despite these differences, the boundaries between the practitioners in the new movement and those of the old feel porous. Some Borān meditators had already been forest or jungle practitioners.[23] In the early days of the forest movement some of the accounts of experiences on the basis of breathing mindfulness were framed in Borān understandings. Verbal expressions and techniques echo those of the manuals and Borān teachings. In a culture steeped in a rich, multivalent symbolism of healing, understandings of the body, and seeing the four elements as applying at all levels of the body and mind, alongside a sense of macrocosm reflected in the microcosm, it would be odd if the traditional ways of expressing meditative transformation had *not* lingered. Their influences were just part of the surrounding world.

Certainly, some meditations discussed in the last chapter start to be conceived and sometimes discussed in more obviously canonical terms, with more stress on insight. But I suspect the old meditative world, filled with myth and folklore, just felt natural—and indeed was itself canonically justified. The universe was seen as filled with spirits and gods as well as animals, while heavenly beings inhabited cosmological realms conceived as planes, open to visitors. All these realms and spirits could be found and known in meditation, chant, and even daily life. Nirvana was evoked as a destination, a city, a place of happiness. It was just how things are (*yathābhūtaṃ*). We see these elements particularly in the older forest teachers. These teachers are all, however, quite distinct from one another: their lives and teachings show how methods and people vary, even in one tradition.

Ajahn Sao Kantasīlo (1859–1942)

The emergence of the forest movement was not associated with one initial teacher or set of teachings. Ajahn Sao Kantasīlo, however, is generally regarded as a founding figure. One of five children, he started to live in a temple when he was twelve, and he ordained at age twenty in the pre-reform monastic orders, which later became collectively known as the Mahānikāya, in Ubon Ratchathani. This is in the Isaan region of northeast Thailand, near the border with Laos, where many other meditator monks liked to settle. Like some others who espoused the forest lifestyle, he reordained in the Dhammayut, the order founded by King Mongkut.

We know little about Ajahn Sao. Clearly uninterested in leaving a personal mark, he appears trackless, as one imagines he would have wanted. He left no meditation manual, and his few talks were largely unrecorded.[24] He rarely gave formal teachings, preferring silence and the occasional pertinent statement as a means of training. He was strict in his Vinaya, asking his fellow monks to join him in rising at 3 a.m. and going to bed at 10 p.m. He went for long periods of *dhutaṅga* walks with his pupil, Ajahn Mun Bhūridatta. His meditation practice was apparently deeply influenced by the methods advocated by Somdet Phra Vanarat Buddhasiri (1806–1891).[25] Buddhaghosa had recommended forty meditation objects for calm meditation.[26] One of the objects, the recollection of the Buddha and his attributes (*Buddhānussati*), was often linked to the breath. Ajahn Sao practiced and taught mindfulness of breathing, often with the syllables BU and DDHO as an anchor for the mind. His pupils, such as Ajahn Mun, and his pupils' pupils, such as Ajahn Lee, also did so. This simple *samatha* practice is still taught, by those who inherited the traditions, in the forest sangha methods that have now spread internationally.[27]

Ajahn Sao was, apparently, an object lesson in the awakening factor of tranquility. Ajahn Mun reported that Sao often experienced great joy in his practice, floating up in the air and descending serenely.[28] He taught mindfulness of body and the recognition that it will eventually be discarded, alongside contemplation of its foulness, as in the viewing of corpses.[29] These meditations lead to the discernment of impermanence, unsatisfactoriness, and no-self, the three signs that produce insight.

One follower, Phra Ajahn Phut Thaniyo, described Ajahn Sao as a "doer not a thinker." A famous story of his teaching method demonstrates one unusual excellence arising from this: he knew when to teach but also when to refrain.[30] When prompted, he addressed very precisely the stage he saw in the meditator concerned—but nothing more. Reminiscing about his time as an attendant novice, Ajahn Thaniyo described Ajahn Sao's handling of a senior monk who had come to learn meditation with him: Ajahn Sao gave him the meditation object of the Buddho repetition. Although the meditator asked for more information, he was told simply to do it and come back when he had done so. There were "no long drawn-out explanations." When the monk had done this, the mind became calm and then very bright. He sent his attention outward: to spirits, ghosts, forests, people, and the numerous visions and different planes of beings that arose as he followed the brightness farther outward. Ajahn Sao's response to his excited accounts was immediate:

> "This isn't right. For the mind to go knowing and seeing outside isn't right. You have to make it know inside."
>
> The monk then asked, "How should I go about making it know inside?"
>
> Phra Ajahn Sao answered, "When the mind is in a bright state like that, when it has forgotten or abandoned its repetition and is simply sitting empty and still, look for the breath. If the sensation of the breath appears in your awareness, focus on the breath as your object and then simply keep track of it, following it inward until the mind becomes even calmer and brighter."[31]

The monk apparently followed these instructions and finally settled down in the state of "approach" or "neighborhood" concentration (upacāra samādhi), a preliminary stage for the attainment of jhāna, where the mind is temporarily free from hindrances but has not yet developed the factors needed to attain the meditation itself.[32] The breath nimitta has usually appeared. Eventually, he got results:

> . . . the breath became more and more refined, ultimately to the point where it disappeared. His sensation of having a body also disappeared, leaving just the state in which the mind was sitting absolutely still, a state of awareness itself standing out clear, with

no sense of going forward or back, no sense of where the mind was, because at that moment there was just the mind, all on its own. At this point, the monk came again to ask, "After my mind has become calm and bright, and I fix my attention on the breath and follow the breath inward until it reaches a state of being absolutely quiet and still—so still that nothing is left, the breath doesn't appear, the sense of having a body vanishes, only the mind stands out, brilliant and still: When it's like this, is it right or wrong?"

"Whether it's right or wrong," the Ajahn answered, "take that as your standard. Make an effort to be able to do this as often as possible, and only when you're skilled at it should you come and see me again."[33]

The monk continued his practices, and the state became stable. When his concentration had become strong, he started to develop discernment and wisdom, knowing the true nature of states as they came and went. Ajahn Sao then approved his progress; the meditator had achieved states of deep calm. But he suggested further development:

> If the mind is forever in that state, it will be stuck simply on that level of stillness. So, once you've made the mind still like this, watch for the interval where it begins to stir out of its concentration. As soon as the mind has a sense that it's beginning to take up an object—no matter what object may appear first—focus on the act of taking up an object. That's what you should examine.

The monk followed Ajahn Sao's instructions and was afterward able to make good progress in insight. As Thaniyo notes, this is the best way to teach meditation on the breath: one stage at a time. Ajahn Sao did not give a talk. There is no explanation of the sixteen stages of breathing mindfulness; all are implied rather than formally explained. The meditator learns through short, appropriate responses as each new stage is reached, finally being given explanation as to how to develop the practice from deep calm to fully developed wisdom.

The story is of particular interest when considering these forest practitioners. Gradual, appropriate teaching, at the right time for the individual concerned, appears to be a hallmark of their teachings, however simple their directness. Whether formally termed esoteric or not, many meditations, meditation involving the breath in particular, are taught in stages, with each stage being given when people are ready for the next. The sixteen stages are certainly there, but unobtrusively so, absorbed as the meditator learns each when he is ready. Ajahn Sao seems to have had a gift in understanding when the time was right for a particular person.

It is an ancient custom for teachers to reveal their attainments to one or two select followers.[34] Ajahn Sao stayed in the Champa cave in Mukdahan from 1915 to 1921 and told his pupil Ajahn Mun that he had lost interest in becoming a *paccekabuddha*, a silent Buddha, his earlier aspiration; he had now seen *dhamma* fully. Ajahn Mun understood that to mean he had become enlightened. Ajahn Sao died at the age of eighty-two in the shrine hall of a monastery in Champasak Province in Southwest Laos, near the borders of Thailand and Cambodia. His death came while he was making the third of the usual three prostrations before the image of the Buddha.[35] After his cremation, his relics apparently became crystals (*sarīradhātu*), a phenomenon associated with those who have achieved their final goal.

Ajahn Mun Bhūridatta (1870–1949)

More information has been handed down about the life of Ajahn Sao's disciple, Ajahn Mun Bhūridatta, than about Sao himself. Mun's position is central; he taught many of the great meditation teachers of the forest tradition, a line that continues to this day. He became legendary in his own lifetime and is regarded as one of the great monastic figures of the last century.[36]

Ajahn Mun Bhūridatta Thera was of Laotian and Thai descent, born the eldest of nine children in 1870 in Khong Chiam, Ubon Ratchatan, Thailand. He died in 1949 at Wat Pa Sutthawat in Sakon Nakhon, aged seventy-nine. He never left Southeast Asia. He had become a novice at the age of sixteen before taking full ordination at the age of twenty-two in 1893. His ordination name, Bhūridatta, is derived from one of the last ten lives of the bodhisatta, in which he is born as a *nāga*, an underwater creature like a snake, able to assume any form at will and possessing miraculous powers.[37] In this rebirth, the bodhisatta worked on the perfection of morality (*sīla*): this certainly suited Ajahn Mun's love of a strict monastic code and evoked well the character of his forest monastic life. He lived in accordance with the *dhutaṅga* spirit, wandering from one place to another.

Several monks wrote accounts of his life. Venerable Ñāṇasampanno, Ācariya Maha Boowa (1913–2011), one of his most famous disciples, wrote the most widely circulated one, long available to an international readership. A world-renowned meditation teacher himself, he subsequently wrote of other figures taught by Ajahn Mun. As we will see, Mun delivered his own highly controversial autobiographical accounts stating stages of spiritual attainment.[38] Ñāṇasampanno, usually known as Maha Boowa, is an eloquent and strong-minded narrator; the events of Ajahn Mun's life are both described and interpreted. Although the account is written in Thai, one senses Western perspectives in mind. The conversational and even anecdotal tone makes Maha Boowa a helpful intermediary. He gives background, lively detail, and where necessary, doctrinal elucidation for some of the features of Ajahn Mun's practice, life events, and interactions that would appear strange to someone unfamiliar with the localized, folk Buddhist practice of Thai villagers. The work looks as if it is intended for a wider and potentially less well-informed audience; the biographer, at any rate, seems to be acutely conscious of the increasingly Western orientation of urban Thais.

It is clear from his biography, however, that Ajahn Mun was thoroughly steeped in a tradition of rural meditative practice. While he has a reputation as being a reformist at the vanguard of moves to change Buddhism, a closer look at his teachings reveals them to be pervaded by the cultures of traditional Buddhist practice. This is old, rural Buddhism: telepathy, healing smallpox through the practice of loving-kindness, miraculous visions, and psychic powers were as natural to him as alms gathering and walks.

Like the villagers who were so resistant to admonitions handed down from Bangkok, Ajahn Mun seems to have let much of the new ideology and its missions pass by. His innovative use of strict *dhutaṅga* practice, and the mix of Vinaya with meditation described by his biographer, conformed to the new spirit of the times; his teachings and worldviews, however, were thoroughly unreconstructed. For him, jungles, caves, and rivers were home to all kinds of beings, ghosts, and spirits; the forest is a jataka world of tree spirits, *nāgas*, and mysterious presences supplemented by local deities. Maha Boowa's biography says that Ajahn Mun communed with these daily, debating them, frequently chanting on their behalf, and offering, where needed, occasional teaching.

This celebratory insistence on such non-modern elements, in a Thailand with eyes increasingly to the Western world, may have been itself a response to the pressures impinging on monastic practitioners at the time. True to his jataka namesake, Bhūridatta, Ajahn Mun had a particular affinity with *nāgas*. He worked hard at propitiating them when staying in their caves, though sometimes he acknowledged a given one as a lost cause. He apparently decided to move on whenever a particularly angry one seemed too entrenched in its ways even for basic *dhamma* teaching.[39] He was, however, compassionate to those in lower rebirths— as ghosts or unhappy spirits—and sometimes visited them, he said.[40]

Ajahn Mun's understanding of the pure *citta* ("mind" or "heart"), the defilements that obscure it, and the way that it can be purified by meditation and a simple way of life are examined in detail against the backdrop of the jungle and the surrounding wildernesses. The forest provides the ground to his work on consciousness: the *citta* is purified and cleansed through chanting, meditation, and teachings to spirits. These clear the jungle thickets and caves around him, just as the deity in his beloved Sutta on Blessings (*Maṅgala-sutta*) irradiates the grove in which he appears.[41]

According to Maha Boowa, Ajahn Mun reached the highest attainments. He "told his circle of close disciples that he attained to the path of Non-Returner in that cave [Saririka Cave]. The writer has decided to take note of it here and is ready for the readers' comments. If there is anything improper with making this fact known, let the writer be blamed for his own heedlessness."[42]

Although Ajahn Mun's life has been subject to great scrutiny, his meditation teachings have been less closely documented. There are, however, multiple anecdotes and reflections of his teachings in accounts of others' attainments. The nun Mae Chee Kaew (1901–1991), for instance, hiked for two weeks with her followers through difficult terrain to meet him in the jungle and was greeted warmly.[43] Like Ajahn Sao, Ajahn Mun was a careful listener, in this case to her dramatic accounts of her journeys in meditation and communications with beings in other realms. He steered her away from some of her psychic adventures with some pertinent and practical advice.[44] It is reported that Mae Chee Kaew herself became enlightened later in life, after further discussions with Maha Boowa.

Ajahn Mun was also friendly with unsympathetic, non-Buddhist hill tribes. They would see him walking slowly and sitting quietly and ask him what he was looking for. He said he wanted to find a bright jewel, Buddho. They decided to look around for it and returned soon, delighted, to confront him: "In reality your mind was already *buddho*, but you wanted us to make our minds as bright as yours . . . you wanted to help us find *buddho* for ourselves!"[45]

There is a collection of his talks, *A Heart Released*, translated by another forest monk, Ajahn Ṭhānissaro.[46] Breathing mindfulness is not the prime meditation apparent in his teaching, but he taught and practiced some versions of it and, like other forest teachers, used the recollection of the Buddha with the breath as a core practice. However, in *A Heart Released*, Ajahn Mun speaks of the Buddha's practice of mindfulness of the body, and hence the breath: "Even the Lord Buddha, when he was about to attain Awakening, started out by investigating the breath—and what is the breath, if not the body?"[47]

A Heart Released is framed in Borān language and teachings. Whether he was formally initiated into such systems, we cannot know. Perhaps he perceived them as simply part of the repertoire of meditations he would have known all his life, taught at monasteries everywhere. *A Heart Released* gives expression to this. In his introduction to this work, Ajahn Ṭhānissaro comments on the quickness and sophistication of Ajahn Mun's intellect, demonstrated in his great learning and a particularly Thai love of wordplay, puns, and multiple levels of meaning. The objects of his word explorations stress a somatic understanding of meditative teaching, linked to the image of the embryo's growth.[48] He takes, for instance, the syllables NA and MO, two of the five NA MO BU DDHA YA, assigning elements to them in the way found in Borān teachings: NA for water and the mother, MO for the father and earth. They are, he says, gradually developed as the embryo in the womb evolves, a process he aligns with meditative development. The body is, first of all, NA and MO, made from the mother and the father. BU is the breath, and DDHA fire and heat, which come after consciousness. The word *namo* means homage, so we must pay homage to our parents. *Namo* is the roots of our heart: *mano*. Quoting the canonical saying, "All dhammas are preceded by the heart, dominated by the heart, made from the heart," he gives this teaching: mind, *mano*, can become homage, *namo*, when the heart and mind are clear.

This is the world of Borān meditation. Ajahn Mun stresses investigation of the body as the basis of the meditation, through the four primary elements, whose associations apply to so many levels of the mind as well. The breath, as one of these, is an aspect of this investigation, in the air and winds that circulate in the body. He describes our body as like a tree overrun by thousands of chameleons, things that drift into the sense doors. We need to guard it all the time.[49] His image of the "five-limbed" body of the human is redolent of the esoteric Fig Tree material described by Bizot in Cambodia and of the "five-branched fig tree" that is the basis of the human mind and body, under constant attack by the defilements.[50]

In *A Heart Released*, Ajahn Mun's use of enumeration and number play is in the Siamese style. He gives a beautiful formulation of the heart as being like the number zero, inherently free. The arhat, like the number zero, can make things bigger, as in the number ten. But freed, it has release from all nine abodes of living beings.

> When connected with anything, it [the heart] instantly proliferates into things elaborate and fantastic. But when trained until it is wise and discerning with regard to all knowable phenomena, it returns to its state as 0 (zero)—empty, open, and clear, beyond all counting and naming. It doesn't stay in the nine places that are abodes for

living beings. Instead, it stays in a place devoid of supposing and formulation: its inherent nature as o (zero), or activitylessness.[51]

Such imagery, vocabulary, and understandings are all central to the old meditations. Multilayered applications of symbology pervade his teaching. There are canonical roots, particularly in the Abhidhamma, cited frequently. Crosby demonstrates that the Borān practice of moving states of consciousness (*citta*) and its associated mental factors (*cetasika*), in and around the body, is rooted in an Abhidhamma understanding of consciousness as mobile and accumulative, with the gradual replacing of unskillful with skillful. The process in time transforms the base metal of the mental states that were there before.[52]

Ajahn Mun terms Buddhahood the inner "Phra," the greatly reverential personal address we saw in the last chapter. There is the teacher within oneself, to be honored when found.[53] Borān meditations feel so deeply embedded in Ajahn Mun's methods that one wonders if any distinction between them and newer teachings would have appeared false or odd to him. Breathing mindfulness is not always specified. But the breath, seen as the element of air, was primary in his understanding of the basic arrangement of the transformation of mental state through a rearrangement of the mental factors in skillful consciousness, in a process felt and circulated both in the mind and in the body.

Ṭhānissaro notes that Ajahn Mun's stress to his followers was always on a direct and immediate contact with the teaching: "If they wanted to know the truth of virtue, concentration, and discernment, they would have to bring these qualities into being in their own hearts and minds."[54] The way Ajahn Mun articulates this is imbued with traditional Southeast Asian perceptions of the relationship between the body and mind, with meditative growth being like the growth of an embryo, an alchemical transformation leading to all elements of the eightfold path in a new birth: ethics (*sīla*), concentration (*samādhi*), and wisdom (*paññā*).[55]

He was clearly aware, however, of attempts to marginalize *samatha*. At the end of one talk, he comments on the old canonical distinction between those who are released through the purification of the heart (*cetovimutti*), through concentration and insight, and those released with or by wisdom (*paññāvimutti*), usually taken as a differentiation between those who primarily follow a *samādhi* path to insight and those for whom insight is predominant. In the canon, he says, both ways need both calm and insight:

> The explanation given by the Commentators—that release through concentration pertains to those arahants [arhats] who develop concentration first, while release through discernment pertains to the "dry insight" arahants, who develop insight exclusively without having first developed concentration—runs counter to the path. The eightfold path includes both Right View and Right Concentration. A person who is to gain release has to develop all eight factors of the path. Otherwise he or she won't be able to gain release. The threefold training includes both concentration and discernment. A person who is to attain knowledge of the ending of mental fermentations has to develop all three parts of the threefold training completely.[56]

Ajahn Mun wants to teach, not make points. Here, however, he is blunt. He clearly felt right concentration, as identified in The Great Sutta on the Foundations of Mindfulness (*Mahāsatipaṭṭhāna-sutta*) with the development of the four *jhānas*, is essential for the path.[57] All path factors, developed fully, are needed for awakening. Even "dry" meditation needs the practice of *jhāna*. The path factors work together in an interrelated manner; no one element can be excluded or downplayed. Aware of the pressures being exerted at the time, he is defending *jhāna* and the great *samatha* traditions of the old meditations.

Cholvijarn points out Ajahn Mun's association with another core Borān understanding: that one can contact beings of a particular level when one attains that level oneself, as indicated by meditations described in the last chapter. At the end of Ajahn Mun's life, apparently, an earlier Buddha and hundreds of thousands of arhats from the past came to visit his solitary meditations and greet him: the explanation is that the brightness of their minds cannot be eradicated, despite their leaving samsara; they come to acknowledge someone attaining their level.[58] Within the style and manner of his life story, it feels entirely natural that his spiritual attainment is articulated within traditional South and Southeast Asian visual and meditative culture.[59] Such framings are sophisticated in their deployment of symbol and the language of dreams, though remain, of course, puzzling to many in the rationalist and literalist West. But this language makes the ineffable vivid and even homely: for Southeast Asians, the enlightened person is one who finds a new family. In Abhidhamma the stage just before awakening is called "change of lineage" or "change of family (*gotrabhu*)."[60] The awakened beings' homage describes the welcome given to a new member who has joined the larger family of all who have attained any stage of path, the *ariyasaṅgha*.

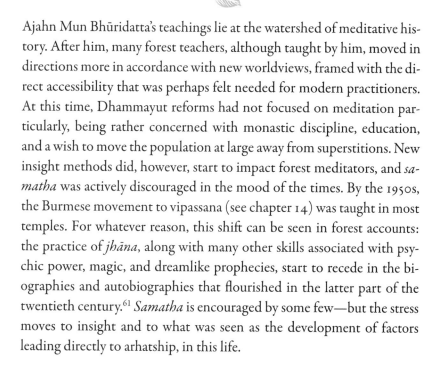

Ajahn Mun Bhūridatta's teachings lie at the watershed of meditative history. After him, many forest teachers, although taught by him, moved in directions more in accordance with new worldviews, framed with the direct accessibility that was perhaps felt needed for modern practitioners. At this time, Dhammayut reforms had not focused on meditation particularly, being rather concerned with monastic discipline, education, and a wish to move the population at large away from superstitions. New insight methods did, however, start to impact forest meditators, and *samatha* was actively discouraged in the mood of the times. By the 1950s, the Burmese movement to vipassana (see chapter 14) was taught in most temples. For whatever reason, this shift can be seen in forest accounts: the practice of *jhāna*, along with many other skills associated with psychic power, magic, and dreamlike prophecies, start to recede in the biographies and autobiographies that flourished in the latter part of the twentieth century.[61] *Samatha* is encouraged by some few—but the stress moves to insight and to what was seen as the development of factors leading directly to arhatship, in this life.

CHAPTER 11

Thailand Forest
Traditions, Part Two

Four Teachers

If you go to a Thai temple, you see jewel-like stories told in beautiful detail on murals, but in a nonsequential manner: the arrangement is multi-scenic, opening up depths of dark, leafy space behind. Some incidents are highlighted and amplified; others, still important, glow from within ever present woodlands. The whole feels three-dimensional and organic, suggesting more, perhaps hidden, worlds. We see such qualities in ways early practitioners of the forest movement interpret practices with the breath.

In this chapter, we shall examine four more teachers from the Thai forest tradition, extending our survey throughout the twentieth century and including the tradition's spread abroad. All four practiced breathing mindfulness in some form or another. They just expressed it in different ways, and they did not, it seems, necessarily follow the sixteen-stage sequence of the sutta. Some do not seem to have used theory a great deal but took it as something worn lightly. An experiential account of their practice, as it occurs, took precedence, along with closely observed illustrative similes. Amid this, they often knew theory well, and in some the language of the old meditations still persisted. By the end of the twentieth century, however, such remnants had mostly dropped away. The practice of breathing mindfulness as a calm practice also receded.

Ajahn Thate (1902–1994), Ajahn Thate Desaransi Phra Rajanirodharangsee

One forest monk deeply imbued in old understandings was Phra Ajahn Thate Desaransi Rajanirodharangsee, who practiced breathing mindfulness, among other meditations, as part of a classic canonical path of calm and then insight. He is not well known now in the West, a fact with which he would have been happy. Renowned for his humility, at the beginning of his autobiography he says he is only writing a biography himself to stop other people from writing about him![1] In that book he says nothing about his meditation attainments, though we know he liked to practice in seclusion in caves and forests.

One of ten children in a rice-farming family in Udorn Thani, Ajahn Thate became a monk when he was taught by both Ajahn Sao and Ajahn Mun. For most of his life he taught and practiced at Wat Hin Maak Peng, near the Mekong River. The simple life there included an alms round and just one meal a day. He held *samatha* sessions two or three times a day. He also undertook extensive teaching in other regions and internationally.

Ajahn Thate's *dhamma* talks give kindly, pragmatic advice. Speaking about the approach to *jhāna* in breathing mindfulness meditation, he understands some people are concerned by visions, of light for instance, either becoming too attached to or too wary of them. He suggests looking at the mental state behind the images, the *jhāna* involved, to see they arise from that and are impermanent. Then one lets visions go spontaneously. He also, sensibly, advises a wholehearted return to the sense-sphere in daily life, with plenty of food and perhaps hard physical work to bring oneself back to the body. This advice looks to be geared to laypeople. For those teaching someone with excessive attachment to *nimittas*, he recommends a strategy of making the practitioner very angry indeed. Any wonderful signs will soon disappear! He finishes this explanation by assuring meditators they really should not take his word for it, but they should have a go at concentration practice themselves and make sure they discuss it afterward.[2]

Such teachings and the tone of his autobiography suggest a quiet but firm man, with deep experience of teaching *jhāna* and breathing mindfulness. After Ajahn Mun's death, he was considered to be the head of the Thai forest lineage until his own death in 1994.

Ācariya Maha Boowa Ñāṇasampanno (1913–2011)

Ajahn Mun's biographer, Ajahn Maha Boowa Ñāṇasampanno, exemplifies the shift to modern trends for insight. When he was born, his father dreamt of a shining knife. This was interpreted to mean that he could either become a master criminal or a great monk of sharp intellect and wisdom—he chose the latter option. Maha Boowa became famous for his blunt approach and uncompromising style. He lived austerely, with one meal a day, long periods of silence, and an alms round. While at one time he also practiced deep concentration, his teachings in his forest monastery, Wat Ba Ban Tat in Udorn Province, Northeast Thailand, emphasized wisdom.

There is a collection of his dhamma talks entitled *Straight from the Heart*, translated by another forest monk, the Westerner Ajahn Ṭhānissaro. In some of these, he enjoins the practice of calm (*samatha*) to offer refreshment and solace for the mind. Here he talks of starting meditation with breathing mindfulness or the mantra BU-DDHO:

> . . . in the beginning stages of the training, the mind is filled with nothing but cloudiness and confusion at all times and cannot find any peace or contentment. We thus have to force it to stay in a restricted range—for example, with the meditation word, "*buddho,*" or with the in-and-outbreath—so as to gain a footing with its meditation theme, so that stillness can form a basis or a foundation for the heart, so that it can set itself up for the practice that is to follow. We first have to teach the mind to withdraw itself from its various preoccupations, using whichever meditation theme it finds appealing, so that it can find a place of rest and relaxation through the stillness.[3]

Such emphasis on giving sufficient rest and sustenance for the mind in *samatha* meditation belies Maha Boowa's reputation as a teacher solely focused on insight teachings. His works certainly incline to mindfulness and wisdom (*sati-paññā*), but he often speaks of deep meditation and stillness and using that to develop discernment. He says humans are like trees and need the water and refreshment of calm.[4] He taught contemplation of the parts of the body, the recollection or bringing to mind of the qualities of the Buddha, and breathing mindfulness as objects to arouse peace:

> In fixing attention on the breath, one may also repeat Buddho in time with the breath as a preparatory repetition to supervise the in- and out-breathing, in order to assist "the one who knows" and make "the one who knows" clear with regard to the breath. Then the breath will appear more and more clearly to the heart.
>
> In particular, it is important to have mindfulness established. One must establish mindfulness to control the heart so that one feels the breath at every moment while it is entering and leaving, whether short or long, until one knows clearly that the breathing is becoming progressively finer with every breath—until finally it becomes apparent that the finest and most subtle breath and the heart have converged and become one. At this stage, one should fix the breath exclusively within the heart, and there is no need to worry about preparatory repetition, for in becoming aware of the breath as entering and leaving, and as short and long, the preparatory repetition is only for the purpose of making the heart become subtle.
>
> When one has attained the most subtle level of breathing, he will be bright, cool, calm, happy and just knowing the heart—and there will be no connection with any disturbing influence. Even if finally at that time the breath disappears, there will be no anxiety because one will have let go of the burden and one will just have knowledge of the heart alone. In other words, it will be non-dual. This is the development of absorption.[5]

Kornfield interestingly observes that this instruction shows some kinship with the development of the heart center in Ajahn Lee Dhammadhāro's teachings, discussed later in this chapter, and with those of Sayagyi U Ba Khin.[6] He comments, "in other words, it seems as if the heart is breathing, and as if the breathing is in the heart."[7]

When this is undertaken, Maha Boowa says that calm and happiness arise and "there will be only one thing influencing the heart, which will be a knowing of the heart alone without any disturbance or distraction, for there will be nothing which can disturb or irritate the heart to make it fall away from this state."[8] This is "the nature of happiness of heart," with nothing to disturb it, free from imagination and thought creations.

Insight, however, is his main teaching, seamlessly arising from this state. He compares it to cutting down a tree in a forest, where creepers and tangles of branches from other trees make felling it difficult. Cutting away all entanglements, it is possible to fell it clean. He warns against attachment to the products of states derived from the cultivation of the *nimitta*, especially the deep peace that thereby arises. With wisdom, the heart "then knows, sees, and follows the truth of all Dharmas in nature, and this knowledge is balanced and no longer inclines to one-sided views and opinions."[9] Maha Boowa is now most widely known for his method, a form of practice that develops, unusually, wisdom first and then *samādhi* afterward. This is not frequently recommended within the canon but composes the second of the four routes described by the Buddha as a path to awakening.[10]

Controversially, Maha Boowa proclaimed his own arhatship, presumably to address the assumption that such an attainment was not possible in modern times. His teaching at the culmination of *Straight from the Heart* stresses finding the "middle (*majjhima*) point" in all dealings, which is possible, he says, at any time and is always accessible when the mind is free.

Ajahn Lee Dhammadhāro (1906–1961)

One of Ajahn Mun's students, Ajahn Lee Dhammadhāro, represents a direct line to the old Thai meditations. Like Ajahn Mun and Maha Boowa's, his formulations were creative, seemingly steeped in both *samādhi* and wisdom. Throughout his life his primary practice was breathing mindfulness. He was intent on bringing forest traditions into mainstream Thai society and the urban areas, where his teachings were widely disseminated and practiced among monastics and the laity. Breathing mindfulness, described in pre-reform terms, is so central to his teachings that it is worth looking at his life and talks in detail.

His autobiography, composed in Thai, reads like an action-packed, picaresque journey, with the occasional drama of a forest life peppered with bizarre encounters and mysterious outcomes. This is no Buddhism laundered for Westerners. It deals with disease, death, magical powers, forests, spells, amulets, cities, minutely explained financial problems, travel hitches, good bargaining deals, seductive women, spirits, and miracles, all with the same even frankness. But Lee exhibits old-style reticence about stating his attainments. As Ajahn Ṭhānissaro says of his autobiography, "if you come to this book in the hope of gauging the level of Ajaan Lee's meditative attainments, you have come to the wrong place."[11]

Ajahn Lee started off an ambivalent monk. His preceptor was Phra Pannabhisara Thera (Nuu), though Ajahn Mun became his main teacher. He ordained, then returned to the lay life and married, but his wife died. He married again, unsuccessfully, and returned to the monastic orders. He was clearly a strong personality—drama, confrontation, and incident were recurrent features of his wandering existence. His telling of his early monastic life is filled with funny anecdotes. In one, he and his fellow young monks are having an all-night competition where they try to out-meditate each other. Ajahn Lee hears a thud and finds one friend lying on his back on the floor, still in the lotus position, fast asleep: he had just keeled over, apparently not having much motivation for the exercise.[12] Throughout his account of travels and meditations, he relates encounters with wild animals and swarms of mosquitoes; he practices loving-kindness, and the danger is averted.[13] Once, an elephant in rut heads for him; he calms the elephant and teaches him the five precepts—with, he claims, some success! He cares for his old father tenderly, and although he chants to dispel bad spirits, he dismisses superstitions about ghosts and malevolent figures. He also cares devotedly for his teacher, Ajahn Mun.

Ajahn Lee loves stories about his skills in winning deals in bargaining and his exciting adventures. At one time a goddess (*deva*) appears while he spends the night in a cave, hoping to entice him. He politely explains that any liaison is impossible; he is a monk. On another occasion some gangsters ask him for magical, protective *gāthās* so they can avoid arrest. He says that, after chanting the verses for a few days, they are remorseful and decide to turn themselves in. He seems to thrive on his wanderings; one senses he never wanted to feel caged. At one time, he recalls, he became very ill indeed, but he recognized it as a karmic illness, for he had once kept a dove and forgotten to feed it. He realized he could only cure the illness by creating good karma. The image of the caged dove recurs throughout his travels.

Despite these great exploits, his main interest is meditation. Most forest ascetics, though clearly loving their natural environment, do not describe it. Ajahn Lee's work by contrast is rich in closely observed commentary on anything he encounters: animals, woods, finances, people, and mountains are all described with the same interest. The *Mahāsatipaṭṭhāna-sutta* teaches that mindfulness should be internal, external, and both internal and external.[14] For Lee, observations move in and out like the breath. Natural phenomena offer lessons to him. He talks of herbs and how to use them and enjoy them. He is particularly interested in trees and their healing properties; he says, living in the forest, he learns how to live with them. If hungry or thirsty, some trees allay his needs; others will quell a fever, and yet others will make him feel disturbed and unhappy—a familiar notion for Thais, who regard the properties of some trees as unhelpful.[15] His comments exemplify the forest meditators' teaching style, of close watching leading to a teaching:

> Some kinds of trees make themselves quiet at night, in ways we can see. We can say that they "sleep." At night, they fold up their leaves. If you go lie under them, you will have a clear view of the stars in the nighttime sky. But when day comes, they'll spread their leaves and give a dense shade. This is a good lesson for the mind: When you sit in meditation, close only your eyes. Keep your mind bright and alert, like a tree that closes its leaves and thus doesn't obstruct

our view of the stars . . . All in all, I can really see what I have gained from living in forests and other quiet places to train the mind. One by one I've been able to cut away all my doubts about the Buddha's teachings. And so, for this reason, I am willing to devote myself to the duties of meditation until there is no more life for me to live. The gains that come from training the mind, if I were to describe them in detail, would go on and on, but I'll finish this short description here.[16]

Such oases for solitary meditation, near animals, trees, herbs, and rivers, are where he feels most at home. He completely supports the practice of scientific investigation. It is, he says, just good observation, and, "As for Dhamma, it is just science: it exists in nature."[17] He then describes, all in the same spare style, deep states of meditation found through practicing breathing mindfulness.

On the night of the full moon—Magha Puja—I decided to sit in meditation as an offering to the Buddha. A little after 9 p.m., my mind became absolutely still. It seemed as if breath and light were radiating from my body in all directions. At the moment, I was focusing on my breath, which was so subtle that I scarcely seemed to be breathing at all. My heart was quiet; my mind still. The breath in my body didn't seem to be moving at all. It was simply quiet and still. My mind had completely stopped formulating thoughts— how all my thoughts had stopped, I had no idea. But I was aware— feeling bright, expansive, and at ease—with a sense of freedom that wiped out all feeling of pain.

After about an hour of this, teachings began to appear in my heart. This, in short, is what they said: "Focus down and examine becoming, birth, death, and ignorance to see how they come about." A vision came to me as plain as if it were right before my eyes: "Birth is like a lightning flash. Death is like a lightning flash." So I focused on the causes leading to birth and death, until I came to the word *avijja*—ignorance. Ignorance of what? What kind of knowing is the knowing of ignorance? What kind of knowing is the knowing of knowledge? I considered things in this manner, back and forth, over and over, until dawn. When it all finally became clear, I left concentration. My heart and body both seemed light, open, and free; my heart, extremely satisfied and full.[18]

Ajahn Lee was a reformist, known for trying to rid villagers of excessive superstition about ghosts; he was member of the Dhammayut.[19] Yet, reading his autobiography is like entering the old Buddhist world of jatakas and Thai vernacular narrative, with inner dramas embodied through encounters with spirits and beings from all realms, as well as magical powers. Wanting to be of service, he decided to travel to towns to make his methods more widely available to laypeople as well as monastics. The Somdet, the head of the sangha, who had also known Ajahn Sao and Ajahn Mun, was particularly impressed and visited him at Wat Boromnivasa, Bangkok. Lee teaches the Somdet breathing mindfulness leading to *jhāna* and gives his rationale for the need for deep concentration states. Lee teaches Somdet in this way:

> "If you don't make the mind take on becoming, it won't give rise to knowledge, because knowledge has to come from becoming if it's going to do away with becoming. This is becoming on a small scale—*uppatika bhava*—which lasts for a single moment. The same holds true with birth. To make the mind still so that samadhi arises for a long mental moment is birth. Say we sit in concentration for a long time until the mind gives rise to the five factors of jhana: that's birth. If you don't do this with your mind, it won't give rise to any knowledge of its own. And when knowledge can't arise, how will you be able to let go of ignorance? It'd be very hard. If you are going to release yourself from becoming, you first have to live in becoming. If you are going to release yourself from birth, you'll have to know all about your own birth."[20]

Controversy trailed Ajahn Lee Dhammadhāro. One night, while in the meditation hall at Wat Supat, relics of the Buddha appeared miraculously for him as crystals. A man walking past said he had seen hundreds of falling stars shower on Wat Supat that evening. Rumors of trickery and fraud started; he disclaimed them all. He took these beautiful emblems, one could say *nimittas* of the durability of the Buddha's teachings, to practical advantage by organizing fundraising events around them. On his near-deathbed in the hospital, he dictated his autobiography. He also wrote a letter expressing his wish that his body be of service when he is gone.

Some of his teachings remain, which have been preserved and translated. One, "Keeping the Breath in Mind," teaches in the old, graduated style, taking great care in establishing the groundwork and ensuring there is a stable basis in breath observation before higher states are attempted: "To practice centering the mind is to build a landing strip for yourself. Then, when discernment comes, you'll be able to attain release safely."[21]

Important to this was establishing the refuge of paying homage to the Buddha, the teaching, and the Sangha. Then, the five ethical precepts are taken before bringing to mind the four divine abidings of loving-kindness, compassion, sympathetic joy, and equanimity, practices he saw as core for teachings of the breath. Ajahn Lee offers two methods to start mindfulness of the breath. The first involves a variation on Buddhaghosa's "counting." This involves taking each pair of in- and outbreath with the syllables BU on the inbreath and DDHA on the outbreath:

> Now you can stop counting the breaths, and simply think *bud* with the in-breath and *dho* with the out. Let the breath be relaxed and natural. Keep your mind perfectly still, focused on the breath as it comes in and out of the nostrils. When the breath goes out, don't send the mind out after it. When the breath comes in, don't let the mind follow it in. Let your awareness be broad, cheerful, and open. Don't force the mind too much. Relax. Pretend that you're breathing out in the wide open air. Keep the mind still, like a post at the edge of the sea. When the water rises, the post doesn't rise with it; when the water ebbs, the post doesn't sink.[22]

He gives guidelines on the manipulation and the learning of healing skills with the *nimitta* when it arises, emphasizing that the meditator can choose whether to follow it or to let it go if they wish:

The bright white *nimitta* is useful to the body and mind: It's a pure breath which can cleanse the blood in the body, reducing or eliminating feelings of pain. When you have this white light as large as the head, bring it down to The Fifth Base, the center of the chest. Once it's firmly settled, let it spread out to fill the chest. Make this breath as white and as bright as possible, and then let both the breath and the light spread throughout the body, out to every pore, until different parts of the body appear on their own as pictures. If you don't want the pictures, take two or three long breaths, and they'll disappear. Keep your awareness still and expansive. Don't let it latch onto or be affected by any *nimitta* that may happen to pass into the brightness of the breath. Keep careful watch over the mind. Keep it one. Keep it intent on a single preoccupation, the refined breath, letting this refined breath suffuse the entire body.[23]

Although framed in simple forest style, the skills deployed with this image—settling it in the heart, the therapeutic properties of the light that arises with breath meditation, a careful sense of a steady base of return—bear the hallmarks of the old meditations.

If you want to acquire knowledge and skill, practice these steps until you're adept at entering, leaving, and staying in place. When you've mastered them, you'll be able to give rise to the nimitta of the breath—the brilliantly white ball or lump of light—whenever you want.[24]

The method he recommends for those less experienced, Method 2, has been partially quoted in chapter 4. Throughout both methods, his instructions are, in spirit and content, pre-reform: an emphasis on bodily suffusion, adjustments of breath length, and flexibility through awareness of the breath moving in and around "resting places" as it enters and leaves the body.[25] A middle way is suggested between being at ease with the breath, not forcing it but not letting it slip away. Images that arise are called "guests": "Before you go receiving guests, you should put your breath and mind into good order, making them stable and secure."[26] He is the one teacher who describes the whole Buddhist path in terms of the breath, with each path factor playing a part.[27] He speaks of the "reality of peace" (*santi-dhamma*); the practice leads in time to experience of the unconditioned (*asaṅkhatā-dhātu*). It does not feel possible to make much of a distinction here between old meditations and the "mainstream" canon and commentary discussions.

Ajahn Lee Dhammadhāro moved toward a far greater emphasis on insight.[28] But all the sixteen stages of breathing mindfulness are found, in organic arrangement, in his manual: breathing mindfulness is seen as a full manifestation of the path, with *jhāna* and insight. The rich Southeast Asian traditions of practice, as well as Ajahn Lee's creative adjustments, bring them fresh expression.

Luang Por Ajahn Chah (1918–1992)

Another of Mun's students, Luang Por Ajahn Chah, can truly be said to have crossed the gulf between East and West. He was of a generation that started to address the problems of transporting Buddhist monasticism, explaining it, and finding new ways of expressing meditative understandings to those who have no background at all in Buddhism: he taught Western monastics, became known internationally, and visited the West himself.

He was born the fifth of eleven children in 1918, in the Lao area of Ubon Ratchatani, Isaan. His was an affectionate family in a farming village, and he was an "ebullient" child with "the gift of the gab."[29] He entered a local monastery at the age of nine, where he learned to read and write for four years before becoming a novice. He ordained in 1939, after one or two romantic setbacks, in which for family reasons he could not marry the girl he would like. He always felt sexual desire to be the most difficult to overcome, but eventually did so later in life when, after nights of struggle, he felt a jewel that freed him had been given him in a dream.[30]

After the death of his father in 1945, he became somber, and he took to meditation seriously. He chose to embrace a wandering lifestyle, walking through Thailand taking teachings. He encountered a few teachers, but it was Ajahn Mun, whom he met a few years before Mun's death in

1949, who seems to have made the greatest impact. Like Mun, Ajahn Chah adopted practices such as eating only one meal a day, sleeping in the open, and conducting extensive walks from one region and monastery to another.[31] Eventually, he returned to his native regions and established a new monastery, Wat Nong Pah Phong.

By the early 1950s his reputation as a teacher had grown: his monastery was filled with monks, novices, nuns, and visiting lay supporters.[32] The Vinaya was his great passion: meditation supported and was supported by its disciplined procedures. Toward the end of his life he placed an increasing emphasis on chanting as a crucial form of *bhāvanā*, encouraging his followers to memorize chants and practice them during the day, a longstanding practice throughout South and Southeast Asia.[33]

Fulfilling the role of the good friend (*kalyāṇamitta*) in meditation was of immense importance to him. Teaching according to the person and their needs was paramount. Ajahn Jayasāro records numerous instances, recounted by his followers, of a life dedicated to others. Ajahn Chah was devoted to his parents and beloved by lay supporters, never taking them for granted, always reminding his followers that they could meditate only because the laypeople sustained them.[34] He had no interest in the "powers that be." Told off by a senior monk at a royal almsgiving for eating out of his simple monastic alms bowl at such a grand occasion, he asks why the senior monk had chosen *not* to eat from his alms bowl, given that he was in front of a Buddha figure of far greater importance than a king.[35] It is thought that a million people attended Ajahn Chah's funeral, including the royal family; at his own monastery, outside his village near Ubon Ratchatani, Isaan, Thailand, there is a *stūpa* for his remains that is open to the public.

Jayasāro's book *Stillness Flowing* (2017) is a magnificent biography that was published in commemoration of its subject's hundredth birth anniversary. It is worth noting that this hardbound volume of 826 pages, in the tradition of this school, opens with a wish for the awakening of all beings. A frontispiece says that it is not for sale but "is a gift of Dhamma, to you, the reader, from lay Buddhists in Thailand, Malaysia and Singapore." Many of Ajahn Chah's *dhamma* talks and plentiful anecdotes about him are included, and many copies are now available online.

With Ajahn Chah, one can see modernity having a considerable impact on forest tradition ways, affecting how teachers within it work, and relate to other monastics and lay communities. He instituted an order of nuns near his own monastery; now monks, nuns, and laypeople are all involved in the meditation teaching. Meditation, including devotional practices and chanting under the general heading of practice (*bhāvanā*), occupy an important role for monks and laity. Despite a recent understanding that this tradition advocates insight rather than calm, Ajahn Chah still regarded calm meditation, leading to the form and formless *jhānas*, as indispensable, with variations according to the teacher. He discusses the *jhāna* factors and the relationship between calm and insight.[36] Describing the means of attaining *jhāna*, he is clearly eager to dispel any sense of exclusivity about this or the vipassana path.[37]

Here is one of his teachings on the *jhānas*:

Seeing while the eyes are closed becomes the same as seeing with the eyes open. There is no doubt about anything at all, merely a sense of wonder. "How can these things be possible? It's unbelievable, but there they are." There will be sustained appreciation (*vicāra*) arising spontaneously in conjunction with rapture, happiness, a fullness of heart and lucid calm.[38]

When the mind becomes calm, *vitakka* and *vicāra* become too coarse to stay with it; then joy, then happiness, are gradually refined. So there is a "gradual movement in stages, that depends on constant and frequent practice." He did not like labels but associates this with the movement to the fourth *jhāna*, which, he says, is always accompanied by mindfulness and wisdom at every stage. He too never disclosed his attainments, remaining silent about the many powers of psychic understanding often attributed to him.[39] The tenor of forest meditation changed, however, with Ajahn Chah. He did receive meditation instructions at Wat Pak Nam from the famous Luang Pho Sot, a teacher renowned for psychic powers and associated with Borān practices; however, there is no obvious evidence of these in his teaching, whatever his private practice.[40] Whether as the result of his temperament or the needs of the people he taught, or simply that he had not had contact with them, the old symbologies and stories have fallen away, replaced by Chah's vivid and direct observation, an astute understanding of the theory he so often decried, and examples derived from simple events in the world around.

The movement has now given rise to extensive monasteries throughout Thailand, and a number throughout the world, largely founded or inspired by his own early Western students, such as Ajahn Sumedho from the United States and Ajahn Viradhammo from Canada. Toward the end of his life Ajahn Chah traveled to the West several times, visiting monasteries set up by his own students in Britain and in other parts of the world. The first of these was Cittaviveka in Sussex, where in 1979 Ajahn Sumedho and Ajahn Viradhammo established the first base for a British sangha, which included nuns, on ten precepts.

Ajahn Chah has had a powerful effect on Western practice. The breath is one among many objects of his teachings. In them he occasionally gives some instructions for breathing mindfulness, saying that it includes all elements of path:

> Compelling the mind to focus on the breath is sīla; the unremitting focus on the breath, bringing to mind a state of lucid calm, is called samādhi; letting go of attachment through contemplation of the focused breath as impermanent, unstable and selfless is called paññā.[41]

His public teachings suggest the breath as a suitable object for meditation, then to be applied to analysis of the five aggregates of form, feeling, identification, formations, and consciousness.[42] Like Ajahn Sao and so many forest meditators, he taught Buddho practice, linking the syllables to the inbreath and the outbreath.[43] He also frequently enjoined mindfulness of breath as a background practice during the day. Ajahn Tiang said that, if there was work going on in the monastery and people wanted to stop to meditate, Ajahn Chah "would ask us if our breath stopped while we were eating or lying down":

How could you be too exhausted to meditate when your breath is so immediate and ordinary? There is nothing more to it than the breath. If you practise and you're mindful, it's nothing more than being with this ordinary breath. That was all he taught. Mindfulness was the main part of it.[44]

Many of Ajahn Chah's talks are now available on the internet. He teaches very much in an insight-based manner—having met him, I can attest to that! But I do not think he would have paid much attention to reformist movements telling him he should be doing so. A man of formidable intelligence, I suspect he taught Western monks and nuns as he saw fit and adapted his teachings accordingly to suit what were Western tastes and styles of the time.[45]

The Forest Sangha Abroad

Since the end of the twentieth century, the tradition has found bases throughout the world.

Western monks and nuns are sometimes termed bridge makers, a skill that is, apparently, a great deal harder than it sounds. A bridge has to be firmly based in two banks and, for the engineering to balance well, have a good keystone, the middle point—perhaps like the *majjhima* place Ajahn Maha Boowa describes as key to the path.

Ajahn Ṭhāṇissaro, once taught by Ajahn Jotika, a student of Ajahn Lee Dhammadhāro, has dedicated his life to translating the works of forest teachers; many works cited in this chapter have been edited and translated by him. He teaches meditation in the Metta Forest Monastery in San Diego, California.

Many students of Ajahn Chah also teach around the world. Ajahn Sumedho and Ajahn Viradhammo use the breath, sometimes with internal Buddho recitation, as a basic platform for calm. The practicality, directness, spontaneity, and love of simplicity of earlier practitioners are there, but the emphasis is largely on insight—though not, I understand, exclusively so.[46] Jack Kornfield, also once a monk with Ajahn Chah, is now renowned as a lay teacher across the United States and internationally.

There are now many nuns in the tradition who have chosen to stay as *sīladhāras*, precept "nuns": those in this line of teaching encourage patience and do not exhibit much interest in particular kinds of status. Some, such as Ajahn Sundarā and Ajahn Candasirī, have earned the honorific Ajahn, a measure of the appreciation with which they are regarded. The shrine hall at Cittaviveka embodies a new, egalitarian strain: the seating area for monks is on one side, for nuns on the other; nuns are not relegated to the back.

Deforestation has ripped apart the native habitat in Thailand, but there are still forest practice monasteries in Thailand—and there are now forest monasteries in Canada, the United States, Australia, New Zealand, Italy, Germany, and many other countries. Monastics from these centers now teach numerous laypeople, who practice as a part of a life in the world.

Ajahn Pasanno, the most senior Ajahn Chah follower in the United States, gives a full explication of the sixteen stages of breathing mindfulness. At the outset, he stresses loving-kindness and the wish for happiness and peace, a tone that informs his elucidation of each stage. Acknowledging the sequence, he suggests experimentation, as each of the sixteen can be an "entry point" that is right for that time.[47] Ajahn Sucitto, a pupil of Ajahn Sumedho, was one of the first monks to come over with him to the United Kingdom. In 2022, Sucitto published a succinct account of the sixteen stages. His teachings also encourage joy in the breath; they are rooted in practical and emotional understanding of each stage and subtle appreciation of the theory involved.[48]

Ajahn Khemadhammo is one of the most senior followers in the United Kingdom, based in Warwick. He has spearheaded a campaign to introduce breathing practices and other types of practice into prisons, with the Angulimala Trust. Ajahn Brahm, also taught at one time by Chah, has founded a temple in Australia and, very controversially, reinstituted the female monastic line in his monasteries. He gives full ordination to nuns, though his moves have not been accepted by his home temples and monasteries, perhaps partly because the Mae Chee order of ten-precept nuns is now regarded so highly on its own merits in Thailand. He teaches his own system of *jhāna* practice, learned in part from Ajahn Chah: he uses the "beautiful breath" as the basis throughout this method, and explains the sixteen stages of the sutta.[49]

This monastic line is not, however, defined by breathing mindfulness.

The Vinaya, openness of the heart, and observation in daily life are paramount: the breath is one among many ways of working within all these areas. It is marked by discipline, *dhutaṅga*, and what Ajahn Viradhammo calls—as Ajahn Lee Dhammadhāro did before him—"the craft of the heart," whereby monastic practitioners are encouraged to surrender to the Vinaya from a point of strength.[50] Viradhammo suggests one can do that in any walk of life: for example, he gave up monastery life to look after his mother for eight years.

In line with modern trends, the lineage has moved more to insight than calm; the practices are usually based on the awakening factors of mindfulness and investigation, leading to wisdom. My impression is that some breathing mindfulness is always taught, but not necessarily in a graduated or structured way. While there are sometimes formal stages, breath awareness is encouraged as a background practice. There is much less emphasis on *jhāna*. Although the forest tradition emerged amid and was influenced by reforms, it had no lack of faith in meditation and nirvana: liberation has always been seen as possible. As has probably become clear, people in this line were not the kind to toe a party line. From the outset they challenged the undermining of *samatha* meditation and, later, the claims of some Burmese "dry" practitioners that *jhāna* was unnecessary. The forest tradition seems like a Vinaya family line. The place of the teacher is central. Each generation has quite distinct characters, but each acknowledges the one before, occasionally reflecting some of its light while revealing their own.

The forest tradition has had multiple generations now within the 150 years that its practitioners have been well recorded. Sometimes at events, you may meet the children, grandchildren, and even great-grandchildren of one family, all with some recognizable features and quirks. Having met many practitioners, monks, and nuns from this tradition—the generations who were taught initially by Ajahn Chah—I can attest to something like that feeling, considering the now long-intertwined branches of the forest tradition. There is a kind of family trait—a liking for direct simplicity, an investigative interest, and a cheerful endurance—in their approach to monastic life and practice.

This must surely be the only line of Buddhist practice that has had first-person comments, biographies, reminiscences, historical meetings, interactions, and teachings so vividly and thoroughly recorded, in a continuous sequence, for over a hundred years. It is an interconnected network of practitioners, and the presence of the older generations, with their crossovers, seems to be felt in those that are new. We know about this through their records, but one imagines such connections are always there in living practice lines.

The teachings of this line show just how varied meditation on the breath can be. Throughout, however—from Maha Boowa's comparison of Ajahn Mun's teaching to the planting of a Bodhi tree, to Ajahn Sucitto's comparison of a good posture to sitting under the canopy of a firmly based tree trunk—the imagery of forests informs their teachings.[51] Ajahn Soṇa, abbot of Birken Forest Buddhist Monastery, British Columbia, compares the tree to a living, growing fountain.

The teaching style is, apparently, different from those of the old meditations, and they do not appear to work in the same way with initiations and stages. There is often an intuitive, unstructured flow to teachings. Ajahn Chah said he did not know what he was going to say before he did: "But after I have finished the Namo invocation and composed my mind, then it comes itself and starts to flow."[52] As he continues, "the Dhamma that comes from the heart flows like water from a spring that never runs dry."[53] But such a method does not mean a lack of sequence or movement: there seems to be something inherently graduated, and even esoteric, about teaching a balanced practice of meditation to the level of either *jhāna* or insight, or both.

Compassion can be the lead that lets a teacher teach something at the time it is right for the meditator, and not before. A sequential, formal element may be present in that teachings unfold and are disclosed over time, even if they are not termed esoteric. Again, Thai forest teachers do not now follow the style of old meditations and do not teach *jhāna* formally to my knowledge. But they take frequent contact with the teacher, consultation, discussion, and friendship as crucially important. This is the kind of care that Ajahn Sao, Ajahn Mun, and Ajahn Chah demonstrated.

Conclusion: Thai Meditation Practice

Southern Buddhist practice is many faceted and is now found in diaspora communities, in lay practitioner groups West and East, and in many secular mindfulness and psychotherapeutic programs. Breathing practices in varied schools, among these, show great variation. Throughout Thai culture in the past, there appear to have been lineages associated with breathing mindfulness that related to one another and borrowed from a shared pool of elements shared with others. Many seem lost now, and few teachers use the language of the old meditations. Breathing mindfulness as a *jhāna* practice is now rare, with the late-twentieth-century insight movements now overwhelmingly evident, powerfully influenced by Western teachers. In Thailand, vipassana and another, streamlined direct approach greatly influenced by teachers of the Burmese insight movement, discussed in the next chapter, are now the most popular methods. Breathing mindfulness in all its styles is still practiced, however, and one cannot know how and where it is taught in old ways.

I have not discussed Cambodia or Laos in this or the preceding chapter, simply because I have had access to less information about them. Both were clearly, before the troubles of the late twentieth century, a place of living Borān meditation for laity and monastics. My only contact with old Cambodian Buddhism involving the practice of breathing mindfulness was during a week at the Manchester Centre for Buddhist Meditation with Venerable Dhammavāro (1889–1999). In the 1970s and 1980s, he used the breath with colors and healing. He taught that all organs have a color; illness occurs when the color is lost. He would have been particularly pleased with the modern ecology movement. He advocated breathing in the color green and breathing it out as a natural way of keeping the heart fresh and "in the middle." It was, he said, the middle color of the spectrum and hence the color our hearts should be. Other colors could be used to address particular imbalances, either with the breath or by drinking water that had rested for specified numbers of days in the sunshine in the appropriate-color bottles: red for colds and mucous problems, blue for fevers and heat. Walking amid greenery and woodlands would change our minds, if we were to link such activities with constant awareness of the breath and let our hearts and bodies be changed by that.

Dhammavāro may have worked out this system himself, using pre-reform understandings of the infusion of healing qualities with the breath: breathing mindfulness appears to encourage exploratory, creative expression.[54] I do not know his influences, but he showed how many ways breathing mindfulness can be interpreted! Dhammavāro was still teaching when he died, in California, at age 110.

There is still much to find out about meditation up to the twentieth century in these regions. Exploring the female perspective, Martin Seeger has given clues to the personal, immediate transmission of meditative teachings in his work on Buddhist nuns in the early twentieth century.[55] Such nuns were usually nonliterate but had a deep knowledge of texts and practice, often learning meditation privately. Many became recognized as arhats. Nuns managed to learn at local monasteries, and apparently practiced *jhāna* and wisdom on the basis of methods once widespread, though less so now.[56]

Most of us are not monastics, and not forest ones: it would not help our daily lives if we stayed up all night to meditate like Ajahn Lee Dhammadhāro and his friends, or refused to take medication for toothache as Ajahn Chah once did to learn about pain.[57] We can always remember the breath, but for many, sustained, sitting breathing meditation for *jhāna* needs to be done at set times of day.

It is worth bearing in mind that, throughout Thailand, where people wanted to watch the breath they seem to have done so, as monk, nun, or layperson. Mae Chee Kau Saetan (1870–1968) moved to Wat Saneha in Nakhon Pathom in 1910. Her role was ancillary, washing and cleaning all day, which was usual for nuns then. She was not encouraged with active meditation instruction. Monks received teaching in the afternoon, while nuns listened at the back. They implemented the practices by themselves at night and asked for guidance later. Despite such difficulties, she became a highly experienced practitioner and, in time, chief advisor to the abbot of the monastery, with eighty *mae chees* under her care. Her daily meditation practice throughout her life focused on breathing mindfulness. Because of this, her biography says she retained "an extraordinarily precise and vast memory," up to her death at 98.[58]

CHAPTER 12

Thailand's Old Meditations Abroad

The Teachings of Nai Boonman Poonyathiro

Thai breathing mindfulness practices did reach the West, primarily through the Thai forest tradition and through Buddhadāsa's idiosyncratic and innovative approach, discussed in chapter 16. In addition, by the latter part of the twentieth century, the Thai government started sending monastics to teach in newly established temples in Europe and the United States, largely in response to Western interest and growing diasporas. All teachers were vetted, however, to ensure that they taught now-obligatory insight methods.

Even so, through luck—or karma perhaps—several old *jhāna* breath meditations of Thailand did survive in the West, by eccentric means. They were taught by Boonman Poonyathiro, who, riding on a happy mixture of chance and determination, found his way to the United Kingdom by motorbike in the early 1960s. The methods of *samatha* breathing mindfulness he introduced there are still being practiced. Although he left the UK in 1974, leaving his two most experienced pupils to teach others, in 1996 he returned as promised—when there was a national center there for the practice of *samatha* breathing mindfulness. Since then, Boonman has visited the UK for the summer nearly every year, and some of his first students are still involved. In a now softened climate, Thai authorities have not only validated his teachings but generously sent relics of the Buddha, which are housed in the center's shrine hall. His teachings are not well known or as widely discussed as the others in this book, so I will spend more time on them.

Boonman Poonyathiro was born in 1932 in the Trat province of northeast Thailand, near Chantaburi and the Cambodian border. When he was born, his father shot a mother gibbon that was nursing an infant to make soup for his wife. But Boonman's mother herself died shortly afterward. Boonman's father blamed his own child for his loss. He left Boonman with his sister and moved away with the rest of their siblings. Boonman was passed around to be nursed, and when he was four, the sister who had become his adopted mother died. He was also bitten by a snake at that time, an event to which he attributes both his good memory and his devil-may-care nature. He turned into a "bad boy," shaming the family and practicing black magic.[1]

After such inauspicious beginnings, Boonman felt the need to propitiate his relatives. He became a monk, retaining the interest in astrology, magic, and psychic powers he had developed when very young but without malign intent. He went to Wat Pailon, Chantaburi, at that time an active meditation monastery, after getting rid of multiple tattoos to obtain entry. He excelled at his Pāli studies and became intent on meditation. At first, he did the calm practice of BU on the inbreath and DDHO on the outbreath.[2] While continuing his studies, he practiced *jhāna* meditations of a kind that, he says, could still be found everywhere in Thailand in the 1950s. The methods were, broadly speaking, the breathing mindfulness techniques he later taught in the UK. The empowerment of amulets on the basis of psychic attainments was also common then in Thailand, and he became adept at skills relating to that.[3]

Because of his wide reading, Boonman decided he needed to learn English and developed a wish to go to the West. In 1957 he went to university in Varanasi, where he learned local meditative techniques. The abbot of a nearby ashram, Phrom Kumari, trained meditators by encouraging them to look at him and then make him disappear, techniques like those Boonman had learned in Wat Pailon as aids to *jhāna* meditation. He met Ananda Bodhi, later Namgyal Rinpoche, who invited him to England, and a man called Ajahn Vichian, who was going to America by motorbike.[4]

In the 1960s, trips to the West were not actively encouraged by the Thai sangha, who had not yet embarked on a program of teaching meditation abroad and who at that time were wholly unsympathetic to old meditations. He had to make a decision: either to return to Thailand to try and get a visa to travel as a monk, with a real possibility he might not, or to go as a layperson. He disrobed and set off with his friend. Many adventures and mishaps followed, including wrongful imprisonment in Iran. He arrived in England in 1963 and, after various jobs such as window cleaning, went to visit Ananda Bodhi at the Hampstead Buddhist Vihara. He was introduced to Maurice Walshe, chair of the English Sangha Trust, and invited to teach meditation.

At that time, he said, he taught "pure" breathing mindfulness, adapting methods he had learned at his monastery—his short autobiography implies that he left some out at that time. He also says that "the technique of how to know and feel the inbreaths and outbreaths I invented myself."[5] He did not teach devotional aspects at first but waited until people wanted them.[6] He could not mention the word *jhāna* at first, as the Thai hierarchy in London would have condemned him outright. In private, he did use the term.[7]

These methods follow the style of the old meditations and, like them, draw on guidelines given in canonical and commentarial texts. Taking Buddhaghosa's four stages of counting, following, touching, and settling, Boonman also teaches four lengths of breath: the longest, to below the navel; the longer, to around the solar plexus; the shorter, to around the throat; and the shortest, to the nasal passage. There is a Cambodian "old meditation" text that emphasizes these areas of the body; as we have seen, it is the Borān style to locate areas around the breath passage. In his method, this makes, in all, sixteen stages for the basic practice. The longest breath loosely corresponds to the entrance to the first *jhāna* and establishing *vitakka* and *vicāra*; the longer to the second *jhāna* and the deepening of joy; the shorter to the third, with the fuller development of happiness and mindfulness; and the shortest to the fourth, where mindfulness and equanimity work together.

When he teaches formless meditation, he takes these breath lengths as starting points for the four stages, again in ascending order. Paul Dennison, one of his first students, has described some of his methods and early teachings. The effects of his practices have been shown to have striking effects on the spindles in brain activity.[8] The lengths gradually "become understood by feel rather than verbal conceptualization and in the same manner as learning a complex piece of music or a Buddhist chant, perhaps in Pāli, the meditator becomes able to simply go to the different stages directly with fluency."[9] The four breath lengths "provide a safe space to develop and enter jhāna and to safely withdraw back to sensory consciousness."[10]

Boonman's statement that these practices could be found all over Thailand up until the 1950s, before the widespread attempts at reform undertaken by monastic authorities, is corroborated by the presence of numerous manuscripts relating to old meditations in temples around Thailand as well as first-person, anecdotal accounts. The overall stress of his teaching methods, then as now, is on a somatic experience of the breath "in the whole body." The awakening factor of joy helps to know the breath in this way. Buddhaghosa's five kinds of joy, ranging from momentary sensations to an overwhelming joy that can suffuse the whole body, are, as we have seen, the traditional starting point of the old meditation traditions. The "body" experiences changes as breathing mindfulness develops: the breath is form (rūpa), and mind is that which relates to it; gradual refinement of the breath means there is an inseparability between the experience of the physical body and that of the breath. This "body" becomes increasingly subtle. Joy enables this process and is itself then made tranquil, falling away as deeper states are attained and equanimity becomes stable. Boonman has sometimes commented that it was a surprise to him at first to see the way that Westerners, with no knowledge of Thai culture and meditative practices, experienced the same effects as monks he had seen in the monastery where he trained in the 1950s.

After taking a class for several years at Cambridge University, in 1973 Boonman became involved with the setting up of the Samatha Trust with Dr. Paul Dennison, L. S. Cousins, Chris Gilchrist, and Dr. Richard Wallis. By then his marriage to an English girl, with whom he had a daughter, had failed. By 1974, he had taught one retreat and had asked for another to be organized. Instead of teaching it himself, however, he asked his two senior students, L. S. Cousins and Paul Dennison, to offer it together, saying he would return when they had set up a national center. They both felt this very significant. Utterly opposed to one another temperamentally, their leadership, together, ensured that the people coming would be very varied. Boonman returned to Thailand and married a Thai woman named Dang, and together they started up a shop selling tektites. The shop also sold dinosaur dung coprolites, which, like tektites, are found throughout Thailand. This was known locally as "Buddha dung": local people felt that even the excrement of the Buddha was enduring and beautiful.

Boonman's Teachings

Boonman's life work, however, is his teaching of meditation. Key to this is the beginning. The meditation starts with taking the longest breath one can comfortably manage—and it may take a couple of minutes to find one's bearings and find this good long breath, which fills the whole body—but it differs slightly from Buddhaghosa's recommendation to count breaths in that the meditator counts to nine on the inbreath itself and from nine back to one again on the outbreath.[11] Again, the attention is very light. The breath can be forced if the counting is too slow. The intention is just to keep the mind on the breath for that long breath, the first of the sixteen stages, and allow it to become even and relaxed as one does so. This stage, the longest of counting, is the baseline of the method: the start to any meditation practice, perhaps even just for a few breaths. After this, a choice is made whether to pursue a long or a short breath for the counting, following, touching, and settling. There can be great variation within this.

Boonman speaks of gangsters—the hindrances—who can attack the meditator sometimes. Some bandits need confronting; others are best avoided if you want to get to your destination. A change of stage or breath length may be necessary to deal with them as is needed. The breath is sustained evenly for a while before another stage of the practice or length of breath is adopted. At the end of the practice there is a return to the longest of counting, ensuring the practice touches base again. It is important to return to the normal breath afterward. Background mindfulness of breath is to be practiced in the day, but it is better to keep it normal. As Boonman says, "then you will remember to be normal too!"[12]

Form (Rūpa) Jhānas

Boonman describes the *nimitta* with the breath as "your friend," who turns up when you might not expect them and guides you into the meditations. He also speaks of the breath *nimitta* as "your friend who takes you to outer space." Placing the mind and exploration hold the first *jhāna*, with the first gradually becoming released by the second, so that even that is no longer necessary. The second *jhāna* is then held by joy (*pīti*). Joy acts as the means to experience the meditation where verbalization is dropping away, and then this, in turn, moves gradually to an increase in happiness. This offers a safe ground within the joy, that steadies it and takes the mind deeper into absorption.

This stage is marked by "internal silence": the third *jhāna* is held by happiness and equanimity, as, to use the canonical image, lotuses under water blossom and are suffused by clarity and contentment.[13] In the fourth *jhāna*, equanimity becomes steady as mindfulness purifies, sometimes increasing in sensitivity and balance. During the time the breath gets ever softer and finer until imperceptible. All experience in the body is immersed by and subsumed in the gentle movement and rhythm. Nothing gets left out: the perception of the body that experiences and knows the breath has changed.

When equanimity is established, the balance is so steady and subtle that mindfulness increases all the time, changing experience as it occurs. Should thoughts, emotions, and feelings arise, they just become part of that.

The Divine Abidings

Before, alongside, and after the *jhāna* and *arūpa* meditations, Boonman teaches the divine abidings, linking them with the breath and, sometimes, the four stages of the meditation. These are crucial to his teaching, as are ways of behaving with mindfulness and alertness in the world.

The breath moves in and out of the body; Boonman teaches that the divine abidings can also do this if they are well established within the breath and felt in the whole body. One practice Boonman gives is "the blessings practice," to be undertaken anywhere. This is to breathe loving-kindness into oneself on the inbreath, and out to other beings on the outbreath. So, the first stage is to breathe in loving-kindness, perhaps with the syllable ME, to oneself, and then breathe it out to all beings, with TTĀ, if that helps. This can be done in meditation or during the day. This will, he says, develop and purify will. Sometimes he teaches variations with the other divine abidings: a few minutes with the breath and loving-kindness, a few with compassion, a few with sympathetic joy, and a few with equanimity. The rise and fall of the breath, and its impermanence, ensures subtle attachments or sentimentality are less likely to arise, and instead genuine feeling arises toward other beings and also to events. Insight into their and your own problems is then likely to arise: vipassana working in *samatha*. Wisdom is also matured as insight into the changing events in the mind and body.

Just as the hindrances show themselves to us mostly through our reactions to people we know and encounter, so openings into the divine abidings often become possible through noticing them in others, particularly on meditation courses, where silence may make their impression deeper. This means that for me the practices with Boonman always feel grounded in the body and the heart. The divine abidings are not taught as abstract ideas but as ways of transforming how one knows one's own mind, breath, and body as well as one's perceptions of others. Within sitting practices, any of the four may lose the sense of the personal as the object becomes limitless. But they need to be authentic and lived, arising from the impingement with other people and the problems and habits of one's own mind and body.

The insights that arise from the divine abidings are deep: hatred may be dispelled when one practices compassion with *samatha* breathing mindfulness and sees and understands the pain of the person, self or other, that is the object of ill will. Sympathetic joy may show a way to help support and sustain oneself or another. Equanimity, with deep insight, may come at the time when it is really best to leave someone or, conversely, when there is an insight that arises that there is something one can usefully do. Without this basis, as a lay practice, the other *jhānas* and *arūpa* meditations just do not have the earth to nourish them and keep them alive. As I understand it, the underlying assumption is that breathing mindfulness may not itself be love, but breath meditations cannot mature without love there to help them.

The sense of selflessness that arises when these are all developed means that the sense of "I" in the sensory world cannot find a place. Other people may give us intimations of this and be our teachers when we see the divine abidings in them; we may enter situations sometimes and find one of the divine abidings by surprise, and see that others respond too. These are all preparations for the meditations on formlessness, if that is the way one wants to go, and to insight, in daily life. The divine abidings can be developed infinitely. This gives the mind a comfortable basis in the spaciousness needed for formless meditation. Or they can arise in odd moments in one's life, ensuring that insight is not harsh, cruel, or selfish. Their subtle presence can and needs to envelop meditation at every level, and particularly be there as a basis for meditation in the formless spheres and the development of wisdom.

Formless (Arūpa) *Meditation*

Only when this basis is established does Boonman teach formless meditation, and only to experienced meditators. "Now," says Boonman, "you may go even further into outer space."[14] Such meditations have never been taught as essential, though they may be for some, or as particularly helpful for others as an antidote to possible attachment to form meditation. It is worth noting how often the Buddha teaches them, alongside form *jhānas*, as well as the divine abidings and the psychic powers: a rich fanning out of possibilities that arise from the fourth *jhāna*. One could say that, within this path, the form *jhānas* are dedicated to purifying feeling; the formless meditations purify cognition, or perception (*saññā*).

Form is defined as anything that can be impinged upon or become an object. The formless meditations transcend that. But to start off with, they may need some handle or means of bypassing usual cognitions. Boonman says that the formless meditations use the brain, rather than the mind and heart needed to sustain the form *jhānas*, but without the usual activities of thinking. It is the exercise and partial abeyance of the cognizing mind (*saññā*), without its usual content. The first formless meditation, infinite space, is considered helpful for this. It is important to remember that, in Buddhist meditation, space is not "dead" emptiness as we conceive it in modern Western cultures. Rather, it is a kind of groundless ground, a potent field or space from which all phenomena and events in the mind and body arise. It is into this they also dissolve. The preliminary "object" leading one to formless meditation may be the infinite skies above, or the space all around, or the depths of the ocean. But it is the process of identifying that object, even rather than the object itself, which allows this meditation to occur. In the style of the old meditations, it can be invoked. As Paul Dennison says, *akāsa*, the word for space, is like the evocation/invocation of the Yogāvacara: *Okāsa*—may it happen.

The method Boonman teaches is based on the old meditation systems and so offers a somatic, joy-based practice. Very occasionally, Boonman also teaches what he calls "psychic power" (*iddhi*) practice, using specific breath techniques long-established in Thailand, given only at appropriate times and to people who are ready. He teaches these formally and with careful boundaries and protocols. The techniques are practiced in the shrine hall, after protective (*paritta*) chanting, and in the presence of others, who act as important witnesses and guardians to the performance. Set times are given for the practices involved, and a sense of ceremony is observed: the techniques are taught in the shrine hall, after the preliminary refuges and precepts are taken to create a safe, magically protected space. Others present watch attentively and without judgment, itself a form of meditative practice. At the end, the meeting draws to a close with a blessing. These are, apparently, old Thai customs and characteristic of the *samatha* style of Boonman's teaching. The tradition also follows another old Southeast Asian custom: not discussing one's level of attainment in meditation with others, except in "reports," or what we call personal consultations on practice. This kind of consultation is essential: the practice can be modified according to needs. Perhaps a more vipassana or a calm orientation is needed, or a different breath length, or a shared silence that suggests a way ahead.

The Role of Joy

Having had close contact with this practice for decades, I do understand why some Southeast Asians were wary of these once widespread practices. For some, though not all, it can produce strong joy in the breath. These effects can be, for some people, dramatic and very cathartic. In the spirit of Borān methods, Boonman encourages joy in the practice right from the outset, and for some people this can involve some shaking and quaking in the body. Among my most cheerful memories of Greenstreete, our meditation center, is hearing one meditator, famous for his powerful experience of joy, bouncing up and down in the upstairs shrine room. Later, he emerged with a serene, alert expression, completely composed. He had at no time in the experience felt any loss of control, could leave his meditation at any time, at will, and felt an increase in mindfulness and alertness to events around. It is my impression that this is one distinguishing feature of the meditations Boonman teaches when compared to some other *jhāna* teachings that have reached the West: the *Patisambhidāmagga* has an interesting passage that describes breathing mindfulness as overcoming shakings and tremblings.[15] Boonman teaches that, through allowing the manifestations of joy a free rein and then calming them through the breath, these phenomena can effect a deeper purification.[16] This strong joy makes the practice very body based; the different lengths of breath allow the practitioner to make sure that they feel in charge and can leave the practice when they need or want to, or take it farther into deeper levels of calm if the time feels right.

In practice, most of us feel lucky if we get some joy, however it comes. For most people it is not so dramatic. But joy is the central, in all senses of the word, factor of awakening. For many Westerners especially, manifestations of joy are not as dramatic as they are for others. Cultures really vary on this. Although Western culture has a strong tradition of charismatic forms of Christianity, even with movements that take their name from "shaking and quaking," we are generally less comfortable with outward physical signs of joy. Those from expressive cultures with more sensitivity to the way hindrances can block the body and the energies there feel no such problem. Such effects are normal for those familiar with charismatic Christian churches. Joy, tears, and some shaking may, surprisingly, accompany unwavering mindfulness and clarity of mind. In calm meditations, steadiness and wisdom are strengthened by such manifestations. What usually happens is that some people, some of the time, feel a bit of shaking in the body and movement, which then quietens as it takes its course, and the factor of tranquility comes into play with the breath. The joy is needed for the hindrances to be shaken away; then it goes. People say this feels as if it washes hindrances away: one woman compared it to the mind being swirled in a washing machine!

I had secretly wanted some of these kinds of things to happen to me when I continued with meditation, but they never did. Then one day I felt myself shaking, with tears streaming down my face. I realized this was not diminishing mindfulness but increasing it: the whole body felt happy and alive, and then steadied itself. The Buddha ascribes the calm of his followers to breathing mindfulness: people feel very peaceful and steady as an aftereffect.[17] Afterward I felt completely settled and clear; the mindfulness felt greatly increased and the body, strong and still. But I can understand how joy-based practices, which clearly were once common throughout Southeast Asia, contributed to the unease felt by some authorities. An international mood of rationalism meant that meditations that could be presented in more scientific, even "detached," terms were seen as more authentically Buddhist. Even now, most books on meditation skirt around *jhāna* or dismiss factors such as joy as subsidiary. The Buddha did not. He constantly taught and practiced *jhāna*, as did his followers. From a purely scientific point of view, studies on those entering *jhāna* on the basis of this and other related practices show an increase in alpha rhythms, high alertness; all those participating report a deep sense of refreshment and restoration. The Buddha says that, when breathing mindfulness is developed and cultivated, "no shaking or trembling occurs in the mind."[18] For some people, there may be some interesting adventures first.

As Ajahn Lee noted, science and mysticism are not in opposition to one another; both depend on good and accurate observation. I have come to see, however, why Southeast Asian monastics and those involved with giving permits to monastics leaving to teach in other countries might want their teachers to be firmly rooted in insight-based methods; their terminology also often borrowed terms gathered from Western science, philosophy, and psychology. I am glad modern research is also doing this for *samatha*.[19]

For many people, however, different kinds of vocabulary and validation are the most effective. Many respond intuitively, without the "head" getting in the way, to the language of the four elements and myth. Such vocabulary itself communicates joy and knowledge. I know several people who say that just experiencing joy once in their meditation was the transformative experience of their lives. It showed what was possible. It also seems particularly suited to lay practice, as the light change of breath length at various stages means that people can practice for a certain period, and then leave it easily. This is a practice for those who need and like deep fuel: the wisdom that arises with breathing practices follows naturally, with the sense of the rise and fall—or at higher stages, the rhythm—of the breath.

Boonman is now ninety-two. His language skills have deteriorated, and he cannot express himself in the same way. But he is there, resting in highly alert equanimity. Paul Dennison sits beside him to give meditation teaching. Boonman still takes reports on meditation. In these he shines a light right into the practice and comments: "Go on with it."

When Boonman Poonyathiro came back to the United Kingdom in 1996 after his twenty-two-year absence, he gave a piece of black tektite to each person who came to the opening ceremony at the shrine hall in Wales. Indochinese tektites are an extraordinary form of a sort of molten glass. Thought until very recently to have come from meteorites from the moon, their real origins are just as dramatic. Volcanic eruptions thousands of years ago spewed out drops of molten lava. These were transformed by the earth's atmosphere into lustrous, ink-black stones of many shapes, which then cascaded throughout remote regions of northeastern

Thailand. Boonman's business later in life involved hunting around for them in remote places and selling them. Converting base metal and finding treasure in unexpected and surprising places is, in my experience, a hallmark of Boonman's teaching.

Boonman teaches according to traditional methods. The body is transformed and seen anew through the breath, leading to practice of *jhāna*, formless meditations, and various powers. In the Siamese manner, the breath is seen to lead to any meditation and to be an accompaniment and support for the full apprehension of path; all sixteen stages occur but are not stated. Boonman is the only international teacher I know of who uses the Thai system of breathing mindfulness as a *jhāna* practice, as part of a full path—though within Theravada countries there are other *jhāna* systems. It represents a once usual kind of practice in Thailand and has a different center of gravity from most now available. It needs consultation and one-to-one interviews with a teacher: this is a lay tradition, and teaching is in the style of the "good friend" (*kalyāṇamitta*). To use the image that introduced this book, it seems like a once healthy and beautiful genus of tree that has been planted and flourishes elsewhere, after being largely eradicated and uprooted in its own terrain.

CHAPTER 13

Myanmar, Part One

*Sagaing, Ledi Sayadaw, and the
Origins of the Insight Movement*

We have talked about the great wave of interest in insight in the twentieth century. We now move back in time and to another region, Burma, known today as Myanmar, to find out how the modern movement began. A few miles from Mandalay, on the other side of the Irrawaddy River, are the natural forests of Sagaing, the country's meditative center. In the nineteenth century, while Mandalay was home to the monarchy and to the administration of Burma before the British arrival, when the monarchy was ousted, Sagaing was the center of Burmese monastic meditation. Throughout this region, numerous hills run in a ridge over the Irrawaddy; there are plenty of other rivers too, historically providing waterways for travel. Stupas are everywhere, a shower of golden teardrops scattered over wooded hills: there are 16,000 in that one area. The land is dry and sparse, and wild animals, though plentiful, tend not to be so dangerous. It is also studded with caves, retreats, and other places for meditation, inhabited continuously by generations of monastics. Since the twelfth century, Sagaing has been held sacred as a place for solitary or communal practice, pilgrimage, and devotion. By the mid-nineteenth century "the hills of Sagaing were honeycombed with meditation caves and dotted with forest monasteries."[1] Still today, it features around a thousand monasteries and nunneries.

Throughout Myanmar, caves are an important location for devotion. They offer cool refuge from scorching sunlight. In some, you walk in darkness along rocky tunnels. Some are covered with frescoes, lit up only by occasional dim lamps, until you penetrate right to the heart of the cave and find the shrine; here, darkness is dispelled by candles, lamps, and the figure of the Buddha at the center. In Myanmar the cave appears to occupy a special role, perhaps a feature of the ancient Mon civilization in the region. In Bagan, one temple has no windows; people bring light in themselves, in the form of candles and electric lamps, causing the paintings of the Buddha's countless past lives as the bodhisatta to flicker into life. Animals, *nāgas*, people, elephants, and golden palaces—all the adventures and exploits of the bodhisatta—surround and animate your awareness as you pass.

It was in Sagaing that the great insight movement emerged, at what appeared to be a time of great darkness for the Burmese. Unlike Thailand, Burma was under siege. Throughout the nineteenth century, British encroachment on all the borders of Burma grew apace, culminating in the deposition of Burma's king in 1885. Colonialism, scientific rationalism, and internal insecurities and tensions were creating the need even for Buddhism, so widely practiced, to look at itself again and reformulate. The caves and temples of Sagaing and elsewhere must have seemed like a refuge from such pressures and a sanctuary in which to face them. Buddhist practice needed to be reconceived, just as it had been in so many places historically. The arid climate here perhaps made it a natural home for the birth of a method of breathing mindfulness known as the "dry" way. Throughout the suttas, the Buddha's teaching is compared to a lamp that is being set up in a darkness where there had been no light:[2] the exponents of the new traditions, often practicing in the caves among the hills, must have felt they were lighting afresh a lamp amid surrounding darkness.

They perhaps did not realize that the simple techniques and tenets they were teaching would offer light elsewhere as well. It was the result of their spark and their development of old methods that Southeast Asian meditations could spread westward. By the beginning of the twenty-first century, they had spread globally, from traditional Buddhist practice into clinics, hospitals, and therapy centers. Multiple and complex factors contributed to the sweeping success of vipassana and its techniques at an international level. The many threads of its origins, however, came together and were made manifest in quite simple ways to understand and experience the breath.

Burmese Buddhism

As we look at the origins of this movement, it is important to have a sense of the particular landscape of Burmese Buddhism. South and Southeast Asian regions were densely interconnected by maritime and riverine means, and since the thirteenth century, the Buddhism that was practiced throughout these regions was largely what we now call Theravada. In Myanmar, several prominent elements were crucial to the style and methods of the teachers we are going to discuss.

Chant and Abhidhamma

The first of these is the role of recital, text, and chanting. As in all South and Southeast Asian regions, these offer a form of practice (*bhāvanā*) that leads into and informs the orientation of meditation itself. But in Myanmar, Abhidhamma, the ancient Buddhist system of psychology and philosophy, is particularly important. The last book, causal relationship (*Paṭṭhāna*), occupies a special role. Its delineation of the twenty-four causes (*paccaya*) that define the relationship between mind, mental states, and matter, is regarded as the highest teaching of the Abhidhamma system. Burmese delight in the rippling waves of *Paṭṭhāna* chanting was noted by the Englishman James George Scott, who wrote *The Burman: His Life and Manners* (1882) under a pseudonym, Shway Yoe, pretending to be Burmese. It was a time when the king at the time, Mindon, was promoting Buddhism with great support. Noting with puzzlement that monastics seemed to spend most of their time in "mystic musings"—what we call meditation now—Scott observes that they also spend considerable periods chanting the *Paṭṭhāna* while telling their rosaries. This, he had been told, would increase the powers (*iddhipāda*) of their mind, crucial factors for the attainment of awakening.[3]

The ebbs and flows of the chant would be familiar to all Burmese, then as now. The chants are considered healing. As elsewhere, the syllables of the books and, when recited, certain texts are held to have properties that can be infused into the meditator and transform them. In Myanmar, this system with its chants is seen as a particularly important practice. The rhythms, waves of repetitive lists, word endings, and phrase clusters of the *Paṭṭhāna* enact ways consciousness, mental states, and matter that arise, sustain themselves in streams of groupings, and then fall away as new mental states and groupings of matter take their place. Volition is central: it governs how these patterns arrange themselves and the way the tides go. As humans, we have currents of skillful, unskillful, and "undeclared" (*abyākata*) mental states: the path to awakening lies in shifting the momentum of skillfulness, so that it overrides the currents of unskillfulness.[4]

In Myanmar more than any other Theravada country, the lists, enumerations, and detail of the Abhidhamma are seen as oral enactments of the currents of human consciousness interacting with matter, in patterns that rise and fall all the time. Understandings derived from Abhidhamma, and the *Paṭṭhāna* in particular, inform teachings on breathing mindfulness practice.

Jatakas and Art

Likewise, possibly even more than in Thailand, the stories of the Buddha's past lives, jatakas, are central. Since the twelfth century in particular, with the great building projects of Bagan, Burmese Buddhism had placed considerable emphasis on these stories. Depictions of all 547 jatakas in friezes of regular, horizontal tiles fill temples, stupas, and monasteries. The bodhisatta ideal and the jataka *imaginaire* were central to the emotional world of practitioners, shaping the rituals, drama, puppet shows, poetry, devotions, and pedagogy that grew around them. Jatakas constituted the core Buddhist texts for centuries. Anyone can cultivate the ten perfections (*pāramis*): one single good act will have karmic consequences, whoever you are. As layperson, monastic, animal, or god, one can always practice the Buddhist path and find awakening, after perhaps many lifetimes. By the end of the eighteenth century, jatakas were the prime source of legal precedent in courts of law.[5]

In Sagaing, the temple art of the region was generously subsidized by textile merchants wishing to make merit and bring good fortune to their families and the region. Alexandra Green notes, "Step into a Burmese temple from the seventeenth, eighteenth and early nineteenth centuries and you are surrounded by a riot of colour and imagery."[6] On often frieze-like registers, jatakas, myths, and vernacular stories filled with nagas, ogres (*yakkhas*), animals, people, and protective deities, ancient and modern, are flanked by protective diagrams and long horizontal lines of textile designs, landscapes, and geometric flowers.

Green shows how deeply such art reflected and inspired Burmese practice. Formulaic distillations of stories, suttas, vinaya incidents, protective configurations, and chants flow around walls and pillars. The paintings celebrate and explain the whole Buddhist path. Friezes, incidents emblematic of qualities, and tableaux echo and supplement each other, just as the separate collections of Abhidhamma, suttas, jatakas, and local stories do.[7] There is something of the Abhidhamma method about this style in Myanmar. Sequence is carefully observed, and the steps of the narrative are scrupulously maintained. The endlessly repetitive motifs and emblems, like Abhidhamma, process with rhythm, movement, and step-by-step change. The cosmology of heavens, humans, and animals is precisely organized around central points to give a three-dimensional enactment of the structure of the universe within the space of the temple. The practitioner is enveloped: this cosmos relates also to the inner world, as it invokes and honors the Buddha and multiple narratives associated with his power.

In jataka stories, beings who are proficient in meditation fly in and out of stories through the air, buoyed by the joy of the Buddhist path. Such powers (*iddhis*) are seen as natural outflows of meditation, as described in The Sutta on the Fruits of Recluseship.[8] *Paccekabuddhas* and meditative recluses in particular excel in these miraculous abilities. Other spirits, the gods of localities and palaces, act as agents within stories, interceding in local affairs and difficulties: the goddess of the parasol in "The Story of Temiya" gives advice to the aspirant bodhisatta, while the goddess of the woods helps him when, in "The Story of Sāma," he is wounded.[9] Stories follow a scrupulously delineated sequence; the hierarchical composition of the cosmos is carefully maintained.

The Figure of the Weikza

Burmese Buddhism also placed considerable emphasis on a figure known as the *weikza*, the inheritor of the powers of such beings, who embodies wisdom, great power, and knowledge.[10] The word derives from *vijjā*, wisdom: such figures ensure that the healing properties of the teaching (*dhamma*) can prevail in times of need. Celestial and human interventions, miraculous events, and protective chants supported a flamboyant, but highly systematic, universe; *vijjā* acted as its protector.

This face of Burmese Buddhism in the early nineteenth century is summarized in stories about a teacher whose pupil, U Nārada (Mingun Sayadaw), was the teacher of Mahāsi Sayadaw, one of the great proponents of the new insight movement; it is possible U Nārada also taught Ledi Sayadaw. Theelon Sayadaw (1786–1861) had started out more interested in theory than meditation: the three threads of practice (*paṭipatti*), theoretical learning (*pariyatti*), and penetrative knowledge (*paṭivedha*) form the plait of Burmese Buddhism, with many teachers, as Gustaaf Houtman points out, following theory lineages as well as practice lines as the means of finding understanding.[11] After a while, he met a monk rumored to be of very high attainment, Kingtawya Sayadaw. Theelon received his teachings every day, as Kingtawya encouraged him to practice in earnest rather than devote himself to theory. Kingtawya gave him this final teaching:

> "We cannot accept the way of teaching if it is not according to the Buddha's teaching and cannot give support to get *jhāna*, supernormal knowledges (*abhiññā*), path and fruition knowledge (*magga-phala*) or *Nibbāna*. The discourses given by the Buddha in reality are complete, and there is no need to discard any part. We can compare own experience with the *Dhamma* scriptures. What we only need is wisdom knowledge. . . . The Buddha's discourses are very real and fresh in essence at this time. We still need faith and effort. When meeting with Buddha Sāsana . . . you need to light up with faith and wisdom, establish mindfulness with effort."

After saying that, he shook off his robe, and left that place by the use of his special psychic power of flying through the sky.[12]

Theelon apparently stood in his tracks, filled with wonder at this vindication of the Buddha's teachings: perhaps enlightenment was indeed possible now. He never saw his teacher again and heard he had died that night. He changed his direction, however, moved to the practice of *jhāna*, the higher knowledges, and then, as instructed, emphasized wisdom and insight. He continued to teach, largely to monastics, and was acclaimed by King Mindon. Later, he was accredited with the same miraculous powers that had so impressed him.

Bodhisattas and Kings

While doubts were being expressed about the possibility of attaining enlightenment in modern times, in the mid-nineteenth century Burmese Buddhism still had a clear center and purpose. Each person sat in the center of a hierarchical yet companionable mandalic universe, stretching out in time and space. Everyone could be on a path stretching lifetimes, and all could search for perfections. It may take many rebirths to perfect oneself, but any single action could contribute to salvation. The bodhisatta embodied this quest. Central to this worldview was the great potency and power of the king, considered a bodhisatta of the present time. Therein lies the problem.

Nineteenth-century politics made this world feel increasingly fragile. As Burma's fortunes declined, it was becoming increasingly clear that a new approach was needed. The British had made deep inroads.[13] After the death of the strong leader King Mindon (1808–1878) and the accession of a new, weak king, Thibaw (1859–1916), amid horrifically murderous familial violence, the next step was inevitable. By 1885 Thibaw had been ousted, unceremoniously taken to the coast in a cart and exiled to India. Burmese Buddhism, like the country, was in crisis: the central character in the Burmese story had been lost. Although Queen Victoria had explicitly tried to protect local religions in the Empire, her directive was ignored amid many Christian influences. These included in particular American Baptist missionaries, unimpressed by the justified caution of the British, who were desperately trying to placate diverse religious loyalties among their acquisitions and to sustain their always fragile empire.[14] The Burmese felt they had to defend their traditions.[15] Whereas the king had chosen leaders for the sangha before, the British now refused to take on this task. The sense that Buddhism may indeed be falling into decline was starting to prevail.

The seeds of the transformation came from within Buddhism itself, in developments that had started in the eighteenth century.[16] In Sagaing, a monk called Waya-zawta had challenged a growing mood of skepticism about the possibilities of a full Buddhist path and the attainment of enlightenment.[17] The earliest "how-to" insight, or vipassana, manuals we have date from the mid-eighteenth century, to a young scholar monk called Medawi (1728–1816). He stresses the three marks and urges for the pursuit of practice on these for the attainment of enlightenment.[18] A later historical work, *Sāsanavaṃsappadīpaka*, written in 1861 by Venerable Paññāsāmi, claimed that people of great supernormal attainments did indeed flourish; it was possible to attain arhatship in this lifetime. Reformers started to establish themselves around Sagaing. One, Ngettwin Sayadaw, the "Bird-Cave Abbot," insisted monks should practice vipassana daily and recommended meditation for the laity.[19] Lay practice around Burma and Shan State is recorded from the nineteenth century.[20]

Ledi Sayadaw (1846–1923)

Amid the colonial-era reforms taking place in Burmese politics, culture, and religion, a radical change in understandings of breathing mindfulness took place. The most significant figurehead in the defense of Buddhism, who did so much to shape and tailor Burmese practice to his country's perceived needs, was Ledi Sayadaw.[21] He was born in Tabayin (Dabayin), a village in the heart of Sagaing. By the time he first ordained, at age sixteen, the British had taken lower Burma, but the area around Mandalay was still ruled by the king. Ledi studied Abhidhamma in Mandalay, near the court. After his first ordination, however, he disrobed, disappointed with the scholarly emphasis, and returned as U Nandaja.

U Nanda, his preceptor, dissuaded him from new interests—fortune telling and the Vedas—and he decided to return to the woods and dedicate himself to meditation. He went first to the forests of Monywa on the Chindwin River and then founded a forest monastery in the Ledi woods, from which he took the name by which he became known. The forest had been haunted by ghosts and frequented by wild beasts, but Ledi, true to his Theravada monastic heritage, suffused it with strong loving-kindness: after, the atmosphere changed and the jungle became habitable.[22] Hundreds of monks joined him, and he taught meditation for thirteen years, while tending also to the pastoral and educational needs of his fellow monks. Eventually, after further retreats, he claimed all five *jhānas* and that he would be a follower of the next Buddha.[23] After a few years he went to the caves near Monywa and Sagaing to help people further their spiritual progress, suggesting enlightenment as a real possibility in this lifetime.

"Meditation," in the Western sense of a seated contemplative practice, had apparently been less widely practiced by the laity. Ledi challenged the perceptions that still made meditation seem difficult. He saw laypeople, as others did, as crucially needed for Buddhism, offering hope for the future as supporters of the sangha and the teaching. Thus, he dedicated himself to ensuring that the full eightfold path was accessible to everyone, monastic and lay.

The Burmese sangha felt they had to address modernity and to present their ancient traditions in terms that would inspire those who had grown up as Buddhists, many of whom were increasingly feeling that Buddhism was in decline. Irrespective of colonial pressures, Buddhist tenets were being reassessed; the sangha also wished to assert Buddhist principle in a world increasingly demanding scientific rationale.[24] The tide of opinion, both among Burmese meditative practitioners and within the international communities requiring rational acceptability in Buddhist theory, made it seem essential that the cognitive, more than the feeling-based, aspects of meditation and daily practice be stressed.[25]

Taking advantage of new printing methods coming to the regions, from the 1890s on Ledi wrote manuals in Burmese—not, as was traditional, in canonical Pāli. These were widely distributed, highly controversial, and became deeply influential. The manuals were in some ways like those produced by Medawi 150 years before, but with a new dimension. Mindfulness, meditation, and particularly vipassana were now in the forefront as a possibility for everyone, lay and monastic. All the richness of Burmese Buddhism, such as the interest in cultivating the ten perfections so constantly taught in jatakas, was still central in a world densely populated by animals and humans, visiting devas from higher realms, local spirits (*nāts*), both benevolent and malign, and the spirits of trees, mountains, and rivers.[26] But practitioners needed insight too: this was taught as essential if enlightenment was to be found in this lifetime, or even if one wanted a good rebirth at the time of the next Buddha.

It should be stressed that Ledi espoused other aspects of traditional Buddhist meditation and training. For instance, he, like Buddhists throughout South and Southeast Asia to this day, encouraged the memorization, recital, and chanting of texts as a basis for, and itself a variety of, meditative practice.[27] There is abundant canonical support for this practice (*bhāvanā*): the repeated memorization and recollection of texts (*anussaraṇa*) leads to serene confidence (*pasāda*), which leads then to gladness (*pāmojja*), leading in turn to purification of the mind (*cittaparyodapanā*).[28] Chanting, listening to, and understanding texts leads to gladness, joy, tranquility of body, happiness, and concentration.[29] While he did not always insist on Abhidhamma as a basis for meditation, his love for this "basket" is shown by the way its presence informs his methods and understanding of how consciousness and matter can be perceived through meditation on the breath.[30]

In 1904 Ledi wrote "A Manual of Breathing Mindfulness" (*Ānāpāna Dīpanī*), in Burmese.[31] It was a crucial work. In it he largely follows a classical pattern of interpretation deriving from Buddhaghosa. According to the traditional convention that one should be asked before providing teaching, he says that he was requested, in March 1904, to offer it to the general public.

He makes clear that he is teaching in accordance with the earliest texts. He starts by saying people should renounce at the age of fifty or fifty-five. The familiar world of jatakas and suttas is invoked. Citing the bodhisatta's jataka rebirths as Makhādeva ("Maghadeva," J 9), Temiya ("Temi," J 539), and King Nemi (J 541), he speaks of the final period of life as when one should practice meditation wholeheartedly and relinquish one's wealth.[32] The sense of the last stage of life as being a time for meditation permeates these stories. They often involve lay kings who renounce, usually in the last stage of life, to take up the practice of meditation.

Makhādeva-jātaka (J 9) describes such an idealized monarch. The king has spent 84,000 years enjoying the "play" of youth, another 84,000 as viceroy, then another 84,000 as king. On seeing a gray hair presented to him by his barber, however, he renounces to practice in a mango grove, and enjoys the "play" of *jhāna* for a further 84,000 years.[33] These mythic fables form a constant in Burmese teaching. Sutta narratives also feature, such as the story of the universal monarch, in which the bodhisatta, as a layman, builds a beautiful city and palace, protects his people, and practices *jhānas* on the divine abidings of loving-kindness, compassion, sympathetic joy, and equanimity for "thousands of years."[34] All Ledi's readers would have known these stories. It is through such appeals to the colorful world of jatakas and the bodhisatta as lay practitioner that Ledi encourages laypeople to find the meditation suitable for them:

> Wise Buddhists of the Present day should try to emulate these distinguished persons of great future destiny and should select and adopt one or other of the practices for spiritual progress.[35]

In early writings, Ledi constantly invokes such characters, familiar and known since childhood for the Burmese, as exempla and guides to support his teachings. The bodhisatta path, of perfections worked on over many lifetimes, is always in the background.

Ledi on Mindfulness of Breathing

What is new is a particular stress on the practice of mindfulness, not just for monastics but also for the laity, whom Ledi saw as providing hope for the future of Buddhism:

> Consider the case of a boatman who has not mastered the art of steering of his boat, floating down the swift and strong currents of a great river, his craft filled with merchandise. During the night, he does not see the towns, havens, and anchorages that lie along

the banks. During the day, although he can see the towns, havens, and anchorages, he is unable to stop and anchor at any of them because he cannot steer his boat, and thus he drifts down to the ocean looking at those towns, havens, and anchorages with longing and admiration.[36]

This, he says, is the drifting that has occurred to beings in the infinitely long samsara, the circle of rising and falling away. It is like people who, though born Buddhist, do not practice meditation, *jhāna*, and wisdom leading to liberating insight.

Mindfulness, he teaches, is primary: it is needed for our capacity to steer through life.

Citing body mindfulness first and then the other three foundations of mindfulness, he lays particular emphasis on mindfulness of the breath according to the traditional sutta:

In the *Ānāpānassati Sutta* (M 118), also of the last fifty, it is shown how the work of mindfulness of the body and the four full absorptions of tranquillity meditation, insight meditation, development of the path, and realisation of fruition (the last two are known as "knowledge of liberation") are accomplished by the practice of mindfulness of respiration alone. It is also the custom for all Buddhas to attain supreme enlightenment through the method of mindfulness of respiration, and having attained Buddhahood, all Buddhas have continued to remain established in mindfulness of respiration without any lapse until they attain Parinibbāna.[37]

To read this, one might be surprised that his methods have been associated so deeply with new insight meditations. His understanding of the sixteen stages is largely based on traditional readings. It is worth looking at his account of them.

For the first tetrad, he takes as his first stage what is usually regarded as the preliminary in the sutta: mindfully breathing out and mindfully breathing in. For him this is a time to fix the attention firmly on the inbreath and the outbreath, by taking the tip of the nose or the upper lip as "the spot of touch."[38] He says it may take one or two hours to ensure that every breath is apprehended in this way, a measure of the attentiveness he accords to every stage of the sixteen.[39] He makes his second stage the differentiation between both long and short breaths; he suggests no alteration in the breath, but rather observation of which is which. Then, in the third stage, the meditator needs to see each breath as the entire breath: from the beginning, such as the tip of the nose, through the middle to the end, at the navel or wherever that may be. There needs to be unwavering attention. In the fourth, where the breath is made tranquil, the mind becomes much more calm and subtle, and the breath seems to disappear: he says he has known many for whom it goes completely. As will be clear from prior chapters of this book, there is not much here that is too different from the commentaries, with their varied interpretations, except for a particular emphasis on the "spot of touch" at the nose or the mouth, which Ledi takes to anchor the mind throughout.[40] This becomes key in much subsequent Burmese meditative practice. There are some innovations in his account of the progress of these stages, but he argued all were in line with ancient text and praxis.[41]

After the fourth stage of first tetrad, he suggests ways of integrating the commentarial stages of counting, following (*anubandhanā*), and settling (*ṭhapanā*), which he sees as aids to this first tetrad. Counting the breaths can be linked to his first stage, as one is simply aware of the "spot of touch." Following can be linked to the second: discerning the length of the breaths. The sign of breathing mindfulness, the counterpart *nimitta* (*paṭibhāganimitta*) described by Buddhaghosa, can then arise. The meditator can move to the settling with the third stage of this cluster, while the fourth consolidates the whole. He recommends that for these stages—experiencing the body of the breath and making it tranquil—constant effort may be needed to refine awareness and see the breath as increasingly delicate until it subsides: "After he has given his attention to counting, when the bodily disturbance has been stilled by the gradual cessation of gross inbreaths and outbreaths, then both the body and the mind become light: the physical body is as though it were ready to leap up into the air." As if to reassure his readers of traditional Buddhist appreciations of the power of joy, he adds: "I have known people whose bodies have risen about the height of four fingers' breadth in the air."[42] In this way, he says, full mindfulness of body is established, and the practitioner can attain *jhāna*.

For the second tetrad, he takes the first stage, of experiencing joy with the breath, as the first and second *jhāna*. The second stage, of experiencing happiness with each breath, is associated with the third. The third stage, of experiencing mental activities with the breath, is attributed to the fourth *jhāna*: with close (*sādhukam*) attention and wisdom, this establishes full mindfulness of feeling. He disagrees with the commentary and says this occurs at access, or neighborhood concentration (*upacāra samādhi*)—a brief but not sustained experience of *jhāna* as well as during *jhāna*. For there is, he says, also joy, happiness, and tranquility at that time.

The third tetrad, mindfulness of *citta*, he takes as attaining mastery and freedom to enter *jhānas* with flexibility and clarity, and so deepen them. "Here, also, while attention continues to be placed on outbreath and inbreath," he writes, "effort is made to completely perceive the mind with wisdom." Experiencing the mind means entering all four *jhānas*, repeatedly, so that the mind becomes clear. Gladdening the mind is focusing on the first and second *jhānas*, repeatedly; stilling the mind is when the heart and mind become very delighted by repeatedly entering the third and fourth *jhānas*. Freeing the mind is ridding the mind of all obstacles by continually entering into and emerging from *jhāna*.[43] He clearly respects and regards this and the second tetrad as important and central to mastery in *samatha* meditation.

He takes the watching of the fourth tetrad, with elements such as contemplating impermanence, as establishing mindfulness of mental objects (*dhammānupassanā-satipaṭṭhāna*): it represents the work on insight. Here again, while attention continues to be placed on outbreath and inbreath, effort is made to see letting go as overcoming unwholesome states, such as covetousness (*abhijjā*) and sorrow (*domanassa*), with wisdom. Elsewhere he vividly compares the sense of impermanence to the flickering scenes of a film—the world's media had been transformed by the arrival of cinema in the 1890s.[44]

Ledi's Innovative Emphasis on Insight

Ledi follows a classical pattern in his stress on the second and third tetrad, the cultivation of *jhānas* through the breath. He says it is essential to have control over the mind and that it can be found through *jhāna* and "making the mind extremely delighted" (*abhippamodayaṃ cittaṃ*). He regards this sequence of practice as ideal. But he now introduces a new element. For, he says, if one finds oneself unable to follow this order of practice, one may proceed to insight from the third *jhāna*. It is permissible to proceed to insight from the second *jhāna*, the first *jhāna*, or from access concentration before *jhāna* is attained, or from the following stage, or even from the counting stage after the wandering tendencies of the mind have been overcome. From any of these stages, one can move to the last tetrad, the practice of insight.[45]

This represents a big change of perspective, introducing greatly innovatory features. He does not reject *jhāna* or the miraculous powers attributed to finding the fourth. His understanding of how vipassana worked involved deep respect for *samādhi*, at that time unchallenged in Burmese Buddhism. Biographies and hagiographies of the many charismatic vipassana teachers are filled with stories of their extraordinary supernatural powers: they were believed to be able to perform great feats, such as being seen in two places at the same time. These skills, so closely related to *samatha* practice of the fourth *jhāna*, were considered part of the natural potency (*iddhi*) of the great teacher and proof of the efficacy of the path: their *vijjā*.[46] They are now, however, completely underplayed in their importance for the practitioner aiming for enlightenment.

Ledi Sayadaw's statement, that it is possible to gain enlightenment even from the basis of the first stages of the breathing mindfulness practice, seems to have had wide effects.[47] Braun notes that this is a classical path for the "dry" meditator (*sukkhavipassika*) as opposed to the "wet" way of *samatha*.[48] And, as we discussed in chapter 6, this sense of possibility is also suggested by the many paths indicated in "The Treatise on Breathing." His presentation of the last tetrad, while based on ancient sources, greatly simplifies the process, making it more accessible, as Braun notes: here, the touch of the breath indicates the earth element, its cohesion the water element, its temperature fire, and its movement air. These are aspects of *rūpa* and, hence, ultimate realities in Abhidhamma terms, whose perception allows the arising of insight.[49]

By the time Ledi composed his *Manual on Insight Meditation* (1915), addressed primarily to Europeans, his position had moved farther. Deep states of concentration are not only unnecessary but even less desirable for, importantly, those with good understanding of Abhidhamma.[50] His expertise in Abhidhamma allowed acceptance of his innovations in breathing practice and of a new "mind-science" for modern times, the practice of *jhāna* being "lower down on the scientific scale."[51] By this time, *samatha* is barely mentioned.

Ledi's manuals set a tone that continues in the inheritors of this tradition: the practice of insight is of paramount importance, for lay and monastics. Those taught by him set up groups and study classes. In Burma generally, new vipassana "hermitages" (*wipathana yeiktha*) became associated with each teacher. These centers were established solely for meditation, a new phenomenon aimed at attracting the laypeople. Each center had, as it still does now, a distinctive feature (*shu-ni*) whereby they distinguished themselves from other groups. The laity were now encouraged by the possibility of finding wisdom that would help them find happiness in this life and be reborn at the time of a future Buddha—or even find enlightenment in this life. Amid this, the new vipassana flourished among monastics and laity. Validated by new scientific comparative work, the techniques were taken to Thailand and then into the international sphere; a sense of pride in the Buddhist heritage reemerged.[52]

It is worth remembering, however, that Ledi's teachings, particularly in the early days, were firmly embedded in the storytelling, protective chants, and custom that provided the background to traditional Burmese practice.[53] He always sustained a sense of a large cosmology and a traditional understanding of levels of consciousness. For him these provided not only a map of heaven realms, spirit realms, meditative heavens, and animal kingdoms but also a way of describing the complexity of the human mind. Humans sit at the center of a large universe, with manifold lives behind them, and rebirth possible in any realm. An intimation of the presence of far higher—and far lower—states of beings and consciousness, within and without, always provides the backdrop to his teachings; chanting for such beings was core to his teachings.[54]

While not stressing the divine abidings, he assumed that extending loving-kindness in all directions means caring for those in all mental states, wherever they are. He openly attacked the beef-eating ways of the British, for instance. In "A Letter on Cows (*Nwa-myitta-sa*)," in 1885, he writes from a cow's perspective, asking why the animals who gave so much milk and support to humans should be so ruthlessly slaughtered.[55] In multiple ways, Ledi defended not only Buddhism's principles and meditative methods but its ethics too: kindness to other beings, within a sense of the vastness of the universe itself, offers the basis of his meditative path. His teaching methods were flexible and did not include the sometimes-strict programs of activities later recommended by some of his followers.

Photographs of Ledi, as those of other meditation teachers photographed at that time, look forbidding. We need to remember that most photographs of people before the 1930s show them as earnestly serious: people saw no need to smile for the camera—perhaps due to waiting for equipment to be set up and during the long exposure needed! It is worth quoting what was noted about him by a British colonial officer: that his fame derived "from a large charity, a thorough knowledge of human nature, a delightful sense of humour and a fine voice. His effortless eloquence held audiences rapt."[56]

Largely in response to constant requests from others, Ledi wrote long expositions and treatises constantly, rapidly, and without error. He apparently used up hundreds of highly sharpened pencils on a daily basis. He went blind at seventy-three, probably the result of too much reading and writing in poor light. He responded by spending more time in meditation, in caves by the Chindwin River, and teaching others. He died in 1923.

Ledi Sayadaw acted as a mediator between different worlds: the colonial and the old Burmese monarchies; laity and monastics; traditional interpretations and modern; the Buddha's teaching and the belief that Buddhism was in decline. He thought—correctly, as it turned out—that the sheer beauty and logic of Abhidhamma made it one of Buddhism's strongest weapons, both within Burma and outside it. In a long poem, *Paramattha Sankhitta*, he condensed the whole of the Abhidhamma into 690 verses. Printed in 1904, its run was 50,000 copies; it was soon reprinted. Thousands of study groups were set up throughout Burma for laypeople; Abhidhamma discussion flourished in the Burmese temples and tea shops.

That Abhidhamma still exercises such a lay appeal to this day in the regions, despite all troubles, is in part a result of Ledi's efforts. Abhidhamma understanding informs not only his but most Burmese meditation teachings. It describes the constant flow of mental states interacting with the physical, itself subject to constant change. It assumes a constant, ever-moving impingement of mind and bodily presence, all the time, making it the most natural tool for investigating meditation: the breath lies at the area of touch between the two. Ledi's practice methods became as successful as his beloved Abhidhamma and were eagerly adopted by the laity. The inheritors of his ways of teaching include lay teachers Saya Thetgyi, Sayagyi U Ba Khin, and Goenka, discussed in chapter 15.

In the next chapter, we shall look at some of the great diversity that arose in Burmese meditation, much of it attributable to Ledi Sayadaw's work and meditative teachings.

CHAPTER 14

Myanmar, Part Two

Five Modern Teachers and the Seeds of Global Breathing Mindfulness

Other teachers, from very diverse backgrounds, also contributed to the defense of Buddhism and the promotion of new ways in Myanmar. We start to see the development of yet more, often highly simplified, insight methods, radical reinterpretations of traditional meditation practice, and a movement toward the assumption that the laity can and should also practice meditation. Both lay and monastics could think about attaining arhatship, "in this very life."

U Nārada (Mingun Sayadaw) (1869–1954)

U Nārada is often credited with establishing the new vipassana methods in their simpler and more direct form: most modern insight teachers look to him or to Ledi Sayadaw as their root teacher.[1] Like Ledi's, U Nārada's roots were steeped in traditional Burmese practice. He was, apparently, taught new direct methods by Aletawya Sayadaw, whom he found in the Sagaing Hills, after finding that few teachers in Myanmar focused on mindfulness. Aletawya is said to have told U Nārada to stick to the foundations of mindfulness as taught by the Buddha. Venerable Nyanaponika Thera also describes a revelatory encounter U Nārada had with a teacher, possibly the same figure, who taught him the four foundations of mindfulness as providing the whole path.[2] Such lines of meditation teachers are wonderfully complex and cross-connected.[3] They also offer surprising genealogies. Aletawya's teacher was Theelon Sayadaw, whose own miraculous conversion to a full *samatha* meditative path, on the basis of seeing Kingtawya Sayadaw, was discussed in the last chapter.

Nyanaponika credits U Nārada with developing the Burmese *satipaṭṭhāna* method, but, he is careful to point out, this is only because "it was in Burma that the practice of that ancient Way had been so ably and energetically revived."[4] After finding his inspiration, he applied great investigation and vigor, and, from energetically following the sutta, "he finally came to understand its salient features. He had found what he was searching for: a clear-cut and effective way of training the mind for highest realization."[5] He is now known primarily for teaching Mahāsi Sayadaw, perhaps the most renowned teacher of the insight movement, whose life and teachings are detailed later in this chapter. Houtman suggests that the center U Nārada founded in Myou Hla in 1911 could be the oldest Wipathana (vipassana) center.[6] He also translated *The Compendium of Abhidhamma* (*Abhidhammatthasaṅgaha*), the twelfth-century Pāli distillation of Abhidhamma principle, which remains the most widely used Abhidhamma manual to this day.

Sunlun Sayadaw Ven. U Kavi (1878–1952)

As noted in the prior chapter, one of the most salient characteristics of modern Burmese Buddhist reform was that laypeople were being encouraged to try meditation. A notable example of success in this was Sunlun Sayadaw, a nonliterate farmer who was married and had four children. Having received little teaching, he found his way to enlightenment on the basis of breathing mindfulness, practicing under a tree in the fields where he worked. The manner of his progress shows a particularly Burmese approach to the experience of the breath, articulated within the frame of references of Abhidhamma. Abhidhamma study had become so predominant that its terms had seeped into popular discourse and, one imagines, became widely known.

His autodidactic approach to meditation notwithstanding, Sunlun did acknowledge Ledi Sayadaw's teachings as having a great effect on his understanding of breathing mindfulness and the path to insight.[7] He had initially found out about meditation from a mill clerk at the offering of a meal (*dāna*) to monks. Concerned about his own lack of education, Sunlun was reassured that he could simply pay attention to the contact of the breath and was told to practice mindfulness of the inbreath and outbreath. He added "noting" to this exercise, saying internally "breathing in" and "breathing out." A friend told him, however, that this was insufficient; he should now be aware of the physical touch (*phassa*) of the breath at all times and guard it with mindfulness. He added a yet further element: scrutiny of the sense-consciousness that arises on the basis of each moment of touch. He also tried to establish constant mindfulness of the impingement of sense-objects in his daily life. This was practiced with an unceasing background awareness of the breath, even when the feelings that arose through such energetic practice were very painful.

In his sitting meditation, the breath *nimitta* arose, taking various forms. He then gained access to heavenly realms—an articulation of the movement to the *jhānas* found throughout South and Southeast Asia—and apparently developed the divine eye (*dibbacakka*), one of the six higher knowledges (*abhiññā*), enabling him to see beings in higher realms. Eventually, through continued practice, he entered on stages of path, attaining enlightenment after becoming a novice monk in 1920. His Burmese hagiography says that, because of his attainments, he could see beings from those in the lowest hells up to the highest heavens and gain insights into the past and future.[8]

Theinngu Sayadaw Ven. U Ukkaṭṭha (1913–1973) also entered monkhood in his forties, greatly influenced by Sunlun's teachings. Another nonliterate meditator, he had married four times while involved in a career punctuated by criminal activity and prison sentences. Shocked by being stabbed during burgling a house, he was gripped with urgency (*saṃvega*). On the encouragement of one of his ex-wives, he began to practice meditation. He experimented with short, middle-length, and long breaths constantly, interspersed with recollection of the Buddha, with practices that continued all day. He took time off just for eating and sleeping. Eventually, after ordaining as a monk, he too was said to become enlightened.[9]

The methods both teachers taught are remarkable: rapid, rhythmic, short breathing while focusing on intense and often unpleasant bodily sensations (*vedanā*) to produce concentration and mindfulness. Their practice is unusual, perhaps, for its taking of what could be called the second stage of the sixteen in The Sutta on Breathing Mindfulness, the short breath, and using it in a particularly energetic form as a basis for the meditation. Meditation systems associated with training the breath tend to require and teach inbuilt mechanisms to ensure that the practice does not go out of balance. The rough, short breath serves that function in these methods; by its very obviousness it ensures that the meditator does not slip into *bhavaṅga*, the passive state of consciousness that, according to the Abhidhamma, arises during sleep and at the end, momentarily, of all thought processes. The short breaths ensure mindfulness of body to prevent this passive state from becoming too dominant.[10]

Kornfield spent three months learning the Sunlun method in the 1970s and describes the breathing like this:

Commence by inhaling. It will be noticed that the breath touches the nostril tip or upper lip. Be keenly mindful of the touch of breath. With mindfulness vigilantly maintained, breathe strongly, firmly and rapidly.... Breathe in air attentively and fully as though water were being drawn into a syringe. Exhale sharply. Full and hard drawing-in of breath helps to establish concentration rapidly. ... When these two [i.e. inhalation and exhalation] are balanced, the touch will be continuous. When they are balanced, the meditator will have reached the stage of smooth, effortless, self-compelled rhythmic breathing.[11]

Both teachers announced their own attainments on stages of the path, a highly unusual practice in Burma, as it was throughout South and Southeast Asia. In Myanmar, such claims are subjected to rigorous and potentially punitive scrutiny: an unsuccessful defense could mean that one's teachings would be banned.[12] It is possible they felt that their innovatory methods, lack of literacy, and inexperience in conventional monastic training made them potential targets of criticism.[13] Their credentials were approved, however, and passed all examinations for textual corroboration. Sunlun and Theinngu's methods continue to be popular in Myanmar.

Webu Sayadaw (1896–1977)

One of the most influential of the new Burmese teachers was Webu Sayadaw. Rumored to be an arhat, he was apparently a hardline and determined teacher. After ordaining at the age of twenty in Mandalay, near where he had grown up in Sagaing, he left his monastery at twenty-seven, after completing his preliminary training. He devoted himself to practice in solitude for four years, then was asked to teach the techniques that supposedly offer a direct method to enlightenment. It was said that he did not sleep at all, abiding always in his awareness of the meditation object. He spent most of the life in the woods, caves, and temples of the Sagaing region, but he did visit Rangoon and Southern Myanmar to impart his teachings. U Hte Hlain, who collected many of Webu's discourses, noted that several points recur frequently in them: ethical behavior, generosity (*dāna*) with skillful volition, awareness of the law of karma, and an aspiration, not to worldly happiness, but only to nirvana. Webu rarely mentioned calm (*samatha*), seeing it as arising in time as a possible by-product.[14]

Breathing mindfulness was his core practice—a short cut, he said, to the goal of arhatship.[15] He took The Sutta on Breathing Mindfulness as his basic text, also with a primary focus on the area in the nostrils where stream of air goes in and out—a common and possibly particularly Burmese reading of "arousing mindfulness in front of the face/mouth." He did not speak English and did not travel much from his native regions. He taught with eloquence and force, using rigorous challenges to impress the practicality of the new methods. In him we start to see the somewhat ascetic style characteristic of many subsequent twentieth-century vipassana teachers. In addition, he does not condone the tacit encouragement to a happy lay life suggested by the many jataka tales and by Ledi, whose examples tend to be of laypeople who renounce at the end of their lives. By contrast, Webu sees urgency and a need to strive for enlightenment in this lifetime as the most pressing imperative for anyone, at any age. Despite this austerity, his teachings are steeped in the narrative literature and spacious cosmology of the canon and commentaries. These form an essential component in his understandings, implying an ethos of loving-kindness toward all beings.[16] His starting point, as that of all the other teachers in this chapter, was *sīla*—the practice of ethical mindfulness and the happiness of a mind free from trouble.

Here is an example of Webu's teachings, from a booklet entitled *What Really Matters*. He stresses the importance of morality in softening the approach to meditation, so the mind then loses harshness. A quietened mind (*nāma*) can then start to know matter (*rūpa*); the practitioner will see matter arising and dissolving in billions of split seconds, all the time, as higher wisdom (*adhipaññā*) develops. The breath, he says, is always evident as the touch of air in or around the "sensitive matter" of the nostrils that register it. Buddhaghosa's emphasis on attentiveness to this area (or the mouth for those who cannot breathe through the nose) had been used to steady calm, leading to *jhāna*. Here, it brings some focus but becomes primarily the site for developing penetrative wisdom:

In this process, the entities touching are matter and the entity knowing the touch is mind. So do not go around asking others about mind and matter; observe your breathing and you will find out about them for yourselves.

When the air comes in, it will touch. When the air goes out, it will touch. If you know this touch continuously, then greed (*lobha*), aversion (*dosa*), and delusion (*moha*) do not have the opportunity to arise, and the fires of these defilements will subside.

You cannot know the touch of air before it actually occurs. After it has gone, you cannot know it anymore. Only while the air moves in or out can you feel the sensation of touch. This we call the present moment.

While we feel the touch of air, we know that there is only mind and matter. We know for ourselves that there is no "I," no other people, no man and woman, and we realize for ourselves that what the Buddha said is true indeed. We do not need to ask others. While we know the in-breath and out-breath, there is no "I" or self.

When we know this, our view is pure; it is right view. We know in that moment that there is nothing but *nāma* and *rūpa*, mind and matter. We also know that mind and matter are two different entities. If we thus know how to distinguish between mind and matter, we have attained to the analytical knowledge of mind and matter (*nāma-rūpaparicched-ñ*).[17]

Webu's question-and-answer sessions seemed designed to shock meditators from complacency: he taught that there was no excuse for a lack of meditation, even for a busy layperson. Through unrelenting cross-questioning, an abrasively challenging style characteristic of some insight teachers, he drove his teachings home. This style is also found in some early Pāli discourses, where it suits the person.[18] He insistently asks one layperson whether they can be aware of their breath now, at the tip of the nose. If so, why not at all times? His repeated confrontations provoke insight: there would be no chance for hindrances to arise, and the creation of the "I" will be seen. He concludes, "So, make a strong effort and keep your attention there."[19]

Concentration, he says, comes naturally from breathing mindfulness—and this will lead to insight.[20] Amid this desire for purity and simplicity of practice, Webu uses sutta, Abhidhamma, and the rich story traditions of Myanmar to impress his teachings: the stories of the universal monarch, his symbolic treasures, and his renunciation are cited as parables for developing the mind.[21]

Webu's reputation in Myanmar was high. He was influential in the new development of lay teaching, discussed further in the next chapter. He urged the layman U Ba Khin to teach, surprised that he had acquired such deep experience in vipassana, and paid respects to Mother Sayamagyi (Mya Thwin), his assistant.[22] He also apparently made a deep impression on S. N. Goenka, who also brought insight methods to an international audience.[23]

Mahāsi Sayadaw (1904–1982)

A very different orientation is presented by another major teacher in this new movement, Mahāsi Sayadaw, whose methods have been one of the most influential in the movement of Buddhist meditative practice into the international sphere. Mahāsi was born in 1904 in Seikkhun village in Upper Myanmar and took the ordination name of Sobhana. After a great deal of study, he went to the Sagaing Hills to practice with U Nārada (Mingun Sayadaw), where he developed a particular interest in the *Satipaṭṭhāna-sutta* and insight teachings. The methods for which he became famous appear to be attributable to U Nārada's teachings.[24] A great scholar of Abhidhamma, Mahāsi was a questioner and editor at the great Sixth Buddhist Council held in Rangoon in 1954.[25]

Mahāsi saw no need for concentration states, apart from momentary concentration (*khaṇika samādhi*), which is briefer than the approach (*upacāra*) concentration described by Buddhaghosa.[26] His great meditation manual, *Manual of Insight*, is based on the seven stages of purification that give the underlying structure of *The Path of Purification*. In that work, breathing mindfulness is one of the forty objects of meditation listed under the second stage, the purification of mind, or heart (*citta*). In his corresponding section, however, Mahāsi says that *jhāna* and even approach concentration are not necessary. He cites a number of sources to explain this, saying that he teaches the path of one who has insight as his vehicle.[27]

For the second stage, after the purification of ethical behavior (*sīla*), the meditator notices the experience of touch or impingement at the six sense doors, contemplating the relationship between mind and matter. At the abdomen, the meditator notices the bodily motion that has breathing as its condition, seeing its rise and expansion and its fall and contraction. The abdomen is more integrated into bodily movement than the nostrils, and hence ensures a constant sense of transience. This motion should be noted as "rising" and "falling." Using standard Abhidhamma categories, he says that the stiffening in the abdomen shows air's characteristic of supporting, the vibrating shows its essential function as movement, and its pushing and pulling shows its impelling nature. The meditator then starts to see matter (*rūpa*) and sees the mind's relationship to that. From there, they will be able to see their impermanence, liability to suffering, and nonself. Thoughts and desires will arise as these processes are observed; they should simply return to the rise and fall of the abdomen, the basic object of mindfulness.[28]

Mahāsi has also become famous for his particular use of observation, or noting (*sallakkhaṇa*), as a key feature of this method.[29] Every time an event arises, it is noticed and labeled: "breathing, " "sitting," "moving," "thinking," "stretching the hand." Concepts and thinking are bypassed, so events are seen just as they are, without interference (*yathābhūtaṃ*). The techniques can sound cold, but practitioners say those who are patient find that, when the labeling is itself dropped, the result is not less feeling but much more. If the process of abandoning labeling is delayed as long as possible, the practice can then lead to greater and more deeply established peace. It is said that the usual verbal "editing" of the mind, which create such a barrier between any event in our experience itself and our perception of it, have been removed.[30]

Like U Nārada, Mahāsi was taught by Aletawya Sayadaw, a student of Theelon. His methods were intensive and rigorous, setting a pattern followed by many Mahāsi schools to this day. Retreats involved long periods of meditation and the application of exercises for the mind as one goes about activities during the day. When he died in 1982 following a massive stroke, thousands of devotees braved the torrential monsoon rains to pay their last respects. His teachings have proved durable; by 2011 there were 564 Mahāsi meditation centers in Myanmar.[31]

Mahāsi's methods do not offer a full breathing mindfulness system and make no claims to. By raising and focusing mindfulness around the point at the abdomen, the practitioner pays less attention to the passage and experience of the whole breath. His methods have nonetheless usually been associated with breathing practice and exercised a radical influence on the transmission of Buddhist practice to the West. Indeed, Mahāsi's heritage has been far-reaching. His student U Paṇḍita Sayadaw (1921–2016) became the chief teacher at the Mahāsi Meditation Center after Mahāsi's death, and U Paṇḍita's book *In This Very Life* is regarded as an authoritative exposition of his method.

In 1953 the Mahāsi rise-and-fall (*yup no phong no*) method was introduced to Wat Mahathat, the main insight monastery in Bangkok, and actively promoted.[32] It is now the most widely practiced insight method in Thailand. There, it sometimes accompanies the view that regards the *Satipaṭṭhāna-sutta* as a "pure" vipassana text, with its techniques offering the sole way to awakening.[33] One common understanding is that *jhāna* predated the Buddha but did not represent the kernel of Buddhist teaching. While few modern scholars or practitioners now subscribe to these assumptions, the preeminence of the sutta is now widespread, though usually without an accompanying rejection of *samatha*.

Mahāsi's teachings were famously transported to the West by Nyanaponika Thera, largely via his book *The Heart of Buddhist Meditation*. Nyanaponika called the method "bare attention," a description that led, in the late twentieth century, to Jon Kabat-Zinn's understanding of mindfulness as "nonjudgmental awareness." Mahāsi's teachings have been adopted worldwide, and many American teachers, such as Sharon Salzburg, Jack Kornfield, and Joseph Goldstein, were taught at some time by him.

Pa Auk Sayadaw (1934–)

The abbot of Pa Auk monastery, in the south in Moulmein, Pa Auk Sayadaw, or Bhaddanta Āciṇṇa, prefers not to give biographical information about himself but rather to focus on his method. We know he trained with Mahāsi and U Paṇḍita. His style—of teaching a full range of canonical *jhāna* practice, where possible, before insight—appears to be the one school of *samatha* within Myanmar. It has, however, proved to be an internationally successful series of techniques. Spending time with other teachers, he developed these "Pa Auk methods." These are characterized by a training in the *jhānas* and formless meditations, for those who are able. Those who find them difficult are encouraged to pursue insight practice through the four elements first.

The breath is a core practice in this teaching, with the orientation and style apparently influenced by Burmese teachings. The tip of the nose, which we see so often in Burmese breathing practices, is considered particularly crucial as the *ānāpāna* spot; the movement through to vipassana is stressed, however, only when the *jhānas* become stable.[34] All aspects of the path are represented, and *samatha* is taught first. He places particular attention on the first four stages of The Sutta on Breathing Mindfulness, weaving each stage with the others to ensure facility and mastery amongst practitioners: so a consciously chosen long breath is applied to experiencing the body and to making the breath tranquil, and a consciously chosen short breath is likewise applied to these stages. Throughout this method, the interweaving and interrelatedness of individual stages of meditation and insight with others are emphasized.[35] Pa Auk draws greatly on traditional teachings. Like some other Burmese teachers, he regards the vision required to see the four elements and the microscopic, evanescent energy fields of matter (*kalāpas*) after the *samatha* practice as the "divine eye" (*dibbacakka*). This is one of the higher psychic knowledges (*abhiññās*) described in The Sutta on the Fruits of Recluseship as arising after the fourth *jhāna*. He terms such skills "supernormal" and not "supernatural," as they are natural capacities found through meditation.[36] The divine abidings are also seen as crucial "protectors" for insight.[37]

Pa Auk systems are practiced in many monasteries throughout Southeast Asia. He has been accorded numerous honors in Myanmar in recognition of his teachings, and his is the most popular single system within Myanmar. International teachers have successfully introduced these methods to the West. Stephen Snyder and Tina Rasmussen were trained in his methods, and their book, *Practicing Jhānas*, communicates some particular features. Shaila Catherine also teaches his style of meditation and has written about these teachings.[38] These teachers have all been accredited by Pa Auk.

Myanmar still has great variety of practices, now almost entirely taught with a vipassana orientation. The breath is sometimes not the main object, but it is a crucial preliminary. The methods devised by Mogok Sayadaw (1899–1962), for instance, use awareness of the breath as a basis for moving on to Abhidhammic analysis, which is used as a tool to examine the arising and falling of mental states.[39]

Burmese and Thai Developments of Modern Breathing Mindfulness

Myanmar was in a very different situation from Thailand, which was never colonized. Thai monastic reforms perhaps arose, in part, in an attempt to ensure this did not happen, and attitudes to meditations involving the breath were linked to cultural changes and history, to which colonialism had a more indirect but meaningful relationship. Burmese teachers, by contrast, operated in a country that had lost political autonomy, and they saw their emergent traditions as ways of preventing Buddhism from falling into a decline. The urgent imperative of Burmese Buddhism's survival seemed dependent on promoting a dynamic new approach. Radically transformed approaches to mindfulness and meditation on the breath, to be undertaken by the laity as well as monastics, were at the center of a project to rescue Buddhism.

It would not be fanciful to say that the resultant stress on breathing mindfulness—in a highly modified form—as well as a new focus on a physical location of the breath's impact on the body offered a turning point in the evolution of the practice of meditation. These various techniques eventually introduced the international community to a simplified genus of breathing mindfulness, both within Buddhism and, later, within secular, clinical settings. Their long-term impact might have surprised those who initially taught these methods: through the transmission of such practices, among others, by various teachers in the late twentieth century, the world started to recognize that the psychological state could be transformed by mindfulness of the breath and, sometimes, stillness within it.

Buddhaghosa had observed that the breath is the only meditation object experienced purely through touch.[40] Upatissa and Buddhaghosa describe the "touching" stage, one stage of *samatha* breathing mindfulness, as focusing on the impact of the breath on the nose or upper lip to arouse calm and unification.[41] Burmese teachers adapted this understanding, taking as their preliminary focus the impact of the breath on one bodily base. In a breathing practice it not only offers a means of finding calm but also gives the most effective means of experiencing the impingement of matter (*rūpa*): through the breath the mind can know the four elements, and hence find insight.

Emphasis on the *ānāpāna* spot, and its adoption as the root to a speedy path, provides a direct point for transformation. Whichever *ānāpāna* spot was taught—the nose or upper lip, the abdomen—a sense of simplicity and accessibility for everyone was preparing the way for international dissemination. All the modern Burmese methods suggested rapid and apparently immediate routes to enlightenment. Mahāsi, through his stress on the rise and fall of the abdomen, offered this through a somewhat different route, introducing a sense of mindfulness, interpreted as nonjudgmental awareness, as a possible constant in anyone's life.

The Heritage of Traditional Buddhisms

In this chapter we have explored the movement that transformed modern Buddhist meditative practice. As I hope is clear, the vipassana traditions developed in a culture steeped in practices, chants, stories, and rituals that still remain a vibrant background in Burmese Buddhism. While some had misgivings about Buddhist teachings about supernormal powers, for instance, the great insight teachers appreciated and worked with their Burmese cultural landscape: both Mahāsi and Ledi speak of *weikzas*, the wizards, with positive associations, integrating their power (*vijjā*) into their very articulation of the noble vipassana wisdom (*ariya weizzā*) to be found through insight and the breath.[42] Sayadaw U Uttamasara (d. 1995), said to be a modern *weikza* practitioner, commented:

> I have heard some criticize [*samatha*'s] value contemptuously. The Buddhas-to-be have all fulfilled the ten kinds of *pāramī* (perfections) by means of practicing *samatha* meditation in their past lives. Passing through the earth and flying in space, and some different kinds of miraculous powers are the outcomes of practicing *samatha* meditation. Therefore, you should regard it as vitally important, and should not look down on it.[43]

Observations made by Scott (Shway Yoe) in 1861 on the resilience of Burmese Buddhism were vindicated. Noting the way that so many young men pass through monastic training, he said, "As long as the men of the country pass through the kyaungs, the teachings of the Western missionaries can have but little power to shake the power of Buddhism over the people."[44] The Burmese resisted all attempts by the British to use the many monasteries for secular purposes, as well as all attempts at secularization within monastic orders.[45]

The forests of remote regions provided a setting for many of the breathing mindfulness methods discussed earlier in this book. In Myanmar, we can look particularly to caves to sense the essence of the way the insight movement took its roots. The Burmese teachers discussed here all felt they were in some way setting upright a lamp that had been overturned, lighting up the gloom of the darkness around. They saw themselves primarily as restorers rather than innovators, though they often explored teaching new methods to achieve this. They all saw themselves as teaching within the eightfold path, and many, particularly in the early days, taught a great deal of calm meditation as well as insight.

Stories, myths, fables from the suttas, chanting, the practice of loving-kindness, and a sense of community, with temples as hubs whose influence radiate outward in villages and towns, all contribute to the background. Insight is a light felt to illuminate, not blot out, this vibrant imaginative and emotional landscape. This cosmology places the human mind within a vast temporal and spatial perspective. There is, as in other Theravada countries, an understanding that higher states of mind may accompany visits from gods of corresponding heavens and, at the attainment of the path, past arahats and Buddhas. Burmese Buddhist folklore, symbolic understandings, and other forms of collective and solitary practice all contribute to meditative development. Awareness of many realms, the importance of generosity and kindness over many lives, and the significance of one moment, the present, in a vast and even measureless landscape, involves a capacious and larger mindfulness. It is an embracing, rather than a rejection, of the possibilities of the mind for alertness, compassion, equanimity, and creative adaptation to the moment.[46] Ethics, generosity, and the happiness arising from the eightfold path are central to this perspective.

It is helpful to remember these roots and this vitally fertile background as we consider the way the international community has embraced the insight paths, sometimes rejecting outright elements long regarded as core to a meditation practice that is well rooted. This can cause real problems: there is a risk a kind of deracination, as subtle psychologies of interdependence and care—the soil that nourishes the meditations—are not always considered important.[47]

The Burmese still love the *Paṭṭhāna*, the Abhidhamma interweaving pattern of causal relations. Their depictions on a twenty-four petal flower can be found everywhere: in leading in rose-like windows in temples, in decorations, in festive mandalas made of kyat notes, in flower arrangements, and in protective mascots and flags. Lay chanting groups enjoy chanting the whole *Paṭṭhāna* chant, which takes forty-five minutes; they can be heard at the sacred sites at Bagan and Mount Kyat. A few years ago, I had to work hard to distract the attention of a young man behind the counter at a perfumery in the small airport in Shan state. He was just so busy trying to learn his *Paṭṭhana* chant, he had not noticed a new customer. His face lit up as he explained it to me! It is in accordance with the principles of this system, of multiple causes and currents influencing any new events, that the great changes in Burmese Buddhism are best understood.

"Colonial discourse represents cultural intersections as a linear process," comments art historian Partha Mitter. "It's like the waterfall, ideas forever flowing downward from the West to the Rest, even though multidirectional flows of cultures have been a known fact of history. Suppose we look at such encounters as a product of reciprocity?"[48] Certainly colonialism played a major part in the Burmese Buddhist developments discussed here, but one should not underestimate local developments or the fact that modernity was never a one-way traffic. New printing presses, increased international contact, and a shift toward scientific rationalism as a worldwide mood, as well as unconnected reassessments of the role of insight in local understandings of Buddhism, were powerful factors. There were complex contributory crosscurrents. Many elements that some international Buddhist teachers underplay now, such as the doctrine of multiple rebirths, karma operating over many lives, contact with spirits from other realms, and an acknowledgment of higher powers, were tenets taken for granted by the vipassana innovators. Features of Buddhism often sidelined now were in early days those that exercised the *most* appeal, both to Burmese Buddhists and to contemporary Westerners.

British rule was oppressive and often unthinking. Ironically, however, a fascination for Indic philosophies also ensured the dissemination of Buddhism and Indic principles worldwide, laying foundations for greater acceptance in the West. The same fissures in society that fostered imperialism from the 1880s also generated among Westerners, at all levels of society, a search for meaning, deeper understandings of psychology, and new intellectual inspiration. Indic religions and Buddhism made a significant, often unacknowledged, impact on late nineteenth- and early twentieth-century philosophy, culture, science, and religious understanding.[49]

Wider literacy and frequent travel to then colonial regions affected all classes in the UK, who were often beguiled by cultures that offered so much that had been lost, unrecognized, or unknown at home. The situation is complex, involving perceptions of the superiority of "mind-training," and the occasional devaluation of traditional understandings of the interconnectedness of mind and body.[50] From the 1880s, however, an interest in the occult, supernormal powers, esotericism, and magic was attracting many in Europe, the United States, and the UK to Indic and Asian religions, philosophies, and practices, manifesting itself in highly diverse ways, from fiction to popular speculation. An American, Colonel Olcott (1832–1907), the first president of the Theosophical Society, became a Buddhist. Helena Blavatsky, author of *Isis Unveiled: A Master-Key to the Mysteries of Ancient and Modern Science and Theology* (1877), ensured that Buddhism and Indic religions were popularly known around the world.[51]

For many in the international community, elements such as rebirth and the exercise of psychic power lay as much behind Buddhism's appeal as its apparently rationalist credentials, however selective their interpretation of such phenomena.[52] This had immediate effect: Ānanda Metteyya (1872–1923), the British-born Charles Henry Allen Bennett, took higher ordination in Burma in 1902. He worked industriously to create a better understanding of Buddhism in England, as well as giving public talks in Asia. At one time a member of the magical lodge the Golden Dawn, he was deeply interested in higher powers, such as awareness of the minds of others, and the nature of rebirth, seeing such phenomena as integral to Buddhist understanding and compassion for other beings.[53] At that period, it appears that it did not occur to many involved, lay or monastic, Asian or Western, to exclude the rich background of psychic and meditative exploration that still characterized Theravada practice: that only came later, and gradually.

Amid such interchanges, it was, however, the dedicated meditation teachers who provided what is known, in Abhidhamma terms, as the strong support (*upanissaya*) for the new methods of meditation.[54] In Abhidhamma, a "strong support" can be a teacher, food, or environment: something that acts as a catalyst for change. In Myanmar itself, these teachers ensured that the methods, while apparently sometimes simple in formulation, were contextualized and validated within the traditional teachings of sutta, Abhidamma, and commentary, even by those who ostensibly downplayed theory.[55] The learning, recitation, and understanding of Abhidhamma, through chant and personal investigation, are all seen as tools to help and invite meditative exploration; directly experiential investigation is then framed in Abhidhamma terms.

It is also worth considering how these teachers taught, for crucial to the emergence of these techniques were the manner and atmosphere in which teachings were given. Some methods are hard-hitting, and some meditative regimes were strict and even "boot camp" style. Many laypeople wanted short periods of strong discipline, as well as immediacy. But ethical courtesies, as in taking the refuges and precepts, chanting, the recitation of texts, generosity, offering food for monastics (*dāna*), recollection of the Buddha, and loving-kindness practice, were also, at that time, considered essential accompanying practices (*bhāvanā*) to balance both insight and calm. While some international meditation schools reject this background, this sense continued in Myanmar: teachings on insight are accompanied by many others—on loving-kindness, ethics, and walking practice.[56]

The situation in Myanmar is deeply troubled now, but the ethos survives, somehow, in some places. A Burmese practitioner who follows one of the apparently more austere styles I've described noted to me the generous atmosphere and the happy, animated chaos in the kitchens and meeting places of the monastery where she learns meditation. She said, "I wish people could see that. The great insight teachers were like our Sayadaw, always looking for ways to help their community!" Kingtawya Sayadaw, the compassionate teacher with apparently *weikza* powers who opened the last chapter, stressed, like other traditional Buddhist teachers, constant attentiveness to the person who is being taught:

> Just like a carpenter makes string measurement in order to make a hole, it can only be normal measurement. However, when he tries to drill a hole practically, there will be crook, straight, shallow or deep, and not follow the exact measurement. Just like the carpenter cannot drill without taking the measurement and so do the Buddha's discourses. There is nothing wrong in the discourse, but the preaching may vary according to the disposition or nature of the listener.[57]

These are some of the many, often overlooked elements in accounts of how the greatly adaptive nineteenth- and twentieth-century Burmese teachers meditated and taught both laity and monastics.

The emergence of the vipassana movement can be seen as a great exercise in ensuring that a number of carpenters, in highly various ways, fitted Buddhist teachings to the needs of their meditators and modern times. Vipassana breathing methods in the late twentieth century became associated with a lessened interest in ritual, a focus on enlightenment in this lifetime, a sense of immediacy, and what was perceived as a scientific worldview. More laypeople saw meditation as something they could try; those in the West with secular inclinations could relate to the new techniques. But the perspective of helping others over many lifetimes, the cultivation of the generosity, awe at the power of the mind in an interdependent universe, and the restorative *jhāna* meditations—all so central to traditional Buddhism—often dropped away as Buddhism traveled. Adaptation was essential, but I do not think it occurred to these early proponents actively to reject, as some do now, so many features that had given the soil for meditation and its associated practices to flourish.

CHAPTER 15

Myanmar's New
Meditations Abroad

U Ba Khin and S. N. Goenka

The Buddha once taught a meditator, Meghiya, who decided to go it alone. He set off to the woods to meditate and got into deep trouble, with thoughts racing and hindrances burgeoning everywhere. Learning the hard way how the wandering thoughts and conflict can creep into all meditations when practiced without guidance, he returned. The Buddha taught him breathing mindfulness among other supporting practices, and Meghiya developed his meditation well.[1]

Care and attentiveness to the whole person are also the hallmark of traditional Buddhist meditative teaching. These principles, however faultily they may have been applied historically, are indicated clearly by the Buddha in suttas about the importance of guidance in learning meditation and the role of the good friend in helping this.[2] All meditators can and do lose their way; help is needed throughout the process of undertaking a breathing mindfulness practice.

This sense of friendly interest in needs is clearly evident in the way techniques for watching the breath moved to the West and the international sphere from the early 1900s. Non-Buddhist countries and practitioners were involved, and so the pioneers had a difficult job: many people disliked religious overtones and wanted "just" a technique. Some notable teachers addressed these barriers with resourcefulness and considerable care.

In this and the next two chapters, we will look at several figures who have taken varied forms or adaptations of breathing mindfulness to the West. In this chapter, we explore two from Burma, now known as Myanmar.

Sayagyi U Ba Khin (1899–1971)

Alertness to individual needs is also clear from accounts given by twentieth-century Western students of U Ba Khin, one of the first Southeast Asians to look directly to the West. One, an American named John Coleman (1930–2012), was among those who took up meditation after being drawn to find meditation teachers in the East who would give them guidance and training. Coleman toured Asia looking for guidance in the 1960s after working, improbably, as an agent for the CIA. He stayed with many teachers to try and find wisdom and peace. It was the lay teacher U Ba Khin, however—whom Coleman described as a "powerhouse of energy," despite U Ba Khin's then being well into his seventies—who made the deepest impression.[3]

U Ba Khin had noticed and responded to Coleman's difficulties in finding stillness in practice during one of his intensive retreats. Coleman, in his keenness, had been too enthusiastic in his note taking and had "missed the whole object of the exercise." Khin tried, through sideways means, to bring him down to earth. While Coleman also consulted many great Buddhist figures in other traditions, he returned to Khin, making a special visit to Rangoon to try again. U Ba Khin clearly spent a great deal of time with him in discussion; Coleman again notes his boundless energy, and willingness to engage.[4] In conversation before the course, Khin told him that, when one finds freedom, "one is entrusted with the energy and efficiency in which compassion and spontaneity compel us to help others."[5] This time, Coleman's attitude to his meditation retreat was different; he dropped attachment to goals and results. He saw his meditation and, by implication, no-self from an entirely new and revelatory perspective: it was not just about him. He kept to his practice and found great calm, but also, through vipassana, experienced "the wild dance of electrons producing a warm glow in my hand, and the same effect was achieved on each part of my person in turn."[6] His whole body started to burn in this dance, with *dukkha* manifest in every particle. With increasing frustration he realized he just could not stop it; his wanting to was making it even more intense. Suddenly, "like a bolt of lightning," he let go. All that remained was quiet: "it was not pleasure as we understand the word: joy comes nearer to expressing the experience."[7] He had frequent private discussions with Khin and received warm approbation for his safe delivery from unhappiness; later, Coleman was asked by Khin to teach in the West.

Khin's own life and teaching were in many ways remarkable.[8] He was born in Rangoon, Burma, during colonial rule. He worked in an accounts office, passing his Accounts Service exam in 1926. When then-Burma was separated administratively from India in 1937, he became the first special office superintendent. That year he met a student of Saya Thetgyi, the lay teacher prized by Ledi Sayadaw, who initiated him in insight methods. He started learning meditation, and by 1941 he was proficient. Webu Sayadaw, discussed in the last chapter, urged him to teach. When Burma became independent again in 1948, he became the first accountant general and at one time was head of four government departments. He started teaching to colleagues in that office, as well as offering vipassana instruction at the International Meditation Centre in Rangoon (Yangon). He was active in the Sixth Buddhist Council, held from 1954 to 1956, in the caves near Rangoon.

Although Khin was never able to travel to the West, he was determined that the methods he taught should have an international reception, and so he sanctioned several teachers to do this job: the black Methodist minister Dr. Leon Wright, Robert Hover, Ruth Denison, Forella Landie, John Coleman, Jan van Amersfoort, and S. N. Goenka. He also, as he wished, managed to take teachings back to India, the homeland of the Buddhism.

The U Ba Khin Method

The techniques U Ba Khin taught were based on Ledi Sayadaw's methods. Like Ledi, he used the breath as a preliminary stage and entrance from which to sweep through the body and its sensations, repeatedly paying attention to their rise and fall and ever-changing movements. He also recommended sustaining a steady point of reference at the *ānāpāna* point, which Ledi had called "the spot of touch," the area where the breath impinges on the nostril or the top of the mouth.[9] This seems important for many Burmese methods to this day, including the Pa Auk *samatha* system. Khin regarded the breath as needed at the outset as a means of arousing basic body mindfulness.

There are four steps to the system. Before embarking on these, one takes the five ethical precepts, an underlying essential in Theravada meditation systems. The first step is then establishing a steady awareness of the point of contact with the breath at the nostril or the upper part of the mouth, to develop concentration and a stable basis for mindfulness. It does not pretend to be a breathing mindfulness exercise, but rather takes the breath, as it is, as a tool to find balance in the conscious and unconscious mind. The attention then moves to the physical body, first as a general awareness—becoming aware of rise and fall—and then in sweeps that scan through the body. At this stage, insubstantiality, movement, and constant arise and fall will become evident. The fourth step involves loving-kindness, letting it arise for oneself and also for all other beings.

The technique draws on the first tetrad of the breathing mindfulness sutta in establishing a calm awareness of the breath, though the orientation is insight based. Its main point of entry into the breath is through, one could say, the first element of the last tetrad of the sixteen stages (the thirteenth stage): watching impermanence on the basis of the in- and outbreath. At the end, a purely *samatha* element is introduced via the practice of loving-kindness, one of Buddhaghosa's calm meditations, to establish kindness and calm in the midst of insight.

Daniel Stuart, a scholar whose recent biography of S. N. Goenka reassesses these insight teachers, shows how some central features of Khin's teaching methods, which seem surprising now, were apparently very effective. One in particular was his arousing of faith in practitioners by active protection, which he effected through the creation of a psychic shield for their initiation into the practice. This was before the meditators whom Khin was teaching had found refuge in the Triple Gem for themselves.

This could also be invoked at times when past karmic influences arose through unhappy *nimittas*, memories, or psychic trouble.

Oddly enough, this new step was connected to a wariness of *samatha* and *jhāna*. U Ba Khin valued the *jhānas* and trained a number of students to master them.[10] He also knew the Abhidhamma interpretation that enlightenment and its moments of fruition necessarily were *jhāna* moments: "It can thus be deduced that the path and fruition states cannot take place without absorption meditation."[11] But he subscribed to a growing suspicion of such states in Burma, which seems to have arisen on the basis that they could lead down some wrong paths and attachment; he felt they were better cultivated at a later stage of practice, when insight had become established. He also felt there were other mechanisms that seemed more reliable than the *jhānas*, which would avoid the need for their practice at all, at the outset: the direct invocation of nonhuman enlightened beings and the use of psychic powers as a means of protection.[12] At that time in Burmese culture, the presence of spirits (*nats*) and *dhāts*, forces for both good and evil whose presence could alter the minds and the bodies of humans, was considered a powerful factor in meditative progress. *Dhāts* needed to be propitiated and, where positive, invoked to protect and guide the meditator in their task. Good *dhāts* could be found through protective recitation and chant; bad *dhāts*, who may be holding the meditator behind, could then be averted.

A worldview of an intricately varied cosmology and the vast perspective of multiple lifetimes underlay this assumption. The understanding is that karma from many rebirths reinforces tendencies and habits (*saṅkhāras*) in this lifetime for any meditator. Many problems that beset people in the early stages can derive from such energies; these may be locked into negative cycles. Khin felt that freeing oneself from their potentially harmful influence could be aided by external agencies, according to a highly sophisticated manipulation of psychic energies.

The understanding that this lifetime is one amid many lives is, of course, found throughout Buddhist and Indic traditions. Here, it is worth remembering again that colonialism was never a one-way traffic of West to East. Rationalist doctrines certainly validated Buddhist doctrine and exercised some appeal, but from the 1890s onward Eastern religions captivated Westerners precisely because of understandings that included reincarnation, karma, and the presence of spirits that could guide and direct those in the present. In the early twentieth century, notions of rebirth and the presence of supernatural beings who could act as agents in people's lives particularly interested those in Britain, the Western country that had most contact with Burma. Favorite authors of the British in India, Burma, and Sri Lanka were Rudyard Kipling, Arthur Conan Doyle, and Edwin Arnold, who frequently included in their works subjects such as rebirth, contact with spirits, and a sense of the active influence of spirit presences and events from the past acting as agents in the present.[13]

Over the last few decades Buddhist teachers have greatly downplayed such doctrines and beliefs. But I remember many people, many decades older than me when I first became interested in Buddhism, whose meditation was informed by their experiences in telepathy, psychic protection, and the recollection of past lives. Their Buddhism and compassion in working with others felt all the richer for this perspective.[14]

In the atmosphere of the time, U Ba Khin's sense that a teacher could exercise an influence over negative *dhāts* might not have seemed as unusual to Westerners as it could now. He believed that a new meditator's progress could take them through painful past karmic influences, perhaps from other lives, which could obstruct progress. Psychic protection provided a safe area that would allow positive *dhāts* to flourish. Such guardianship, he felt, made *jhāna* less essential; he used the power of experienced meditators to support the invocation and guardianship of these beings. One might say that U Ba Khin understood the need for trust and faith in meditation, arousing these in those he taught.

A central collaborator in this work was a married laywoman, Mya Thwin, also known as Mother Sayamagyi (1925–2017), who acted as his assistant. She learned his methods in 1953 and made speedy progress. Like her teacher, she was validated by Webu Sayadaw, who paid deep respects when he met her.[15] Mother Sayamagyi appears to have ensured this safety net was established when teachings were given and acted in what appears to have been a magnetic polarity with U Ba Khin, alert to meditators' problems as she sensed their past karma and difficulties it might bring to the meditation. She also taught his method and was regarded as his direct lineage holder, founding the International Meditation Centre in the UK in 1979 as well as several other centers.[16]

The modern mindfulness movement, in part a highly successful adaptation of U Ba Khin's teachings, clearly has interesting roots. While the aforementioned aspects have fallen away now in its teaching, to my knowledge, the U Ba Khin system flourishes. For instance, the modern body scan of the mindfulness movement is a highly successful adaptation of U Ba Khin's teachings. And one element that has clearly been retained is its precise technical formulation of the possible insight found through mindfulness of the breath:

> Whenever we breathe in or out, the in-coming and the out-going air touches somewhere in or near the nostrils. The sensitive matter (*kāyapasāda*) registers the touch of air. In this process, the entities touching are matter and the entity knowing the touch is mind. So don't go around asking others about mind and matter; observe your breathing and you will find out about them for yourselves. When the air comes in, it will touch. When the air goes out, it will touch. If you know this touch continuously, then wanting (*lobha*), dislike (*dosa*), and delusion (*moha*) don't have the opportunity to arise and the fires of greed, anger, and delusion will subside.[17]

There is an articulation of one's perception of the breath as the contact between the mind (*nāma*) and breath (*rūpa*). There is also the sense of momentary manifestations of mind and, with the notion of *kalāpas*, its interaction with a constant evanescence of momentary phenomena in matter. An acute awareness of impermanence (*anicca*) that characterizes the system's later stages is informed by the detailed Abhidhammic terminology that underpinned the inception of this system.

U Ba Khin may not, as is sometimes claimed, have inaugurated meditation for laypeople in modern times—there is evidence of that from the late eighteenth century in Thailand and Sri Lanka, with roots possibly earlier than that; we do not know the situation before then. But his championing of the laity as the protectors of Buddhism and his active promotion of their meditative path ensured that the Burmese and many international meditators saw meditation as a lay practice and the goal of arhatship as a realistic possibility. In that regard he changed popular perceptions of the practice of meditation in Southeast Asia generally, and his methods traveled, often through his students, to those in the West.

S. N. Goenka (1924–2013)

An immensely influential disciple of U Ba Khin, S. N. Goenka, brought Buddhist meditation to thousands—and perhaps millions—of international meditators through adaptations intended to make the techniques of meditation available to those in other traditions as well as in Buddhism. This extraordinary man was a successful Indian businessman who started meditation training in Burma, where he had grown up steeped in a profoundly religious Hindu family. A deeply devotional background left its imprint: he cried on reading stories of the god Krishna on his mother's lap. His dad was a devotee of Śiva. Like many Indic children, he combined worship of both throughout his childhood. But Buddhism was already exerting an appeal. He visited the Mahamuni temple in Mandalay, Burma, with his grandfather (Baba), where later in life he remembered sitting silently with him:

> When I joined my very first *vipaśyana* course at the age of thirty-one, the atmosphere of silence and calm aroused the karmic forces (*saṃskār*) of my childhood, pulling them out of me like a magnet. The karmic perfections of my previous lives were surely with me, but it is also evident that *vipaśyanā* agreed with me as well as it did because of the influence of the meritorious seed planted in my mind when sitting cross-legged and silent with Baba at the Mahamuni Temple.[18]

Suffering from bad headaches and various psychosomatic illnesses, he consulted U Ba Khin, hoping for a cure, and was refused. U Ba Khin said that he was there to teach spiritual matters, so he told Goenka to go away. When he later learned from U Ba Khin, Goenka found that meditation did indeed cure his headaches, but as a by-product when that was not the goal.

Sensing an innate connection to Ledi Sayadaw, Goenka told friends late in life that he believed he must be this great teacher's rebirth: Ledi Sayadaw died eight months before Goenka was born in 1924.[19] He carried on Ledi's work with a creativity and vision that they certainly both shared:

> I am merely a medium. Dhamma is doing its own work. "The clock of Vipassana has struck," Sayagyi often said. "At this time many people endowed with abundant pāramitā have been born in India and in the other countries of the world. The ticking of this vipassana clock will attract these people towards Dhamma."[20]

Goenka is often seen as a secular teacher, enabling many to practice meditation who would be put off by Buddhist background. It can seem puzzling that such a spiritual and respectful communicator of Buddhist practice, including some quite traditional elements, has come to be associated with a secularism that significantly downplays chanting, devotions, and *jhāna*. Stuart's biography highlights and helps clarify the complexity of factors involved in assessing this great figure: Goenka, in stages, not only adapted his practice for Westerners but, over a period of time, made various decisions that ensured it could be undertaken, not only by the numbers of Indic and devotional practitioners attracted to his teaching, but also by those in the West, for whom such features could be off-putting.[21]

On his videos, gravitas and a sense of the profundity of spiritual practice inform Goenka's content and delivery. He too focuses on the *ānāpāna* spot: it is, he says, the gatekeeper and watchman. The focus is again on touch: the in- and outbreath at the nostrils. Goenka's way of teaching breathing mindfulness thus follows U Ba Khin's method in some regards, in that, rather than widening the attention in breath meditation to encompass the flows of the breath in the body as Borān meditations often do, he teaches repeatedly that a "small area" is sufficient to feel contact or touch.[22] There is, however, a particular emphasis throughout on awareness of the breath as a healing, restorative agent providing calm as well as insight. An emphasis on loving-kindness at Goenka retreats remains strong, always as an accompaniment to the teachings on the breath.

Goenka conveys a sense of great presence: benign, vigilant, and mindful. His precision, attentiveness to the audience, and sense of focus are palpable. He does not advocate changing lengths of breath. "Do nothing," he says. "Just remain aware." The depth of his voice, his resonant and slow, measured style, and a sense of his great devotion and care for those he is teaching pervade both his teaching and his attitude to breath. There is something Indic in the sense of awe, yet the style also feels Western, in its application of technical terminology framed in scientific terms and its appeal to the practical and even rationalist, cognitive areas of the mind as well as emotional bases.[23]

He stresses happiness and harmony right from the outset: the sense of calm that imbues his delivery is strong, and thus, implicitly, the stages of the sixteen in the sutta concerned with joy and happiness are evoked. In the videos, he is concerned to remove agitation and worry. He describes his meditations as the "kindergarten" of vipassana, but it is serenity that is communicated, particularly for laypeople: "However busy you are, you can spend ten to fifteen minutes . . . every day, every morning or evening [just observing the breath]." It is worth remembering that the Buddha usually taught calm (*samatha*) practices to "busy" lay practitioners.[24]

The practices of loving-kindness and compassion remain crucial to Goenka's methods today. At the end of many videos, he chants three times the opening of the great blessings verses—"*Bhavatu sabba-maṅgalaṃ*" (may there be good fortune)—and, as he delivers his teachings on the breath, repeats, "be happy, be happy." A sense of protection, from his background understanding of the responsibilities of the teacher and the magical traditions with which he was familiar, informs his teachings, even when oriented toward a secular audience.

Unlike U Ba Khin, Goenka did not feel himself to be directly in contact with supernatural forces, but he did feel such powers were part of his heritage through the karmic streams of merit that his teacher had transmitted to him. He also saw the guidance of a teacher and a strong foothold in the eightfold path as crucial to a balanced meditative development. In this regard, he had considerable psychic sensitivity to his meditators' mental states. In one revealing essay, he describes his first experience of teaching a meditation course in English rather than his native languages, Burmese and Hindi, in the Himalayas. He found he could not speak, feeling a dark block in the room that made him unable to open his mouth. This happened a second day. On the third, he discovered that a student listening in the adjacent room was practicing with a human skull and a bloody knife nearby, having just made an animal sacrifice to accumulate tantric power. Goenka, with great difficulty, persuaded him to throw them away. When the man did this, the weight lifted. Goenka experienced a surge of the healing power of goodness from the Himalayas, where he felt he had spent many lifetimes in meditation, and from those present. His English flowed uninterruptedly for an hour, and the course was the success it might not have been otherwise.[25]

Goenka felt a strong commitment to the Indian population, whom he believed had "forgotten" Buddhism centuries before. For his Indic audience, he impressed the importance of the *dhāt* and the *weikza*, associated in Myanmar with magical traditions and lineages that enabled someone to be guarded in meditation. In all his insight teachings he drew on the ritual symbolism of his youth to establish protective fields for those he taught, so that the "element of nibbāna" (*nibbāna dhātu*) would both shield and guide his followers; students in turn formally committed themselves to his guidance.

Like Ledi, Goenka saw the ancient Indic ideal of four stages, of a full and happy lay life leading to renunciation, as an exemplary mode of living.[26] In his Indic teachings as well as others, he reiterates a point made elsewhere among the early vipassana teachers, that the mind can become tired with insight and need recharging in some way. The breath is seen as the restorer to the main purpose of the meditation: the acquisition of insight. It feels like a nurturing, supporting presence throughout the meditator's investigation into what is, for Goenka, the primary purpose of the practice—seeing rise and fall in phenomena in the mind and body. Chant, devotions, and the strong protective bond between teacher and pupil were a marked feature of his Indic teachings. In all his talks, for the

East or the West, there is a repeated emphasis on loving-kindness. While the breath meditation formed his core technique, it was accompanied by many features associated with traditional calm meditation.

Goenka was visionary in his anticipation of the effects media would have on our lives: he allowed his teachings to be recorded as he gave them and, it seems, saw that visual and aural media could record and communicate a great deal more than was credited at the time. His teaching and methods seem a good example of awareness of the breath as what one could call a *samatha* in vipassana practice: a practice dedicated to rise and fall, but always coming back to the restful and restorative properties of the breath to give strength, fuel, and good feeling.

In the twenty-first century, Goenka's method's success has brought some problems caused, in effect, by its very suitability to so many people and its popularity. At one time very large numbers were admitted to intensive Goenka retreats, and a few episodes were recorded of people experiencing psychotic dissociation after them. Most who attend, however, are more than happy with the practice and the retreats, often making a life-long commitment to this method. But with the tight schedule and the fact that retreats are conducted in silence, it involves a kind of intensity that does not work for all temperaments. No technique or meditative regime suits everyone; some people are simply unsuited to the method and need a less rigorous schedule and more personal contact.

Some meditators did not realize that they were becoming unbalanced. Chances to speak alone with a teacher, particularly at the end of the course, to ensure people are well based to return to the world, sort out most difficulties; one-to-one discussions tend to reveal this. However, one suspects that there were, at one time, just too many people on some courses for sensitive or vulnerable practitioners to be identified.

The incidents were a shock to the Goenka movement, but they have actively and conscientiously addressed the problem. A caveat is given now that those who are in difficulties with mental disturbance should not attend ten-day retreats: they are intensive, and the organizers ask for a commitment from those attending to abide by their guidelines.[27] I spoke to one meditator on his return after a very happy monthlong retreat in the UK for experienced practitioners. There were three assigned interviews with teachers for each participant; all were told that they could make a consultation at any time if they were worried or needed help. Goenka groups are now vigilant: faced with a problem that can happen to any group, using any method, where large numbers are involved, their rapid response has been to their credit.

Goenka's teachings continue to be widely practiced and admired throughout the world. He lay great store on ethical foundations: he did not, for instance, think people should be charged money for the meditation teaching.[28] The sixteen stages described by the sutta are not taken step by step and are not intended to be, though the principal elements described by the Buddha are implicit. There is less overt emphasis on joy and happiness; rather, they appear to be seen as incidental by-products of the method, supported by an underswell of repeated loving-kindness practice.

By and large, meditation centers associated with Goenka's name tend not to use chanting or devotional practices now. There is a strong emphasis, however, on the need for the five precepts. The techniques have been taught successfully in many prisons and remand centers and have transformed Buddhist chaplaincy.

U Ba Khin and S. N. Goenka made an incalculable contribution to the spread of Buddhist meditation techniques, with innovations, to new settings and peoples. Their care for those they taught and their unswerving loyalty to the principles of older Buddhist traditions are also worth noting.

CHAPTER 16

Two Innovators

Ajahn Buddhadāsa and Ayya Khemā

Toward the end of the twentieth century the world discovered Buddhist meditation, in varied forms, from many Buddhisms. All kinds of methods and practices started to reach the West. A different kind of meditator emerged: one for whom Buddhism was completely new and for whom meditation may offer a way of dealing with problems in an often secular world. For that very reason, the next two teachers feel difficult to classify.

In this chapter, we look Ajahn Buddhadāsa and Ayya Khemā. Much as U Ba Khin and Goenka adapted Burmese practices for the world at large, both these teachers address new kinds of practitioners: traditional Buddhists wanting a modern approach and those who have never had contact with Buddhism before.

Ajahn Buddhadāsa, Phra Dharmakosācārya (Nguam Indapañño) (1906–1993)

The markedly independent approach of the twentieth-century Thai monastic Phra Dharmakosācārya (Nguam Indapañño), known more usually as Buddhadāsa, makes him difficult to pigeonhole in any category. He remained in Thailand throughout his life. But, while he is often bracketed with the forest tradition monks, he falls outside them in many ways, both geographically and in style, showing an appeal that allowed his teachings to travel widely. Ajahn Buddhadāsa became internationally renowned for his teaching of breathing mindfulness. Born in Chaiya District, Southern Thailand, to a second-generation Chinese father and Thai mother, at the age of seventeen he went to Bangkok, full of idealism about Buddhist life there. He was deeply disappointed with the quality and commitment of the monastic life and training in the capital. He returned to his home region and learned from the rich methods of meditation still widely available at that time. Never demonstrating any interest in the usual hierarchical prestige associated with leaders in Thai monastic life, there he founded a meditation monastery, Suan Mokkh, when he was twenty-six.

A scholar as well as a meditation monk, Buddhadāsa had particular understandings of Buddhism that helped reshape it for the twentieth and twenty-first centuries, though not without controversy. He felt breathing mindfulness was particularly good to teach in the West: it carried no baggage and contained a full path. His ideas were widely disseminated, alongside a no-nonsense attitude to meditation that appealed to sometimes more secular Westerners, enabling them to feel a sympathy for a new outlook on Buddhist understanding. He did not place much emphasis on ritual, devotional Buddhism, or in particular, an acceptance of the doctrine of life-to-life rebirth. Buddhadāsa preferred to stress demonstrable features in this life that correspond to rebirth: the various ways we regenerate and become different in this lifetime. He felt that all religions were innately the same and that, when one had penetrated dhamma, there "was no religion." His radical teachings proved very attractive to a Thai urban elite moving away from old Buddhism; students alienated from traditional Buddhism flocked to his talks: "Buddhadāsa's 'scientific' Buddhism was the science of ultimate timeless truth, with meditation as an integral 'technology.'"[1]

The flavor of some of his published teachings are insight based, but Buddhadāsa also taught *samatha* and *jhāna*: he felt calm and insight supported each other. Particularly notable was his careful adherence to all the sixteen stages of breathing mindfulness. He felt each was important and that a full path involves developing, appreciating, and exploring them all. It is certainly possible, he said, just to do the first tetrad and the last, thereby not seeing the full *samatha* fruition of the practice, but he did not consider that route more desirable. He speaks of concentration in a realistic way, saying we find it naturally when we want to shoot a gun or set ourselves to a problem that we enjoy.[2]

His *Mindfulness of Breathing*, constantly being reprinted, sometimes under different titles, is a meditator's exegesis of the great sutta, going through each phase in turn. It is invaluable as a guide for practitioners of any style of breathing mindfulness. Its ambition is direct and stated: to describe all the stages of breathing mindfulness, as recounted in the sutta, as a means of finding awakening. Throughout his work he stresses the practice of mindfulness in daily life, consultation, suitability of practice to individual, and the development of calm leading to insight.[3] At the end of his book, he speaks of nirvana. This, he says, can be temporary (*sāmāyika-nibbāna*)—a taste in one's life: "The greatest possible benefit of the practice of mindfulness is that without having to die we will have *nibbāna* in this very life . . . Through practicing *ānāpānasati* we will receive the most satisfying sort of *nibbāna*—cool in body, cool in mind, cool in all aspects."[4]

Buddhadāsa drew widely on many traditions. He had a humanist and even universalist attitude to practice, consciously attempting to make his method acceptable on an international scale. This strategy has ensured that his teachings continue to be popular well into the twenty-first century. Jack Kornfield, writing of him while he was still alive, notes that he advocated a "meditation-in-action" in "a natural meditation done throughout one's daily activities." Buddhadāsa felt a strong need for adaptations in modes of teaching as well as content for modern times. Kornfield explains how Buddhadāsa did not see himself as a meditation master so much as a "good friend who provides a suitable place to live and some good advice on how to allow the natural development of wisdom to take place."[5] Buddhadāsa commented, "At a higher level, this close bond should be one of affection based on reason, insight and compassion." He is cautious, too: "Teacher and disciple should not, however, be too much attached to each other—otherwise troubles may arise which will be detrimental to the practice in general." He also strongly encouraged laypeople to meet in groups, as communities are so greatly needed in alienated modern societies.[6]

A big part of his approach was to encourage people to see clearly how *any* desire leads them to suffering, and that meditation is deeply grounded in the development of the whole eightfold path.

Buddhadāsa's approach earned him many followers but also courted deep controversy. His ideas on rebirth have been criticized by the many who feel that Buddhism without a karma doctrine loses its heart; Buddhadāsa felt, however, that the emphasis should be on eliminating views of any kind:

> Meditation brings the elimination of wrong views. More and more we see the uselessness of striving for personal gain or happiness in the constantly changing world outside ourselves and realize the peace of mind that comes from non-striving. This natural unfolding of the path, of morality, of clear view, and unselfishness is Buddhadasa's way of approaching Dharma. It is clear, simple, and unmystical, leading to the joy of wisdom, the end of suffering.[7]

His humor was apparently strong. In a video interview with Larry Rosenberg, his translator and meditation pupil, he says, "Of course breathing is happening, but you will see that no matter how hard you look, there is no 'breather' to be found anywhere!" Upon which his warm, large smile enters the interview.

Though Buddhadāsa does evince overlaps with the Thai forest tradition, such as a liking for directness as shown by Ajahn Chah, his approach is distinctive, associated with new understandings of Buddhist theory as well as meditation. He forged a highly successful path following his own understandings of traditional text and practice, and his teachings continue in Thailand and internationally.[8] Suan Mokkh, his monastery, is still a meditation center and continues to attract people who want to find out about his teachings and meditate in its idyllic setting. There is a Spiritual Theater there, where art from Zen, Tibetan, and East Asian traditions sits comfortably with Southeast Asian: Buddhadāsa was not keen on old divides remaining divisive.[9]

Ayya Khemā (1923–1997)

Most of the teachers discussed in this book have been men, but there have also been many female teachers of Southeast Asian breathing mindfulness traditions. A number of nuns were regarded as having attained enlightenment in the twentieth century.[10] In the late twentieth and early twenty-first century, there have been more women teachers in general. Ayya Khemā (1923–1997), a nun, has earned a particular international respect, which has continued well after her death. She is interesting for numerous reasons, but perhaps primarily because she represents a new kind of meditator—someone who discovered Buddhist teachings, for herself, having come from a Western, or perhaps more precisely, international background, without Buddhist roots. Somewhat counter to the trends of the late twentieth century, her sympathies lay toward calm practice. She apparently had an adaptive style of teaching that placed a great deal of emphasis on personal discussion. Whatever her level of attainment, about which she did not speak, her attitude to breathing mindfulness exhibits a maturity and warmth that make her teachings very approachable to Westerners.

Ayya Khemā was born Ilse Kessel, and she saw some of the worst and most dramatic events of the twentieth century. Her early life was one of uprootedness and worry. She was Jewish, born in Berlin in 1923, and was fortunate to escape from Germany in 1938, on the Kindertransport to Glasgow, Scotland. Her parents escaped to Shanghai and, when the war broke out, she was put on a boat to meet them. Reunited with her family, she was happy and fulfilled. A picture from her autobiography, taken when she was nineteen, shows a vivacious and beautiful young woman smiling confidently at the camera.[11] But the war reached even there: Shanghai became occupied by Japan, and her family was moved to the ghetto. One day they were bombed by American pilots missing their target. She claimed that, seeing so many die in that incident, she lost her fear of death. But her father, the mainstay of her life, was broken by these events, and died five days before the end of the war. So devastated at first that she could not even cry, she had a further blow when a few months later her mother remarried to another Jewish exile, to whom she then devoted all her attention. Ilse developed feelings of isolation and married a fellow German exile. After the war and the birth of their first daughter, they moved to California, where they had a son in 1949.

She had begun to have strong spiritual yearnings, however, which she could not share with her husband. They divorced, and in Tecate, Mexico, she married again, this time more happily. She traveled constantly and widely, continuing her interest through study and visits to temples, and she received teachings from Phra Khantipālo (1932–2021), a British monk she met in Australia. Photos from this time show someone delighting in her family—there seems no lack of joy and contentment in her lay existence. Later pictures of her with a grandchild confirm that that appreciation never diminished.[12] According to her accounts, her life was fulfilled and eventful. She explains her openness and description of this personal detail in her autobiography: "I don't find these private things so much worth the telling, but they belong to my development and show that for a long time I lived the same life as many other women, with the same problems and entanglements, and with the same risks that are always involved in separations and changes."[13]

When her children had grown more, however, her yearnings for an investigative, meditative life increased. Her daughter married young, as a teenager, in a partnership that proved successful, and her son went to university. She hoped to combine family life and marriage with meditation and her quest for teachings but, she said, it proved impossible. She was too committed to her search, and her husband was not comfortable with his wife teaching meditation. Although uneasy about her involvements, he was, she says, a natural adventurer, and went to live in Nepal.

Ilse's spiritual path was highly unusual and involved constant travel. She spent several years with Khantipālo, and studied Vinaya, suttas, and insight methods. She had a strong wish to develop *jhāna* but could find no teachers. While receiving her teachings, she worked entirely from canonical recommendations about meditation found in the suttas and made considerable progress. However, she wanted some verification that the powerful experiences she was having were on the right track. While in Sri Lanka, she heard about the Most Venerable Matara Ñāṇarāma

Mahāthera (1901–1992), a meditative monk highly experienced in insight. She was discouraged from visiting him, being told it would take two days' journey and a long walk to get to his monastery. By chance, however, he was visiting a doctor nearby. She immediately went to discuss her meditation with him. He listened carefully to her account of her experiences in the four *jhāna*s and formless-sphere meditations. He reassured her: not only were her attainments valid and true, but she must now teach them, for she had learned a nearly "lost art."[14]

Her interest was eclectic: she stayed for a while at the San Francisco Zen Center and the Tassajara Zen Center and spent three weeks learning vipassana meditation in Burma with U Ba Khin. The flavor of these methods and schools left an imprint on her teaching style, even though she moved to different kinds of practice. The spare immediacy and direct delivery of her teachings, as well as a constant recourse to the three signs of existence as her primary frame of reference, were perhaps in part the result of a temperamental leaning, but also in part learned through these early contacts.

The pull to become a nun became powerful, and Ilse went to Thailand, Khantipālo's previous home. There she practiced and studied with Tan Ajahn Singtong for three months, then went to Sri Lanka, where she met Nyanaponika Thera and Nārada Mahā Thera. She founded the Wat Buddha Dhamma forest monastery in New South Wales, Australia, in 1978, and invited Phra Khantipālo to be the abbot. In 1979 she was ordained and given the name Ayya Khemā. She went on to coordinate the first ever conference of Buddhist nuns in 1987 and was the first ordained Buddhist ever to address the United Nations in New York. She reestablished the Nyanatiloka Mahāthera's Island Hermitage, in Sri Lanka, for Western women. After its completion in 1984, she kept it going for five years but, once again confronted with war, was forced by the turmoil of the time to leave in 1989. Her German students started a center in Germany, where she died.

Ayya Khemā's teachings are geared to those who wish to practice as part of a busy life as well in the quiet of a meditation retreat or a monastic forest lifestyle. *Khemā* means safety and security. It is also the name given to one of the Buddha's two chief female nuns. The ancient Khemā, famously, became ordained after seeing a form of her beautiful body, created by the Buddha, decaying and falling into old age; she mastered all aspects of wisdom. One can feel this emphasis in some of her namesake's talks, some of which are available on the internet.

She gives a rare and helpfully female perspective, talking openly about her lay life and the responsibilities of teaching. Speaking about celibacy, she says it is a great help if one sees it, not as a negative, but as a way of being "independent of the emotions of others." This makes equanimity, as well as joy, possible. If one acts constantly on sense desires, she said, one becomes dependent on outside sources, but one needs to find joy and happiness inside, not outside: "We carry the inner joy within." As a warning lest it might seem very easy, she notes that monastic life needs to cultivate inner joy so it does not become drudgery, as without that inner life it does not work.

Significantly, she regarded teaching as a purificatory path in itself. She gives an account, rare among Buddhist teachers, of how it demands vigilance: constant mindfulness is needed to ensure one's own ego does not get in the way. "There is nobody teaching," she says in one of her videos. "If you do not watch that position, you are in trouble." She points out that one either grows or deteriorates—nothing stands still in the universe: "As a teacher you have that responsibility to yourself but to everyone who has contact with you."[15] There is richness in her understandings of life in the world. At one time she steeped herself in Kabbalah and the Zohar, her own cultural roots, which I suspect supported the depth and emotional warmth of her teachings.[16]

She taught *jhāna* and formless meditation, usually starting with breathing mindfulness. While some teachings were given in talks, she tended to offer teaching privately according to individuals; her emphasis was on sutta interpretation. She certainly taught the sixteen stages in a formal sense, but only occasionally, as a pattern for understanding development. She took the two central tetrads for the deepening of *jhāna* and formless meditation, two stages at a time for each.[17] Breathing mindfulness, she says, is extraordinary for one thing: it goes on whether "I" is there or not.[18]

Some of the teachers discussed in this book practiced in austere monastic conditions, often assuming those they taught also had such a background. Ayya Khemā, mindful of lay practice, does not reject the world of the senses and the joys found there. Rather, she teaches the importance of mindfulness within those experiences. She speaks of four kinds of happiness: that of the senses, of the devas, of deep meditation, and of insight. All of these are valid. She says there is, however, an ascending order of depth and purity at each level. This is particularly important for those who pursue breathing mindfulness in a lay life. For, as she points out, the Buddha does not condemn happiness in sensory experience: such pleasure just needs mindfulness so that it does not lead to craving and attachment. The happiness of devas, she teaches, is possible for everyone. She describes this as the heaven that arises when happiness is found within, through loving-kindness and compassion, which can in turn transform one's relationships with others and with the environment. Deeper still is the great peace of the happiness of quiet meditation. And highest of all is the happiness provided by insight—on the basis of the other three. If there is this sense of balance and strength found through a secure basis found in daily life and calm meditation, then insight will be peaceful and not cause sharpness or hatred.[19]

In a YouTube video she gives a meditation instruction for the divine abiding of loving-kindness: encouraging people to adapt this method to the instructions for loving-kindness, in the traditional style, that they know, she incorporates a new element: the breath.[20] She introduces a technique of breathing in peace toward oneself and breathing out loving-kindness to others, somewhat like Boonman's. When this is established, she encourages practitioners to link this to the exercise of awareness of the traditional objects of loving-kindness practice (as taught by Buddhaghosa): first the one close to you, then a friend, and then someone for whom you feel hatred, or, in her addition to the traditional instructions, someone whom you feel dislikes you. There is a sense of the interdependence of calm and insight: she notes that the loving-kindness practice can find you "knowing . . . in a different way."[21]

According to Leigh Brasington, one of her longtime practitioners, she was strict and even formidable. But, he says, she was also "like a grandmother," attentive to the different needs of each person present on her courses. Even on large courses, while the open meetings were aimed at everyone, she had regular personal interviews with meditators to give private instruction. For those that wished, there was a chance to take the five precepts formally before the return to ordinary life; people could pick flowers in the garden for offerings if they wished. Such ceremonies at the end of courses are intended as a way of helping the transition back to life afterward; she evidently saw the end of the retreat as important, a time for people to get ready for the outside world.

Leigh Brasington continues in her line, and follows broadly the pattern of her courses, with some new features. Brasington's books on the subject give guides to her methods and to his own developments, as he brings *jhāna* practice mostly to Western audiences.[22] Ayya Khemā was unusual in her "do-it-yourself" style: such experiments tend not to work. She had, however, recognized a pressing need to find validation for herself when she had attained various meditation stages, and clearly saw the risks involved. She encouraged constant consultation while developing meditation. Brasington also stresses the importance of one-to-one discussion about meditation practice.

At the outset of her autobiography, Ayya Khemā engagingly gives us her birth sign, Virgo. It is denoted by a young woman holding a sheaf of wheat. As the adaptable, mutable earth sign, it is associated with hard work, fertility, and purity in service. Ayya Khemā's talks communicate the purity of her contact with the canon, leavened by a sense of earthy groundedness and attentiveness to others' needs.

CHAPTER 17

Sri Lanka, the Homeland of Theravada Buddhism, and Some Reflections

In the last few chapters, we have looked at the lives and methods of several twentieth and twenty-first century practitioners. The tradition and community in which I have long practiced is in there, so it has felt like trying to describe the countryside of various regions in the UK and then including the place that I have chosen as home. I know many people who thrive in their very different systems, which are home to them. They have chosen to sit under a species of tree that is quite different from the one I have found most supportive but are very happy there!

Before moving on to the final chapter of this book, which opens out from Buddhism to other traditions, it seems helpful to take an interlude for reflection, both on one area left out of this study and then, generally, on breathing mindfulness systems as they are found.

Sri Lanka

The area of Sri Lanka has been mentioned often in this book, but not explored on its own. This richly verdant island of Sri Lanka, once Ceylon, used to be known as Serendib—from which, for its spices, foods, and maritime breezes, we derive the word *serendipity*. Throughout the first millennium, it was a Buddhist heartland as, apparently, the first great region outside India where Buddhism traveled. King Aśoka sent his son Mahinda to found temples and monasteries there around 200 B.C.E. Artifacts, teachings, and texts came with him.[1]

The island gave a base for Buddhaghosa, and indeed, for what we now call Theravada, in the twelfth century. Literary forms based on Buddhist story and legend, particularly jatakas, have flourished throughout history.[2] But there have been, apparently, times when Buddhism has lapsed; ordination lines, texts and manuscripts had to be imported from Southeast Asia in the sixteenth and late eighteenth centuries.[3] Despite this and recent troubles, Buddhism still pervades the island. There is great emotional engagement and participation in devotions, festivals, chants, pūjas, preachings (bana), and many other activities. On full-moon days laypeople spend the time in temples, dressed in white, taking extra precepts. Anne Blackburn has shown how recitation, chanting, and learning were perceived as essential practices in early modern Sri Lanka, as they still are today throughout South and Southeast Asia; these traditions are still very much alive.[4] As is vibrant Helatuwa discussion—a system of cheerful and argumentative debate among monks and laity, who together unpack stories and jatakas in a creative method claimed to predate the commentaries.[5]

Methods of breathing mindfulness in Sri Lanka, while in part revived now, are less documented. The Yogāvacara handbook, discussed in chapter 9, was found in the late nineteenth century in Sri Lanka. It possibly dates from sixteenth-century attempts to revive Buddhism on the island when the sangha and teachings had lapsed; by the nineteenth century, however, its particular methods had passed into decline.[6] It is often said that Sri Lankans historically did not practice meditation. But at the end of the eighteenth century, the Siyam Nikāya brought numerous practices as well as artifacts in an attempt to revive Buddhism on the island. Throughout the nineteenth century, forest monasteries were revivified by Burmese monastic lineages settling in the island. Elizabeth Harris, a Buddhist scholar who lived in Sri Lanka, argues on the basis of her close reading of letters, diaries, and comments that "meditation" as we understand it now was practiced in the nineteenth century, certainly by monastics and probably by the laity.[7]

Sri Lanka was also colonized and needed to defend its Buddhism, as Burma did. Leaders were alert to defend Buddhist understandings against Western influences, and a number of debates with Christians were felt to vindicate their position.[8] Sri Lanka has long been attractive to Westerners: the German teacher Nyanaponika Thera trained and taught a great deal in Sri Lanka; his book, *The Heart of Buddhist Meditation*, is still used widely. Nowadays, breathing mindfulness remains one of the most popular methods of meditation on the island, along with that of loving-kindness. Venerable Balangodo Anandamaitreya Mahāthera (1896–1998) often taught this practice.[9]

One layperson, Godwin Samararatne (1932–2000), who taught near Kandy, was renowned. Bhikkhu Bodhi writes: "he embodied the twin virtues of loving-kindness and compassion, maitri and karuna."[10] He did not apparently teach *jhāna*, but he taught both insight and some calm, linked to perception of the breath. He sees the breath as the friend helping us at birth; awareness of it helps us at death. His attitude toward its movement in and out of the body appears infused with loving-kindness:

> Sometimes I like to refer to our breath as our friend. If you make a connection with your breath as a friend, then whenever we think of our friend, the friend will help us to experience the present moment. Whenever we are lost in thoughts about the past and the future and there is confusion and disorder in our minds, you only have to think of your friend and immediately you can experience the present moment . . .
>
> Our friend shows us our state of mind, helps us find awareness of the body, and if we are nice to it, it helps us overcome problems and difficulties.[11]

There seem to have been times when meditation has lapsed in Sri Lanka, in the twentieth century and before, but one needs to be wary of this assertion. As Cousins notes, "if an anthropologist is not a meditator and is plainly uninterested in meditation, most meditators will say little on the subject to him."[12] Traditional *samatha* certainly was practiced on the island up to the 1970s and 1980s. It was a feature, if rare, in forest monasteries, with meditation discs (*kasiṇa*) used as aids to calm. This is less evident now, though such practices perhaps still continue in some places.[13] Such traditions were perceived as generally lost in the late twentieth century.

Ñāṇarāma, the teacher who encouraged Ayya Khemā, believed many methods had now gone, but attempted to revive *samatha* practices.[14] Insight-based meditation is popular now: Goenka methods have exercised the most appeal in the last seventy years, though Ajahn Brahm has had some success with practices associated with *jhāna*.[15] Yuki Sirimane describes a number of insight lay meditators attaining, apparently, levels of path.[16]

I have been able to find less information about methods on this island. But there is something about Sri Lankan meditation that feels open to possibility. The pattern since the twentieth century, at least, has been for two practices, loving-kindness and mindfulness of breathing, both for a *samatha* and an insight path, but there is little evidence of old styles of *samatha*.[17] At any rate, laypeople do now meditate, however one classifies "meditation," and whatever the incidence.

In *Freed Freedom* (1986), a laywoman writes a series of letters to her teacher, who responds with advice on how to find the next stages. She sees him only occasionally; meditation teachings are primarily given through this correspondence. She starts with breathing mindfulness, in what appears to be a Goenka method, tries some other methods too, has powerful psychic experiences, and is steered through stages of practice in response to her questions and accounts of her meditation. Finally, she is credited by her teacher, Venerable Nayako Thero, as finding stream entry, the first stage of path.[18] Her identity is kept anonymous to protect her love of solitude.[19] A love of privacy and quiet characterizes many Sri Lankan meditation teachers and practitioners.[20] It seems likely more meditation has gone on, there and in other Buddhist regions, than we know about now.

An Ambrosial Practice: Some Reflections

We can now move on to an overview. Is it possible to gain a sense of Theravada methods as part of a whole? The eightfold path gives a compass and map to help us to find ways of making breathing mindfulness right for us. The Buddha said he had found anew a forgotten path. I remember once walking through the bush in New Zealand and being inspired by the kauri trees, thousands of years old: they were so stately and magnificent there was a temptation to wander. But the bush paths were needed to protect the walker: in New Zealand, as in India at the time of the Buddha, if one strays too far from the path they can get very lost! The methods of all these teachers give us paths. And they all require our compass—the eightfold path—as a support and as a means of directing the meditation and grounding it in daily life.

While asking people about their methods and researching these last chapters, it felt important to find out how the methods were taught, as much as what the content was. Does the method I do develop maturity and love? Does it help give happiness and direction? Does it give help at times of uncertainty? And, crucially, are teachers flexible to people's differing needs? The great beauty of The Sutta on Breathing Mindfulness lies in its capacity to suggest many ways. It shows us how to dissolve forms as well as to find joy in what is there, the familiar. The sutta offers ever new ways and lights on our breath. Simple awareness of the breath, as we have seen, is the guide that keeps us on the path in meditation, however unfamiliar the terrain. The teachers and traditions here have found different ways of realizing the discourse, and in their very diversity, to me, there seems to be health.

The breath is an extraordinary object for meditation: we can see in the different approaches the full differences between a *samatha* and a vipassana path. It lies at the balance of the conscious and the unconscious, the known and the unknown, "me" and the outside world. It goes in and out, and both out and in: awareness of the breath never lets us get stuck in any mental state. It is the familiar thread that offers a safe way through the explorations of *jhāna*; but it also goes, all the time, and shows us how to release. The breath is more than ourselves, always familiar yet always elusive: it takes us into our own self but suggests the infinite and a path of love.

There has been a deforestation of meditative practice. Sadly, politics, active moves toward modernity, and a culture of reforms in the 1950s attempted, often successfully, to impose a meditative monoculture in many regions. Much has been lost. It is oddly coincidental that this endeavor accompanied the literal end of the old "Jungle Village" era in Thailand and elsewhere, with the start of the "Forest Invasion" period and its industrial and systematic tree culling.[21] Apparent reforms, modernity, and in some cases, civil violence, war, and a sometimes-cold rationalism have also damaged so many lineages and traditions. But, as I hope has become clear, some ways of using the breath as the basis of a spiritual path have remained. Usually, awareness of the breath offers the main focus of meditation. But sometimes it is part of a mosaic, sometimes a thread that sustains mindfulness and background awareness, and sometimes a stage, between others, to which the meditator returns. The ancient soil of a rich system of practices is still latent.

Breath meditations are understood and described in manifold terms: with Abhidhamma in Burma (Myanmar), or local magical traditions in Thailand, with Borān practices themselves informed by canonical principle. Abhidhammic observation might lend precision and clarity to one stage in particular of the sixteen, explored in its fullness to reveal a full path: perhaps that is the way of U Ba Khin and Goenka, helped by the important inclusion of loving-kindness, the *samatha* practice that keeps it steady. Innovators such as Buddhadāsa seem inspired by the sutta itself: he adapted the sixteen stages so that there is less emphasis on *jhāna* and more on a direct insight. His immediacy and clarity of observation make breathing mindfulness particularly approachable for those who do not relate to traditional practices, such as chanting, or who want to be true to the sutta but do not wish to practice *jhāna*. His stress on the full sixteen follows the pattern of the ancient styles. Ayya Khemā, also inspired by the sutta, taught in various ways according to the person, adapting as she saw fit.

But what is it that unites these teachers and what they teach? How do they work, and for what ends? What strikes me is the underlying attitude of care and service in all teachers discussed in this book. They follow the path that has helped them and teach it to help others. Some teachers know how to adjust their teachings to the person, or to encourage their practitioners to find ways of adjusting them for themselves: as Goenka points out in one of his teachings, one has to find one's own path.[22] Many teachers cite and use jatakas or tales of the universal monarch: the path may be better seen as one of many lives, and selflessness as a dedicated commitment to service, without thought for oneself. I have seen this commitment in people who have taught me, and that is why I persevered; how a method is taught can be the secret as to whether and how it works for you.

All these methods, the practitioners would say, can lead to enlightenment. The breath arouses calm and also, inevitably, insight, through its rise and fall, unsatisfactoriness, and the fact it is not owned, or self. How they achieve this would, I imagine, differ greatly. Three gates to awakening are described for this final step: perception of *anicca* leads to the signless (*animitta*; literally, "without *nimittas*"). Charles Hallisey translates this as "dependent on nothing else."[23] The perception of *dukkha* leads to the desireless, and the perception of *anattā* to emptiness.[24] Here I can only conjecture. The U Ba Khin path looks to me very much like a signless path; Burmese lay methods in some way represent entry into the thirteenth stage of the sutta. After establishing the first cluster of stages, to do with the body, watching impermanence with the in- and outbreath offers the route that is taken to lead to insight. I sense Boonman's method would go the desireless route. It is through concentration, and becoming skilled in entrance into and emergence from *jhāna*, that desires are increasingly refined. The suffering at each level of experience becomes more subtle, and desires are gradually shed, until the mind is ready to discern desire arising and how it causes suffering. I would not like to hazard a guess about the others.

Some contemporary practitioners of these methods aspire to arhatship—enlightenment—in this lifetime. Some take a vow to be either an arhat, one who becomes awakened after hearing the teaching of a buddha; a *paccekabuddha*, sometimes called a "silent" buddha, who finds their own way but does not teach a full path to others; or a bodhisatta, who aspires to Buddhahood. These goals may take many lives. The last two in particular offer a long path. In that very length some see more chances for compassion, teaching, or care of others, whichever of the three aspirations. For such practitioners, the idea of enlightenment "in this very life," popular with so many, may not look very appealing. What about dedication to service, what many feel is a really heroic path? One can choose a life of dedication to others, whether one follows an arhat, *paccekabuddha*, or bodhisatta path, however those goals are framed.

One may not even articulate one's goal. There is just a feeling that by offering service you are finding your true path, giving back and fostering in others what has given so much to you. That seems to be the case with the teachers described here, whatever their private goal. Many lifetimes, or one? Many possibilities can fulfill this goal of service. I remember Venerable Anandamaitreya giving a talk in Manchester in the 1980s. He said that his body felt as it if was ready to cease working, but that his path to help other beings would continue; as it happened, he lived for many more years. But he did not see death as the end of his path. This is a matter of personal choice, and I do not feel that any method is better, unless it is the right one for the person involved.

This seems important when we talk about the goals of a meditative practice. Most of us, perhaps, stumble upon meditation practice for some sense of "dealing with stress" or finding "well-being." But in time, the path itself changes us, and we feel a sense that we are happily part of something measureless, much larger than ourselves, that is leading us and supporting us when we need comfort, fuel, and direction. The breath fills us with awe: it is our very life force and indeed is, like the Borān meditations say, an honorable presence, or more simply, our lifelong friend.

At the beginning of the book, I suggested that the Buddha wanted plentiful options for his meditators. His teachings on breathing mindfulness encourage that. The instructions of the sutta remind me a little of medieval recipes, which mysteriously but correctly say one should take the "right" amount of a particular ingredient and mix it with others. Personal judgment and a sense of flexible appropriateness are key; if we befriend the breath, it can lead us and suggest what to do. In the next chapter, we will see how other traditions, within and beyond Buddhism, explore, deploy, and occasionally, honor the breath.

CHAPTER 18

Breath Meditation Across Buddhism and Beyond

In South and Southeast Asian Buddhism the breath is a primary vehicle of observation and basis for meditation, at all stages of the path. This preeminence does not seem to be found in other Buddhisms, but many traditions also have teachings that routinely use the breath. It seems a good chance here to suggest, in brief, a larger landscape of how the breath is perceived and understood in these traditions, as well as a few outside of Buddhism altogether. Their teachings show fascinating comment on posture, on how to enter and emerge from meditation, and on the identification of the effects of breath meditation, which is often described in radically different ways. They also show us that as humans we share a common life: our breath.

Indic Traditions of the Breath

Given this book's anchoring in The Sutta on Breathing Mindfulness, it makes sense for our first port of call to be the Indic. How was the breath understood, cultivated, and used in Indic cultures at the time of the Buddha? We know only a little from Pāli sources. In the *Mahāsaccaka-sutta* (M 36), the Buddha describes some practices he undertook before his awakening. He implies they are wrong and unhelpful: all involve holding the breath, with alarming consequences. He even attains what he calls a *jhāna* in the varieties of this practice and arouses great mindfulness and ardor; but he sees that this does not lead to liberation and is mortifying the body. Apart from that, other contemporary breathing practices are not discussed.

As Professor Florin Deleanu, a scholar in Buddhist meditative texts, points out, breath control is not the same as breathing mindfulness.[1] Two early *Upaniṣads*, which appear to date from around the sixth century B.C.E., a couple of centuries before the historical Buddha, are interesting here. Although Patrick Olivelle, a professor in Hinduism, notes that such dating is usually based on a house-of-cards principle of comparison, it is generally agreed they were composed well before the time of the Buddha.[2]

The first, the *Bṛhadāraṇyaka Upaniṣad*, is particularly ancient. In it the breath is one of the vital powers found in human beings, and it is associated too with four others: speech, sight, hearing, and mind. Breath is the Ayāsya (Invincible or Life-Wind). It has five manifestations in the human body, in breaths that move in, up, and around. The essence of the bodily parts is breath: any bodily part that loses breath, withers. What constitutes the self (*ātman*) is speech and mind plus breath, the child of the other two as parents: "Whatever someone does not know is breath, for breath is what he does not know. By becoming that, breath helps him." Breath is also the child of the sun and the sky: "The waters are the body of breath, and that moon up there is its luminous appearance. So the extent of the waters and of that moon is the same as the extent of the breath . . . those who venerate them as infinite win a world without limit." Such mythic passages communicate the closeness that characterizes these texts—*upaniṣad* means "[with the teacher] sitting just beside."

The possibly later *Chāndyoga Upaniṣad*, speaking of the superiority of the breath over other functions, says: "This breath in here and that sun up there are exactly the same. This is warm, and so is that."[3] These are not explicit meditative instructions. The verses suggest, however, the kind of experience possible through perception of the breath and could well have accompanied meditations of the kind found in particular in yoga systems now.

Pranayama (*prāṇāyāma*) exercises often introduce a yoga session: the word is made up of the Sanskrit words for the breath (*prāṇa*), and control (*yāma*) and is linked to a sense of the breath as the vital life force in all beings. The sense of living immediacy is reinforced by the use of deictic pronouns "this" and "that," used to refer to things "here" and "there."[4] The breath is central to Indic understandings and to the practice of Hindu traditions.[5] It is a manifestation of Brahma, who breathes the universe into existence and breathes it out again: awareness and respect for the breath offers the means whereby union with him may be found.

The capacity of language to evoke, as well as describe, is there in the Buddha's instructions for breathing mindfulness; it is difficult not to see some influence. Breathing practices of various kinds are found throughout Indian yoga systems and are considered an integral part of the bodily exercises involved. After the Buddha's death, the sixteen occur frequently in Indian Buddhism, in the Sanskrit *Dhyāna Sūtras* particularly, called variously the sixteen "excellent practices" or the "sixteen limbs."[6] The six aids or "means,"[7] which have been discussed in part in earlier chapters, were probably compiled later: counting (*gaṇanā*), following (*anugama*), the settling (*sthāpanā*), observation (*upalakṣana*), turning away (*vivarta*), and purification (*pariśuddhi*). This last leads to the final stage of seeing the path (*darśanamārga*), in effect stream-entry and the assurance of enlightenment within seven lifetimes.[8]

With the Buddha, we have apparently a new, comprehensive practice. It involves awareness of the breath, at all times: *ānāpānasmṛti* includes body, feelings, heart or mind, and events as they arise and fall. The putting together of "breathing" and "mindfulness" is new. Pāli understandings of *sati* seem quite different from earlier understandings of the word *smṛti* in Sanskrit. Discussing the Indic roots of the term, Konrad Klaus has shown that *smṛti* can mean deliberately adverting to an object, and a kind of noting.[9] But the Buddha's use of the term is wider and more all-compassing, covering an awareness that is both protective and alert, that may be there at all times.[10] Right mindfulness includes memory, the usual Sanskrit understanding of *smṛti*. In Sanskrit it retains this primary usage after Buddhism, in non-Buddhist texts.[11] Mindfulness involves an intuitive, constant awareness that may be present throughout all activities: where mindfulness is established, the attention is fine and the practice continuous. The Buddha even practices mindfulness when asleep.[12]

Such a capacity is not apparently attributed to *smṛti* in Sanskrit texts, whatever practices preceded the Buddha.

After the death of the Buddha, as Buddhism traveled, breathing practices clearly did as well.[13] Vasubandhu's *Abhidharma-kośa* includes the full sixteen stages. It includes various aids, again in a comparable manner to the commentaries: counting, following, touching, settling, observing (*upalakṣana*), changing (*vivartanā*), observation of skillful roots, and purification (*pariśuddhi*).[14] In *The Treatise on the Foundation for Yoga Practitioners* (*Yogācāra-bhūmi-śāstra*), a vast meditation manual from the Yogācāra traditions of philosophy, the breath is considered the best object for the thinking type of person, as it is in Pāli Buddhism.[15] It is said to be so in five ways: through counting, through observing the five aggregates at each stage of the breathing process, observing dependent arising as it occurs in the breath, observing the four noble truths, and observing the sixteen stages of breathing mindfulness. Creative investigative methods have started to be used with mindfulness of the breath, as one sees in twentieth-century developments in this practice.

Chinese Traditions of the Breath

One of the first extant Buddhist texts we have is a translation of *The Sutta on Breathing Mindfulness* (*Anban shouyi jing*) translated by An Shigao (fl. 148–180 C.E.).[16] A translation by Kumarajīva (350?–409?), in what is apparently a more accessible Chinese, seems to have been particularly influential. Kumarajīva was born in Kucha and became a monk when he was seven. He traveled to Northwest India to have contact with traditional Indic Buddhism and was there converted to the Mahayana. He was then responsible for setting up the first systematic means of translating Buddhist texts into Chinese, becoming one of the major figures in overseeing this process.

Kumarajīva compiled the *Sutra on the Concentration of Sitting Meditation* largely from Indic sources, although no single text corresponds to his.[17] The extent to which it is pure translation or represents Kumarajīva's teachings is not clear; it may represent his creative synthesis of material from several sources, in order to integrate the Mahayana path clearly within Chinese Buddhism. The last section is based on the path to Buddhahood, though the methods throughout are largely the same, whether one's aspiration is to be an arhat or a buddha. The sixteen stages are seen as part of this larger path. They are much as described in the sutta, but subtly adapted and interpreted afresh:

1. Being mindful of the inbreath (in six ways analogous to the six aids described above).

2. Being mindful of the outbreath, using the same six.

3. Awareness of the long and short breath (corresponding to stages 1 and 2 in the Pāli sutta).

4. Mindfulness of the pervasion of the full inbreath and outbreath in the whole body, The mind feels the breath in the whole body (stage 3).

5. Eliminating various unfavorable physical functions and hindrances, such as restlessness and sleepiness (apparently, making the breath tranquil—possibly stage 4).

6. As the body becomes light, soft, and fitting for meditation, the "mind experiences joy": the meditator now has full mindfulness of body, and with joy can approach the mind and its mental states (stage 5).

7. One experiences comfort or happiness (stage 6).

8. When one experiences mental activities, one is mindful of the breath. Different types of mind are known: whether it is polluted or unpolluted, and whether it is distracted or still (apparently, stages 7 through 9).

9. The joy that arose before was spontaneous and unintentional. Now, mindful of one's own mind, one gladdens the mind intentionally, to liberate oneself from defilements (stage 10).

10. When the mind is concentrated, one should also be mindful of the inbreath and outbreath; if it is not settled, one settles it (stage 11).

11. When the mind is free, be mindful of the inbreath and outbreath (apparently, stage 12).

12. When observing impermanence, be aware of the inbreath and outbreath (stage 13).

13. Observing rise and fall (apparently corresponding still to stage 13).

14. Observing release from binding desires (apparently corresponding to stage 14).

15. Observing cessation; the suffering of binding defilements disperses. The spot where one is becomes "peaceful" (stage 15).

16. Observing letting go. This is the abandoning of all lust, defilements, the five aggregates, and the conditioned world (stage 16).

Slight shifts in grammar and interpretation have transformed the list. The orientation, though not the substance, feels different. Stages are now defined by the *need* for awareness of the inbreath and outbreath, with mindfulness of the breath a necessary purifier within each stage. These effects are also now spelled out in doctrinal terms, with one stage flowing through to the next. There are also some apt new Chinese touches. For the lengths of breath, he describes someone in great terror, running: they will have a short breath. Another person, released from jail or just out of peril, finds in their relief their breath becomes long. For his fourth stage, "one perceives the breath pervading all pores, down to those on the toes, just like water soaking into sand." During the outbreath one also experiences the breath in all pores, "from those on the feet to those on the head." The breath in the whole body is like the holes of a lotus root filled with water, or a fishing net soaked in water. In his eleventh stage, if the mind does not feel free, one needs to use the breath to ensure it becomes so, like painstakingly pulling cockleburs off of a sheep.

There must have been considerable variety in early Chinese meditative practice. The *Yogalehrbuch*, an anonymous Sanskrit text found at Qizil, Xinjiang Province, China, is particularly interesting for its treatment of breathing mindfulness. While apparently based on Sarvāstivādin understandings, its treatments of meditation objects follows Buddhaghosa's pattern. The imagery, however, is like those of early Buddhist Chinese manuals, with consecrations, sprinklings by Buddhas, beings emerging from lotus flowers to offer guidance, streams of milk allaying suffering and unhappiness, and trees of crystal—presumably derived from the Indian notion of the world tree, described also in the West as the *axis mundi*: the human body. The meditator sits on a diamond throne, and the body becomes like a diamond. Its guided evocation of breathing mindfulness practice illustrates this method.

All visual images are susceptible to change and transformation within the mind's eye of the practitioner. Each of the sixteen stages becomes a vivid tableau, providing a fluid, dynamic visualization of flow and change.[18] In language oddly anticipatory of Vajrayāna and the old meditations of Southeast Asia, this is how the last four stages of the sixteen are described, after the mind has been gladdened and known:

> Strings of pearls go out all around from his head; through the silk cloth and strings of pearls . . . in a similar way appear countless world systems, filled with crystal shrine-halls, and inside these Lord Buddhas with many hundreds of followers. Similarly . . . they envelop their followers and abide, while experiencing freedom (i.e., freeing the *citta*).
>
> Then the inbreaths and outbreaths become covered with diamonds. The world crumbles into dust—at the vision of impermanence.
>
> Then thirdly . . . the inbreaths and outbreaths set the whole world on fire—at the vision of letting go.
>
> Like a mass of foam, it afflicts the whole world seething with these very flames—at the vision of dispassion.
>
> . . . the body of the practitioner of yoga . . . he sees the mass of foam crumbling and coming to peace, as if sprinkled with cool water—at the vision of cessation.
>
> At the time of emerging there arises a palace covered with pearls and the body of the yoga practitioner therein (is similarly covered) with pearls. The Lord ties a silken cloth around his head and says:

'Mindfulness of breathing should be practised in this way. If it is practised in this way, it is very complete.' Devas fill the whole sky and release a rain of flowers and jewels.

This is the practice of breathing mindfulness for the present time.[19]

Practices concerning the breath were already familiar in China, where there was a preexistent system of practice and philosophy, Dao (Tao), with highly sophisticated exercises involving breathing linked to meditation. Harold Roth notes that *qi*, pervasive in Chinese practice, can be translated as "vital breath"; cultivating the breath is central to "Inner Cultivation."[20] These employ the "vital breath," which places particular emphasis on the *dantian*, the area below the navel, as the source of *qi*, the life force, which can be used for training and healing the mind and body; the *dantian* comes to be known as a "cinnabar chamber." Breath exercises are very early. The "fasting of the mind" narrative in *Zhuāngzǐ*, dating from the period between 476 and 221 B.C.E., gives this advice for awareness of breathing:

> Unify your attention
> Don't listen with your ears, listen with your mind;
> Don't listen with your mind, listen with your breathing.
> Listening stops at the ears; the mind stops at what it can objectify
> As for your breathing, it becomes empty and waits to respond to things.
> The Way gathers in emptiness.
> Emptiness is attained through the fasting of the mind.[21]

The *Zhuāngzǐ* also contrasts the common way of breathing—from the throat—with the deep breathing—"from the heels"—of the genuine person (*zhēnren*), who is true and authentic, a follower of the Dao.[22] Breathing practices were involved.

A stable, balanced posture also seems a crucial element in ensuring flow in the Dao exercise known as "revolving breath":[23]

When you enlarge your mind and let go of it,
When you relax your vital breath and expand it,
When your body is calm and unmoving:
And you can maintain the One and discard the myriad
  disturbances,
You will see profit and not be enticed,
You will see harm and not be frightened by it.
Relaxed and unwound, yet acutely sensitive,
In solitude you delight in your own person.
This is called "revolving the vital breath":
Your thoughts and deeds seem heavenly.[24]

A more recent work, *The Secret of the Golden Flower*, shows the interplay of Daoism with, apparently, some Buddhism. This seventeenth-century book (1688–1692) describes a way of practice, an inner alchemy (*neidan*) bringing integration and transformation. It describes the silent cultivation of breathing while sitting and contemplation. The doctrines and procedures behind the practices are infused with Daoism, Buddhist Yogācāra understandings of the storehouse consciousness of our minds (*ālayavijñāna*), and Chinese alchemy. The light that arises within the body is circulated, with the breath, so that the energies and mind of the practitioner are transformed. The breath, watched gently, is perceived as transmuting the base metal, one's hindrances, so they can contribute to the "light" of the golden flower, which rests in the heart: "The breath is one's own mind; one's own mind does the breathing."[25] The text quotes a passage that has long been popular for Daoists and Buddhists:

> The breathing that passes through the nose is external breathing, which is a phenomenon of the physical body. Only when the mind and the breathing rest on each other is this the true breath. The venerable Prajnatara [considered the twenty-seventh ancestor of Chan Buddhism] said, "Breathing out, I do not follow myriad objects, breathing in, I do not dwell on the elements of body or mind."[26]

Breathing Mindfulness in Zhiyi's Tiantai

Particularly important in the history of Chinese Buddhist breathing practice is the work of the sixth-century teacher Zhiyi (538–597), the founder of Tiantai Buddhism (Jp., Tendai), who advocated breathing mindfulness techniques that are still undertaken today.[27] In the *Foundations for Developing Buddhist Tranquility (Śamatha) and Insight (Vipaśyanā)*, Zhiyi says that five adjustments are necessary: "adjust diet, sleep, breath, body and mind." These adjustments prevent obstacles in establishing *jhāna (dhyāna)* and wisdom *(prajñā)*. He has a practical, body-based approach, placing great care in describing how one should enter and leave breathing practice. Delineating carefully the physical posture required, he suggests adopting a relaxed, straight back and, while keeping hands and legs stable, limbering up the body while sitting, by stretching and moving it around, so it feels ready. One should consciously expel turbid air and get the breath to feel in tune with the body, while also shutting the eyes. The body should be neither too loose nor too tight.

He describes four different kinds of breath for entrance into calm meditation *(dhyāna)*. The first, windy, is noisy as it passes through the nostrils, and it is associated with confusion. The second is gasping, where the breath is silent but irregular and broken. The third is lopsided: the breath is silent and not broken, but not steady, so the mind tires. Eventually, from these three, "silent, unbroken and even breathing" is found, "smoothly passing in and out of the nostrils; regulated and balanced; through which the mind attains tranquility, stability, and joy in meditation." This evenness is obtained by focusing on the navel area, relaxing the body, and visualizing the vital energy from below the navel *(qi)*, which "goes in and out of the body through the pores freely and smoothly, without any obstruction."[28] Bodily adjustment is the coarse or obvious level, the breath is the middling, and mind the more subtle. While reaching the stage of abiding in concentration, any one of the three may become out of balance and need attention. When the practice goes well in *dhyāna*, the three become unified, free from conflict, and in harmony. The stage of emerging is discussed with comparable care. The mind should be relaxed, the mouth open to exhale, and the air visualized, freely and effortlessly exiting through the hundred channels of the pulse:

> Then, move the body gently—first the shoulders, then the hands, the head, the neck, and finally the crossed legs, making sure that they are relaxed. Next, massage the skin of the body; rub the hands together and use them to warm the eyes before opening them. Do not leave your seat until your body has returned to its regular temperature. Otherwise, if hurriedly getting up after the mind has been concentrated, the subtle quietness [and warmness] that remains can cause headache and stiffness in the joints similar to the symptoms of consumptive disorder. This may also cause agitation and restlessness. Therefore, such matters must always be kept in mind when emerging from meditation.[29]

This care for every stage and respect for the *qi*—the alignment of the body and consideration of the Chinese understanding of various pulses in the body—make the practice highly distinctive. The sixteen stages of the Pāli sutta have found a new formulation, embedded in Chinese medical and meditative understanding. In his manual, the breath is used as object for the cultivation of both calm and insight, as the two constantly balance one another. Both calm and insight are used as the basis of healing "most illnesses," through awareness of the *dantian* and the soles of the feet and the balancing of the four elements in one's mind and body. Adaptations in the breath offer the basis of a healing system linked to syllables associated with parts of the body. Twelve kinds of breath, Zhiyi says, can adjust various bodily imbalances, though little information is given about each one. But "if you can skillfully employ *śamatha* and *vipaśyanā*, there are no illnesses that cannot be cured."[30] He stresses it is important to emerge from the subtle to the everyday and the coarse:

> Inhale and exhale sequentially;
> Adjust the coarse to enter the subtle harmoniously.
> Like skillfully training a horse,
> Let it stay still or move accordingly.

Zhiyi's practices are still actively pursued in China and elsewhere to this day.

Other Eastern Asian Buddhist traditions also employ the breath, though rarely as a foreground practice. The Pure Land schools sometimes link the breath to the internal utterance of the *nianfo*, the recital of the name of the Buddha Amitābha, whose name will bring about a rebirth in a Pure Land, a paradisical state for after death that is also associated with the purity of the mind itself. There are various methods for linking the *nianfo*, or the *amituofo*, to the breath. Here is one:

> Hold your hands on your lap with the back of the right hand resting on the palm of the left hand, and with thumb tips slightly raised and lightly touching. Eyes may be lightly closed or slightly open . . . posture is very important, so sit upright comfortably without slumping or leaning forward. Hold the head at a slightly downward tilt with the chin pulled in just a little. In this position, begin chanting "Amituofo" aloud or silently. Breathe in through the nose, pulling the air down into the deepest part of the lungs while distending the diaphragm and then slowly breathe out through the nose. Breathing should be natural. Try to use your diaphragm to pull the air deeper into your lungs instead of breathing shallowly. In silent chanting, the tip of the tongue lightly touches the back of the upper teeth, and the teeth and lips are held as usual.[31]

The adoption of the traditional concentration (*samādhi*) posture, of right hand resting on left, align this with Indian Buddhisms, with the chant as the foreground focus and the breath as the object of background awareness. Interestingly, all the Buddhist breathing traditions discussed in this section stress the importance of an upright back, explaining this need in different ways. Cheng Wei-An describes another way of conducting breathing practice as the basis for Pure Land chant. Here, the meditation is said to lead to the experience of "mind-only," a core *Cittamātra* doctrine, that holds that all events and appearances are the product of mind.

When the mind feels peaceful and the breath regular, the practitioner visualizes themselves in a circular zone of light:

> … then visualize the breath going in and out of your nose as you silently recite the Buddha's name once with each breath. You should regulate the breath so that it is neither slow nor hurried, the mind and the breath reinforcing each other, following each other in and out. Whether walking or standing, reclining or sitting, proceed in this manner without interruption. If you always "secretly recite" in the above manner, focusing the mind over a long period of time, there will no longer be a distinction between the breath and the recitation—your body and mind merging with empty space. When recitation is perfected, the mind-eye will open up and *samādhi* is suddenly realized. This is the state of Mind-Only Pure Land.
>
> Commentary. This method is similar to Counting the Breath Meditation, which is one of the Six Profound Dharma Doors [leading to nirvana]. It utilizes the counting of each breath to regularize inhaling and exhaling. Each breath, whether in or out, is accompanied by a silent recitation of the Buddha's name, in an even manner, neither too slow nor too fast. Otherwise, the recitation could become an obstacle to achieving one-pointedness of mind. Through this kind of uninterrupted recitation, the mind becomes pure, free of distractions, and merges with the unimpeded immensity of empty space—everything is Mind-Only. And, if the mind is pure, the environment is also entirely pure—as far as we are concerned.[32]

Breathing Mindfulness in Zen

While putting little or no emphasis on the sixteen stages, awareness of the breath is also key to the tradition most widely known as "Zen" in the West, which originated as the Chan schools of China and also traveled to Korea as Seon and Vietnam as Thiền.[33]

If you enter a Japanese Zen temple, you walk between two terrifying warrior presences who flank the entranceway (*Niōmon*). On your right is Naraen Kongō, with his mouth open, uttering the Sanskrit syllable "A," the first letter of the alphabet. He represents the first breath of life. The one on the left, Misshaku Kongō, has his mouth closed, representing the last letter, "UM," and our last breath. Together, A and UM symbolize our two great unknowns: the birth and death of all things. They act as guardians of the gate to the sacred space.

There is scant evidence of the sixteen stages of the sutta being adapted or developed. In these systems, the breath is part of a larger awareness of events in the mind and body. Some Zen practices, though not all, use the breath as an aid to meditation. This account is of a three-step process: the adjustment of the body, the adjustment of the breathing, and the adjustment of the mind:

> The benefits of Zen meditation are closely tied to the practice of breathing. Generally speaking, Zen doesn't recommend any complicated, strenuous breathing exercises as in Yoga. Zen's breathing exercise is called "observation of breath count" (sūsokukan). In this exercise, the practitioner counts an in-coming breath and an out-going breath. Before counting the breath, the practitioner breathes in through the nostrils and breathes out through the mouth a couple of times. Then one starts counting breaths, but this time breathing in through the nostrils and breathing out through the nostrils. The breath count is performed while performing an abdominal breathing: one brings in air all the way down to the lower abdomen, and breathes out from there. This exercise has the effect of infusing one's mind-body with fresh life-energy and expelling a negative toxic energy out of the practitioner's system. For this reason, it must be done in a place where there is ample ventilation. A key to performing breathing exercises successfully is just to observe the in-coming and out-going breath.[34]

A modern Rinzai teacher, Meido Moore, provides extensive and systematic trainings that link the breath to bodily movement within martial arts systems, according to Rinzai methods. He explains, for instance, exercises linking the syllables related to our first and last breath to the inbreath and the outbreath. A can be awakening and clarifying, internally or externally recited with the inhalation; UN (UM), uttered with the exhalation, is powerfully strengthening and grounding.[35] These serve to activate and circulate the energy of the *dantian*. Variations on this include a very gentle exercise to perform before going to sleep, allowing the intonation of the syllables in turn to accompany each inbreath and outbreath. The mantric breaths must be felt in the entire body, and the breath is deep. As he says, "Simple, effective practices like this are treasures."[36] A four-breath practice and an eight-breath also engage the two syllables, for specific purposes, thus allowing the mind to experience "non-duality" and enter concentration easily.[37]

Other practices include *dantian soku*, a means of allowing the breath to collect at the *dantian*, apparently a traditional Zen exercise that enables the flow of *qi* (ki) to radiate throughout the body.[38] The system is linked closely to bodily experience and a sense of a rapid awakening effect through dramatic but simple breath work, for various and specific purposes. There is, for instance, an exercise for group breathing, with the participants all timing their deep inhalations and exhalations together under the direction of the teacher; the leader must be highly experienced in meditative concentration (*samādhi*) to be equipped to lead this practice. Many methods and applications are described: all are designed to play a central role in a classically Rinzai Zen path.

Some Zen practitioners do sometimes use the "counting" stage of Indic Buddhism. Philip Kapleau was a practitioner in the Sanbo Kyodan tradition, which incorporates koans, the enigmatic statements designed to unsettle conventional thinking, into Sōtō practice, though koans are more usually associated with Rinzai Zen. He recommended counting up to the number ten within each inbreath and within each outbreath, as a preliminary to settling the mind.[39] In practice, the attitude in these traditions is often to take the breath as an event, as any other, simply to be noticed and observed. The Sōtō teacher Shunryu Suzuki (1904–1971) says it is through the contact with the breath that we can locate the formation and dissolution of the "I":

> What we call "I" is just a swinging door which moves when we inhale and when we exhale. When we practice zazen, our mind always follows our breathing. When we inhale, the air comes into the inner

world. When we exhale, the air goes out to the outer world. The inner world is limitless, and the outer world is also limitless. . . . actually there is just one whole world. . . . The air comes in and goes out like someone passing through a swinging door. . . . What we call "I" is just a swinging door which moves when we inhale and when we exhale.[40]

The Vietnamese teacher Thich Nhat Hanh (1926–2022) did teach all sixteen stages as part of a syncretic Buddhist approach.

Breathing Mindfulness in Tibet

Breathing mindfulness appears at first sight to feature less frequently in Mahayana traditions.[41] The breath does not appear so often as the primary focus in Tibetan practices, where visualizations, mantras, and tantras often form the foreground components. But many Tibetan traditions have a rich relationship with breathing mindfulness and creative techniques associated with it.[42] A number of breathing techniques, such as the famous vase breathing, arose from Tibetan meditative experience. As one practitioner said to me: "Where will you *not* find the breath in Tibetan practice?"

Tibetan religion generally has a number of breath exercises, linking color, the channels of the body, and cakras within the body with awareness of the passage of the breath. Tantras were popular in Northern India at the time of the greatest dissemination of texts and practices in the latter part of the first millennium, so much of the patterning is Indic. But preexisting Bön traditions in Tibet appear to have also contributed. Such practices are often esoteric, but some are generally available.

The Tibetan Bön teacher Tenzin Wangyal Rinpoche (1961–) teaches some of these for modern practitioners.[43] The nine breathings of purification work with three channels of light within the body: blue as the central column, red as the left, and white on the right. The breath is imagined moving through specific channels, held slightly, and then released with the exhalation. The mind rests in spacious peacefulness when the channels have been cleared. He also describes various kinds of winds within the body, connected to the cakras: breathing mindfulness moves into other practices and other ways of using the breath. He also explains vase breathing, which is of two types. One is intense *tummo* meditation, to generate internal heat. The other is more relaxed and associated with calm meditation and mantra.[44]

The relationship with the sixteen stages of the breathing mindfulness sutta is possibly not so strong in Tibet. This has been attributed to the fact that, when the sources where the Tibetans found them—the *Abhidharma-kośa* and *Yogācārabhūmi-sūtra*—reached them, the practice tradition for breathing mindfulness had been lost and so was an understanding of its key role in establishing the four foundations of mindfulness. The breath is considered important, however, as a preliminary calm (*samatha*) practice.[45] It is employed in various ways in some Gelug, Kagyu, and Nyingma schools.

Geshe Gedün Lodrö (1924–1979), teaching calm and insight, explained its role in great detail, particularly with regard to posture. The straight back and relaxed shoulders are required to ensure that, with the breath, the body can control the noxious winds, associated with the four elements, of coarse mental states: hatred, jealous and envy, desires, and distractions all have their own elements and passages. As with Borān meditations and those of Zhiyi, the posture itself is seen as a means of allowing negative states to be overcome and positive energies and flows to be channeled, though all describe this process in radically different ways according to various medical traditions concerning the mind and the body. Lodrö then suggests three stages of breath meditation for preliminary calm: observing the in- and outbreaths; counting the breaths in twenty-one cycles; and then breathing exercises apparently based on Indic yoga systems, of breathing in through the left nostril and out through the right nostril three times and then reversing this—a means of dispelling "bad winds."[46] Particularly important is an exercise to purify motivation, as the practice is dedicated to other beings:

> Meditators should imagine or manifest their own impure motivation in the form of smoke, and with the exhalation of the breath should expel bad motivation. When inhaling, they should imagine that all the blessings and qualities of Buddhas and Bodhisattvas, in the form of bright light, are inhaled into them. This practice is called purification by way of the descent of ambrosia.[47]

In his question-and-answer session, Geshe Gedün Lodrö points out that suitability to the person governs how these are taught.[48] This is a preparatory stage; care is maintained in his discussion about the more usual Tibetan objects of *dhyāna* practice.

In Vajrayāna, teachings are esoteric, with the efficacy of many predicated on preliminary undertakings and the bodhisatta vow. The practitioner's opening of the heart and commitment to this informs all practices, shaping their content, meaning, and outcome. Mindfulness of breathing plays a major part in some of these meditations, often as a precursor, in the generative stage, or as a concluding practice. But there is great variety. The Namcho lineage within the Nyingma tradition, one of the four oldest Buddhist schools in Tibet, introduces calm (*samatha*) alongside the "crossing the peak" (*tögal*) practice. It is sometimes termed "the practice of clear light" or "the practice of transcendence," one of the highest initiate stages; the breath plays a key element for calm in this meditation.

The Drukpa Kagyu lineage, founded in the Tsang region of Tibet by Tsangpa Gyare (1161–1211), uses mindfulness of breathing as an introduction, in what is called the sūtra stage, as well as what they characterize as the even more refined state of Mahāmudra and tantra.[49] Again, the preliminaries stress the importance of posture alongside the practice of breathing mindfulness, clearly seeing an inextricable link between the two. The *samādhi* posture is advised and described with care to ensure that the channels of energy flow well in the body. The seven points of the posture are explained: the legs crossed "like woven threads," the hands in the concentration posture, the spine erect like a column of gold coins, shoulders spread "like vulture's wings," the throat curved like a hook and the tongue rolled up, the teeth and lips slightly opened, and the gaze steady.[50] The body should sit "Comfortably, loosely, and lightly."[51] Straightness of body straightens energies and flows in the body.

The breath is treated as the primary support for the yoga of one-pointedness and the tantra stage. The author says that an "inconceivable number" of meditations on the breath are taught in the pith instructions of the tantra. He does explain some familiar from Indic Buddhism. While the sixteen stages do not feature, the system recommended is that found in Vasubandhu and early Indian Abhidharma

(*Abhidharmakośa*): of counting, following, settling, realizing, transforming, and purifying or perfecting.[52] Some of these we have seen
already in this book. He explains counting, suggesting being gentle,
focusing on the breaths, and, for diamond (*vajra*) recitation, counting
each breath with the attention resting on the nostrils. Quoting from
tantric sources, he recommends that one should count up to a hundred
thousand times, "repeating the breath count silently: 'His impaired
lifespan recovers five years. There is no doubt about this.'"[53] "Coming and going" is the following of the breath, as one learns to "merge
the breath with cognizance" and follow it down to the navel and back
again. For the settling, the attention rests on "the breath spreading
throughout the entire body and returning."[54] Realizing is seeing the
breath as nonobjectifiable; transforming changes the conceptual mind
into "another objective support" for calm (*śamatha*). In the last stage,
purifying or perfecting, the conception of subject and object dissolves
and is purified.

Further exercises involve consultation and homage to a guru, before
introducing the inbreath with the sacred syllables and transforming
them while invoking others: AH and HUM. The vase breathing is then described, again after supplicating the teacher. This involves making a kind
of round of the breathing, by expelling stale air then drawing in upper air,
then lower, merging them below the navel and holding them, then gently breathing in more. Gradual exhalations can accompany this, but the
intention is to sustain non-distraction as the breath becomes like a circle.
He notes there are great benefits and dangers in this practice, which needs
a teacher.[55] Eventually, the mind and breath become stable, and deeper
states of concentration are achieved.[56] Practiced diligently, such meditations ensure long life and, he says, the recollection of past lives.

This account can only suggest some of the manifold ways the breath
is deployed in Tibetan practices. Some derive and trace their source back
to the earliest *suttanta* sources, but others have clearly emerged as creative meditative developments, either as background to other practices
or in the use of the breath in novel and purposeful ways for specific meditative effects. It is striking how closely they resemble some Thai *śamatha*
meditations.

The Breath in Non-Buddhist Traditions

In ancient Greek mythology, the beautiful mortal princess, Psyche, whose name means "breath" or "spirit," roamed around, suffering terribly trying to find her husband, Eros, love. When they married, Eros having been pierced with one of his own arrows, realized that she must not see his face, for as a mortal, she would not survive. He insisted she visit him only at night. But she does try and catches a glimpse of his face and so is condemned to years of restless wandering until they are reunited and she is made immortal.

The transformation of the breath, and hence the psyche, through love, is acknowledged and explored by many religious traditions, with the breath as a background awareness being an element in a number of spiritual exercises. In Sikhism, for instance, mantras are linked to the breath, as they are throughout Indic traditions: the practitioner should "enshrine the mantra Vāh gurū in his heart, repeating it with every breath in and every breath out, and thereby fixing it within his inner being (man)."[57]

The Old Testament begins with an evocation of breath, as the "breath of God moves over the face of the waters" (Genesis 1.2). The Hebrew word used, *ruah*, denotes the divine breath. Jewish mysticism also places great emphasis on the breath in prayer and spiritual exercises: Adam was made man by the breath of God, and the job of the human is to find and attune oneself to that divine breath.

Breathing techniques become, at different times, part of Christian spiritual practice. St. John of the Cross (1542–1591), describing how God gave the gift of breath to the soul, says that he did so in the hope that it would find its way back to God:

> Nor is it to be thought possible that the soul should be capable of so great a thing as that it should breathe in God as God in it, in the way of participation. For granting that God has bestowed upon it so great a favor as to unite it to the most Holy Trinity, whereby it becomes like God, and God by participation, is it altogether incredible that it should exercise the faculties of its understanding, perform its acts of knowledge and of love, or, to speak more

accurately, should have it all done in the Holy Trinity together with It, as the Holy Trinity itself? This, however, takes place by communication and participation, God Himself effecting it in the soul, for this is "to be transformed in the Three Persons" in power, wisdom, and love, and herein it is that the soul becomes like God, Who, that it might come to this, created it to His own image and likeness.[58]

Elizabeth Harris finds significant consonances between accounts of Buddhist form and formless meditations and the contemplations of St. John of the Cross.[59] Pointing out the centrality of the breath in key passages in the New Testament, Ruben Habito says, "Christian spirituality is literally a life led in the Spirit, or Breath, of Jesus Christ."[60]

In practice, the Christian tradition sometimes takes the breath as a background awareness associated with counting a rosary or linked to chant. As in Buddhism, this latter practice, of chanted formulas, is considered powerful and best conducted with the help and support of a spiritual advisor.[61] One extraordinary passage from the *Philokalia* shows that the breath, linked to the repetition of Kyrie eleison, Christe eleison ("Lord have mercy, Christ have mercy") must have been employed in the early days of Christianity as an aid and support to devotions. It says the breath that comes in inevitably envelops the heart:

Thus, breathing is the natural way to the heart. And so, having collected your mind within you, lead it into the channel of breathing through which air reaches the heart and, together with this inhaled air, force your mind to descend into the heart and remain there. Accustom it, brother, not to come out of the heart too soon, for at first it feels lonely in that inner imprisonment. But when it gets accustomed to it begins on the contrary to dislike its aimless wandering outside, for it is no longer unpleasant and wearisome for it to be within. Just as a man who has been away from home, when he returns is beside himself with joy at seeing again his children and wife, embraces them and cannot talk to them enough, so the mind, when it unites with the heart, is filled with unspeakable joy and delight. Then a man sees that the kingdom of heaven is truly within us; and seeing it now in himself, he strives with pure prayer to keep it and strengthen it there, and regards everything external as not worthy of attention and wholly unattractive.

When you thus enter into the place of the heart, as I have shown you, give thanks to God, and praising his mercy, keep always to this doing, and it will teach you things which in no other way will you ever learn.[62]

This path of love found in prayer, through the repeated practice, takes the practitioner to states that invite ever deeper investigation. *Jhāna* practitioners might recognize something here about both the reticence people feel about entering states of seclusion (*viveka*) and also their great reward. The stages of union with God described by another mystic, St. Teresa of Avila, carry a comparable resonance. Cousins has shown the way her four stages of prayer correspond closely to the descriptions of *jhāna* in the Buddhist tradition.[63]

Sufism also sometimes links the breath with chant and meditation. The poet Jalāl al-dīn Rūmī (1207–1273) wrote a famous poem, "Only Breath," in which the breath describes itself as living everywhere, staying nowhere, yet visiting all.[64]

This chapter can only give brief vignettes of some ways breathing practices have been employed in Buddhist and non-Buddhist religious traditions outside of Theravada Asia. This exercise shows how meditation on the breath informs the practices and symbology and theory of multiple systems. Awareness of the breath, in the background or the foreground, is informed by understandings of the body and medicine, healing technologies, and theoretical systems proper to the tradition concerned. Many are also pervaded by a sense of profound devotion and humility: the breath opens us to the infinite yet is so intimately personal. I am not going to begin to try comparisons, as the contributory factors are far too complex, and the exercise would risk diminishing all. But the breath does not seem far away from most meditative practice and even prayer.

Its omnipresence, its rise and fall, its place at the threshold of conscious and unconscious processes, and its propensity to arouse and reflect deep calm, make it perhaps the most natural meditation object—and we always have to let go at the last, as we do at death.

Within Buddhism, the verbs associated with the sutta's sixteen stages—making tranquil, experiencing the whole body, experiencing joy, happiness, and gladdening, until the final "watching" of ceasings and letting go—have manifold depths and reverberations of meaning, in practice and in theory. The breath is how we relate to ourselves and the world, and these verbs show us how we may do so as part of a Buddhist path. Its universality is encapsulated for me in the following passage. All practitioners have days when the breathing practice goes awry or feels impossible. But sometimes you just know it is taking you to calm and wisdom. Peter Cornish, a semi-blind Tibetan Buddhist, described his practice at the cliff-top Dzogchen Beara center on the coast of Southwest Ireland. Clearly informed by decades of intensive training, his fine writing is, however, simple, showing the purifying calm that can arise, alongside wisdom in rise and fall, with meditation on the breath:

It was in those pre-dawn mornings that I developed my technique for calming the mind. Sitting, observing my breath coming and going through not quite closed lips. Hearing the air in my teeth was the sound of the sea. Like waves washing a long sandy shoreline in the shimmering light of dawn. The inbreath, drawing the backwash into the ocean of being. Briefly holding. Uniting. Then the wave of the outbreath breaking on the sand, on the primordial strand of existence. With a sweep of white freshness, it wipes out the footprints of the wandering mind.

When there comes a storm in the ocean of the mind, the surf of the breathing increases and the breakers grow louder. Then the wind that blows words to whip up the surface begins to die down and the ocean calms slowly. The sound of the breakers whispers "ssssssssh" with each other-breath, as the breeze of mental activity dies, and rogue thoughts that lap at the end dissolve into freedom.[65]

Conclusion

The Forest of Breathing Mindfulness in Theravada

Trees preside over all the major events of the Buddha's life: his birth took place under a sal tree, his first experience of meditation came to him under a rose-apple tree, his awakening was under the Bodhi tree, and the entry into nirvana at the passing away of his body occurred in the sal grove at Kusināra. Past Buddhas chose manifold trees for their awakening, but all Buddhas teach and practice breathing mindfulness.[1] It is good to appreciate each tree for its own merits, and to take shelter under the one that suits you. I hope this book has helped to give a sense of some of the distinctive characters of different breathing mindfulness traditions, as each can provide shelter and support in its own way.

As we return at the end to Theravada Buddhism, it is possible, I hope, just to step back and see that woodlands are complex and rich, with tangled branches, different kinds of ground cover, and different characters, supported by so many plants, shrubs, lichens, mosses, fungi, and relationships—the way we conduct our lives, how we relate to others in that, and how we understand. The Buddha taught people according to their temperament and disposition. I hope this book has shown how his teachings have been developed and taught so variously, according to people's needs. The profusion of methods and teaching styles involved in breathing mindfulness bears testament to the tradition's vitality and capacity to adapt.

Some systems do not work with one another and need to remain distinct—as the Buddha indicated in describing the many paths his followers pursued. For instance, "dry" methods sometimes do not work well with "wet," to use an ancient distinction.[2] Some people really are not suited to an insight practice; others feel uncomfortable with a primarily calm-based one. The systems appear to have their own balances. We could say that genotypes and phenotypes, even within species, may adapt and change to suit their conditions, but still fulfill the principles of healthy growth. And there are still many features of this forest that may take time to find, or which thrive in the shade. Some schools are esoteric, and some give teachings only when the practitioner is ready. Many prefer only to discuss one's practice with teachers. There are mysteries in this forest that remain intact, ready to disclose themselves only when the time is right.

In South and Southeast Asian Buddhism, how to perceive the breath as part of a meditative path has been expressed and taught in manifold ways, depending on the background, the language, and even the symbologies of those who watch the breath. For some, in Borān meditations, the breath is described and understood with poetical language that speaks directly to the heart, in systems where it is treated with reverence. Many such teachings are esoteric. Other teachers describe the breath simply as our friend, there to help us if we are mindful of it. For others, it is scrutinized closely for characteristics defined in Abhidhamma terms, or those of analytic suttas. In all systems, however, contact with the breath, based on present experience, keeps the practice grounded and offers inherent balance. The Buddha's sixteen stages have grown in different ways, in different people and different soils.

The forest embodies the wilderness and untamed potential of the human mind; it is also where we find resolution and quiet. The varieties of breathing mindfulness systems, and the people who undertake them, feel like vibrant, organically connected woodlands. Any intentions I had to find some taxonomy were soon happily confounded. There is just so much apt variety. Some features do emerge. Taking the factors of awakening as an analytic tool, one could say that some methods are strongly based in investigation and vigor; others in joy, leading to tranquility. All stress mindfulness, some concentration, and equanimity.

There is some difference in styles as to whether the breath is felt in the whole body or at one point of "touch." Whether breath lengths are adjusted can be another element. Burmese traditions emphasize the *ānāpāna* spot, the point of contact—something akin to Buddhaghosa's touching. This is usually the tip of the nose or the upper part of the mouth. Other styles follow the breath from the nose to below the navel, and teach a somatic sense of the breath's suffusion, felt within the whole body. Some do all of these at different times. There are many possibilities, and many levels of experience. Common to *samatha* traditions is a sense of subtle happiness and the area of feeling in the breath: a path unfolds through that. Those based more on insight move to refining tools of identification. There is a letting go as an investigation of the point of contact in terms of the four elements, or awareness of impermanence, is undertaken.

A *Dhammapada* verse says that there is no *jhāna* without wisdom and no wisdom without *jhāna*.[3] Yet, throughout these discussions, there has been debate about the practice of *jhāna*. Is it needed? Is it suitable for modern laypeople? Does it arouse too much attachment? The layman Mahānāma, a stream-enterer, said he could not rid himself of defilements; the Buddha said that having *more* practice in *jhāna*, with its higher happiness, would cure him (M 14). Another householder, Citta, encourages his old friend Kassapa, an ascetic but not a Buddhist follower, by stating his attainments in the four *jhānas*; Kassapa decides he should change his course.[4] Right concentration appears sometimes without a mention of *jhāna*.[5] Is *jhāna* necessary to attain the path? To me it seems so, but as some insight teachers suggest, it may be a by-product that comes in time.

From early times, multiple kinds of paths were described.[6] Bhikkhu Bodhi has shown, in a compassionate study of the kinds of awakening and how they might relate to attainment of *jhāna*, that *jhāna* may not always be needed for some routes to enlightenment.[7] The "dry" way, favored by many now, is vindicated in early texts.[8] It has brought many people internationally to breathing mindfulness through often direct and approachable methods. But there has also been a trend that threatens classical, often more intuitive and body-based, practices. Paul Dennison notes that nineteenth-century reforms throughout Theravada regions, associated with Mongkut's endeavors, "set in motion the near destruction of some of the most valuable and subtle understandings of Buddhist meditation, in particular *jhāna* meditation."[9] Certainly, the exclusion of *jhāna* as a possibility for laypeople is not in accordance with early teachings.[10] The nature of *jhāna*, known in its fullness, can feel like a mystery, and understandings of this state vary deeply in modern meditation systems. Perhaps it is best seen as not so much a state but an area, a moment of peace, that offers a window into what is possible. It seems like an attuning, with relief, to a restorative bandwidth. The body and mind can adjust and, with time, become more deeply engaged and transformed by that. Anyone is lucky who gets a sense of that. It seems to me that the more important question is not whether *jhāna* is necessary, but which kind of practice you prefer and would like to do.

Everyone needs to find balance in their meditation, whatever their system or goal. All the principles needed are distilled in the sixteen. The factors of awakening are our guide through the breath. These seven, which the Buddha linked closely with the sixteen stages, inform breathing mindfulness. Being happy in one's own tradition, and feeling at home there, seems key. Throughout this book, it has felt just as important to find how teachers taught as what they taught. Most of us know when someone has helped us, and it may be in surprising ways. Sometimes it is something they said, perhaps as a chance remark; sometimes it is just by watching them and noticing them; and sometimes it is through hearing a talk. Sometimes it is just through a feeling of friendship and compassion, where you sense the person will not be surprised or shocked. In the breathing mindfulness sutta, the Buddha gave a recipe for success in following this practice. And, as with all recipes, it may need adaptation and adjustments as you find out what works for particular people and temperaments. The methods described here have been developed on the basis of deep meditative and teaching experience. Finding one that you trust is the key to breathing mindfulness practice. Teachers are needed to help us with that.

People sometimes need different emphases at different times. The mood toward direct, insight methods clearly answered needs that felt pressing for many in the twentieth century, as they do now. But there are those who need and benefit from a different kind of practice. The richness of breathing mindfulness meditation in these areas, now taught internationally, lies in its adaptability. Concentration practices give fuel, a fact so often noted by insight teachers in this book. Theravada systems are usually steeped in centuries of understanding about how Buddhist practice works with people and their temperaments. For all these regions, chant, devotion, the practice of ethics, and theory give depth, warmth, and direction to practice.

Just as important for nearly all the systems that teach breathing mindfulness are what we do before and after it. The divine abidings are often taught as a preliminary, they can be there sometimes during a breathing practice, and they can follow it. The simple BU-DDHO chant, *samatha* in feeling, nonetheless provides its reassurance through its simple rise and fall—the ever-present repetition of breath as an impermanent, often unsatisfactory and irregular, movement in our lives.

In South and Southeast Asia there has been a great depletion that now I think is recognized by everyone involved. The forest tradition lost not just its habitat in the twentieth century but also some of its old practices, particularly old methods of breathing mindfulness. Buddhist practices seem to have a habit of replenishing themselves, however. When rainforests are depleted or eliminated, their presence can be discerned by flowers, shrubs, and plants that provided the habitat on which the old trees depended; they make the soil fertile and able to nourish new growth.[11] At a time of great worry and fear in so many cultures, the old meditations offer an emotional base that is hard to find in other meditative systems. Southeast Asian culture and practice still teems with its regenerative foliage and flora: perhaps these can help return to growth some of the "trees" that benefited from them.

In the West, experiments are still ongoing, as some Westerners are not comfortable with many practices and theories intended to nourish and direct growth. People do not always relate to the refuges and precepts or to some understandings, such as karma working over lifetimes, that Asian Buddhists always felt important. Immediacy is valued.[12] The move to secularism has ensured the worldwide acceptance of Buddhist meditation, in quite unforeseen ways. It is noticeable how many teachers, even those termed secular, introduce a reformulation of the three jewels. Many stress community and friendship now, as well as the basic practice. Modern teachers tend to teach not just breathing mindfulness but plenty of other things as well. Many, for instance, teach the divine abidings, often undertaken during the day, lightly and linked to the breath, as well as in seated meditation.[13] I imagine this has happened because it is needed. Underneath this, taking refuge in the Buddha, the teaching, and the community is important, in some way. Everyone has vulnerabilities. Some refuge, deeper than our usual "self," is needed for us all; a teacher is there to help us find this.

A greater emphasis on the inherent radiance of the mind is also evident. This very idea has been a skillful means that many breathing mindfulness teachers find useful, as it helps people trust their own innate wisdom and capacity to do the practice. Knowing also that, when there is mindfulness, other factors of awakening are possible is a great encouragement, as people so often underestimate their own progress. Stories and immediate examples are an important part of Buddhist teaching, now and as they were in the past. Secular Buddhism and associated modern insight methods are sometimes criticized, but their adaptability, rearticulation of principle, and humor have supported Buddhism's travel to the international stage. I do not know if it is possible to practice breathing mindfulness without smiling sometimes at the whole process. But I think that would make it much harder!

One main difference now is that practitioners are often not monastics living in extreme austerity. But monastic seclusion was not an isolation: the teachers in this book frequently express gratitude to those who support them and help them in many ways. Now there are many lay practitioners, who find support and balance for their meditation through different means: their families, care for others, pets, crafts, sports, and skills. Skillful consciousness can be found in many things. Anything of this kind can help breathing meditation, as "The Treatise on the Breath" indicates. We all breathe. We may not have the monastic code, but we do have five precepts. These are not always popular now, as we associate being "good" with negative feelings. But their intention, as Ayya Khemā points out, is to allow happiness to arise without worry or fear; they help loving-kindness and care. They protect and are there to prevent us from harm. Other supporting factors for lay people are community, or sangha in its modern understanding as a group of friends in the dharma, and dharma discussion. The level of Buddhist lay involvement with texts, debates, and stories is impressive and widespread.

Generosity has also provided the greatly nourishing foliage and undercover of Buddhism in practice. Generosity was seen, in the past, as an essential foundation for meditation. It has lost its role sometimes in Western interpretations, but we can still find ways of giving, however small. Most of us do not live in forests but in crowded cities, where we go on underground trains and have to stand in long lines. But the human race is nature too, and the same principles apply! Our breath is one thing we share, with ours and other species. It makes us part of nature. We can still be generous, and we can find that the movement out to others, and letting go of self, helps the movement in, to perception of the breath, as well. Watching the breath is a lifelong process of maturation, as other aspects of the eightfold path can be woven in with it, in meditation and in the daily round.

Throughout all forms of Buddhism, gods, trees, lakes, rivers, people, and animals exist in constantly interactive dances of mutual exchange.[14] The richness of our landscape, however we articulate that, becomes a natural part of the practitioner's experience of breathing mindfulness: we may need "native species" of plants in stories, myths, and adaptations of how we understand sensitivities around us to help this happen, but meditation on the breath tends to foster sensitivities that help our mindfulness of what is inside, what is outside, and what is both inside and outside us, wherever we are. It feels right that new stories, tellings of teachings, myths, and histories emerge from these perceptions.

Another recent factor is that many people learn meditation online if they cannot go to groups. Although it is better to have personal contact, ways around that are found by people going on meditation days or retreat weeks with their teacher or organization so that they can practice with other people. All these adjustments seem to me like ensuring the ground cover is there in a forest. In the West, the soil might need experimentation before our mycorrhizal network, at ground level, can offer the supports and nutrients that are needed. The eightfold path is there to help us do that.

If you look up in a forest, there is something called, evocatively, "crown shyness." This is the practice whereby trees like to leave a good space all around the boughs and leaves of others at sky level. As you walk in old woodlands, in hot sunshine or rain, you are sheltered by a generous canopy of branches. But raise your eyes, and you see the pattern of these lines of space between each tree, letting in the light and air. Trees are opportunistic: if the bough falls off one, another will fill the space. Who knows what is going on at ground level, as trees feed and support one another but also fight for territory? At the roots of all of us are dark impulses to grab, reject, and pull: that must be there in trees as well. But at the top, trees find the sky, air, and rain. They leave openings all around, seen in changing dapples and shafts of light through leaves and boughs so that rain, sunshine, and sky are known throughout the forest. They respect the growth of other trees who share their soil and with whom each one communicates, all the time, through exchanges of fungi mycelia. They stand alone but leave spaces for each other, as branches and undergrowth intertwine.

When a mother tree, who sustains and supports the others around, dies and decays, she leaves her memories to mulch the soil, remaining as underground micronutrients and networks of knowledge from which later trees may benefit.[15] This only has to happen a few times before the soil becomes "ancient," diverse, fertile, and self-sustaining. We have such soil in the heritage of teachers behind us; the many ways the eightfold path can be fulfilled seem like the apparent tangle of interconnections that surround, move underground, and nourish the trees. These are always regenerating and learning.

The Buddha said his teaching was well taught, capable of being seen, for any time, "come and see," leading onward, and to be known each person for themselves. It is just like the breath. All the mysteries of how we form our self, and how we can let that go, are hidden in the simple passage of our most basic bodily function. One day this friend, the breath, will go: the Buddha told his son that, if he practiced breathing mindfulness, it will be "not unknown." If we are aware of it and listen to it, ever-elusive yet always inviting, it reassures, steadies, and shows the way ahead. Each breath has its own story—an arising, a texture, and a feel; then it subsides to give way to another. The Buddha showed a path through an ancient forest: our breath, always a new landscape, helps us find it.

Appendix A

Thai Forest Tradition

In this table, some teachers in the Thai "forest" traditions are arranged by dates of birth (not relative seniority in their respective orders). The title "Ajahn" is an honorific given to a very experienced teacher.

NAME AND MONASTIC LINEAGE	LOCATIONS	TEACHERS AND/OR INFLUENCES
Ajahn Sao Kantasīlo (1859–1942); Mahānikāya/Dhammayut	Died in Champasak Province, SW Laos, paying homage to a Buddha image	Somdet Phra Vanarat Buddhasiri (1806–1891), a founder of the Dhammayut
Ajahn Mun Bhūridatta (1870–1949); Dhammayut	Born in Isaan, Thailand. Wandered through Thailand, Burma, and Laos	Ajahn Sao Kantasīlo
Ajahn Thate Desaransi Phra Rajanirodharangsee (1902–1994); Dhammayut	Udon Thani, Wat Hin Maak Peng, near Nong Khai, Thailand	Ajahn Sao Kantasīlo; Ajahn Mun Bhūridatta

NAME AND MONASTIC LINEAGE	LOCATIONS	TEACHERS AND/OR INFLUENCES
Ajahn Buddhadāsa, Phra Dharmakosācārya (1906–1993); Mahānikāya	Suan Mokkh, Chaiya District, Southern Thailand	(discussed in chapter 16)
Ajahn Lee Dhammadhāro (1907–1961); Dhammayut	Born in Ubon Ratchatan, traveled widely in Thailand	Ajahn Mun Bhūridatta
Ajahn Maha Boowa (Bua) Ñāṇasampanno, Phra Dhammavisuddhimaṅgala (1913–2011); Dhammayut	Udon Thani and Mukdahan, Thailand; regarded as an Ajahn Yai, head monk of forest lineage, 1994–2011	Ajahn Mun Bhūridatta
Ajahn Chah (1918–1992), Phra Bodhiñāṇathera; Mahānikāya	Ubon Ratchatan, Thailand	Ajahn Lang; Ajahn Kinaree; Ajahn Mun Bhūridatta
Ajahn Sumedho (1934–), Phra Sumedhacārya; Mahānikāya	Seattle, US; Cittaviveka, Sussex, UK; Amaravati Buddhist Monastery, Hemel Hempstead, UK	Ajahn Chah
Ajahn Khemadhammo, Phra Bhavanaviteht (1944–); Mahānikāya	Forest Hermitage, Warwickshire, UK	Ajahn Chah
Ajahn Viradhammo, Luang Por Viradhammo (1947–); Mahānikāya	Tisarano Buddhist Monastery, Perth, Ontario, Canada	Ajahn Chah
Ajahn Ṭhānissaro (1949–); Dhammayut	Metta Forest Monastery, Valley Center, US	Ajahn Fuang Jotiko (1915–1986), a pupil of Ajahn Lee Dhammadhāro
Ajahn Sucitto (1949–)	Cittaviveka, Sussex, UK	Phra Alan Nyānavajīro; Ajahn Sumedho
Ajahn Pasanno, Phra Bodhiñāṇavidesa (1949–); Mahānikāya	Amaravati Buddhist Monastery, Hemel Hempstead, UK	Ajahn Chah

Other renowned teachers include:

Ajahn Brahm, Visuddhisaṃvarathera (1951–), abbot of Bodhinyana Monastery, Serpentine, Australia, who has founded a new order of Buddhist nuns;

Ajahn Amaro, Phra Videsabuddhiguṇa (1956–), abbot of Amaravati Buddhist Monastery, UK;

Ajahn Jayasāro, Phra Dharma Bajranyanamuni (1958–), biographer of Ajahn Chah;

Ajahn Sujāto (1966–), Australia, cofounder with Ajahn Brahm of a new order of Buddhist nuns.

Two Western women are longstanding *sīladhāra* nuns, having taken ten precepts in 1979 at the then Chithurst Monastery, later Cittaviveka. They are Ajahn Sundarā (1946–) and Ajahn Candasirī (1947–).

Appendix B

Burmese Meditation Teachers

This table records some Burmese monastics and, where known, meditative influences or teachers; they are listed according to date of birth, not seniority in their order.

TEACHER	LOCATIONS	TEACHER OR MEDITATIVE INFLUENCES
Medawi (1728–1816)	Mandalay	Wrote the first meditation manual in Burmese in 1754
Theelon Sayadaw (1786–1861)		Kingtawya Sayadaw
Ngettwin Sayadaw, "Bird-Cave" Abbot	Sagaing Hills	
Ledi Sayadaw (1846–1923)	Born in what is now Monywa district, Mandalay; lived in Sagaing caves by Chindwin River	U Nanda-dhaja Sayadaw; San-Kyaung Sayadaw

TEACHER	LOCATIONS	TEACHER OR MEDITATIVE INFLUENCES
U Nārada (1868–1955), Mingun Jetavana Sayadaw	Myanmar	Aletawya Sayadaw (a disciple of Theelon Sayadaw), also known as U Mañjūsa
Sunlun Sayadaw Ven. U Kavi (1878–1952)	Myanmar	Influenced by Ledi Sayadaw methods
Webu Sayadaw (1896–1977)	Sagaing; Yangon	
Mogok Sayadaw Ven. U Vimala (1899–1962)	Amarapura, Mandalay	Sayadaw U Zagara; Pathamagyaw Sayagyi, U Ohn
Mahāsi Sayadaw (1904–1982)	Born in Seikkhun, Sagaing; lived in Moulmein, Thaton, and Yangon	U Nārada (Mingun Sayadaw)
Theinngu Sayadaw Ven. U Ukkaṭṭha (1913–1973)	Yangon	Read a book by Sunlun Sayadaw; took advice from friends
U Paṇḍita Sayadaw (1921–2016)	Yangon	Mahāsi Sayadaw
Pa Auk Sayadaw, Bhaddanta Āciṇṇa (1934–)	Since 1981, abbot of Pa Auk monastery (after Venerable Aggapañña)	

This table lists some influential lay teachers from Myanmar:

LAY TEACHER	LOCATIONS	TEACHER OR MEDITATIVE INFLUENCES
Saya Thetgyi (1873–1945); celibate lay teacher	Yangon, Myanmar	Saya Nyunt, a lay teacher; Ledi Sayadaw
Sayagyi U Ba Khin (1899–1971); lay teacher	Yangon, Myanmar; India; worldwide	Ledi Sayadaw
S. N. Goenka (1924–2013); lay teacher	Born in Mandalay; taught in Myanmar, India, and worldwide	U Ba Khin
Mother Sayamagyi (1925–2017); lay teacher	Born in Myanmar; taught worldwide	U Ba Khin

Glossary

Key

In the main text, most words with counterparts in Merriam-Webster Dictionary are used in Anglicized form, except in quotes:

arhat = *arahat*; jataka = *jātaka*; karma = *kamma*; nirvana = *nibbāna*; samsara = *saṃsāra*; koans = *koāns*. Brahmā, Mahāyāna, and Theravāda are spelled in Anglicized forms: Brahma, Mahayana, and Theravada. Vipassana (*vipassanā*), now an English term, is in roman type. Sutta (sutta) and Vinaya are also in roman type.

Terms

Abhidhamma: The philosophical and psychological system that composes the third "basket" of the Buddhist teaching.

abhiññā: Higher, meditative powers considered available to some meditators through the practice of calm and insight. There are six, the first five being such magical powers as flying, hearing faraway sounds, penetrating the thoughts of others, remembering past lives, and the divine eye, which sees beings passing away and being reborn; the sixth is the destruction of the defilements, and thus awakening.

arhat: A being who is "worthy," has eradicated the defilements, and has attained awakening. Arhats achieve enlightenment by hearing the teaching of a buddha; following this path is one of the three possible choices or lineages of Theravada practice.

bodhisatta: The being attached to awakening. One who is on a path to Buddhahood, over many lives, in which they develop the ten perfections. Jataka stories, popular throughout Theravada regions, describe the bodhisatta's adventures and experiences as they cultivate these; following this path is one of the three choices, or lineages, of Theravada practice.

Brahma: A god from the meditative heavens; gods are reborn in these realms on the basis of practicing *jhāna* and the divine abidings of loving-kindness, compassion, sympathetic joy, and equanimity.

breathing mindfulness (*ānāpānasati*): The system of breath meditation in sixteen stages taught by the Buddha in The Sutta on Breathing Mindfulness (M 118). The *ānāpāna* spot is the point of contact with the breath, usually the tip of the nose or the mouth.

deva: A deity, usually from the sense-sphere heavens, who "shines"; these divinities are reborn in their heavens on the basis of their faith, morality, generosity, and investigation.

dhamma: The teaching, the path, law; the teaching of the Buddha and second refuge in what is known as the Triple Gem of Buddha, Dhamma, and Sangha. It can also be translated as truth, law, or justice.

formless (*arūpa*) meditation: The four formless meditations are sometimes developed after the form (*rūpa*) *jhānas*.

jhāna: One of four deeply alert *samatha* meditations. In these states of calm, the mind becomes "secluded" from the sense-sphere. The mind's hindrances—longing for the senses, ill will, sloth and torpor, restlessness and worry, and doubt—are temporarily overcome as the factors of adverting, exploring, joy, happiness, and equanimity arise for the first *jhāna*. Adverting, exploring, joy, and happiness are gradually dropped as equanimity deepens and mindfulness increases. The four *jhānas* are the first four of the eight attainments.

karma (*kamma*): An action, intention, or volition that produces effects in the future.

nāga: A creature in Buddhist myths who is half-human and half-snake.

nikāya: A monastic division or lineage. A *nikāya* is also a collection of canonical texts.

nimitta: A mental object that arises in meditation. Calm meditations develop the *nimitta* to enter *jhāna*. *Nimitta* has visual associations in other meditative contexts. For breath meditation, its meanings are more fluid.

nirvana (*nibbāna*): The highest goal and the cessation of suffering.

paccekabuddha: A silent buddha. One who finds awakening for themselves but does not teach a full path to awakening; following this path is one of the three choices or lineages of Theravada practice.

pārami: Perfection; a supreme quality or excellence needed to become a buddha. There are ten: generosity, virtue, renunciation, wisdom, vigor, forbearance, truthfulness, resolve, loving-kindness, and equanimity. They are cultivated by laypeople.

path (*magga*): The path to awakening. There are four stages of awakening: stream entry, once-return, never-return, and arhatship. The whole path is described as eightfold because it is has eight factors: "right" view, intention, speech, action, livelihood, effort, mindfulness, and concentration or meditation.

rūpa: Form or pertaining to form. The term has two main usages: the four *jhānas* (meditations)—the first four of the eight attainments— are called *rūpa jhānas*, as they still have some vestiges of form, in the sense of a visual object or bodily experience. The word also applies to matter, one of the basic realities of the Abhidhamma.

samatha: Calm, peace. There are four stages of calm, known as the four *jhānas*, and four that are formless meditations.

sangha (*saṅgha*): The community of those who have attained stages of the path, the community of monks and nuns, and the third refuge in what is known as the Triple Gem: Buddha, Dhamma, and Sangha.

stream-enterer (*sotāpanna*): One who has attained the first stage of the path and so has "entered the stream."

sutta: A teaching or discourse of the Buddha. Sutta is a generic term for the collections that form the second "basket" of the Buddha's teachings.

Vinaya: The Buddhist monastic code. Vinaya is the first of the three "baskets" of the Buddha's teachings.

vipassana: Insight meditation.

Abbreviations

DP   Dictionary of Pāli. Margaret Cone. 3 vols. Pali Text Society: 2001; 2010; 2020.

Editions used are Pali Text Society, cited by volume and page number:

AN   *Aṅguttaranikāya*
Asl   *Atthasālinī*
Dhp   *Dhammapada*
DhS   *Dhammasaṅgaṇi*
DN   *Dīghanikāya* (page references are to DN; the numbers of individual suttas are noted by D 1, etc.)
Ja   *Jātaka* commentary (page references are to Ja; the numbers of individual stories are noted by J 1, etc.)
Miln   *Milindapañha*
MN   *Majjhimanikāya* (page references are to MN; the numbers of individual suttas are noted by M 1, etc.)
Nidd   *Mahāniddesa*
Patis   *Paṭisambhidāmagga*
Patis-a   Commentary on *Paṭisambhidāmagga (Saddhammapakkāsinī)*
SN   *Saṃyuttanikāya*
Th   *Theragāthā*
Thī   *Therīgāthā*
Ud   *Udāna*
Vin   *Vinaya*

Vism   *Visuddhimagga* (references are first to the Pāli and then, in parentheses, to the Ñāṇamoli translation, according to its method: e.g., Vism 3.25 for chapter 3, paragraph 25).

Notes

Prelude

1. Books I have consulted on the extraordinary network of interdependency in ancient woodlands include Simard 2021, Shrubsole 2023, and Vohlleben 2023.

1. Introduction

1. Ja 1.58.
2. *Mahāsaccaka-sutta* (M 36), Ñāṇamoli and Bodhi 2001: 341–342 (MN 1.246–247).
3. Varjirañāṇa writes: "The mind which is wholly given to a single perception of a salutary kind becomes purely radiant and illuminant in its original state." (Vajirañāṇa 1975: 56). The *Niddesa*, a canonical commentary, says that it affects the temporary suppression (*vikkhambana*) of the hindrances to meditation but does not cut them off (see Nidd 1.7; Cousins 2022: 5). See also Cousins 1973; Gethin 2019; Cousins 2022: 5–50.
4. Bodhi 2000a: 2.1774 (SN 5.321).
5. Dixon 2015.
6. See, for instance, *Mahāsakuludāyi-sutta* (M 77) for various meditative practices and approaches validated and approved where appropriate.
7. See Shaw 2006a: 194–198; Anālayo 2003, 15–30 (on the four foundations of mindfulness); 2013: 237–240.
8. See an unusual inclusion of "space" amid practice on the four elements (MN 1.420–426), the recollection of good friends where one expects the *saṅgha* (AN 5.336), or the use of imagery appropriate to the person addressed (AN 1.206–211; Shaw 2006a: 196). These suggest on-the-spot improvisation of

a kind we see practiced by some forest teachers, such as Ajahn Chah (see chapter 11).

9. Halvor Eifring (2016) stresses the importance of investigating context and background in both nurturing and understanding different meditative techniques. See also Skilton, Crosby, and Kyaw 2019 for a rounded overview of current research in this crucial area. As we go to press, I have been alerted to David L. McMahan's recent examination of comparative Buddhist contexts. He highlights the crucial role of context and delineates ways that an understanding of setting, practitioner base, and intention needs to inform our interpretations of various forms of meditative praxis (see, for instance, McMahan 2023: 49–59).

2. Vocabulary

1. AN 4.358; Nidd 1.360. See also Vism 3.122, 8.238.
2. Ṭhānissaro, in his opening remarks to Dhammadhāro 1990: 7–8.
3. Ṭhānissaro, in his opening remarks to Dhammadhāro 1990: 8.
4. See Shaw 2021a: 68–70.
5. Sucitto 2022: 41.
6. Thanks to Dr. Francis Beresford, Professor Peter Harvey, and Dr. David Jolly for conversations on this.
7. Sucitto 2022: 40.
8. Sucitto 2022: 44.
9. See, for instance, the discussions on Ajahn Dhammadhāro (chapter 11), Boonman Poonyathiro (chapter 12), and Godwin Samararatne (chapter 17). See also Salzburg 2023.
10. See Cousins 2022: 6–7.
11. Viradhammo 2017: 16.
12. Buddhadāsa 1997: 49.
13. Cousins 2022: 11–14.
14. Pasanno 2017.
15. Sucitto 2022: 71.
16. Anālayo 2019: 85.
17. Buddhadāsa 1997: 84–85.
18. Vism 114 (3.119).
19. DN 2.290–315 (D 22); see Vism 84–89 (3.1–28).
20. See Cousins 2022: 14–17.
21. Dennison 2022: 26–28.

3. The Sutta on Breathing Mindfulness

1. MN 3.78–88. Cousins (2015: 1) prefers mindfulness *with* in- and outbreathing to mindfulness "of." For translations of this text, see Ñāṇamoli and Bodhi 2001: 941–948; Shaw 2006a: 153–158.

2. See MN 3.111–120.

3. Detective work and analysis on this subject are extensive and complex. I cite discussion only occasionally, where obviously helpful. See Deleanu 1992; Dhammajoti 2008; Kuan 2008; Ñāṇamoli 1998; Cousins 2015; Cousins 2022: 111–132; Shaw 2016a; Anālayo 2019, 2021.

4. MN 3.80 (translated in Shaw 2006a: 153; see also Ñāṇamoli and Bodhi 200: 942).

5. These are the four stages of finding the path. Stream entry is the first stage, when doubt is eradicated. More defilements go at the next stage, "once-return," after which the practitioner has only one more rebirth. At the third stage, "never return," the practitioner will enter *nibbāna* at death. The fourth stage is enlightenment or awakening, arhatship. The Pure Abodes are considered the most noble heavens, as all beings there are destined for awakening.

6. MN 3.82.

7. DN 1.71.

8. Cousins 2015: 2.

9. SN 5.311–41. Anālayo (2021: 14–17) discusses the use of the word concentration (*samādhi*) in suttas concerned with this practice.

10. Cousins 2022: 121.

11. MN 1.301. The *Vibhaṅga* says that *upekkhāsatipārisuddhiṃ* means mindfulness "purified by" equanimity. Other interpreters, taking this as a *dvandvā* linkage, translate it as "mindfulness and equanimity." Both translations are grammatically valid (Vibh 271); Shaw 2020: 54.

12. See Shaw 2020: 71–89. The *Dhammasaṅgani* (DhS 10–30) describes eight types of skillful consciousness: all are characterized by right mindfulness, as are all right *jhāna* moments, their fruits, path moments, and the fruits of path. In this work, mindfulness is never described as being a factor (*cetasika*) in the *kiriya*, functional consciousnesses of the ordinary person, or unskillful consciousness: right mindfulness is present, however, in all skillful consciousness, *jhāna* and its results, moments of path and their results, and in the functional consciousness of enlightened beings, which produces no karmic result.

13. For a full discussion, see Gethin 2019.

14. See Shaw 2020: 71–89.

15. Gunaratana 1991: 155.

16. See, for instance, SN 5.314; MN 1.421.

17. Ud 34–37; Nidd 1.360.

18. One early text says this means "on the nose-tip," or "the appearance of the face" (*nāsikagge vā mukhanimitte vā*; Patis 1.171; Ñāṇamoli 1982: 172). See Cousins 2022: 112; Anālayo 2019: 16–17, 236–238.

19. MN 3.82 (S. Shaw trans.).

20. MN 3.82 (S. Shaw trans.).

21. Vism 256 (8.111); Vism 409 (13.9); Vism 451 (14.78). For discussion, see Ñāṇamoli 1976: 1.497–498, n. 26.

22. MN 3.82–83 (S. Shaw trans.).

23. MN 3.83 (S. Shaw trans.).

24. See Kuan 2008: 65–66. Cousins (2022: 120) also argues they are modes of addressing the breath.

4. How a Small Detail Reflects the Whole

1. Ja 1: 58; M 26; M 36.

2. Ud 34–37; Cousins 2022: 19, 76–78. The sequence is illustrated by the pattern of Buddhaghosa's manual (see chapter 8).

3. See chapters 6, 7, and 8.

4. "Following" (*anubandhanā*) is one of the ways of working with the breath described by Upatissa and Buddhaghosa (see chapters 7 and 8).

5. Buddhadāsa 1997: 49.

6. Dhammadhāro 1990: 32–33, Method 2.

7. Here, it is like the "counting" stage, an aid for breathing mindfulness explained in chapter 8.

8. Nyanaponika 1962: 108.

9. Nyanaponika 1962: 87–99.

10. Cousins 2022: 114; 259, n. 13 and n. 14. He notes that Sarvāstivādin interpretations take the word "understands" for all the sixteen stages.

11. For related comment, see Anālayo 2019: 31–37.

12. Cousins 2022: 259, n. 13. Chinese texts predating the arrival of Buddhism stress the benefits of a long breath. Harold Roth (2016: 189) notes recommendations from a medical text discovered in a tomb that was closed in 168 B.C.E., the Shiwen (Ten Questions): "The way to inhale qi [the vital breath]: it must be made to reach the extremities so that essence is generated and not deficient ... Breathing must be deep and long, so that new qi is easy to hold."

13. Cousins 2015: 124–5.

14. Cousins 2022: 113.

15. *Seyyathāpi bhikkhave dakkho bhamakāro va bhamakāranteva vā dīghaṃ vā añchato dīghaṃ añchāmi't I pajānāti, rassaṃ vā añchato rassaṃ añchāmi'ti pajānāti* (MN 1.56; D 2.291).

16. DP 3.625.

17. See chapter 14.

18. See Kyaw 2019. I am grateful to her for discussions about this method.

19. See Dennison 2022: 101–103.

20. MN 2.243.

21. Ja 1.58.

22. See Dennison 2022: 93–95.

5. Sixteen Ways of Knowing the Breath

1. See SN 5.67–70, 5.99.

2. Dennison 2022: 27.

3. SN 5.70–72.

4. Cousins 2022: 113.

5. For varied comment see Anālayo 2019: 16–25; Cousins 2022: 112; Cousins 2015: 1–2.

6. Giustarini 2023: 278–280. The alliteration *sato-assasati* creates an association between "mindfulness" and "he breathes," rather like the association between breath and food produced by the alliteration *ana-anna* in the *Bṛhadāraṇyaka Upaniṣad* (Olivelle 1996: 20).

7. Sucitto suggests it is why people can be put off breathing mindfulness practice. Anālayo (2019: 24) says: "Just being mindful of inhalations and exhalations can become a summary of the whole trajectory" of the breathing mindfulness practice.

8. Vism 350 (11.37).

9. Sucitto 2022: 29.

10. Buddhadāsa 1997: 82.

11. Anālayo 2019: 4–5, 28–29, 54–55, 98–99, 120–121.

12. Four is the number of protection; each four has four modes. The sixteen feel designed to be a protective series. The understanding appears to be that these modes, if balanced, can be found in all sorts of different ways.

13. Florin Deleanu (1992: 49) notes, "The sixteen bases represent a very old technique dating back, most probably, to the very early days of Buddhism."

14. Giustarini 2023: 280.

15. Cousins 2015.

16. I would like to thank Professor Peter Harvey for pointing this out. See Shaw 2021a: 80–82.

17. Shulman 2022.

6. The Treatise on Breathing

1. SN 2.155–157.

2. For more discussion of various early interpretations, see Cousins 2015 and 2022: 111–132. Some later interpretations will be discussed in this book.

3. "In other words, practice of any of the four *satipaṭṭhāna*s has the potential of leading to liberation"(Anālayo 2013: 235).

4. Ñāṇamoli 1982: 162–207 (Patis 1.162–196).

5. *Satokārī*; Ñāṇamoli 1982: 175 (Patis 1.175). See DP 1.676.

6. For a neurological account of this process, see Dennison 2022: 78–80.

7. S. Shaw trans. See also Ñāṇamoli 1982: 164–165 (Patis 1.162–163).

8. See chapter 2.

9. See Bodhi 1978: 244–248.

10. On the five hindrances see, for instance, AN 1.3. On the Buddha's recommendations to Mahāmoggallāna, see AN 4.85–88.

11. AN 3.317. See also SN 5.154. Seclusion is considered essential to find the object of the mind (*cittassa nimitta*; AN 3.422–423). For discussion, see Weerasekera 2024: 47–71. *Nimitta* means a target, sign, or mark (DP 2.589–592).

12. Thate (Ṭhānissaro trans.) 1994: 9. See chapter 11.

13. This simile is used as the key image for a stage of breathing mindfulness discussed by Upatissa and Buddhaghosa, called the "touching" (*phusanā*), a mode of working with the breath for the attainment of *jhāna* where it is associated with focus. The image is applied to the attention on the point of contact with the air—the nose-tip or mouth—before the settling phase.

14. S. Shaw trans. Ñāṇamoli translates this as "not unrecognized."

15. S. Shaw trans.; see also Ñāṇamoli 1982: 172 (Patis 1.171).

16. S. Shaw trans.; see also Ñāṇamoli 1982: 1.177–178 (Patis 1.177).

17. This continues the extract above.

18. Soma 1998: 47.

19. Ajahn Brahmali remarked on this at a talk at Balliol College, University of Oxford, UK, on May 24, 2023.

20. Nyanatusita 2021: 1.422.

21. For more on this verb and its function here, see Ñāṇamoli 1998: 138, n. 74.

22. Ñāṇamoli 1982: 186 (Patis 1.185–186).

23. Ñāṇamoli 1982: 173 (Patis 1.173).

24. Dhp 382; Ñāṇamoli 1982: 172 (Patis 1.171).

7. *The Path to Freedom* (*Vimuttimagga*)

1. For Upatissa's instructions on breathing mindfulness, see Nyanatusita 2021: 1.415–437. An excellent introduction to the work places it in its larger context (Nyanatusita 2021: 1–118). Bhikkhu Nyanatusita has disrobed and now uses his given name, P. D. H. Prins. In direct quotes I have changed his translations of some terms to line up with translations in this book. So, for instance, the "wind" element becomes the "air" element; for the "sign" I have used *nimitta*.

2. Nyanatusita 2021: 417; 417–418, n. 614. For discussion of this expression in practice, see Anālayo 2019: 16–17.

3. Ñāṇamoli 1982: 165–166 (Patis 1.164).

4. Cousins 2022: 116.

5. Nyanatusita 2021: 1.419–420.

6. See Ñāṇamoli 1982: 185–186 (Patis 1.185–186) and Nyanatusita 2021: 1.422.

7. AN 4.34.

8. These stages are found in Sanskrit Buddhist literature (see chapter 18).

9. Nyanatusita 2021: 1.426.

10. See chapters 8 and 9.

11. Nyanatusita 2021: 1.437.

8. Buddhaghosa

1. See Ray, 1998. Buddhist stories, in contrast to other Indic tales, are by this time overflowing with nautical imagery, travel across waters, and wonder at the ocean's treasures (see Shaw 2012).

2. See Ñāṇamoli 1976: xx–xxvii.

3. For Buddhaghosa's styles of writing and exegetical approach, see Heim 2018: 96–106.

4. Heim 2018: 104.

5. Heim 2018: 49–59. She cites his discussion of the "ocean of methods" elsewhere (Heim 2018: 52; Asl 11). For a modern account of working on meditation with Buddhaghosa, see Rose 2022.

6. Vism 278 (8.190–193) for this and the other images.

7. For varied perspectives, see Anālayo 2019: 16–35. He also gives comment on the use of counting and the use of the "tip of the nose" in breathing mindfulness

methods in his account of Chinese versions of the text (Anālayo 2019: 227–239).

8. See Cousins 2022: 115–116.

9. Vism 273–274 (8.172).

10. Vism 280–281 (8.199).

11. See AN 4.107; Shaw 2020.

12. Vism 283 (8.208).

13. Ñāṇamoli 2022: 8.211.

14. Vism 284 (8.211).

15. See the teachings of Ajahn Thate and Ajahn Lee in chapter 11.

16. Vism 285 (8.214–216).

17. The reciters of the *Dīghanikāya* and the *Saṃyuttanikāya*, for instance, had differing understandings of access *jhāna* (Vism 8.179).

18. Vism 275 (8.180).

9. Thailand

1. For accounts of movement between Buddhist regions in the first millennium, see Guy 2014, and for early developments, Skilling 2012a.

2. Throughout South and Southeast Asian Buddhisms, boundaries between what westerners call "meditation" and recitation, chant, offerings, and devotional practice are fluid. Gethin says of the commentaries, "In effect, what we call 'meditation' is presented as a continuum from simple devotional acts and contemplations through to the most advanced spiritual practices and attainments" (Gethin 2004: 214). On the crucial role of many forms of cultivation (*bhāvanā*), see Crosby 2014: 55–59; Shaw 2021a: 120–132; Cousins 2022: 3; 178–179.

3. See, for instance, Crosby 2014: 146–149.

4. See Crosby 2014: 203–240 for extensive analysis of modern contexts. One could describe these systems fully as the old, pre-reform, Tai-Khmer meditation (kammatthan) tradition(s); I am very grateful to Professor Rupert Gethin for his suggestions about this. Historically, the areas involved were largely Tai and Khmer regions (Kourilsky 2024). As we go to press, I have been sent this article; it says the word Borān (*porāṇa* in Pāli), tends, apparently, to have some negative connotations of being old-fashioned in Thailand (Kourilsky 2024: 96–97). Perhaps negative connotations will change as these methods become more widely accepted again.

5. Bizot notes the way the *kammaṭṭhāna*s relate closely to *Visuddhimagga* classifications (see Bizot 1992: 48–50). For examination of related terminology see Crosby 2013: 154–156, n. 26.

6. See Cousins 2022: 155–174.

7. Crosby 2020: 1–8; Cousins 2022: 155–174, 176–179.

8. Seeger 2018: 173.

9. See Seeger 2018: 170–176 for amulet empowerment.

10. Rajadhon 2009: 207–237; Dennison 2022: 35–39.

11. Dennison 2022: 111–137; McDaniel 2013: 203–209, 219–221; Schedneck 2023: 51–60.

12. Some *gāthas* appear to date from fourteenth-century Sri Lanka. A yantra chanting manual contains fourteen stanzas, which it says originated from Ceylon at the time of King Devanampiyatissa; it distills all the qualities of the Buddha into one chant (Rajadhon 2009: 300–301). McDaniel (2013: 104–109) notes some difficulties in the very use of the term "esoteric." The word is derived from the Greek word, "inner." Susceptible to many scholarly interpretations, it is usually applied to hidden teachings, revealed only to select initiates.

13. Mon Maha Ongkam, for instance (the mantra of OM), is learned by heart for emergency use; old people that know it do not reveal it (Rajadhon 2009: 284).

14. McDaniel 2013: 119.

15. Dennison 2022: 22–29; Crosby 2020: 55–65.

16. Dennison 2022: 146–147.

17. See Skilton and Choompolpaisal 2014 and Choompolpaisal 2021 for fluidity and blending in Borān techniques.

18. See Crosby 2020: 42–60. For discussion of the magical use of syllables and their function in encapsulating, ordering, and distributing teachings and text, see Skilling 1997; Skilling 2012b; Schnake 2016; Dennison 2022: 113–129.

19. Crosby 2014: 138.

20. Crosby 2020: 30–34, 141.

21. See Bizot 1976; 1992. For a full bibliography of his work, see Crosby 2000. French scholars such as C. Becchetti, Olivier de Bernon, and F. Lagirarde have continued his work (Becchetti 1994; Bernon 2000; Bizot and Lagirarde 1996).

22. See Skilling 2012b for Thai distillation of textual culture through sacred syllables; Dennison 2022: 113–129.

23. See Cousins 2022: 169–174.

24. See Bizot 1976. In Bizot's work, the inbreath, outbreath, and unbreath of an embryo are described.

25. This passage is discussed in Cousins 2022: 167–168 (see Bizot 1992 for the full text).

26. Rhys Davids 1896. For discussion of Sri Lanka, see chapter 17.

27. For varied comment, see Bizot 1992; Crosby, Skilton, and Gunasena 2012; Crosby 2013: 9; Kemper 2019; Cousins 2022: 155–160. It was translated under the title *Manual of a Mystic* by F. L. Woodward (1916).

28. See Cousins 2022: 167–168.

29. An *anulom*, literally something circling to the right, or noncontradictory, also refers to the filament that purportedly emerges from between the eyes of a Buddha-to-be.

30. See Skilling 2012b.

31. McDaniel 2013: 72–120.

32. For the chant, see Siddhiñāṇo 1995. It is recited by monastic and lay practitioners at Wat Mahathat, Bangkok, an insight-based temple not usually considered a home for Borān meditation.

33. Walker 2022: 65.

34. Paul Dennison (2022: 112–137) outlines many features from a practice perspective.

35. Choompolpaisal 2021.

36. Cholvijarn 2019: 5–6, 378.

37. See Skilton and Choompolpaisal 2014; 2015.

38. For translation and discussion of the breathing mindfulness section, see Skilton and Choompolpaisal 2015.

39. For full discussion, see Cholvijarn 2019: 106–142.

40. The ten *kasiṇas* are the four elements, four colors, enclosed space, and consciousness.

41. For a survey of these skills, see Shaw 2006a: 86–100; also Cousins 2022: 11–14.

42. Bizot gives a detailed account of various forms of *nimittas* in Bizot 1992: 51–56. See also Crosby 2019; Crosby 2020: 48–60. *Nimittas* in Siamese and Laotian practice are discussed in detail in Choompolpaisal 2019.

43. See Cousins 2022: 7–11 for Abhidhamma and commentarial explanations of the role of the *nimitta*.

44. Skilton and Choompolpaisal 2014.

45. See, for instance, Crosby 2013: 92–97.

46. Skilton and Choompolpaisal 2014: 211.

47. Skilton and Choompolpaisal 2014: 93.

48. See Vism 126 (4.34). Buddhaghosa describes guarding the *nimitta* like protecting the embryo of a universal monarch. In Cambodian texts, meditation and spiritual development are compared more explicitly to the growth of the embryo; see Bizot 1976, in the "fig tree" material where the growing "body" of

the meditator is depicted in yantras balancing the five elements, aligned as the five *jhāna* factors.

49. Crosby 2013: 93–94.

50. For the five kinds of joy, see Vism 143–144 (4.94–99). Bizot notes the preeminence of this list and other features of Buddhaghosa's discussion in Cambodian manuscripts (Bizot 1992: 47–56). On the more general role of joy and happiness in meditation, see Arbel 2015.

51. Vism 143–144 (4.96).

52. See Skilton and Choompolpaisal 2015: 225–227; Crosby 2020: 45, 58–60, 150–152; Cholvijarn 2023: 104–105.

53. The perception of the four elements—not including space—within the body becomes the last of the forty meditation objects described by Buddhaghosa.

54. Skilton, Crosby, and Kyaw 2019: 6.

55. Cholvijarn 2019: 114; Crosby 2020: 54–60.

56. DhS 40–51. See Shaw 2006a: 33–34.

57. See Skilton and Choompolpaisal 2014; 2015. Crosby 2020: 111–119.

58. See DhS 9–20.

59. Skilton and Poompaisol 2015: 222; Cholvijarn 2019: 114.

60. Skilton and Poompaisol 2015: 216, 221–222. The nine are: the top lip, the nasal septum, the tip of the nose, between the eyes, between the eyebrows, the crown, the root of the tongue, the heart (*hadaya-vatthu*), and the navel. The navel is last here but first in Suk's list, apparently because that is how the method is taught. Modern teachings of the nine bases vary the locations and order (Cholvijarn 2022: 38–39).

61. Cholvijarn 2019: 114.

62. See chapter 6.

63. See DN 2.210–211.

64. Jones 2020: 129.

65. See Shaw 2006a: 101–108; M 1.58; AN 1.38–42; DhS 263–264; Th 567–576.

66. Cholvijarn 2019: 113–119.

67. AN 2.47–49.

68. The intention of the Manomayiddhi system is for practitioners to obtain the "mind-made" body—an *iddhi* said to be possible after the fourth *jhāna* and the Divine Eye—in order to visit other realms, both below and in the heavens. They can then obtain knowledge (*vijjā*), understand *kamma*, and eventually attain nirvana (Cholvijarn 2023: 94–96).

69. The bases are associated with auspicious qualities. Here is the full list: the navel "appeases all suffering"; the chest is where rebirth consciousness is joined

with the Dhamma of wholesomeness, unwholesomeness, and neutrality; the end of the throat is for "sleeping"; the eyes are the origin of the "wisdom eye ... seeing good and evil"; between the eyebrows is "purifying the mind"; the top of the head is "the house of patience and graciousness"; the occipital part of the head is for "mindfulness ... the controller of feeling and all abnormal thoughts"; and the base just above the navel is for quelling all unwholesome thoughts and fostering wholesome ones (Mettanando 1998: 301; Cholvijarn 2019: 130–131). See also Cholvijarn 2022.

70. Skilton and Choompolpaisal 2014; 2015.

71. Cholvijarn 2019: 50–55.

72. Compilation of Dhamma sermons 2012: 69, quoted in Cholvijarn 2019: 39.

73. Cholvijarn 2019: 176.

74. For the fluidity and creatively investigative applications of canonical and commentarial Buddhism, see Gethin 2004.

75. Dhammakāya 2005: 25–27.

76. Although a nonliterate farmer's daughter growing up at a time of little formal education for women in Thailand, Chandra Khon-nok-yoong became a renowned teacher. She found meditation while working as a maid, when allowed to sit in on a session in Sammā Arahaṃ practice by her employers. She listened to teachings whenever she could. Eventually, she moved to Wat Pak Nam and was singled out for her meditative skills. She was renowned for her mindfulness and higher knowledges (abhiññā).

77. Venerable Nicholas Ṭhānissaro, a longstanding practitioner, tells me the emphasis has moved to other samatha objects. Focus is on the bodily centers on the breath passage, with mindfulness sustained by other means. A greater emphasis is accorded to the spheres of crystal, or light, and how these can be worked with to arouse calm and, thence, insight. The key element is "bringing the mind to the centre of the body from that starting point [the meditation object]" (email, 12/18/23). The center of the body and the area of the navel are key to the system. In the Borān manner, here the physical body finds other bodies within bodies, leading to the dhammakāya, the body of the teaching, and thence nirvana (Cholvijarn 2019: 114–118).

78. See, for varied contributory factors, McDaniel 2013: 100–120.

79. Translation in Cousins 2022: 172.

10. Thai Forest Traditions, Part One

1. Th 350–354; Thī 39–62; SN 1.197–206. For detailed discussion, see Schedneck 2011: 4–5.

2. The *Maṅgala-sutta* (Sn 257–269) and the *Mahāsamaya-sutta* (D 20; DN 2.235–262), key protective (*paritta*) texts, are given in woodlands in the presence of deities (*devas*).

3. See DN 1.71.

4. Soma 1998: 63; Miln 369.

5. Jayasāro 2017: 461–462.

6. Gombrich 1988, 156–160.

7. Tiyavanich 2018: xxiii-xxxiv.

8. Tiyavanich 2018: xxxii-xxxiv. See also Jayasāro 2017: 26–41; Baker and Phongpaichit 2005: 47–80.

9. See Taylor 1993; Crosby 2014: 270–272.

10. Dennison 2022: 233–235.

11. See Crosby 2020: 60–65, 182–183.

12. Tiyavanich 1997: 29–31.

13. See Skilton and Choompolpaisal 2014: 84.

14. Crosby 2020: 141–172.

15. Taylor 1993; Tiyavanich 1997.

16. AN 3.343; Vin 4.183. Taking a decision to live in forests, at the roots of the tree, and in the open air respectively constitute the eighth, ninth, and tenth of the austerities described and sanctioned in the Pāli canon.

17. Vism 71 (2.48).

18. AN 1.10 for *pabhassara-citta*. It is worth noting, however, that experiences of a pure radiance in the mind are not yet enlightenment itself, as Maha Boowa points out to Mae Chee Kaew (Sīlaratano 2009: 193–197).

19. For an examination of the many facets of Buddhist auto/biographical writing, see Covill, Roesler, and Shaw eds. 2010.

20. The others are killing another human being, theft, and sexual intercourse.

21. Translations of Thai works or English compositions are in PDF form on sites like Access to Insight and Buddhanet. There are numerous YouTube videos of teachings and recollections.

22. Kornfield 1977.

23. Taylor 1976: 116–120.

24. He had made a resolve to become a silent buddha (*paccekabuddha*), who attains Buddhahood but rarely teaches others (Nyanasampanno [Ñāṇasampanno] 1976: 12).

25. Buddhasiri's manual, "The Four Objects of Meditation That Give Protection," recommended loving-kindness, recollection of the Buddha, contemplation of the foul, and recollection of death.

26. These comprise objects 31, 21, 11–20, and 27. See Vism 110 (3.104–105).

27. See Giustarini 2024 for discussion of canonical precedence for this practice.

28. Nyanasampanno (Ñāṇasampanno) 1976: 11–12.

29. Th 393–398; Th 567–576; DN 2.295–297.

30. I am grateful to Paul Dennison for pointing this out to me.

31. Ṭhāṇissaro 1997. All references to this story are derived from this unpaginated resource.

32. See Vism 126 (4.32–33); Vism 137–138 (4.74–78).

33. Ṭhāṇissaro 1997. This story has all been quoted from this unpaginated resource.

34. For an ancient example, see *Parosahassa-jātaka* (J 99); Shaw 2006b: 1.405–407.

35. Jayasāro 2017: 720.

36. Taylor 1993: 75–109.

37. Ja 6.157–217.

38. See, for instance, Ñāṇasampanno 2005: part 3.

39. Nyanasampanno (Ñāṇasampanno) 1976: 184–185.

40. Nyanasampanno (Ñāṇasampanno) 1976: 175–177.

41. Sn 257–269.

42. Nyanasampanno (Ñāṇasampanno) 1976: 31–32.

43. Sīlaratano 2009: 144.

44. Sīlaratano 2009: 144–145.

45. Nyanasampanno (Ñāṇasampanno) 1976: 144–146.

46. See Ṭhāṇissaro's "Introduction" in Bhūridatta 2016.

47. Bhūridatta 2016: §8.

48. Bhūridatta 2016: §4.

49. Bhūridatta 2016: §10.

50. Bizot 1976; for an account, see Cousins 2022: 156–172.

51. Bhūridatta 2016: §15.

52. Crosby 2019: 142–143.

53. Nyanasampanno (Ñāṇasampanno) 1976: 217.

54. Ṭhāṇissaro's "Introduction" in Bhūridatta 2016.

55. See, in particular, Bizot 1976.

56. Bhūridatta 2016: §17; Patis 2.92–103; Patis-A: 281, 584. For comment, see Cousins 1984; Cousins 2022: 102–109, 257, n. 24.

57. See DN 2.313–314.

58. Nyanasampanno (Ñāṇasampanno) 1976: 190–192. For comment and the doctrinal understanding of this, see Cholvijarn 2019: 83–85.

59. For discussion of this capacity, see also Nyanasampanno (Ñāṇasampanno) 1976: 90–91.

60. Ñāṇamoli 1982: 67–68 (Patis 1.66–68); Vism 672 (22.5).

61. Skilton and Choompolpaisal 2014: 84.

11. Thai Forest Traditions, Part Two

1. Tate (Thate) 1993: 18–20.

2. Thate 1994: 8–11.

3. Ñāṇasampanno 1994: "The Conventional Mind, The Mind Released" (unpaginated).

4. Ñāṇasampanno 1994: "Investigating Pain" (unpaginated).

5. Quoted in Kornfield 1977: 168–169.

6. Kornfield 1977: 168–169, n. 10. See Jayasāro 2017: 327–331 for Ajahn Chah's teachings on this subject.

7. Kornfield 1977: 169, n. 11.

8. Kornfield 1977: 169.

9. Quoted in Kornfield 1977: 182.

10. AN 2.157. See Kornfield 1977: 164–183.

11. In Dhammadhāro 2012: 14.

12. Dhammadhāro 2012: 25–26.

13. When the bodhisatta is reborn as a deer, he radiates loving-kindness when a human king wants to kill him; the king cannot do it (*Nandiya-jātaka*; J 385). See also Nyanasampanno (Ñāṇasampanno) 1976: 34–36.

14. DN 2.292.

15. See Rajadhon 2009: 314–321.

16. Dhammadhāro 2012: 123–124.

17. Dhammadhāro 2012: 124.

18. Dhammadhāro 2012: 50–51.

19. Tiyavanich 1997: 205–206.

20. Dhammadhāro 2012: 91–92.

21. Dhammadhāro 1990: 16.

22. Dhammadhāro 1990: Method 1, 24.

23. Dhammadhāro 1990: Method 1, 26.

24. Dhammadhāro 1990: Method 1, 27.

25. Dhammadhāro 1990: Method 2, 34. Ajahn Lee suggests coming to know "resting spots of the breath," citing Borān centers: the nose-tip; the middle of the head; the palate; the base of the throat; the breastbone, or tip of the sternum; and the navel, or the point just above it. He recommends adjusting the length

of the breaths as a skill in flexibility, suggesting four such ways: (a) in long and out long, (b) in long and out short, (c) in short and out long, and (d) in short and out short. The meditator should find what is comfortable or, ideally, "learn to breathe comfortably all four ways because your physical condition and your breath are always changing."

26. Dhammadhāro 1990: Method 2, 37. Ajahn Lee is relaxed about the possibility the breath *nimitta* might not arise and reassures that the practice still works. But if images do come, the meditator can learn facility then "in making them [*nimittas*] small, large, sending them far away, bringing them up close, making them appear and disappear, sending them outside, bringing them in. Only then will you be able to use them in training the mind."

27. Dhammadhāro 1990: Method 2, 39–40. Skills in the breath are described entirely in terms of each path factor. He concludes: "A mind intent only on issues related to the breath, not pulling any other objects in to interfere, until the breath is refined, giving rise to fixed absorption and then liberating insight right there: This is *Right Concentration.*" He says all the four noble truths may be found in the breath. "Being constantly mindful and alert to all aspects of the breath, is the path to the disbanding of stress [*magga*]."

28. See, for instance, Kornfield 1977: 256–270.

29. Jayasāro 2017: 22.

30. Jayasāro 2017: 34–40, 80.

31. Jayasāro 2017: 59–62.

32. Jayasāro 2017: 161–207.

33. Jayasāro 2017: 258–260, 270–271. On listening, memorization, and chanting as Buddhist practice, see Shaw 2021a: 20–33.

34. Jayasāro 2017: 178.

35. Jayasāro 2017: 182.

36. Jayasāro: 2017: 360–374.

37. For Chah's caution with regard to *nimittas*, see Jayasāro: 2017: 357–360.

38. Jayasāro 2017: 360–361.

39. Jayasāro 2017: 172–176, 356–357.

40. Jayasāro 2017: 113–114. Jayasāro records an incident of Chah's attunement to psychic powers, despite his refusal to enter into this subject much. As Chah predicts, a mysterious light reveals to all present the boundaries of the new ordination ground (Jayasāro 2017: 126–127).

41. Jayasāro 2017: 322. See also Chah 2007; Jayasāro 2017: 327–331.

42. Chah 1982: 13–14, 103–104.

43. Chah 2011: 1.12.

44. Quoted in Jayasāro 2017: 146–147.
45. For appropriateness in teaching and varied methods, see Jayasāro 2017: 413–422.
46. See, for instance, Sumedho 1997.
47. Pasanno 2017.
48. Sucitto 2022.
49. Brahm 2006: 81–102.
50. See Viradhammo 2015.
51. See Nyanasampanno (Ñāṇasampanno) 1976: 221–222; Sucitto 2022: 40; Dhammdhāro 1990: 11, 70.
52. Jayasāro 2017: 194–195.
53. Jayasāro 2017: 195.
54. Color plays some role but to my knowledge does not feature obviously in documented Borān systems. Southeast Asians enjoy some play with color systems, however, assigning one to each day of the week, for instance.
55. Seeger 2018.
56. Mae Chee Kaew, for instance, did not practice breathing mindfulness, from the evidence of accounts, but did attain *jhāna* and the path, according to her meditation teacher.
57. See Jayasāro 2017: 117–118.
58. Seeger 2014: 172.

12. Thailand's Old Meditations Abroad

1. Poonyathiro 2003: 8.
2. Poonyathiro 2003: 18.
3. Poonyathiro 2003: 20.
4. Poonyathiro 2003: 32.
5. Poonyathiro 2003: 50.
6. Poonyathiro 2003: 48.
7. Dennison 2022: 3.
8. Dennison 2022: 1–17, 21–48.
9. Dennison 2022: 94; see also Dennison 2022: 59, 101–103.
10. Dennison 2022: 82.
11. Some Zen practices also use counting in this way with the breath. See chapter 16.
12. Summer meditation course at the Samatha Centre, Greenstreete, Powys, UK, August 2019.
13. For images for each *jhāna*, see DN 1: 73–76 (translated in Shaw 2006a: 70–71).

14. Summer meditation course at the Samatha Centre, Greenstreete, Powys, UK, August 2007.
15. Ñāṇamoli 1982: 185 (Paṭis 1.184–185). As we see in Part 5, Ledi Sayadaw describes this stage under the fourth stage of breathing mindfulness, before the entry into *jhāna*.
16. Cousins (2022: 21–24) notes that such phenomena are associated with *jhāna* practice from ancient times, as are "visions" of gods visiting and miraculous events.
17. SN 5.315–316.
18. Bodhi 2000a: 2.1769 (SN 5.316).
19. See, for instance, Dennison 2019.

13. Myanmar, Part One

1. Pranke 2010: 460.
2. See SN 1.173.
3. Scott (Yoe) 1882/1989: 35–36. They are desire (*chanda*), strength (*viriya*), mind (*citta*), and investigation (*vimaṃsa*).
4. Crosby 2020: 149.
5. See Tun 1986.
6. Green 2018: 1.
7. Green 2018: 20–24, 148–160; Skilling 2012b.
8. *Sāmaññaphala-sutta* (D 2); DN 1.76–85. See Bodhi 1989: 44–51, 154–161; Shaw 2006a: 65–68. For the crucial importance of *iddhi*s in early Buddhist discourse, see Gethin 1992: 97–103.
9. *Mūgapakkha-jātaka* (J 538; Shaw 2006b: 179–221; Appleton and Shaw 2015: 1.51–80); *Sāma-jātaka* (J 541; Shaw 2006b: 274–310; Appleton and Shaw 2015: 1.119–146).
10. Patton 2020: 12–17.
11. Houtman 1985: 90–91.
12. Hlaing 2013: 8. On Theelon's apparently coincidental development of comparable interests with Htuthkaung Sayadaw (1799–1881), see Houtman 1985: 91–93.
13. See Braun 2013: 19–34.
14. For extensive study of the impact of American Baptist endeavors, see Kaloyanides 2023.
15. Crosby 2021: 139–143.
16. See Braun 2013: 66–72. Braun points out that, within Burma itself, controversies regarding, for instance, Abhidhamma predated colonialist interventions.

17. Pranke 2010: 455–456. Such early attempts to reinstate vipassana predated colonialism.

18. Pranke 2010: 457–459.

19. Pranke 2010: 460.

20. For analysis of nineteenth-century Burmese practice see Crosby 2014: 162–163 and, in its wider context in the region, Crosby 2021. See also Houtman 1985 and 1990 for detailed analysis of the interplay between text and practice.

21. For his life story, see Patrick Given-Wilson 2021.

22. Braun 2013: 38–40.

23. According to Abhidhamma understanding, there are five form-sphere *jhānas*, with the second being exploration (*vicāra*) without initial application (*vitakka*).

24. See Braun 2013: 79–84.

25. Crosby describes ways that mind cultivation was emphasized as Buddhism became known internationally, at the expense of somatic meditative practices unifying mind and body (Crosby 2020: 15–27).

26. See Houtman 1990: 12–16, 26–54 for nineteenth-century Burmese practice and the profound impact of the educational and political background: "During the colonial period Buddhism provided a very powerful idiom of opposition to colonial rule" (Houtman 1990: 36).

27. See Stuart 2024.

28. AN 1.206–207. See Shaw 2021a: 20–23 and Giustarini 2023 for listening as a Buddhist practice.

29. DN 3.141.

30. For Ledi's role in revolutionizing Burmese lay understandings of spiritual progress through Abhidhamma, see Braun 2013: 102–121.

31. Braun 2013: 136–144.

32. For translations, see J 9 (Shaw 2006b: 26–30; Ja 1.137–139); J 539 (Shaw 2006b: 179–221, Appleton and Shaw 2015: 51–80; Ja 6.1–30); and for J 541, Appleton and Shaw 2015: 147–185 (Ja 6.95–129).

33. Shaw 2006b: 26–30.

34. *Mahāsudassana-sutta* (D 17; DN 2.169–199).

35. Ledi 2011: 14.

36. Ledi 2011: 17–18.

37. Ledi 2011: 22–23.

38. Ledi 2011: 29.

39. Ledi 2011: 27–28.

40. He calls the third stage the settling, or fixing, stage. Through his stress on the tip of the nose it sounds like a development of Buddhaghosa's third stage,

touching (*phusanā*). Ledi omits mentioning this as a stage but integrates it by using it as the basis for a natural movement to the settling (*ṭhapanā*) (Ledi 2011: 29–30).

41. He takes the outbreath as the first, in accordance with some commentaries. He says, for his first stage, "it is not yet possible to perceive such details as the lengths of the out-breaths and in-breaths." For him, the second stage covers the long breath and the short breath. The other two stages of the first four are the same (Ledi 2011: 27).

42. Ledi 2011: 40.

43. Ledi 2011: 45–46.

44. Braun 2013: 156.

45. Ledi 2011: 53.

46. See Stuart 2020: 47, 281, n. 76.

47. A comparable route had been suggested in early commentaries. See Soma 1998: 47.

48. Vism 666–667 (21.112); Braun 2013: 137–139. See also Cousins 1996: 48–50.

49. Braun 2013: 140–141.

50. Braun 2013: 141–142.

51. Crosby 2021: 147–148.

52. See Crosby 2021: 203–234.

53. See Stuart 2024 for the crucial importance of chant for Ledi, as well as U Ba Khin, discussed in chapter 15.

54. In the twentieth century, challenges both to Abhidhamma and the presence of other realms increased the "scientification" of traditional Buddhism (Crosby 2021: 156–159). The process is ongoing, however, and examination of scientific principle and Buddhism is itself always changing.

55. Braun 2013: 35–39.

56. Quoted in Braun 2013: 4.

14. Myanmar, Part Two

1. Braun 2013: 161.

2. Nyanaponika 1962: 86.

3. For close analysis of practice and theory lineages in nineteenth and twentieth century Burma, see Houtman 1990: 90–93.

4. Nyanaponika 1962: 86.

5. Nyanaponika 1962: 86

6. Houtman 1985: 90–91.

7. Braun 2013: 160; 227, n. 53. Kornfield 1977: 83–115.

8. This information is derived from Kyaw 2019.

9. See Kyaw 2019.

10. See Dennison 2022: 169–210 for research on breathing practices and *jhāna*, revealing an association between the breath lengths and brain activity.

11. Kornfield 1977: 103.

12. See Crosby 2017; Kyaw 2019; Crosby 2021: 154–159.

13. Houtman 1985: 95, 100; Kyaw 2019.

14. Explained by Roger Bischoff in Webu 1995, Part I: "Introduction."

15. Webu 1995, Part 1.

16. For the centrality of loving-kindness and compassion in canonical teachings, see Aronson 2008.

17. Webu 1995, Part 1: *What Really Matters*. For a striking but contrasting parallel, see Dhammadhāro 1990: 76.

18. SN 3.106–109. See Shaw 2006a: 53–56.

19. Webu 1995, Part 2: *Work without Wavering!*

20. This is the second route to enlightenment suggested by Ānanda in an early sutta (AN 2.157): vipassana preceding *samatha*. The normative first route is *samatha* first and then insight. The other two routes are calm and insight "yoked together" and "dhamma excitement." Webu appears to be suggesting the last option.

21. Webu Part II, 1995, 2: *Work without Wavering!*

22. See Stuart 2020: 45; Khin 1999: 87.

23. See Stuart 2020: 63–64.

24. See Houtman 1990: 269–270.

25. For study of Mahāsi's hagiography and biography, see Houtman 1990: 195, 202, 214–220.

26. See Mahāsi 2016: 45–92; Tan 2011: 312–314. See also Cousins 2022: 17–19.

27. Mahāsi terms this *suddha-vipassanā-yanika* or *sukkah-vipassanā-yanika*.

28. See Kornfield 1977: 51–81 and 57–58 for the basic method.

29. See Nyanatusita 2021: 423–425, n. 639. Mahāsi develops commentarial advice. Upatissa takes observing (*sallakkhaṇa*) as a way of steadying the *nimitta* in meditation. Buddhaghosa takes "observing" and "turning away" as means of making *jhāna* familiar by finding mastery there before insight (Vism 286 [8.222]).

30. Particular thanks to the practitioners who discussed this with me.

31. Kyaw 2019.

32. Cholvijarn 2019: 24–25.

33. This supposition is in part based on a possible translation of the word used to describe the path of the four foundations of mindfulness, *ekāyana*.

Commentaries suggest several alternative meanings. One is that it offers the "only way" to awakening. Most scholars and practitioners now prefer other, also commentarial, options. Anālayo suggests "direct way" (Anālayo 2013: 11–12) or "direct path" (Ñāṇamoli and Bodhi 2001: 145). Many prefer "that goes in one way only," or "leading only one way" (for discussion, see Gethin 1992: 59–66). A famous Upaniṣadic image of the passage of rivers and rivulets leading down to the ocean, could be read to support both latter interpretations; the image is also there in Buddha's suttas, in the inevitability of the path leading to awakening (*Chāndogya Upaniṣad* 6.10; Olivelle 1996: 153; M 73). Whatever the translation, the exclusion of *samatha* is not implied. The extended version (*Mahāsatipaṭṭhāna-sutta*, D 22) *defines* right concentration as the four *jhānas* (D 22; DN 2.313). The shorter Sutta on the Foundations of Mindfulness (M 10) does not mention *jhāna* but cites several meditations usually seen to involve it.

34. Pa Auk 2010: 29–55.

35. I am grateful to Venerable Tikkhañāṇa Thera, trained in Pa Auk Sayadaw's teachings, for information about this (conversation, Oxford, 06/25/2024).

36. Sneyder and Rasmussen 2009: 48–49. For a firsthand account of some advanced meditations and their undertaking, see Jeon 2018.

37. Sneyder and Rasmussen 2009: 117–118.

38. See Catherine 2008.

39. Kyaw 2012; Kornfield 1977: 209–254; Cousins 2022: 186.

40. Vism 114 (3.119).

41. See chapters 7 and 8.

42. Patton 2020: 122–123. Patton's account of modern perspectives notes that some suspicion has perhaps inevitably been directed to these figures, supposedly associated with, by the mid-twentieth century, discredited *samatha* meditations and psychic powers (Patton 2020: 120–127). See also Crosby 2014: xii.

43. Quoted in Patton 2020: 122. Modern exponents of this tradition apparently link the breath to exercises in visualization, such as of images of pagodas (Patton 2020: 124).

44. Scott (Yoe) 1882/1989: 38.

45. Crosby 2021: 148.

46. For discussion of Buddhist cosmology, see Gethin 1998: 112–132 (with table, 116–117); Collins 1998: 291–297; Harvey 2013: 32–36 and Shaw 2021a: 92–100.

47. See, for instance, Schedneck 2015: 166–167.

48. Mitter and Moxey 2013.

49. See Almond 1988.

50. See Crosby 2021: 135–152.

51. Blavatsky 1877.

52. See Cousins 1994; Almond 1988.

53. On the significance of loving-kindness, see Bennett, 1923: 105. Bennett systematically trained himself in past-life recollection. He was revered by occultist Aleister Crowley and became a cult figure in magical circles (Harris 2024). I am grateful to Dr. Elizabeth Harris for discussion about this and the inevitable, if mild, "stand-off" that emerged between Theosophy and Buddhism in the UK (Talk, Buddhist Society, London, April 27, 2024).

54. The ninth causal relationship (*paccaya*), of strong support (*upanissaya*), is active when liberation acts as a strong foundation for the arising of new events (see Sumanaphala 1998: 84).

55. Houtman notes ways that insight practices were validated through text in the early twentieth century. In Myanmar, as elsewhere, practice traditions are considered paramount (Houtman 1985: 101).

56. See, for instance, Dhammasāmi 1999.

57. Quoted in Hlaing 2013: 7. For the importance of suitability to temperament in the assignation and teaching of meditation in Pāli Buddhism, see Shaw 2016b.

15. Myanmar's New Meditations Abroad

1. See Ud 34–37; Shaw 2006a: 24–27.

2. See, for instance, AN 3.316; Shaw 2006a: 8–12, 49–53.

3. Coleman 1971: 65.

4. Footage from a 1950s BBC film gives a glimpse of his relationship with a student experiencing deep absorption (Khin 2013).

5. Coleman 1971: 215.

6. Coleman 1971: 217.

7. Coleman 1971: 219.

8. Houtman 1990: 206–214.

9. See Kornfield 1977: 233–255.

10. Stuart 2020: 90.

11. Quoted in Stuart 2020: 137–139.

12. Stuart 2020: 137–139.

13. See, for instance, Cousins 1994; Almond 1988; Shaw 2014. See, for instance, Rudyard Kipling's "The Finest Story in the World" (1891) and *Kim* (1901) for sympathetic treatments of reincarnation. A best-selling novel by the son of Sir

Edwin Arnold, Edwin Lester Arnold, called *The Wonderful Adventures of Phra the Phoenician* (1890), shows repetitive character traits and patterns resurfacing through all the reincarnations of his hero in different periods of British history.

14. I refer here primarily to Connie Waterton, Russel Williams, and Ralph Beresford, among others, at the Manchester Buddhist Society, Sale, UK, and John Ryder in Cambridge. The Sale Buddhists had been taught by Venerable Kapilavaddhu.

15. Khin 1999: 87.

16. Braun 2013: 226–227, n. 45.

17. International Meditation Centre 2023.

18. Quoted in Stuart 2020: 11–12.

19. Stuart 2020: 9.

20. Quoted in Stuart 2020: 236.

21. Stuart 2020. Stuart's biography also includes many of Goenka's teachings.

22. See Stuart 2020: 204–205. See also Goenka's rationale for the orientation of his teachings (Stuart 2020: 241–249).

23. Goenka 2014; Goenka 2020.

24. See Shaw 2006a: 129–134, 195–197.

25. For his first-person account of the incident, see Stuart 2020: 235–240.

26. Stuart 2020: 13.

27. Dhamma.org 2023.

28. See Braun 2013: 226–227, n. 45.

16. Two Innovators

1. Tiyavanich 2007: 14.

2. Kornfield 1977: 120.

3. Buddhadāsa 1997: 100–107.

4. Buddhadāsa 1997: 106–107.

5. Kornfield 1977: 118.

6. Buddhadāsa 1997: 127.

7. Kornfield 1977: 119.

8. Larry Rosenberg and Bhikkhu Anālayo draw on his methods and develop them in different ways (Rosenberg 2004; Anālayo 2019).

9. Amaro 2013: x–xii.

10. For a study of eight female accredited arhats, see Seeger 2018.

11. Khemā 1997: 36. For Khemā's autobiography, recounted by herself, see Khemā 1991.

12. Khemā 1997: 213.
13. Khemā 1997: 48.
14. I am very grateful for discussion with Leigh Brasington about this and for information derived from his firsthand experience of learning with Ayya Khemā.
15. Khemā 2014. See also 1987: 110–113.
16. Khemā 1997: 142–143.
17. Conversation with Leigh Brasington, August 2023.
18. Khemā 2001: 69. For some of her basic teachings concerning mindfulness of breathing, see Khemā 1987: 6–8.
19. Khemā 1987: 105–114.
20. Khemā 1996.
21. Khemā 1996.
22. See, for instance, Brasington 2015.

17. Sri Lanka, the Homeland of Theravada Buddhism, and Some Reflections

1. See Gombrich 1988: 137–171 for pre-nineteenth-century Ceylon; Gombrich 1988: 173–210 for nineteenth and twentieth centuries; see Holt 2004 for a concise history of Buddhism on the island.
2. See Obeyesekere 2004.
3. See Crosby, Skilton, and Gunasena 2012 for the Siam Nikāya mission from Thailand and meditation teachings in the eighteenth-century Kandyan Court.
4. Blackburn 1999.
5. I am grateful to Robert Adkins for information about this, from his recent time being a monk there.
6. See chapter 10 for discussion of Rhys Davids 1896. For discussion of nineteenth-century Sri Lankan Buddhism, see Harvey 2013: 376–385; Crosby 2013: 106–118.
7. Harris argues, on reading nineteenth-century commentator Robert Spence Hardy, "that formal meditation was present in lay practice but was not central, and that the monastic Sangha considered the *jhāna*s to be part of their self-understanding, even if their practice of them was limited" (Harris 2019: 212). The breath appears to be included. See also Crosby 2013: 34–39.
8. See Harris 2006 for a fuller picture of this process.
9. He taught various forms of loving-kindness practice in the Samatha Centre, Manchester, in 1982 and 1983, accompanied by awareness of the breath.
10. Bodhi 2000b.
11. Samaratne 2002: 22.

12. Cousins 2022: 178.

13. L. S. Cousins practiced *kasiṇa* meditation at a *samatha* monastery in the east of the island, Kalugala, in 1981. This beautiful place of retreat, like some others, was destroyed in the wars. The monastery where my husband spent a retreat in 1982, Kudumbigala, was evacuated.

14. Crosby 2020: 212–215.

15. I am grateful to Dr. Rajith Dissanayake for information on this subject. For an account of some forest monasteries, see Nyanatusita 2018. For Brahm's teachings, see chapter 11; Brahm 2006.

16. Sirimane 2016.

17. See Cousins 1996: 37.

18. Ganarama 1986.

19. Ganarama 1986: 2.

20. For some accounts of private female lay practice in Sri Lanka, see Snell 2001.

21. Tiyavanich says the Jungle Village period ended in Thailand in 1957, around the same time as in other Southeast Asian regions (Tiyavanich 2007: xxii). It is striking that this coincides with widespread meditative reforms in Thailand. By the 1960s, "any organized teaching of the old *samatha* practices had all but disappeared, certainly in Thailand and Burma, but soon across South and Southeast Asia and eventually worldwide" (Dennison 2022: 2).

22. Stuart 2020: 203–204.

23. Hallisey 2015: 28.

24. See Harvey 1988.

18. Breath Meditation Across Buddhism and Beyond

1. Deleanu 1992: 50.

2. Olivelle 1996: xxxiv–xl.

3. Olivelle 1996: 100 (3.2).

4. Olivelle 1996: xxxii.

5. Olivelle 1996: l–li.

6. See Deleanu 1992: 51.

7. Deleanu 1992: 52–54

8. Deleanu 1992: 53–57. This interpretation is slightly different from Buddhaghosa's, with the settling in effect being his "touching" (*phusanā*).

9. See Klaus 1992.

10. See, for instance, Gethin 1992: 36–44; Anālayo 2003: 46–61; Anālayo 2013: 21–38; Shaw 2020: 38–57.

11. Olivelle understands the Sanskrit word *smṛti* as meaning "a textualized form of memory" (Olivelle 2011: 168). In practice, this usually means "tradition," applicable to the traditions of memorization involved in the recitation of texts. For conjecture as to ways this background could have shaped the Buddha's understanding of the term, see Shaw 2020: 17–26.

12. MN 1.249. See Bronkhorst, 1993: 27. Bronkhorst references the *Maitrāyaṇiya Upaniṣad*, where yoga on the breath (*prāṇāyāmaḥ*) is encouraged (Bronkhorst 1993: 47; for discussion of breath restraint, see 47–53; 64–68). On mindfulness in Buddhist vocabulary, see also Shaw 2021b: 319–320, n. 38.

13. Anālayo has conducted extensive research on Chinese (Āgama) translations, some of which could predate the Pāli (see Anālayo 2003; Anālayo 2007; Anālayo 2019: 155–244).

14. Pradhan 1975 (AKBh 341.6–8).

15. Nidd. 1.360.

16. Zacchetti 2008.

17. Yamabe and Sueki 2010: *Zuochan sanmei jing* (Taishō no. 614).

18. Yamabe and Sueki 2010; Schlingoff 1964.

19. This translation, from the German, of sections of Schlingoff 1964, is by Amanda Lindop and L. S. Cousins (1998).

20. Roth 2016: 188.

21. Translation from Roth 2016: 189 (*Zhuāngzi* 4/10/1–3); 201, n. 13.

22. Roth 2016: 189; 201, n. 14.

23. Roth 1999: 109–112.

24. Translation of verse 24 of the *Inward Training* (*Nei-yeh*), a collection of verses on breath meditation and the nature of the way (Dao) (Roth 1999: 92–93; 110–111).

25. Cleary 1991: 23.

26. Cleary 1991: 68.

27. Donner and Stevenson (1993) provide extensive discussion of this work, known as the *Mohe Zhiguan*, which recommends finding calm through awareness of the breath.

28. Guan 2020: 63.

29. Guan 2020: 66.

30. Guan 2020: 115.

31. Wuling 2006.

32. Cheng 2000: 23–24.

33. See Nan 1997: 80–83.

34. Nagatomo 2020.

35. Moore 2020: 94.

36. Moore 2020: 97.

37. Moore 2020: 111–116

38. Moore 2020: 60.

39. Kapleau 2000. This loosely aligns with Poonyathiro's methods, of counting within each breath (see chapter 12).

40. Suzuki 1997: 148.

41. Deleanu 1992: 46. Deleanu notes, with examples, ways that the role of mindfulness of breathing becomes significantly diminished in Mahāyāna Buddhisms (Deleanu 1992: 46–48).

42. See, for instance, practical instructions given by Gelug teacher Alan Wallace (Wallace 2016).

43. Wangyal 2011.

44. Wangyal 2011.

45. Zahler 2009: 80; 108.

46. Lodrö 1998: 26–27.

47. Lodrö 1998: 29.

48. Lodrö 1998: 33.

49. Abboud 2014.

50. Abboud 2014: 22–23.

51. Abboud 2014: 25.

52. *Abhidharma-kośa* takes the counting and following much as Pāli commentaries do. The settling here is concerned with finding the breath at two points—say the tip of the nose and the feet—and experiencing it as a whole (*Abhidharma-kośa*: 6.12d). For discussion of breathing mindfulness in this work, see Chadha 2015.

53. Abboud 2014: 145.

54. Abboud 2014: 144.

55. Boonman Poonyathiro teaches a comparable Thai technique.

56. Abboud 2014: 147–150.

57. Myrvold 2016: 108.

58. John of the Cross 2000 (1584): 152–153.

59. Harris 2018.

60. Habito 2006: 53–55.

61. I am grateful to Canon Dr. Robin Gibbons for discussions on this.

62. Kadloubovsky and Palmer 1992: 33.

63. Cousins 1989.

64. Rumi (Barks trans.) 1995: 32.
65. Cornish 2014: 145–146.

Conclusion

1. See Vajirañāṇa 1975: 227–228. Gotama Buddha particularly favored concentration (*samādhi*) based on breathing mindfulness (SN 5.317–320). For the various trees under which Buddhas become enlightened, see Ja 1.29–48.
2. See Gombrich 1996: 96–134.
3. Dhp 372. See also Gethin 1992: 344–350; Anālayo 2003: 72–79. Gethin points out that *jhāna* meditations are "at the heart of early Buddhist meditation theory and, at least as far as the Theravāda tradition goes, they continue to occupy a central place in the meditation theory of the Abhidhamma and commentaries" (Gethin 1992: 347). One sutta (AN 2.157) describes four routes to enlightenment: calm first, then insight; insight first then calm; the two "yoked together"; and what is described as dhamma excitement. This last the *Paṭisambhidāmagga* interprets as the ten defilements of insight (*vipassānupakilesa*): stages of attachment or misunderstanding that can occur at each stage of wisdom until the goal is attained (Paṭis 2.100; Vism 663–638 [20.105–130]; Cousins 2022: Appendix A; see also Tan 2011: 320–324). Both insight paths and calm paths have some potential and perhaps inevitable passing problems; these can be overcome. Cousins uses the image of the corkscrew to suggest ways that insight and calm can circle around, finally producing awakening (Cousins 2022: 108–109).
4. SN 4.300–2.
5. See, for instance, SN 5.197–98.
6. See Gethin 2019 for discussion of varied understandings regarding *jhāna* and the richness of variety of paths in early texts.
7. Bodhi 2004. See also Cousins 2022: 71–94.
8. See AN 2.157; Cousins 1996; Cousins 2022: 43–50.
9. Dennison 2022: 232.
10. See MN 1.340; Gethin 2004: 213–214; Shaw 2006a: 12–15.
11. See Shrubsole 2023: 33–35; 92: in the UK, the presence of woodland shrubs and plants, like bracken and bluebells, as well as lichens, mosses, and ferns, is often the best indicator of ancient rainforest.
12. See, for instance, Schedneck 2015.
13. See Khemā 1996; Kornfield 2023; Salzburg 2023. For Boonman, see chapter 14.
14. Theravada is usually thought not to have a developed sense of interdependence, compared to other Buddhisms. Western theoretical discourse, however, tends to exhibit less knowledge of those areas where understandings of

interrelatedness are deeply embedded. We have seen this at multiple levels, from the personal to the cosmological, in chapter 9 on old meditations in Thailand and in chapter 14 on Myanmar. Abhidhamma teachings of the complex networks of interrelationships (*Paṭṭhāna*) pervade Burmese Buddhism yet are not known well to western scholars. The profusely interactive, interrelational stories of jataka literature discussed in chapter 12 are also less known internationally, as are the transference of merit and blessings rituals of collective *bhāvanā*. The Theravadins did not formulate a doctrine of interpenetration as found in Huayan philosophy; interdependency between divine, animal, spirit, and human realms, however, within the natural world, permeates theory and personal practice.

15. See Simard 2021.

Bibliography

Romanized transliterations for Pāli, Burmese, Sinhalese, and Thai names vary, as do the names by which some teachers are known. To avoid confusion, a common alternative spelling or name is sometimes put in parentheses after the author or subject.

Abboud, Gerardo. *The Royal Seal of Mahamudra: A Guidebook for the Realization of Coemergence.* Volume 1. Boulder, CO: Shambhala Publications, 2014.

Almond, Philip C. *The British Discovery of Buddhism.* Cambridge: Cambridge University Press, 1988.

Amaro, Ajahn. *Small Boat, Great Mountain: Theravada Reflections on the Natural Great Perfection.* Redwood Valley, CA: Abhayagiri Monastery, 2003.

Anālayo, Bhikkhu. *Early Buddhist Meditation Studies.* Volume 1. Barre, MA: Barre Centre for Buddhist Studies via CreateSpace Independent Publishing Platform, 2017.

——. *Mindfulness of Breathing: A Practice Guide and Translations.* Cambridge: Windhorse Publications, 2019.

——. "Mindfulness of Breathing in the Saṃyuktāgama." *Buddhist Studies Review* 24, no. 2 (2007): 137–50.

——. *Perspectives on Satipaṭṭhāna.* Birmingham, UK: Windhorse, 2013.

——. *Satipaṭṭhāna: The Direct Path to Realization.* Birmingham, UK: Windhorse, 2003.

Appleton, Naomi, and Sarah Shaw. *The Ten Great Birth Stories of the Buddha: The Mahānipāta of the Jātakatthavaṇṇanā.* Foreword by Peter Skilling. Chiang Mai, Thailand: Silkworm Books, 2015.

Arbel, Keren. "The Liberative Role of *Jhānic* Joy (*Pīti*) and Pleasure (*Sukha*) in the Early Buddhist Path to Awakening." *Buddhist Studies Review* 32, no. 2 (2015): 179–205.

Arnold, Edwin Lester. *The Wonderful Adventures of Phra the Phoenician*. London and Boston: Chatto and Windus, 1891.

Aronson, Harvey B. *Love and Sympathy in Theravāda Buddhism*. 2nd ed. New Delhi: Motilal Banarsidass, 2008.

Baker, Christopher, and Pasuk Phongpaichit. *A History of Thailand*. Cambridge: Cambridge University Press, 2005.

Becchetti, C. "Une ancienne traon de manuscrits au Cambodge." In *Recherches nouvelles sur le Cambodge*, edited by François Bizot, 47–62. Paris: L'École française d'Extrême-Orient, 1994.

Bennett, Alan (Metteyya). *The Wisdom of the Aryas*. London: Kegan Paul, Trench, Trubner, 1923.

Bernon, Olivier de. "Le manuel des maîtres de kammaṭṭhān: étude et présentation de rituels de méditation dans la tradition du bouddhisme khmer." PhD dissertation, Lille University, 2000.

Bhūridatta, Ajahn Mun. *A Heart Released: The Teachings of Phra Ajaan Mun Bhūridatta Thera*. Translated, with an introduction, by Ṭhānissaro Bhikkhu. Dhammatalks.org, 2016. https://www.dhammatalks.org/books/HeartReleased/Contents.html.

Bizot, François. *Le chemin de Laṅkā*. Textes bouddhiques du Cambodge 1. Paris: L'École française d'Extrême-Orient, 1992.

———. *Le figuier à cinq branches*. Recherches sur le bouddhisme khmer II, Publications de L'École française d'Extrême-Orient 107. Paris: L'École française d'Extrême-Orient, 1976.

Bizot, François, and François Lagirarde. *Saddavimala: la pureté par les mots*. Paris and Chiang Mai: L'École française d'Extrême-Orient, 1996.

Blackburn, Anne M. "Magic in the Monastery: Textual Practice and Monastic Identity in Sri Lanka." *History of Religions* 38, no. 4 (1999): 354–72.

Blavatsky, Helena. *Isis Unveiled: A Master-Key to the Mysteries of Ancient and Modern Science and Theology*. New York: J. W. Bouton, 1877.

Bodhi, Bhikkhu. *The All-Embracing Net of Views: The Brahmajāla Sutta and its Commentaries*. Kandy, Sri Lanka: Buddhist Publication Society, 1978.

———. *The Connected Discourses of the Buddha: A Translation of the Saṃyutta Nikāya*. 2 vols. Somerville, MA, and London: Wisdom Publications/Pali Text Society, 2000a.

———, trans. *The Discourse on the Fruits of Recluseship (Sāmaññaphala Sutta): The Sāmaññaphala Sutta and Its Commentaries*. Kandy, Sri Lanka: Buddhist Publication Society, 1989.

———. "The Jhānas and the Lay Disciple according to the Pāli Suttas." Buddha-Sasana, June 14–30, 2004. https://www.budsas.org/ebud/ebdha267.htm.

———. "Tributes to Godwin: In Memorium Acharya Godwin Samararatne (1932–2000)." Buddhist Publication Society newsletter (April 2000b). https://www.godwin-home-page.net/Tributes/Bodhi.htm.

Brahm, Ajahn. *Mindfulness, Bliss, and Beyond: A Meditator's Handbook*. Somerville, MA: Wisdom Publications, 2006.

Brasington, Leigh. *Right Concentration: A Practical Guide to the Jhānas*. Boston and London: Shambhala Publications, 2015.

Braun, Erik. *The Birth of Insight: Meditation, Modern Buddhism, and the Burmese Monk Ledi Sayadaw*. Chicago: Chicago University Press, 2013.

Bronkhorst, Johannes. *The Two Traditions of Meditation in Ancient India*. Delhi: Motilal Banarsidass, 1993.

Buddhadāsa, Bhikkhu. *Mindfulness with Breathing: A Manual for Serious Beginners*. Somerville, MA: Wisdom Publications, 1997.

Catherine, Shaila. *Focused and Fearless: A Meditator's Guide to States of Deep Joy, Calm, and Clarity*. Somerville, MA: Wisdom Publications, 2008.

Chadha, Monima. "A Buddhist Epistemological Framework for Mindfulness Meditation." *Asian Philosophy* 25, no. 1 (2015): 65–80.

Chah, Ajahn (Phra Bodhinyāna Thera). *Bodhinyāna: A Collection of Dhamma Talks*. 3rd ed. Ubon Ratchathani, Thailand: Wat Nong Pah Pong, 1982.

———. *The Collected Teachings of Ajahn Chah*. 3 vols. Harnham, Belsay, Northumberland: Aruna Publications, 2011.

———. "On Meditation." Transcript, translated anonymously. Dhammatalk, Wat Nong Pah Pong, Ubon Ratchathani, Thailand, 2007 (updated June 2008). https://www.ajahnchah.org/book/On_Meditation1.php.

Cheng, Wei-an. *Training the Monkey Mind: A Guide to Pure Land Practice*. Translated by Dharma Master Suddhisukha. New York and San Francisco: Sutra Translation Committee, 2000. http://www.buddhanet.net/pdf_file/monkeym.pdf.

Cholvijarn, Potprecha. "Buddha, Dhamma, and Saṅgha *Yantras*: An Ayutthaya Period Meditation Manual from Wat Pradusongtham." *Journal of the Siam Society* 9, no. 1 (2021): 63–82.

———. "Manomayiddhi: Power of Mind Meditation." *Journal of the Siam Society* 111, no. 1 (2023): 93–110.

———. "Meditation Manual of King Taksin of Thonburi." *Journal of the Siam Society* 110, no. 1 (2022): 31–47.

———. "The Origins and Development of Sammā Arahaṃ Meditation: From Phra Mongkhon Thepmuni (Sot Candasaro) to Phra Thep Yan Mongkhon (Sermchai Jayamaṅgalo)." PhD dissertation, University of Bristol, 2019.

Choompolpaisal, Phibul. "Boran Kammatthan (Ancient Theravāda) Meditation Transmissions in Siam from the Late Ayutthaya to Rattanakosin Periods." *Buddhist Studies Review* 38, no. 2 (2021): 225–252.

———. "*Nimitta* and Visual Methods in Siamese and Lao Meditation Traditions from the 17th Century to the Present Day." *Contemporary Buddhism* 20, no. 1 (2019): 152–183.

Cleary, Thomas. *The Secret of the Golden Flower: The Classic Chinese Book of Life.* New York: HarperSanFrancisco, 1991.

Coleman, John E. *The Quiet Mind.* London: Rider and Company, 1971.

Collins, Stevens. *Nirvana and Other Buddhist Felicities.* Cambridge: Cambridge University Press, 1998.

Cornish, Peter. *Dazzled by Daylight.* Cork: Garranes Publications, 2014.

Cousins, L. S. "Buddhist *Jhāna.*" *Religion* 3 (1973): 115–31.

———. *Meditations of the Pali Traditions: Illuminating Buddhist Doctrine, History, and Practice.* Edited by Sarah Shaw. Boulder, CO: Shambhala Publications, 2022.

———. "The Origins of Insight Meditation." In *The Buddhist Forum*, Vol. 4, edited by T. Skorupski, 35–58. London: School of Oriental and African Studies, 1996.

———. "*Samatha-yāna* and *Vipassanā-yāna.*" In *Buddhist Studies in Honour of Hammalava Saddhatissa*, edited by D. Dhammapāla and other hands, 56–68. Nugegoda, Sri Lanka: Hammalava Saddhatissa Felicitation Committee, 1984.

———. "The Stages of Christian Mysticism and Buddhist Purification: *Interior Castle* of St. Theresa of Avila and the *Path of Purification* of Buddhaghosa." In *The Yogi and the Mystic: Studies in Indian and Comparative Mysticism*, edited by Karel Werner, 103–20. London: Curzon Press, 1989.

———. "The Sutta on Mindfulness with In and Out Breathing." In *Buddhist Meditative Praxis: Traditional Teachings and Modern Applications*, edited by K. L. Dhammajoti, 1–24. Hong Kong: Centre of Buddhist Studies, 2015.

———. "Theravada Buddhism in England." In *Buddhism into the Year 2000: International Conference Proceedings* (editor unnamed), 141–150. Bangkok and Los Angeles: Dhammakāya Foundation, 1994.

Covill, Linda, Ulrike Roesler, and Sarah Shaw, eds. *Lives Lived, Lives Imagined: Biographies of Awakening.* Somerville, MA: Wisdom Publications, 2010.

Crosby, Kate. "Abhidhamma and *Nimitta* in Eighteenth-Century Meditation Manuscripts from Sri Lanka: A Consideration of Orthodoxy and Heteropraxy in *Borān Kammaṭṭhāna*." *Contemporary Buddhism* 20, no. 1 (2019): 111–151.

———. *Esoteric Theravada: The Story of the Forgotten Meditation Tradition of Southeast Asia.* Boulder, CO: Shambhala Publications, 2020.

———. "Heresy and Monastic Malpractice in the Buddhist Court Cases (*Vinicchaya*) of Modern Burma (Myanmar)." *Contemporary Buddhism* 18, no. 1 (2017): 199–261.

———. "The Shared Origins of Traditionalism and Secularism in Theravada Buddhism." In *Secularizing Buddhism: New Perspectives on a Dynamic Tradition*, edited by Richard K. Payne, 135–161. Boulder, CO: Shambhala Publications, 2021.

———. "Tantric Theravāda: A Bibliographic Essay on the Writings of François Bizot and Others on the Yogāvacara Tradition," *Contemporary Buddhism* 1, no. 2 (2000), 141–193.

———. *Theravada Buddhism: Continuity, Diversity, and Identity.* Oxford: Wiley-Blackwell, 2014.

———. *Traditional Theravada Meditation and Its Modern-Era Suppression.* Hong Kong: Buddha Dharma Centre of Hong Kong, 2013.

Crosby, Kate, Andrew Skilton, and Amal Gunasena. "The Sutta on Understanding Death in the Transmission of Borān Meditation from Siam to the Kandyan Court." *Journal of Indian Philosophy* 40, no. 2 (2012): 177–198.

Deleanu, Florin. "Mindfulness of Breathing in the *Dhyāna Sūtras*." *Transactions of the International Conference of Orientalists in Japan* 37 (1992): 42–57.

Dennison, Paul. "The Human Default Consciousness and Its Disruption: Insights from an EEG Study of Buddhist Jhāna Meditation." *Frontiers in Human Neuroscience* 13 (2019): 178.

———. *Jhāna Consciousness: Buddhist Meditation in the Age of Neuroscience.* Boulder, CO: Shambhala Publications, 2022.

Dhammadhāro, Ajahn Lee. *The Autobiography of Phra Ajaan Lee.* 3rd ed. Translated from the Thai by Ṭhānissaro Bhikkhu. Dhammatalks.org, 2012. https://www.dhammatalks.org/Archive/Writings/Ebooks/TheAutobiographyof PhraAjaanLee_181215.pdf.

———. *Keeping the Breath in Mind and Lessons in Samadhi.* 3rd ed. Translated from the Thai by Ṭhānissaro Bhikkhu (Geoffrey DeGraff). BuddhaNet, 1990. www.buddhanet.net/pdf_file/breathmind.pdf.

Dhammajoti Bhikkhu. "The Sixteen-Mode Mindfulness of Breathing." *Journal of the Centre for Buddhist Studies, Sri Lanka* 6 (2008): 251–88.

Dhammakāya Foundation (author unnamed). *Second to None: The Biography of Khun Yay Maharatana Upasika Chandra Khon-nok-yoong.* Bangkok: Dhammakāya Foundation, 2005.

Dhammasāmi, Khammai. *Mindfulness Meditation Made Easy.* Penang, Malaysia: Inner Path, 1999.

Dixon, Graham. "Assertion and Restraint in Dhamma Transmission in Early Pāli Sources." *Buddhist Studies Review* 32, no. 1 (2015): 99–141.

Donner, Neal, and Daniel Stevenson. *The Great Calming and Contemplation: A Study and Annotated Translation of the First Chapter of Chih-I's Mo-Ho Chih-Kuan.* Honolulu: University of Hawai'i Press, 1993.

Eifring, Halvor. "Introduction." In *Asian Traditions of Meditation*, edited by Halvor Eifring, ix–xv. Honolulu: University of Hawai'i Press, 2016.

Ganarama, Venerable. *Freed Freedom.* Mitirigala, Sri Lanka: private publication/ Amazon, 1986.

Gethin, R. M. L. *The Buddhist Path to Awakening: A Study of the Bodhi-Pakkhiyā Dhammā.* Brill's Indological Library 7. Leiden, Netherlands: Brill, 1992.

———. *Foundations of Buddhism.* Oxford: Oxford University Press, 1998.

———. "The *Jhānas* in the Buddhist Path to Liberation: the Theravāda Perspective." In *Meditación y contemplación: Caminos hacia la paz (Budismo Theravada y mística Teresiana)*, edited by F. J. S. Fermín, 177–206. Burgos: Grupo Editorial Fonte, 2019.

———. "On the Practice of Buddhist Meditation according to the Pāli Nikāyas and Exegetical Sources." *Buddhism in Geschichte und Gegenwart* 9 (2004): 201–221.

Giustarini, Giuliano. "Meditative Listening in the Pāli Buddhist Canon." *Numen* 70 (2023): 254–285.

———. "The Sleep of the Good: Meditation on Buddho in the Sudattasutta and Its *Aṭṭhakathā.*" *Kervan: International Journal of African and Asiatic Studies* 28, no. 1 (2024): 303–322.

Given-Wilson, Patrick. "Ven. Ledi Sayadaw: A Talk Given by Patrick Given-Wilson." Pariyatti. YouTube, October 14, 2020. https://www.youtube.com/watch?v=qgCKCYixx_g.

Goenka, S. N. "Anapana Meditation for All (English—10 mins) (with Subtitles)." Vipassana Meditation. YouTube, October 28, 2014. https://www.youtube.com/watch?v=Oh5ii6R6LTM&t=18s.

———. "Introduction to Anapana Meditation." Vipassana Meditation. YouTube, July 24, 2020. https://www.youtube.com/watch?v=eyM_c3wSh8s.

Gombrich, R. F. *How Buddhism Began: The Conditioned Genesis of the Early Teachings.* London and Atlantic Highlands, NJ: Athlone Press, 1996.

———. *Theravada Buddhism: A Social History from Ancient Benares to Modern Co-lombo*. London: Routledge and Kegan Paul, 1988.

Green, Alexandra. *Buddhist Visual Cultures, Rhetoric, and Narrative in Late Bur-mese Wall Paintings*. Hong Kong: Hong Kong University Press, 2018.

Guan, Venerable Zhen, trans. *Foundations for Developing Buddhist Tranquility (Śamatha) and Insight (Vipaśyanā) (by Master Zhiyi)*. Kong Meng San Phor Kark See Monastery, China: Dhamma Propagation Division, 2020.

Gunaratana, Henepola. *Mindfulness in Plain English*. Taipei: Buddhist Educa-tional Foundation, 1991.

Guy, John. "Introducing Early Southeast Asia." In *Lost Kingdoms: Hindu-Buddhist Sculpture of Early Southeast Asia*, edited by John Guy, 3–13. New York: Metro-politan Museum of Art, 2014.

Habito, Ruben L. F. *Healing Breath: Zen for Christians and Buddhists in a Wounded World*. Somerville, MA: Wisdom Publications, 2006.

Hallisey, Charles. *Therigatha: Poems of the First Buddhist Women*. Murty Classi-cal Library. Cambridge, MA: Harvard University Press, 2015.

Harris, Elizabeth J. "Ananda Metteyya/Allan Bennett 1872–1923." *St. Andrews Encyclopedia of Theology*, March 14, 2024. https://www.saet.ac.uk/Buddhism /AnandaMetteyyaAllanBennett.

———. "Buddhist Meditation and the British Colonial Gaze in Nineteenth-Century Sri Lanka." *Contemporary Buddhism* 20, no. 1 (2019): 200–222.

———. "John of the Cross, the Dark Night of the Soul, and the Jhānas and the Arūpa States: A Critical Comparative Study." *Buddhist Studies Review* 35, no. 1–2 [special issue: *Buddhist Path, Buddhist Teachings: Studies in Memory of L. S. Cousins*] (2018): 65–80.

———. *Theravāda Buddhism and the British Encounter: Religious, Missionary, and Colonial Experience in Nineteenth-Century Sri Lanka*. London: Routledge, 2006.

Harvey, Peter. *An Introduction to Buddhism: Teachings, History and Practices*. 2nd ed. Cambridge: Cambridge University Press, 2013.

———. "'Signless' Meditations in Pali Buddhism." *The Journal of the International Association of Buddhist Studies* 9, no. 1 (1988): 25–52.

Heim, Maria. *Voice of the Buddha: Buddhaghosa and the Immeasurable Words*. Ox-ford: Oxford University Press, 2018.

Hlaing, Dhammācariya U Htay. "Theelon Sayadaw (1786 A.D.–1861 A.D.): A great meditation master in old Burma." Translated by Aggācāra Dhamma Distribu-tion Group. Wikipitika. Fandom, September 2, 2013. https://tipitaka.fandom .com/wiki/Theelon_Sayadaw, 2013.

Holt, John Clifford. "Sri Lanka." In *Encyclopedia of Buddhism*, edited by Robert Buswell, 2.795–799. New York: Macmillan, 2004.

Houtman, Gustaaf. "The Burmese Wipathana Meditation Tradition Self Conscious: A History of Sleeping Texts and Silent Buddhas." *Groniek* 92 (1985): 87–105.

———. "Traditions of Buddhist Practice in Burma." PhD dissertation, School of Oriental and African Studies, University of London, 1990.

International Meditation Centre. "Anapana Meditation." International Meditation Centre in the Tradition of Sayagyi U Ba Khin and Mother Sayamagyi. https://www.ubakhin-vipassana-meditation.org/anapana-meditation.

Jayasāro, Ajahn. *Stillness Flowing: The Life and Teachings of Ajahn Chah*. Malaysia: Panyaprateep Foundation, 2017.

Jeon, Hyunsoo. *Samatha, Jhāna, and Vipassanā: Practice at the Pa-Auk Monastery— A Meditator's Experience*. Translated by H. Jun. Somerville, MA: Wisdom Publications, 2018.

John of the Cross, St. *A Spiritual Canticle of the Soul and the Bridegroom Christ*. 1584. Grand Rapids, MI: Christian Classics, 2000.

Jones, Christopher V. *The Buddhist Self: On Tathāgatagarbha and Ātman*. Honolulu: University of Hawai'i Press, 2020.

Kadloubovsky, E., and G. E. H. Palmer, trans. *Writings from the Philokalia on Prayer of the Heart*. London: Faber and Faber, 1992.

Kaloyanides, Alexandra. *Baptizing Burma: Religious Change in the Last Buddhist Kingdom*. New York: Columbia University Press, 2023.

Kapleau, Philip. *The Three Pillars of Zen: Teachings, Practice, and Enlightenment*. New York: Anchor Books, 2000.

Kemper, Steven. "Anagarika Dhammapala's Meditation." *Contemporary Buddhism* 20, no. 1 (2019): 223–246.

Khemā, Ayya. *Being Nobody, Going Nowhere: Meditations on the Buddhist Path*. Somerville, MA: Wisdom Publications, 1987.

———. "Breathing in Peace." Talk at Green Gulch Farm Zen Center, June 29, 1996. Audio, 18:16. Dharma Seed. https://dharmaseed.org/talks/7980/. 1996.

———. *I Give You My Life: Autobiography of a Western Buddhist Nun*. Boston, MA: Shambhala Publications, 1997.

———. "Sister Ayya Khema's Biography (parts 1–4 together) 1991 (English)." Reuben. YouTube, February 18, 2014. https://www.youtube.com/watch?v=iYW8YNYa75o.

———. *Visible Here and Now: The Buddha's Teachings on the Rewards of Spiritual Practice*. Boston, MA: Shambhala Publications, 2001.

Khin, Sayagyi U Ba. *The Anecdotes of Sayaygi U Ba Khin.* Trowbridge, Wiltshire, UK: The Sayagyi U Ba Khin Memorial Trust, UK, 1999.

———. "Sayagyi U Ba Khin, BBC (Budismo Birmanês) 1950s." Oldstudent Behappy. YouTube, May 29, 2013. https://www.youtube.com/watch?v=V_2zfQyA9c.

Kipling, Rudyard. "The Finest Story in the World." 1891. The Kipling Society. https://www.kiplingsociety.co.uk/tale/the-finest-story-in-the-world.htm.

———. *Kim.* London: Macmillan, 1901.

Klaus, Konrad. "On the Meaning of the Root SMṚ in Vedic Literature." *Wiener Zeitschrift für die Kunde Südasiens* (1992): 77–86.

Kornfield, Jack. "Breathe Love in, Breath Love Out Meditation." Jack Kornfield. YouTube, January 29, 2021. https://www.youtube.com/watch?v=mNg9eRfsUoY.

———. *Living Buddhist Masters.* Santa Cruz, CA: Unity Press, 1977.

Kourilsky, Gregory. "The Kammatthan Buddhist Tradition of Mainland Southeast Asia: Where Do We Stand?" *Journal of the Siam Society* 112, no. 1 (2024) 85–130.

Kuan, Tse-fu. *Mindfulness in Early Buddhism: New Approaches through Psychology and Textual Analysis of Pali, Chinese, and Sanskrit Sources.* London: Routledge, 2008.

Kyaw, Pyi Phyo. "The *Paṭṭhāna* (Conditional Relations) and Buddhist Meditation: Application of the Teachings in the *Paṭṭhāna* in Insight (*Vipassanā*) Meditation Practice." Conference Proceedings of the 2nd International Association of Buddhist University Conference: Buddhist Philosophy and Praxis, May 31 to June 2, 2012. http://www.undv.org/vesak2012/iabudoc/07Pyi PhyoKyawFINAL.pdf

———. "The Sound of the Breath: Sunlun and Theinngu Meditation Traditions of Myanmar." *Contemporary Buddhism* 20, no. 1 (2019): 247–291.

Ledi Sayadaw. *Manual of Mindfulness of Breathing (Ānāpāna Dīpanī).* Wheel Publication no. 431–432. Translated by U Sein Nyo Tun and edited by S. S. Davison. Kandy, Sri Lanka: Buddhist Publication Society, 2011. https://www.bps.lk /olib/wh/wh431_Ledi_Manual-of-Mindfulness-Of-Breathing.pdf.

Lodrō, Geshe Gedün. *Calm Abiding and Special Insight: Achieving Spiritual Transformation through Meditation.* Ithaca, NY: Snow Lion Publications, 1998.

Mahāsi Sayadaw. *Manual of Insight.* 1945. Translated by the Vipassanā Mettā Foundation Translation Committee, Somerville, MA: Wisdom Publications, 2016.

McDaniel, Justin. *The Lovelorn Ghost and the Magical Monk: Practicing Buddhism in Modern Thailand.* New York: Columbia University Press, 2013.

McMahan, David L. *Rethinking Meditation: Buddhist Meditative Practices in Ancient and Modern Worlds.* Oxford: Oxford University Press, 2023.

Mettānando Bhikkhu. "Meditation and Healing in the Theravāda Buddhist Order of Thailand and Laos." Unpublished PhD dissertation, Hamburg University, 1998.

Mitter, Partha, and Keith Moxey. "A Virtual Cosmopolis: Partha Mitter in Conversation with Keith Moxey." *The Art Bulletin* 95, no. 3 (2013): 381–392.

Moore, Meido. *Hidden Zen: Practices for Sudden Awakening and Embodied Realization*. Boulder, CO: Shambhala Publications, 2020.

Myrvold, Kristina. "Nām Simran in the Sikh Religion." In *Asian Traditions of Meditation*, edited by Halvor Eifring, 103–121. Honolulu: University of Hawai'i Press, 2016.

Nagatomo, Shigenori. "Japanese Zen Buddhist Philosophy." In *The Stanford Encyclopedia of Philosophy* (Spring 2020), edited by Edward N. Zalta. https://plato.stanford.edu/archives/spr2020/entries/japanese-zen/.

Nan, Huai-Chin. *Basic Buddhism: Exploring Buddhism and Zen*. Newburyport: Red Wheel/Weiser, 1997.

Ñāṇamoli, Bhikkhu. *Mindfulness of Breathing (Ānāpānasati): Buddhist Texts from the Pāli Canon and Extracts from the Pāli Commentaries*. 1952. 6th ed. Kandy, Sri Lanka: Buddhist Publication Society, 1998.

———. *The Path of Discrimination (Patisambhidāmagga)*. Oxford: Pali Text Society, 1982.

———. *The Path of Purification*. 2 vols. Berkeley, CA, and London: Shambhala Publications, 1976. (Chapters and paragraphs are denoted in parentheses after the Pāli Vism page reference.)

Ñāṇamoli, Bhikkhu, and Bhikkhu Bodhi. *Middle Length Discourses of the Buddha: A Translation of the Majjhimanikāya*. Somerville, MA: Wisdom Publications, 2001.

Ñāṇasampanno, Maha Boowa (Ajahn Nyanasampanno). *Arahatta Magga, Arahatta Phala: The Path to Arahantship*. Translated by Bhikkhu Sīlaratano. DhammaTalks .net, 2005: https://www.dhammatalks.net/Books/Maha_Boowa_The_Path_to _Arahantship.htm#PART%203.

———. *Forest Dhamma: A Selection of Talks on Buddhist Practice*. Translated by Bhikkhu Paññāvaddho. Bangkok: Sathirakoses–Nagapradipa Foundation, 1973.

———. *Straight from the Heart: Thirteen Talks on the Practice of Meditation*. Translated by Bhikkhu Ṭhāṇissaro. Access to Insight, 1994: https://www.accesstoin sight.org/ati/lib/thai/boowa/straight.html.

———. *The Venerable Phra Acharn Mun Bhuridatta Thera, Meditation Master*. Translated by Siri Buddhasukh. Bangkok: Mahamakut Rajavidyalaya Press, 1976.

Nyanaponika, Thera. *The Heart of Buddhist Meditation: A Handbook of Mental Training Based on the Buddha's Way of Mindfulness.* London: Rider and Company, 1962.

Nyanatusita, Bhikkhu. *Buddhist Forest Monasteries and Meditation Centres in Sri Lanka: A Guide for Foreign Buddhist Monastics and Lay Practitioners.* Buddhist Publication Society, April 2018. https://www.bps.lk/olib/mi/mi008.html.

———. *The Path to Freedom (Vimuttimagga).* Hong Kong: Centre of Buddhist Studies, University of Hong Kong, 2021.

Obeyesekere, Ranjini. "Sinhala, Buddhist Literature." In *Encyclopedia of Buddhism,* edited by Robert Buswell, 2.777–778. New York: Macmillan, 2004.

Olivelle, Patrick. *Language, Texts, and Society: Explorations in Ancient Indian Culture and Religion.* New York: Anthem Press, 2011.

———. *The Upaniṣads.* Oxford and New York: Oxford University Press, 1996.

Pa Auk Sayadaw. *Knowing and Seeing.* 4th ed. Moulmein, Burma: Pa Auk Monastery, 2010.

Pasanno, Ajahn. "Engaging the 16 Steps of Breathing Meditation." Abhayagiri Monastery. YouTube, June 21, 2017. https://www.youtube.com/watch?v=Dp FaHoHYtKI.

Patton, Thomas Nathan. *The Buddha's Wizards: Magic, Protection, and Healing in Burmese Buddhism.* New York: Columbia University Press, 2020.

Poonyathiro, Boonman. *From One to Nine.* Bangkok: private publication, 2003.

Pradhan, Prahlad, trans. *Abhidharmakośabhaṣyam of Vasubandhu.* Patna, India: Jayaswal Research Institute, 1975.

Pranke, Patrick. "On Saints and Wizards: Ideals of Human Perfection and Power in Contemporary Burmese Buddhism." *Journal of the International Association of Buddhist Studies* 33 (2010): 453–88.

Rajadhon, Phraya Anuman. *Essays on Thai Folklore.* 3rd ed. Bangkok: Institute of Thai Studies, Chulalongkorn University, 2009.

Ray, Himanshu Prabha. *Winds of Change: Buddhism and the Maritime Links of Early South Asia.* New ed. New Delhi and Oxford: Oxford India Paperbacks, 1998.

Rhys Davids, T. W. *The Yogāvacara's Manual of Indian Mysticism As Practised by Buddhists.* London: (Pali Text Society) H. Frowde, 1896.

Rose, Ian. *Loosening the Tangle: A Meditator's Guide to the Visuddhimagga.* Llangynllo, Powys, UK: Samatha Trust, 2022. https://samatha.org/sites/default /files/2023-05/Loosening%20The%20Tangle%20by%20Ian%20Rose.pdf.

Rosenberg, Larry. *Breath by Breath: The Liberating Practice of Insight Meditation.* Boulder, CO: Shambhala Publications, 2004.

Roth, Harold. "Meditation in the Classical Daoist Tradition." In *Asian Traditions of Meditation*, edited by Halvor Eifring, 185–206. Honolulu: University of Hawai'i Press, 2016.

———. *Original Tao: Inward Training (Nei-Yeh) and the Foundations of Taoist Mysticism*. Translations from the Asian Classics. New York: Columbia University Press, 1999.

Rumi, Jelaluddin. *The Essential Rumi*. Expanded ed. Translated by Coleman Barks. New York: HarperCollins, 1995.

Salzburg, Sharon. "Breath Meditation." InsightTimer App, 2023. Audio, 09:49. https://insighttimer.com/sharonsalzberg/guided-meditations/breathmeditation.

Samararatne, Godwin. *Talks on Buddhist Meditation*. Wheel Publication no. 448–449. Kandy: Buddhist Publication Society, 2002.

Sayadaw, U Pandita. 1993. *In This Very Life: The Liberation Teachings of the Buddha*. Translated by Venerable U Aggacitta. Edited by Kate Wheeler. Boston, MA: Wisdom Publications, 1993.

Schedneck, Brooke. "Forest as Challenge, Forest as Healer: Reinterpretations and Hybridity within the Forest Tradition of Thailand." *Pacific World Journal of the Institute of Buddhist Studies* 13 (2011): 1–24.

———. *Living Theravada: Demystifying the People, Places, and Practices of a Buddhist Tradition*. Boulder, CO: Shambhala Publications, 2023.

———. *Thailand's International Meditation Centers: Tourism and the Global Commodification of Religious Practices*. London, UK: Routledge, 2015.

Schlingoff, Dieter. *Ein buddhistisches Yogalehrbuch: unveränderter Nachdruck der Ausgabe von 1964 unter Beigabe aller seither bekannt gewordenen Fragmente*. 1964. Düsseldorf: Haus der Japanischen Kultur EKO, 2006.

Schnake, Javier. "Letters and Numbers: Protective Aspects in the *Vajirasāratthasaṅgaha*." In *Katā Me Rakkhā, Katā Me Parittā. Protecting the Protective Texts and Manuscripts* edited by Claudio Cicuzza, 157–196. Bangkok and Lumbini: Fragile Palm Leaves, 2016.

Scott, James George (Shway Yoe). *The Burman, His Life and Notions*. 1882. Arran, Scotland: Kiscadale Publications, 1989.

Seeger, Martin. *Gender and the Path to Awakening: Hidden Histories of Nuns in Modern Thai Buddhism*. Copenhagen: NIAS Press, 2018.

———. "Orality, Memory and Spiritual Practice." *Journal of the Oxford Centre for Buddhist Studies* 7 (2014): 153–90.

Shaw, Sarah. "And That Was I: How the Buddha Himself Creates a Path between Biography and Autobiography." In *Lives Lived, Lives Imagined: Biographies of Awakening*, edited by Linda Covill, Ulrike Roesler, and Sarah Shaw, 15–41. Somerville, MA: Wisdom Publications, 2010.

———. *The Art of Listening: A Guide to the Early Teachings of Buddhism.* Boulder, CO: Shambhala Publications, 2021a.

———. *Buddhist Meditation: An Anthology of Texts.* London: Routledge, 2006a.

———. "Crossing to the Farthest Shore: How Pāli *Jātakas* Launch the Buddhist Image of the Boat onto the Open Seas." *Journal Oxford Centre for Buddhist Studies* 3 (2012): 128–156. http://jocbs.org/index.php/jocbs/article /view/29/31.

———. Review of *Encountering Buddhism in Twentieth-Century British and American Literature*, edited by Laurence Normand and Alison Winch. *Buddhist Studies Review: Journal of the UK Association for Buddhist Studies* 31, no. 1 (2014): 146–151.

———. "Has Secularism Become a Religion?" In *Secularizing Buddhism: New Perspectives on a Dynamic Tradition*, edited by Richard K. Payne, 29–55. Boulder, CO: Shambhala Publications, 2021b.

———. *The Jātakas: Birth Stories of the Bodhisatta.* Penguin Global Classic. Harmondsworth, London: Penguin, 2006b.

———. "Meditation Teaching and Suitability: The Depiction of Temperament in Pāli Canonical Text and Commentarial Narrative." In *Asian Traditions of Meditation*, edited by Halvor Eifring, 122–144. Honolulu: University of Hawai'i Press, 2016b.

———. *Mindfulness: Where It Comes From and What It Means.* Boulder, CO: Shambhala Publications, 2020.

———. "Southern Buddhist Meditation: The Ānāpānasati-*Sutta*." In *Contemplative Literature: A Comparative Sourcebook*, edited by Louis Komjathy, 265–396. New York: State of New York Press, 2016a.

Shrubsole, Guy. *The Lost Rainforests of Britain.* London: William Collins, 2023.

Shulman, Eviatar. "The Play of Formulas in the Early Buddhist Discourses." *Journal of Indian Philosophy* 50, no. 4 (2022): 557–580.

Siddhiñāṇo, Phramahāsomboon. *Yod Phrakantraipidok [The Peak of Tipiṭaka] and Gathachinbanchorn, Transliterated into Romance Characters.* For the Buddhavihara Temple. Birmingham, England. Bangkok: Saddhammika, 1995. Private publication.

Sīlaratano, Bhikkhu. *Mae Chee Kaew: Her Journey to Spiritual Awakening and Enlightenment.* Udon Thani, Thailand: Forest Dhamma, 2009.

Simard, Suzanne. *Finding the Mother Tree: Uncovering the Wisdom and Intelligence of the Forest.* London: Penguin Random House, 2021.

Sirimane, Yuki. *Entering the Stream to Enlightenment: Experience of the Stages of the Buddhist Path in Contemporary Sri Lanka.* Sheffield, UK: Equinox Publishing, 2016.

Skilling, Peter. "At the Heart of Letters: Aksara and Akkhara in Thai Tradition." In *80 that Mom Rajawong Suphawat Kasemsri [Felicitation volume for MR Suphawat Kasemsri on his 80th Birthday],* edited by Weerawan Ngamsantikul, 443–441. Bangkok: Rongphim Deuan Tula, 2012b.

———. "Introduction." In *How Theravada Is Theravada? Exploring Buddhist Identities,* edited by Peter Skilling, Jason A. Carbine, Calusio Cicuzza, and Santi Pakdeekham, xiii–xxx. Chiang Mai: Silkworm Books, 2012a.

———. *Mahāsutras: Great Discourses of the Buddha.* Vol. 2: Parts 1 and 2, *Sacred Books of the Buddhists XLIV.* Oxford: Pali Text Society, 1997.

Skilton, Andrew. "Meditation and Its Subjects: Tracing *Kammaṭṭhāna* from the Early Canon to the *Boran Kammathan* Traditions of Southeast Asia." In *Contemporary Buddhism* 20, no. 1–2 (2019): 36–72.

Skilton, Andrew, and Phibul Choompolpaisal. "The Ancient Theravāda Meditation System, *Borān Kammaṭṭhāna*: Ānāpānasati in Kammatthan Majjima Baeb Lamdub." *Buddhist Studies Review* 32, no. 2 (2015): 207–229.

———. "The Old Meditation (*boran kammatthan*), a Pre-reform Theravāda Meditation System, from Wat Ratchasittharam: The *Pīti* Section of the Kammatthan Matchima Baeb Lamdap." *Aséanie* 33 (2014): 83–116.

Skilton, Andrew, Kate Crosby, and Pyi Phyo Kyaw. "Terms of Engagement: Text, Technique and Experience in Scholarship on Theravada Meditation." *Contemporary Buddhism* 20, no. 1 (2019): 1–35.

Snell, Helle. *Buddhist Women Meditators in Sri Lanka.* Wheel Publication no. 443–445. Kandy, Sri Lanka: Buddhist Publication Society, 2001.

Sneyder, Stephen, and Tina Rasmussen. *Traditional Concentration Meditation As Presented by Pa Auk Sayadaw.* Boston, MA: Shambhala Publications, 2009.

Soma Thera. *The Way of Mindfulness: The Satipatthana Sutta and Its Commentary.* Access to Insight, 1998. http://www.accesstoinsight.org/lib/authors/soma/wayof.html.

Stuart, Daniel M. "Local Cure, Global Chant: Performing Theravadic Awakening in the Footsteps of the Ledi Sayadaw." *Numen* 71, no. 2–3 (2024): 256–302.

———. *S. N. Goenka: Emissary of Insight: Lives of the Masters.* Boulder, CO: Shambhala Publications, 2020.

Sucitto, Ajahn. *Breathing Like a Buddha.* Hemel Hempstead, UK: Abhayagiri Monastery, 2022. https://www.abhayagiri.org/books/650breathing-like-a-buddha.

Sumanaphala, G. D. *An Introduction to Theravāda Abhidhamma.* Singapore: Buddhist Research Society, 1998.

Sumedho, Ajahn. *Mindfulness: The Path to the Deathless.* Hemel Hempstead, UK: Amaravati Buddhist Publications, 1987.

Suzuki, Shunryu. "Zen Mind." In *The Meditative Way: Readings in the Theory and Practice of Buddhist Meditation,* edited by Rob Bucknell and Chris Kang, 146–158. London: Curzon, 1997.

Tan, Uncle. *A Collection of Mahāsī Sayādaw's Discourses on Meditation, by the Most Venerable Mahāsī Sayādaw (Chaṭṭha Saṅgīti Pucchaka Agga Mahā Paṇḍita).* 2nd ed. Yangon, Myanmar: Buddhasāsana Nugaha Organization, 2011. Private publication.

Taylor, James L. "Cosmology, Forest Monks and Sangha Reconstruction in the Early Bangkok Period." *Journal of the Siam Society* 64, no. 2 (1976): 104–150.

———. *Forest Monks and the Nation-State: An Anthropological and Historical Study in Northeastern Thailand.* Singapore: Institute of Southeast Asian Studies, 1993.

Ṭhānissaro Bhikkhu, trans. "Ajaan Sao's Teaching: A Reminiscence of Phra Ajaan Sao Kantasilo transcribed from a talk by Phra Ajaan Phut Thaniyo." Access to Insight, 1997. https://www.accesstoinsight.org/lib/thai/phut/sao.html.

Thate, Ajahn (Phra Rajanirodharangsee, Ajahn Tate). *The Autobiography of a Forest Monk.* Edited by Bhikkhu Ariyaseko. Chiang Mai: Wat Hin Mark Peng, 1993.

———. *Thate: Steps along the Path by Phra Ajaan Thate Desaransi (Phra Rajanirodharansi).* Translated by Ṭhānissaro Bhikkhu. Access to Insight, 1994. https://www.accesstoinsight.org/lib/thai/thate/stepsalong.html.

Tiyavanich, Kamala. *Forest Recollections: Wandering Monks in Twentieth-Century Thailand.* Honolulu: University of Hawai'i Press, 1997.

———. *In the Cool Shade of Compassion: The Enchanted World of the Buddha in the Jungle.* Boulder, CO: Shambhala Publications, 2018.

———. *Sons of the Buddha: The Early Lives of Three Extraordinary Thai Masters.* Somerville, MA: Wisdom Publications, 2007.

Tun, Than, ed. *The Royal Orders of Burma, AD 1598–1885.* Volume 5 (1788–1806). Kyoto: Centre for Southeast Asian Studies, Kyoto University, 1986.

Vajirañāṇa, Mahāthera. *Buddhist Meditation in Theory and Practice: A General Exposition According to the Pali Canon of the Theravada School.* 2nd ed. Kuala Lumpur: Buddhist Missionary Society, 1975.

Viradhammo, Ajahn. *The Contemplatives' Craft: Internalizing the Teachings of the Buddha.* Perth, Ontario: Tisarana Buddhist Monastery, 2017. https://forestsangha.org/teachings/books/the-contemplative-s-craft?language=English.

———. "The Craft of the Heart." Abhayagiri Monastery, October 17, 2015. https://www.abhayagiri.org/reflections/89-the-craft-of-the-heart.

Walker, Trent. *Until Nirvana's Time: Buddhist Songs from Cambodia.* Boulder, CO: Shambhala Publications, 2022.

Wallace, B. Alan. "02 Asanga's Method of Meditation on Mindfulness of Breathing." Talk presented at Meditation Retreat on Shamatha, Vipashyana, Mahamudra, and Dzogchen, Lama Tzong Khapa Institute, Italy, March 29–May 24, 2016. SBI Media, March 30, 2016. Transcript and audio, 41:55. https://media.sbinstitute.com/courses/spring2016/02/.

Wangyal Rinpoche, Tenzin. *Awakening the Sacred Body: Tibetan Yogas of Breath and Movement.* Carlsbad, CA: Hay House, 2011.

Webu, Sayadaw. "The Essential Practice: Dhamma Discourses of Venerable Webu Sayadaw." 2 parts. Translated by Roger Bischoff. Access to Insight, 1995: https://www.accesstoinsight.org/lib/authors/webu/wheel375.html.

Weerasekera, Indaka Nishan. *The Notion of Solitude in Pali Buddhist Literature: Finding a Space in the Crowd.* London: Bloomsbury, 2024.

Woodward, F. L. *Manual of a Mystic: Being a Translation from the Pali and Sinhalese Work Entitled the Yogāvachara's Manual.* London: Pali Text Society, 1916.

Wohlleben, Peter. *The Power of Trees: How Ancient Forests Can Save Us If We Let Them.* Vancouver, BC: Greystone, 2023.

Wuling, Venerable Shi. *In One Lifetime: Pure Land Buddhism.* Chicago: Amitabha Publications, 2006.

Yamabe, Nobuyoshi, and Fumihiko Sueki. *The Sutra on the Concentration of Sitting Meditation.* Honolulu: University of Hawai'i Press, 2010.

Zacchetti, Stefano. "A 'New' Early Chinese Buddhist Commentary: The Nature of the *Da Anban Shouyi Jing* (大安般守意經) T 602 Reconsidered." *Journal of the International Association of Buddhist Studies* 31, no. 1–2 (2008): 421–484.

Zahler, Leah. *Study and Practice of Meditation: Tibetan Interpretations of the Concentrations and Formless Absorptions.* Ithaca, NY: Snow Lion Publications, 2009.

Index